CHILD LABOR LEGISLATION

IN THE

SOUTHERN TEXTILE STATES

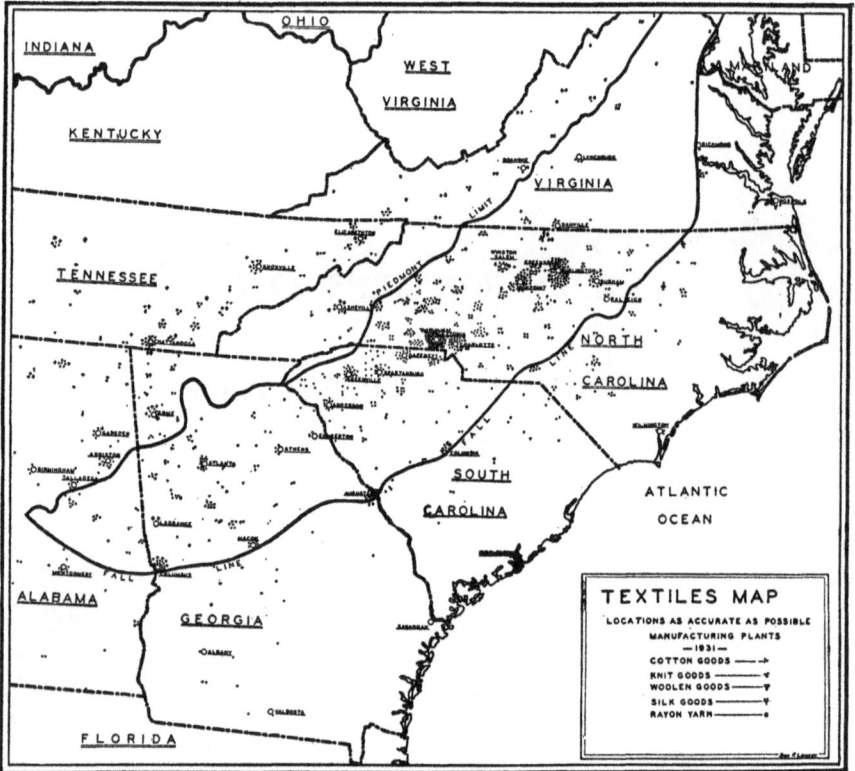

From Lemert's *The Cotton Textile Industry of the Southern Appalachian Piedmont*

TEXTILE MANUFACTURING PLANTS IN THE SOUTH—1931

CHILD LABOR LEGISLATION
IN THE
SOUTHERN TEXTILE STATES

By

ELIZABETH H. DAVIDSON

CHAPEL HILL
THE UNIVERSITY OF NORTH CAROLINA PRESS
1939

PREFACE

THE HISTORY of child labor legislation in the South illustrates the social changes that have taken place there in the last half century. Beginning in the days of "Bourbon" rule, the wave of reform nevertheless lagged until the rise to power of a new generation in politics. Although distinct from the movement for public education, it came hand in hand with it, and the success of one was accompanied or followed by that of the other. In this study I have undertaken to trace the growth of the child labor reform movement in the South from its obscure beginnings in the 1880's through the failure of the federal amendment and the enactment of more or less satisfactory state laws. The history of child labor legislation is not yet complete. Both the laws and the agencies for their enforcement have imperfections which future legislatures may endeavor to remove. But the period of bitter criticism and violent defense of the employment of children closed more than a decade ago.

I wish to acknowledge my indebtedness to a number of people for the assistance they have given me in making this study. I owe thanks especially to the late Professor William K. Boyd of Duke University, under whose direction I did my work, and to Mr. Paul H. Buck of Harvard for his helpful advice during the months I spent in Cambridge. I wish also to express appreciation for the co-operation of the officers of the American Federation of Labor and the National Child Labor Committee, and to Mrs. Edgar Gardner Murphy and Mrs. Alexander J. McKelway. They made accessible for my use valuable materials without which this study would have been impossible. I also received help from the librarians of the Department of Archives and History of Alabama, the Department of Archives and History of Georgia, and the North Carolina Historical Commission, as well as from many other people too numerous to mention here who have contributed in some way to my work.

E. H. D.

CONTENTS

TABLES

CHILD LABOR LEGISLATION

IN THE

SOUTHERN TEXTILE STATES

CHAPTER I

THE PROBLEMS OF CHILD LABOR LEGISLATION

A STUDY of child labor legislation in the South cannot be separated from some consideration of the textile industry because it was the chief nonagricultural occupation in which large numbers of children were employed over an extensive area. The problem of children in southern mines has never been acute, and up to the present time the children who work on farms and form by far the largest part of juvenile breadwinners have not been subject to legislative control.

The four leading states included in this study are North Carolina, South Carolina, Georgia, and Alabama. They are chosen because they are the most important, in the order named, in the production of textiles, and because in them larger numbers of children once found industrial employment than in any other section of the South. The cotton manufacturing region coincides largely with the Piedmont section, and therefore does not include the entire area of any of these states, but the regulation of child labor through legislation involved each state as a whole rather than a section of it.

Child labor was in no sense a problem peculiar to the South. It had appeared in the earliest manufacturing enterprises of the northern states, and the spread of industry in the South produced the same result. The rapid industrial expansion of the United States in the latter part of the nineteenth century, of which the rise of cotton manufacturing in the South was only a part, brought more and more children into industrial employment. Some of the old manufacturing states had already passed laws to restrict employment below certain ages, but as factory expansion became more general they found it necessary to revise and extend these statutes, while the states which had no laws were forced, for the most part reluctantly, to enact them.

The movement for child labor reform was part of the general reform wave which began late in the nineteenth century and spread rapidly in the early years of the twentieth. Critics directed their shafts against the evils of big business and corrupt municipal government. The fights for prohibition and women's rights, reform of marriage and divorce laws, and the enactment of pure food laws loomed large in the early twentieth century. The demand for better educational facilities, for juvenile courts, for city playgrounds, and for health protection for children were all a part of the same movement which created a demand for the abolition of child labor in industry. The publicity given these reforms and the enormous amount of propaganda spread in their behalf were made possible only by the contemporaneous growth of popular magazines. It was chiefly through the flood of weekly and monthly periodicals that the agitation for reform was constantly forced on the attention of a growing reading public.[1]

There are only a few characteristics of the child labor struggle in the South which differentiate it from the movement in the nation at large, and even in them the difference is largely one of degree rather than of kind. The laissez faire attitude of the state governments toward industry was slower to yield in the South than elsewhere, because manufacturing on any considerable scale was a comparatively recent development there. The child labor reform movement of the twentieth century originated in the South, but because interest in it spread rapidly in the North and because publicity came chiefly through periodicals which were published in the North—there were almost no southern magazines—the southern people were touched by a resentment of what they called "northern interference." This was a natural feeling on the part of a people still sore from the wounds of civil war and reconstruction, and included not only a dislike of northern child labor reform, but also of northern criticism of the South's handling of the Negro question and, to a more limited degree, of northern efforts to benefit the educational situation of the South.

The most marked difference between the two sections was in the character of cotton mill employees. The tendency of the native southern whites who went to the mills to work was toward a greater individualism than was found among the workers in the northern mills. Their unwillingness to submit to undue control by either state or labor union meant that they would make fewer demands for labor legislation and those demands could be more safely disregarded. But even here they were not entirely different from the northern textile workers who were always slow to form unions and showed little ability to keep their organizations functioning. When, in the later period of reform, the southern millowners raised the cry of state rights against the demands for federal legislation, they were merely taking refuge in the time-honored plea of the minority facing defeat.

The criticism to which southern manufacturers were subjected for the employment of child labor was a repetition of that which had been made in England a hundred years earlier and in New England

[1] H. U. Faulkner, "The Quest for Social Justice," in *A History of American Life*, XI, 110-203, *passim*.

more recently. In an article published in 1929,[2] Harriet L. Herring reviewed the history of the criticism of the cotton mill systems in the several localities where that industry has become highly developed. She reached the conclusion that criticisms always follow a certain cycle. An industry at the beginning of its development excites little notice from either an economic or social standpoint; in a second phase it attracts attention and praise for local reasons; next, adverse criticism is mingled with favorable; in the fourth stage the industry undergoes a period of rapid growth, violent attacks of criticism, and vigorous defense; this is followed by the calmer completion of legislation already begun for regulating the industry, and a dying down of old arguments; finally there is a period of economic quiescence or actual decline.

In the ante-bellum South there was a period of cotton mill development in which the industry went through the first two stages of the cycle of criticism. Prior to 1840 there were a few small mills which received almost no notice. Then there was a period of development in which a relatively small circle of people began to look to cotton manufacturing as a means of economic and social salvation for the South.[3] An argument much used in favor of building more mills was that they provided a suitable means for needy women and children to earn a living.[4] The third stage of the cycle, in which the employment of such people was subjected to criticism, was not reached before the Civil War.

The events of the Civil War and Reconstruction intervened to check mill development between 1860 and 1880. It is the theory of Professor Broadus Mitchell that the ante-bellum industry was completely eclipsed by these events. While some of the mills of the old era survived, they were few and unimportant, and it was not until 1880 that a reawakening of interest and new development of industry began. Mitchell says that the slow recovery from Reconstruction, the financial panic of 1873, and the high price of both machinery and cotton served to delay the development of manufacturing. According to the Census of 1880, only St. Louis and Baltimore were prominent southern manufacturing cities. Neither of them was in reality southern nor did either count cotton manufacturing among its six leading industries.[5] Mitchell attributed the change after 1880 to political defeat, which brought the leaders of the South to turn their attention from unprofitable national politics to economic de-

---

[2] "Cycles of Cotton Mill Criticism," in *South Atlantic Quarterly*, XXVIII (1929), 113-25.   [3] *Ibid.*, p. 119.
[4] Broadus Mitchell, *William Gregg: Factory Master of the Old South*, pp. 24 ff.
[5] Mitchell, *The Rise of Cotton Mills in the South*, pp. 61-63.

velopment. The process, he believes, was not an unanticipated or accidental development, but was deliberately planned.[6]

One may disagree with Professor Mitchell as to the effect of the Civil War on the cotton manufacturing industry. A comparison of figures in Table I shows that in the four principal manufacturing states of the South there was only a very moderate increase in cotton manufacturing between 1850 and 1860. In the next decade there was a decrease in the number of establishments in each state except Georgia, and in capital in both Alabama and North Carolina, but in all of the states there was an increase in the value of the product. The figures for 1870 are of little value, however, because of the conditions that prevailed at the time the census was taken. The year 1880 shows an increase in the number of mills in all four states, North Carolina leading with sixteen in excess of her former number. The increase in value of output was in each case larger than

TABLE I[7]

GROWTH OF COTTON MANUFACTURING 1840-1890

State	Number of Mills	Capital	Value of Products
Alabama			
1840	14	$ 35,575	$ 17,547
1850	12	651,900	382,260
1860	14	1,316,000	1,040,147
1870	13	931,000	1,088,767
1880	16	1,246,500	1,228,019
1890	13	2,853,015	2,190,771
Georgia			
1840	19	$ 573,835	$ 304,342
1850	35	1,736,156	2,135,044
1860	33	2,126,103	2,371,207
1870	34	3,433,265	3,648,973
1880	40	6,348,657	6,481,894
1890	53	17,664,675	12,035,629
South Carolina			
1840	15	$ 617,450	$ 359,000
1850	18	857,200	748,338
1860	17	801,825	713,050
1870	12	1,337,000	1,529,937
1880	14	2,776,100	2,895,769
1890	34	11,141,833	9,800,798
North Carolina			
1840	25	$ 995,300	$ 438,900
1850	28	1,058,800	831,342
1860	39	1,272,750	1,046,047
1870	33	1,030,900	1,345,052
1880	49	2,855,800	2,554,482
1890	91	10,775,134	9,563,443

[6] *Ibid.*, pp. 79, 88-90.
[7] U. S. Bureau of the Census, "Textiles," in *Report on Manufacturing Industries in the United States,* Eleventh Census, 1890 (Washington, 1894), pp. 188-89.

in the preceding decade. Even allowing for the unreliability of the figures for 1870, there is indication of the continuity of the industry before and after the war, although the rate of increase after 1880 was far greater than before.

The building of cotton mills was regarded in 1880 much as it had been in 1840, as an enterprise which would provide economic uplift for the masses of white people. A mill was sometimes a sort of community project, begun by an individual who hoped to benefit not only himself but his neighbors as well. If employment was furnished to many poor people, the condition of the community was improved in a corresponding proportion. Sometimes this aspect of the question took on almost a religious fervor, so that the building of a mill was in a way regarded as a public philanthropy.[8] The years around 1880 began the period of praise without adverse comment in the cycle of criticism. "The press, the politician, the preacher, and the forerunner of the community booster joined forces with the business interests to urge the building of mills."[9]

There were reasons enough why the building of mills should make rapid strides, once the movement was begun. In spite of the long tradition of New England in cotton manufacturing, the South had certain natural advantages. The proximity to the supply of raw material and the abundance of undeveloped water power were two outstanding arguments in favor of building factories. To many people farming was not profitable. Cotton was the staple crop of a large area and much of the time the price was low. What was hardship to the farmer was a boon to the manufacturer, and the number of mills erected varied inversely with the price of raw material. Added to these advantages was an abundant supply of cheap labor, much of it drawn from the farms which were burdened with the production of a single unprofitable crop.[10]

The South's rapid development as a manufacturing section began to attract attention in the North in a few years. In 1887 the Edwin Alden Company of Cincinnati, which compiled directories of newspapers throughout the United States to be used for advertising purposes, published a directory, its explanation for doing so being that the rapid growth of commercial prosperity, the increase in population, and the extensive building of cotton factories, rolling mills, and manufactures of various kinds was making the section a profitable field for advertisement. "Many of the Southern cities and towns have the appearance of a New York or New England town, they are so full of the hum of activity and business. . . . There is a steady

[8] Mitchell, *The Rise of Cotton Mills in the South*, pp. 96-106, 128-36.
[9] Herring, *op. cit.*, p. 119.
[10] Mitchell, *The Rise of Cotton Mills in the South*, pp. 137-44.

and permanent improvement in every line of industry throughout this entire section."[11]

Returning prosperity and the increased demand for cotton goods made the capital already invested in mills productive of good dividends. The price of the finished goods went up more rapidly than the price of raw material; some factories ran day and night. This prosperity drew capital, leading to the more rapid expansion of a paying industry.[12] Mitchell believes that three fourths of the capital invested in cotton mills in 1881 came from the South, much of it in the form of small investments by men of moderate means. Machinery was secured by exchange for stock in the company. By 1880 the South was ready to welcome northern assistance and bids for investments were made in the form of special exemptions from taxation. Southern advantages were advertised and leading men went north to interest investors.[13]

The race with New England begun in the 1880's was won before the end of the first decade of the twentieth century. The average cotton crop of South Carolina at that time was 500,000,000 pounds. Once Massachusetts would have bought it up at seven cents a pound, paying into the state $35,000,000, and making $100,000,000 on its manufacture. But at the peak of her prosperity South Carolina was making her own cotton into cloth and keeping the $100,000,000.[14]

The figures in Table II, compiled from government reports on the consumption of cotton, show that in 1850 the southern mills consumed 13.5 per cent of the cotton used in manufacturing in the United States, as against 74.8 per cent consumed in New England. In 1860 the South's part was 11 per cent as compared with New

TABLE II[15]

BALES OF COTTON CONSUMED IN THE UNITED STATES

Year	Cotton States	New England	All Other States
1840	71,000	158,708	6,817
1850	78,140	430,603	66,763
1860	93,553	567,403	184,454
1870	68,702	551,250	176,664
1880	188,748	1,129,498	252,098
1890	538,895	1,502,177	477,337
1900	1,523,168	1,909,498	440,499
1910	2,292,333	2,016,386	490,234
1920	3,714,403	2,418,828	628,976

[11] Central South Advertising Mediums, Introduction.

[12] Mitchell, The Rise of Cotton Mills in the South, pp. 146-47.

[13] Ibid., pp. 232-38.

[14] J. A. B. Scherer, Cotton as a World Power, pp. 340-41.

[15] Louis Bader, World Developments in the Cotton Industry, pp. 59-60; Scherer, op. cit., p. 422.

England's 67.1 per cent. In 1870 the figures show that the South used only 8.6 per cent and New England 69.2 per cent. In 1880 these figures changed to 12 per cent for the South and 72 per cent for New England; in 1890 to 21.4 per cent for the South and 59.6 per cent for New England; in 1900, 39 per cent for the South and 49 per cent for New England. In 1910 the South reached 47 per cent and New England took second place with only 46 per cent. By 1920 the South was over the 50 per cent mark for the whole United States.

The figures in Table III do not show the same growth for spindles as for cotton consumed, but the development on the part of the South was so rapid that for three decades after 1880 the number of spindles increased on an average each decade by 2.7 times as many as in the previous decade.

TABLE III[16]

ACTIVE COTTON SPINDLES IN THE UNITED STATES

Year	Cotton States	New England	All Other States
1840	180,927	1,597,394	506,310
1850	264,571	2,958,536	774,915
1860	324,052	3,858,962	1,052,713
1870	327,871	5,498,308	1,306,236
1880	561,368	8,632,087	1,459,988
1890	1,570,288	10,934,297	1,879,595
1900	4,367,688	13,171,377	1,933,167
1910	10,494,112	15,735,086	2,037,664
1920	15,230,983	18,287,424	1,962,546

The growth of manufacturing was accompanied by a corresponding increase in the number of workers employed. Table IV shows the numbers employed in 1870 and after.

This increase in the number of employees took place with practically no foreign or northern immigration. With few exceptions the workers in the mills were native southern whites.[17] They have been frequently designated by the vague name of "poor whites." This is an ill-defined term about which there is so much difference of opinion as to make unwise its use in connection with the cotton mill population. The mills of the ante-bellum South had drawn their operatives from the great body of nonslaveholding whites. They were for the most part poor, illiterate, and unsuccessful as farmers. Most of the factory work was done by the women and children of such families.[18] The new mills of the 1880's drew their operatives

[16] Ibid.

[17] U. S. Bureau of Labor, Report on Condition of Woman and Child Wage-Earners in the United States, VI, 125. Hereafter cited as Woman and Child Wage-Earners.

[18] Mitchell, William Gregg, pp. 24 ff.; George White, Statistics of the State of Georgia, pp. 574-75.

TABLE IV[19]

NUMBER AND PER CENT OF OPERATIVES IN SOUTHERN MILLS

State	Men	Per cent	Women	Per cent	Children	Per cent	Total
Alabama							
1870	303	29	445	43	284	28	1,032
1880	384	26.5	631	43.5	433	30	1,448
1890	735	35	852	41	501	24	2,088
1900	3,152	38	2,743	33	2,437	29	8,332
Georgia							
1870	1,147	40	1,080	38	619	22	2,846
1880	1,853	30	2,951	47	1,411	23	6,215
1890	3,849	37	4,005	39	2,460	24	10,314
1900	7,309	40	6,495	36	4,479	24	18,283
South Carolina							
1870	289	26	508	45	326	29	1,123
1880	661	33	772	38	585	29	2,018
1890	2,849	36	3,070	38	2,152	26	8,071
1900	13,418	44	8,673	29	8,110	27	30,201
North Carolina							
1870	258	18	916	63	279	19	1,453
1880	764	24	1,727	53	741	23	3,232
1890	2,788	33	3,656	42	2,071	25	8,515
1900	12,780	42	10,364	35	7,129	23	30,273

from the same class. A study made by the Bureau of Labor of the United States in 1907-8 indicated that 75.8 per cent of the women and child employees in cotton mills had spent their early childhood on the farm, 20.2 per cent in villages, and 4 per cent in cities. Those who were reported as coming from villages were usually members of cotton mill communities.[20]

The small farmers came to the mill villages willingly. They were often discouraged by poor crops and low prices. They hoped for comforts and better wages in the mills. The regular pay, with its opportunity to handle money, which was rare on the farm; the promise of better houses, better food and clothing; the contact with other people all made the prospect of mill life attractive. Some families came because they hoped to give their children a chance to rise through the better educational and economic opportunities they expected to find in the mill villages. Still more came because the members of the family were largely women and children who could expect employment. Widows with families and disabled or worthless and idle men all hoped to live by the work of the younger hands. For many of these families the change was advantageous. This was especially true for the smaller number who came from the remote

[19] U. S. Bureau of Labor, *Woman and Child Wage-Earners*, VI, 45-46.
[20] *Ibid.*, I, 119-20.

mountain districts, where some of them lived in extreme poverty and isolation. It was true in a lesser degree for the lowland farmers who had lived near the mills.[21]

Some of the millworkers returned to the old life, but the large majority of them, once in the mill village, never went back to the farm permanently.[22] The mill population remained essentially a rural people, however. New groups coming directly from the country were continually moving into the villages, and practically every family had friends or relatives still working on the land.[23]

The mill village was a paternalistic institution. The system was in many respects a reproduction of the great ante-bellum mill of William Gregg at Graniteville, South Carolina. When the farmers moved to the mill they were supplied with company houses, and the company-owned village became a characteristic of the cotton manufacturing industry. The custom arose from necessity, for the worker had no money to build or buy a home and there were not houses enough even in the towns to care for the influx of working population.[24] The mill villages were not all alike, however. In a study made in North Carolina, four types of mill communities are described. There is the rural mill, usually rather small, in the open country near a stream that furnishes water power. The houses in such a village are as a rule of a poorer type and unattractive in appearance. The community is not incorporated and the administration under county regulations may devolve on the mill authorities. The people who live there are isolated and illiterate, and belong to the poorest class of mill operatives. Their restlessness is exemplified in the frequent moves they make from one such mill to another; yet their whole attitude is one of hopelessness and indifference toward any attempts to improve their condition.[25]

Of a different type is the incorporated cotton mill town which frequently contains a number of mills and has a municipal government of its own. Some of the workers own their own homes and others are fairly permanent residents of the town. But even here there is a high degree of mobility of population and a resulting indifference to community life and progress. The greatest organizing force in such a town is the church, for here mill people are not segregated from other occupational groups as they are in other types of mill communities.[26]

---

[21] *Ibid.*, pp. 120-23; Holland Thompson, *From the Cotton Field to the Cotton Mill*, pp. 114-16.

[22] August Kohn, *The Cotton Mills of South Carolina*, p. 26.

[23] Broadus Mitchell, "Why Cheap Labor Down South," in *Virginia Quarterly Review*, v (1929), 484.

[24] J. J. Rhyne, *Some Southern Cotton Mill Workers and Their Villages*, p. 21.

[25] *Ibid.*, pp. 37-42, *passim.*   [26] *Ibid.*, pp. 43-53, *passim.*

The third type is the suburban mill village, located on the outskirts of a city. Such a village may be under the municipal control of the city and yet be in many respects a separate community. The homes which are built by the mill company are fairly good, though the tendency in recent years has been to make them much more attractive and comfortable than formerly. The village has its own churches and is therefore cut off from contact with other groups through that channel. In such communities as this the mill companies have come to carry on social welfare work, providing in some instances day nurseries, playgrounds, swimming pools, and hospitals.[27]

The fourth type of mill community, of which fewer are found than of the others, is the unincorporated company town. The government is carried on under county laws, but in accordance with the wishes of the mill authorities, since the mill corporation owns everything in the town. In such a place the corporations may be very liberal in the types of houses built, the support given to churches and schools, and the welfare work done through social directors.[28]

In the smaller mills there has always been a considerable degree of personal contact between worker and employer. While the white employee was characterized by a strong individualism, he also showed a tendency to look to the millowner as a friend and advisor. This attitude is well exemplified in the case of a small North Carolina mill whose records and correspondence have been in part preserved. The mill was closed at one time, and the letters of former employees seeking to return show their feeling of friendship for the owner and reliance on his advice in personal as well as business matters.[29]

As the mill grew to the point where the personal relationship became slight if it were maintained at all, social welfare work began to appear. It was not carried on in all mills, however. A recent study of three hundred North Carolina mills showed that approximately 20 per cent had one or more welfare workers, 35 per cent had at some time employed such workers, and 40 per cent had at some time contributed to the support of public schools. Over half of the mills had never at any time provided for any kind of welfare work.[30]

Contributions to the support of schools was the chief form of welfare work. In the rural mill village or unincorporated towns, the mills paid the ordinary property tax and exercised practically no control over the administration of the school. In the unincorporated towns owned by the mill, company schools were frequently subsidized

---

[27] *Ibid.*, pp. 54-59, *passim.*   [28] *Ibid.*, pp. 60-64, *passim.*
[29] Correspondence of the Morgan-Malloy Mill, Laurel Hill, N. C., in Duke University Library.   [30] Rhyne, *op. cit.*, p. 29.

by the mills. This inevitably meant that the company would control the policies of the school and regulate the employment of teachers.[31]

The farm families who came to work in the mills were for the most part ignorant of the laws of sanitation and health, illiterate, poverty-stricken, and sadly in need of instruction "in better methods of living." The mills furnished them houses, water, and light at a nominal price and fuel at cost, and frequently provided nurses and social workers to aid by their advice and teaching. The cheap homes were almost universally provided and millworkers accepted them as a matter of course. The welfare work they regarded with indifference. While a large part of the mill population became settled workers, capable of caring for their own interests, many of them remained shiftless and irresponsible and constantly in need of the guidance which the mill officials offered through their welfare agencies.[32]

The company which provided employees with mill-owned houses at low rent, fuel at cost, free medical attention, gardens, and a company store to supply all wants found them dependent, uncomplaining, and slow to make demands for improvements in hours and wages. What was at first a blessing later became a means of restraint.[33] The wages in the mills were low. Even after considering the number of ways in which the paternalistic system lessened the cost of living, the scale of wages was at a minimum. With all or most of the members of a family at work, children in competition with the elders, the income was only sufficient to support tolerable existence.[34]

The employment of large numbers of children and women has been characteristic of the textile industry in all of its stages. The appearance of child labor in the South as the industry developed and the proportion of children employed before restrictive legislation was made effective was in no way unusual. Reference to Table IV shows that in the four states under consideration the proportion of child employees averaged about 26 per cent in 1880, and that it was slightly less in 1890, due to a relatively larger increase in the number of men, but that in 1900 the proportion of children was again about 26 per cent. The actual numbers employed increased rapidly. In the leading textile states there were 4.9 times as many children employed in 1900 as there had been in 1880. Census figures do not include children under ten years of age, although it was generally recognized that some were employed. The estimates of the total number of children employed vary widely. Table V gives the

[31] *Ibid.*, pp. 30-31.   [32] *Ibid.*, pp. 34-35.
[33] Mitchell, "Why Cheap Labor Down South," in *Virginia Quarterly Review*, v, 483-88; Edgar Gardner Murphy, *Problems of the Present South*, pp. 123-24.
[34] Mitchell, *The Rise of Cotton Mills in the South*, p. 230.

number and per cent of children employed in the cotton mills of the several southern states in 1900. The census figures indicate that a relatively large number of young children were employed in southern mills. Whereas in the North only 17.2 per cent of the total number of children between the ages of ten and fifteen, inclusive, were under fourteen, in the South 57.5 per cent of the total number in that group were under fourteen.[35]

TABLE V[36]

COTTON MILL OPERATIVES 10 TO 15 YEARS OF AGE IN SOUTHERN MILLS—1900

State	Number of Operatives	Number of Operatives 10-15 years Old	Per Cent of Operatives 10-15 years Old	Per Cent the Southern Operatives 10-15 Form of Whole Number in Cotton Mills in U.S.
Delaware............	751	121	16.1	0.3
Maryland...........	4,009	1,052	26.2	2.4
Virginia............	2,648	543	20.6	1.2
North Carolina.......	30,717	9,445	30.7	21.3
South Carolina.......	26,821	8,049	30.0	18.1
Georgia.............	16,544	4,552	27.5	10.2
Kentucky...........	769	208	27.0	0.5
Tennessee...........	1,803	443	24.6	1.0
Alabama............	9,049	2,747	30.4	6.2
Mississippi..........	1,636	411	25.1	0.9
Louisiana...........	703	184	26.2	0.4
Texas...............	777	209	26.9	0.5
All Other S. States....	240	57	23.8	0.1
				63.1

After the passage of restrictive legislation and before enforcement became effective, there was a tendency to conceal the number of children employed. While a great many children were openly employed in violation of the law, methods were sometimes used to evade the spirit of the law while conforming to its letter. Children were allowed to work as helpers without having their names on the pay roll. This was often done in the Carolinas, where the early laws only prohibited "employment" of children under certain ages and did not specify "permitting" or "suffering" to work. Since many attempts were made to deceive the agents of the United States Bureau of Labor in making the study of woman and child labor in 1907-8, it may be assumed that similar deceptions were practiced in regard to census figures.[37] The results of the investigation of the Bureau of

[35] U. S. Dept. of Commerce and Labor, *Census Bulletin No. 69*, "Child Labor in the United States," pp. 43-44. Hereafter cited as *Census Bulletin No. 69*.

[36] *Ibid.*, pp. 42-43.

[37] U. S. Bureau of Labor, *Woman and Child Wage-Earners*, I, 187-97.

Labor in 1907 after each state had adopted a twelve-year age limit, with certain exceptions in South Carolina and Georgia, best illustrate the extent of child labor. The investigations covered a representative group of mills in each of the leading cotton manufacturing states. The following table gives the percentages of those employed.

TABLE VI[38]

PER CENT OF CHILDREN EMPLOYED UNDER LEGAL AGE

State	Per Cent of Establishments Employing Children under Legal Age, 12	Children Employed under 12		Number of Establishments Investigated
		Per Cent of Total Number of Children	Per Cent of Total Number of Operatives	
Alabama.........	61.5	6.1	1.27	13
Georgia.........	64.5	3.6	.58	31
South Carolina...	91.7	12.3	2.81	36
North Carolina...	74.6	8.6	1.77	59

These figures do not include children employed under legal exceptions. They include only those admittedly under the legal age or positively proved to be so. The investigators were convinced that if there had been any adequate method of proving the ages of children the percentages would have been considerably higher. Even these figures are evidence of the ineffectiveness of child labor laws without provision for inspection or enforcement.

The figures in Table VII are based on the investigation of 4,091 children in southern mill families. They indicate the relation of child labor to the school and home life of mill children under fifteen years of age.

TABLE VII[39]

PER CENT OF CHILDREN SIX TO FIFTEEN YEARS OF AGE IN COTTON MILL FAMILIES AT WORK, AT SCHOOL, AT HOME

Age Group	At Work	At School	At Home
6-11................	24.6	40.5	34.9
12-13...............	87.8	8.3	3.9
14-15...............	96.2	1.9	1.9

The effect of employment on literacy is indicated in Table VIII.

[38] *Ibid.*, p. 171.　　　　　　[39] *Ibid.*, p. 237.

TABLE VIII[40]

PERCENTAGE OF ILLITERACY AMONG MILL CHILDREN

State	Mill Children Unable to Read and Write		White Children 10-14 Years of Age in State at Large Unable to Read and Write
	Under 14 Years	14-15 Years	
Alabama..............	65.5	46.5	15.3
Georgia..............	42.7	28.2	10.4
South Carolina.......	50.3	31.9	14.8
North Carolina.......	53.8	39.8	16.6

According to the reports made by the mill companies in North Carolina, the illiteracy among operatives over a period of nine years was as follows:

TABLE IX[41]

PERCENTAGE OF ILLITERACY AMONG MILL EMPLOYEES IN NORTH CAROLINA

Year	Adults	Children
1896.............	19	33.5
1900.............	18	32
1904.............	15	22

The high rate of illiteracy among southern workers was paralleled by a low rate of school attendance so that those who could read and write had little education beyond that point. In the North the age group with the highest proportion in school was ten years with 89.9 per cent. In the South it was eight years with 27.7 per cent.[42]

The problem of child labor included not only the fixing of a definite age limit but also the regulation of the hours and conditions of labor under which children should be permitted to work. In some respects this proved one of the most difficult phases. For a time after the revival of the cotton mills began, it occurred to no one to question the desirability of employing children whose parents wished them to work. Boys were employed in "doffing" and sweeping and girls in spinning. The doffers removed the bobbins as they were filled with thread and replaced them with empty ones. The spinners were principally engaged in connecting the ends of broken threads. When called on to defend the system of child labor, the employers pointed out that this was very light work. The boys were busy only

[40] Ibid., pp. 244, 250.
[41] N. C. Bureau of Labor, Tenth Annual Report, 1896, p. 59; Fourteenth Annual Report, 1900, p. 183; Eighteenth Annual Report, 1904, p. 83.
[42] U. S. Dept. of Commerce and Labor, Census Bulletin No. 69, p. 62.

intermittently and played, sometimes in the mill and sometimes in the yard, during their spare time. The spinning required closer attention but little muscular exertion.[43]

Hours of work were long in all mills. A movement to shorten them for all workers developed simultaneously with the demand for child labor legislation. In the first annual report of the Bureau of Labor of North Carolina,[44] the hours in the mills were shown to range from eleven to over twelve a day. A report of a representative of the American Federation of Labor in Alabama in 1901 showed the average workday for twenty-one mills to be eleven and a quarter hours.[45] There were frequently day and night shifts and the spinning department, which employed most of the children, was kept in operation at night more often than any other part of the mill.[46] For this reason night work became a serious phase of the child labor problem.

In estimating the wages received by cotton mill operatives in the earlier years of mill development, it is necessary to take into consideration that much of their pay was "in kind." The whole mill village usually had certain privileges on the company's property. Besides the low rent, wood might be cut on the company's land, cows pastured there, and gardens grown. The company often owned and operated a store from which the employee bought what he needed. Even the churches and school might be supported to a large extent by company money.[47] These things lessened the amount of wages necessary to pay in cash.

Another factor bearing on wages was that the mills employed families rather than individuals. Since the corporations owned the dwelling houses of the mill people, they wished to have in each one as many operatives as possible. A family which did not furnish as many as three workers was not regarded as an asset. The records of the Turnersburg Mill,[48] a small North Carolina factory employing between twenty-five and thirty-five hands, show that in the first few years of the new century the work was all done by a few families whose names were entered in a group on the company books. When one member of a family dropped out for a time, another would take his place. The price of the merchandise which a family bought each week at the company store was deducted from the pay of some of

[43] Kohn, *op. cit.*, pp. 121-22; Thompson, *op. cit.*, pp. 226-27; Scherer, *op. cit.*, p. 328.   [44] Pp. 148-52.
[45] Irene M. Ashby-Macfadyen, "Cotton Mills in Alabama Visited between Dec. 8, 1900 and Jan. 14, 1901," Report to A. F. of L., in Letter File, Box 252. Hereafter cited as "Cotton Mills in Alabama."
[46] Thompson, *op. cit.*, p. 229.
[47] Mitchell, *The Rise of Cotton Mills in the South*, p. 225.
[48] Time Book, in Duke University Library.

its members. A fairly large part of the workers appear to have been children, judging from the wages paid.

One company required the head of the family to sign a contract that all children under a certain age were to be sent to school and all over that age were to be put to work in the mill unless excused by the mill superintendent.[49] Such regulations prevented children of the mill villages from finding employment or making contacts elsewhere. Since employment was a family matter, many small children were brought into the mills by their mothers because there was no other place to leave them. Such children began by helping parents or older sisters, even though they were not on the pay roll themselves. This was the origin of the system of "helpers" and nonemployed workers which complicated the gathering of statistics. The wage of such a child was not paid directly to him but was included in the pay of some other member of his family.[50]

It is impossible to estimate closely the wages of children according to age. Various statements made by the reformers estimated that children received as little as ten or twenty cents a day.[51] Actual wages were low and the competition of child labor was generally regarded by the labor unions as lowering the standard for adult workers. At the Morgan-Malloy Mill in Laurel Hill, North Carolina, the time books for the 1890's show that some children were paid from ten or twelve cents a day up. Most of them received twenty or twenty-five cents, and some thirty. The average for all the workers, including adults, was usually around forty cents a day.[52] In the Turnersburg Mill about 1903 the wages of most workers were approximately fifty cents a day. A few, probably the younger workers, received from twenty cents up.[53] In North Carolina the wages paid over a period of twelve years, as shown in the reports to the Commissioner of Labor, are given in Table X.

The problems presented by child labor in textile mills began to command attention almost as soon as the period of rapid expansion of mills began. If one accepts the date of 1880 which Professor Mitchell sets as the year in which the beginning of this development occurred, it was only about three years before the first demands for labor legislation appeared and six years before the first restrictive law was passed. The period of adverse criticism mingled with favor-

[49] This was the Pelzer Contract, quoted by A. J. McKelway in his manuscript, "History of Child Labor Legislation in the South," and frequently referred to in other places. The manuscript, hereafter referred to as "McKelway's Account," is in a collection of papers and letters in the possession of Mrs. McKelway.

[50] Kohn, op. cit., p. 115.

[51] Atlanta Constitution, Nov. 10, 1897, Dec. 3, 1899.

[52] Time Book, in Duke University Library.

[53] Ibid.

TABLE X[54]

DAILY WAGES IN NORTH CAROLINA COTTON MILLS 1896-1908

Year	Skilled Men	Unskilled Men	Skilled Women	Unskilled Women	Children
1896...........	$ .99	$ .67	$ .66	$ .47½	$ .31
1900...........	1.72	.51	.84	.39	.32
1904...........	2.13	.62	1.04	.49	.41
1908...........	2.50	.79	1.30	.66	.57

able, which occurred in the eighties and early nineties, developed with the rapidly expanding industry into the next stage of bitter attack and defense of the system of child labor at the opening of the new century.

[54] Compiled from N. C. Bureau of Labor, *Tenth Annual Report*, pp. 57-59; *Fourteenth Annual Report*, pp. 182-83; *Eighteenth Annual Report*, p. 83; *Twenty-second Annual Report*, p. 168.

CHAPTER II

ALABAMA, 1887-1903: THE PIONEER

ALABAMA was the first southern state to enact a child labor law during the new manufacturing era. It was not as the result of widespread demand for reform that the restrictive measure was passed. In each of the states the new industrial trends caused a number of labor measures to be proposed in the legislatures. In Alabama in the 1880's there were few cotton manufacturers to oppose the restriction of child labor, while the operators of iron and soft-coal mines had not many places to offer children. Neither was there any strong labor group to demand legislation. During the legislative session of 1886-87 Senator Daniel Smith of Mobile introduced three bills for the protection of children. The first was to prevent the employment of children under fourteen years of age in shows or for any indecent or immoral purpose, or in any occupation injurious to health or dangerous to life. The second bill was directed against the torture, neglect, or abandonment of children. The third bill was "to prevent the compelling of women and children, or the permitting of children under fourteen years of age, to labor in a mechanical or manufacturing business more than ten hours in any day."[1] Similar bills were introduced in the House by Representative T. G. Bush of Mobile.[2] Bush had taken part in the movement to regulate whiskey licenses and to reform the city government in Mobile. He was the president of the Mobile and Birmingham Railroad and later had extensive interests in several iron companies in northern Alabama.[3]

The bill relating to the hours of employment of women and children was reported favorably in the Senate and on the third reading it passed by a vote of nineteen to one, the only opposition coming from Jefferson Falkner, the member for Coosa, Chilton, and Elmore counties.[4] The House amended the bill so as to forbid the employment of children under fifteen in mines, and changed the hours from ten to eight. With these changes the measure was passed

[1] Ala., *Journal of the Senate*, 1886-87, p. 330.

[2] *Daily Register*, Feb. 2, 1887.

[3] T. M. Owen, *History of Alabama and Dictionary of Alabama Biography*, III, 271-72.

[4] Ala., *Journal of the Senate*, 1886-87, pp. 354, 405.

without an opposing vote.[5] The Governor approved the new law on February 28, 1887.

The terms of the law provided that "whoever compels a child under eighteen years of age or a woman to labor in a mechanical or a manufacturing business more than eight hours in any day, or permits a child under the age of fourteen to labor for more than eight hours in any day in any factory, workshop or other place used for mechanical or manufacturing purposes of which he has control, or whoever shall work or permit to be worked in a coal or iron mine, or mines, children under the age of fifteen years of age, shall be fined not more than fifty dollars nor less than five dollars."[6]

The passage of this law received scant attention from press or public. The measures for protection were proposed by the members from Mobile County, where there were no cotton mills or mines. The committees handling them were headed by men from nonmanufacturing regions.[7] The fact that there was practically no opposition to the bill in either house indicates a lack of interest or ignorance of the measure on the part of those concerned with the employment of children and women. The Mobile *Daily Register* showed some interest in the matter and during the time when the bill was under consideration it published at length an article quoted from the *Philadelphia Record* dealing with the growth of woman and child labor, but made no comments on it. The arguments advanced by the *Record* were primarily economic rather than humanitarian.

Since the pressure for factory labor was becoming more intense from year to year, child labor should be prohibited and laws against it adequately enforced. According to an article quoted in the *Register,* "Just as the prevention of imported labor from other countries under contracts based upon wage systems not suited to this free country would improve the condition of men who work in mines or build railroads, or engage in other forms of unskilled labor, so the abolition of child labor would be followed by a widening of the field for the labor of women. Employers should not be allowed to force down the wages of the grown mother or sister by pitting against her in the struggle for existence the poor children who ought to be in school, and who are physically dwarfed and mentally benumbed by the drudgery imposed upon them. . . . There ought to be no cessation in the effort to keep infants out of the factories. If no place were thereby made for girls out of work who are old enough to

[5] Ala., *Journal of the House of Representatives,* 1886-87, p. 1046, hereafter cited as *Journal of the House; Daily Register,* Feb. 26, 1887.

[6] Ala., *Acts of the General Assembly,* 1886-87, pp. 90-91.

[7] Ala., *Journal of the Senate,* 1886-87, p. 354; *Journal of the House,* 1886-87, p. 999.

work, still the humane side of the matter ought to engage the mind of every thinking man and the heart of every good woman."[8]

Although Alabama had taken the first step toward child labor legislation, it proved to be a false start. At the next session of the legislature in 1888-89 a bill was introduced by Senator J. H. Parker from Elmore County to repeal the act in so far as it related to Elmore.[9] The bill passed and was sent to the House where Representative M. E. Pratt of Autauga County proposed an amendment to have his county included in the bill. This amendment was adopted and the bill became law. Elmore County was the seat of a cotton mill established in 1866. Its senator had cast the only opposing vote to the Act of 1887. In Autauga the Prattville Cotton Mill had been established in 1887.[10]

In November, 1894, a bill was introduced in the Senate to repeal the Act of 1887 in so far as it related to Etowah County, and a similar bill was started through the House.[11] After having been favorably reported, the Senate bill was amended so as to apply to the whole state, and was passed by a vote of twenty to six.[12] The House concurred in the repeal[13] and the Governor approved it on December 5, 1894.[14]

The repeal of the first restrictive measure on the employment of children caused even less comment than had its passage. The press of the state said nothing and if the friends of the law were concerned over its repeal they were silent. It is not probable that the act was ever effective for there was no provision for machinery to enforce its terms. Although the later reformers held it up as a precedent and praised the state for being the first to prohibit child labor, there is no evidence that the statute was ever more than a dead letter.

The only explanation of the repeal was made by the advocates of child labor reform. The Dwight Manufacturing Company of Massachusetts began building a large mill in Etowah County in 1895.[15] It was to satisfy the demands of this and similar interests

---

[8] Feb. 20, 1887.

[9] Ala., *Journal of the Senate*, 1888-89, p. 469.

[10] Ala., *Journal of the House*, 1888-89, pp. 840, 841, 864, 922; U. S. Bureau of Labor, *Woman and Child Wage-Earners*, VI, 189.

[11] Ala., *Journal of the Senate*, 1894-95, p. 62; *Journal of the House*, 1894-95, p. 71.

[12] Ala., *Journal of the Senate*, 1894-95, pp. 105, 123, 214.

[13] Ala., *Journal of the House*, 1894-95, pp. 203, 246, 276.

[14] Ala., *Journal of the Senate*, 1894-95, p. 257; *Acts of the General Assembly*, 1894-95, p. 18.

[15] U. S. Bureau of Labor, *Woman and Child Wage-Earners*, VI, 190. This is based on statements in the *Textile Blue Book* for 1895-96, p. 47.

that the law relating to the hours of labor was repealed.[16] If enforced, the eight-hour law for children under fourteen might have interfered seriously with the interests of the mills, but considered in the light of later developments it seems unlikely that the law was effective. In that case the only reason for repealing the act must have been the desire to clear the statute books of all labor legislation.

The first active demands for labor legislation in Alabama began to develop toward the end of the century. Widespread labor organization in the South was nonexistent at this time, but the American Federation of Labor began a campaign for organization of the southern working classes soon after the repeal of the Law of 1887. The Federation had gone on record at its first annual convention in 1881 as opposing child labor,[17] and continued to take this position at each successive meeting. This had little influence on southern workers who had scarcely any representation in the national gatherings. At the convention of 1890 there were only three delegates from the southern states, one from Louisiana, one from Tennessee, and one from Alabama.[18] In 1898 an editorial in the *American Federationist*,[19] the official publication of the Federation, described the repeal of the Alabama law as the "Crime of '94-5." The writer, Samuel Gompers, states that he was in the South organizing garment workers at the time of the repeal, which he heard of "by the merest accident." He called the attention of the Birmingham workers to the action of the state. "It was owing to this incident as much as to any other," he wrote, "that the A. F. of L. two years ago last year, sent organizers through the South with a view of securing the organization of the workers and the passage of laws limiting the hours of labor in Alabama and Georgia."

Organized labor encountered enormous handicaps in trying to promote labor legislation in the South. Local unions were few, and those few were poorly organized. The first attempt at organization on a large scale was made by the representatives of the Federation in 1898, but the effort was not productive of lasting results. The local leaders were for the most part men of scant education and no political influence. Their letters amply testify to their willingness but also indicate a woeful incapacity for leadership in a legislative

[16] Irene M. Ashby-Macfadyen, "The Fight Against Child Labor in Alabama," in *American Federationist*, VIII (1901), 153; U. S. Industrial Commission, *Report of the Industrial Commission on the Relations and Conditions of Capital and Labor*, VII, 619, hereafter cited as *Report*.

[17] "Report of the First Annual Session, 1881," in *Proceedings*, American Federation of Labor, p. 3.

[18] "Report of the Tenth Annual Session, 1890," in *Proceedings*, pp. 7-9.

[19] IV (1898), 278; also U. S. Industrial Commission, *Report*, VII, 619.

reform movement.[20] Furthermore, the organization of labor unions was an unpopular movement with the large majority of the people in the South. According to one of the earlier organizers in Georgia, the general public had the idea that unionism, strikes, and lockouts were synonymous.[21] N. F. Thompson of Huntsville, Alabama, the secretary of the Southern Industrial Convention, in a long article presented as testimony before the United States Industrial Commission in 1900, declared that labor organizations were the greatest existing menace to the government. He claimed to represent the opinion of a considerable portion of the southern public.[22] The operatives in cotton mills showed little inclination to organize. The formation of unions among textile workers has always been one of the weak points of the Federation of Labor, and its efforts in the South proved to be no exception to this.[23]

There were sporadic attempts to enact child labor legislation all through the 1890's in Alabama. The first progress made was in restriction in the mining industry. In 1891 the position of inspector of mines was created.[24] The next session's new mining law forbade the employment of women and boys under ten in the mines.[25] In 1896-97 this age limit was raised to twelve years. The bill was brought about as a result of an investigation of the mines of the state by a committee of the House. The report of the committee did not refer to the employment of children, and it is not probable that many were employed, since the coal mined was bituminous and offered few occupations to children.[26]

In 1897 several child labor bills were presented and lost. Thomas H. Smith of Mobile introduced a series of bills for the protection of children, one of which proposed to prohibit the employment of children of twelve and under in any mechanical, mercantile, or manufacturing establishments.[27] These bills were reported to have come from the Mobile Society for the Propagation of Christian Knowl-

[20] A district organizer in Florence, Alabama, wrote to President Gompers of the A. F. of L.: "I have had Several interviews with our Representatives about factory laws Child Labor in factory and restore the law that they repealed not to allow children under fourteen years to work in factorys and Compolsion Education they say that they agree with me but it was very hard to get a measure through the Legislature like that I told them to take other States for example."—G. W. Osborne to Samuel Gompers, May 1, 1898, A. F. of L. Letter File, Box 97. This is a fair example of what the local organizers wrote.
[21] Will H. Winn to Gompers, May 14, 1896, A. F. of L. Letter File, Box 84.
[22] *Report*, VII, 756.
[23] *American Federationist*, VII (1900), 17.
[24] Ala., *Acts of the General Assembly*, 1890-91, pp. 1362-65.
[25] *Ibid.*, 1892-93, p. 611.
[26] *State Herald (Age Herald)*, Jan. 26, 1897.
[27] Ala., *Journal of the Senate*, 1896-97, p. 496. Smith was a lawyer serving his only term in the Senate at this time. See Owen, *op. cit.*, IV, 1595.

edge.[28] W. T. Cofer of Cullman County proposed prohibiting girls under fifteen working in cotton or woolen mills.[29] Still another bill presented November, 1898, in the House by Luther C. Jones, a labor union member from Lee County and president of the Trades Council of Phoenix, and in the Senate by Dr. J. A. Hurst, a Populist from Etowah County, failed to be reported from the committee in the House, although it passed the Senate after some opposition by a vote of twenty-six to six.[30] It would have limited the hours in the mines and factories to ten a day and prohibited employment of children under eight years of age.[31]

The growth of the labor organizations by 1898 is shown not through any success in securing a child labor law, but through the introduction of several measures relating to labor. In addition to the child labor bill mentioned, Jones introduced a bill to regulate hours of labor in mines and factories, a bill to prohibit the employment of children under twelve in mines and factories, and a bill requiring firms and corporations to provide seats for women employees.[32] After the Christmas recess still another bill was presented to forbid the employment of "children of certain ages in cotton factories in the State before sunup or after sun down."[33]

In the debate in the Senate on the bill to limit the employment of children to ten hours a day, efforts were made to exempt Madison, Walker, Bibb, and Perry counties, which were all cotton mill centers.[34] The *Age Herald* of Birmingham approved the twelve-year bill, saying that it might keep out of the state "a few stony-hearted capitalists," but that it was "a righteous bill nevertheless."[35]

The promotion of child labor legislation by organized labor began to take definite form in 1900. The American Federation of Labor in accordance with its national policy began to urge on local labor leaders the support of measures to regulate child labor. Although this type of law was labor legislation, it had a strong humanitarian appeal which would win it support from people who would not under other circumstances approve such measures. The leaders of labor were aware that they could secure allies from among the non-laboring groups for the enactment of such laws. In 1898 Pres-

[28] Irene M. Ashby-Macfadyen, *Child Labor in Alabama*, Report to the Executive Committee of the State on the History of Child Labor Legislation in Alabama, p. 4.

[29] Ala., *Journal of the Senate*, 1896-97, p. 337.

[30] *Ibid.*, 1898-99, pp. 126, 155, 200-1; *Journal of the House*, 1898-99, p. 104; Ashby-Macfadyen, *Child Labor in Alabama*, p. 4; Owen, *op. cit.*, III, 876.

[31] *Daily Register*, Nov. 22, 1898; *Woman and Child Wage-Earners*, VI, 19.

[32] Ala., *Journal of the House*, 1898-99, p. 167.

[33] *Ibid.*, p. 1178.

[34] *Age Herald*, Dec. 2, 1898.   [35] Dec. 3, 1898.

ident Gompers wrote to a local Alabama leader, "If there are but a few organizations in the South, which will cooperate with each other and concentrate all their efforts without regard to partisan preferences and prejudices and insist upon the passage of the law restricting the hours of labor of children to say ten per day, it can be accomplished. . . . If partisanship is left in the background and men will consistently and persistently demand the ten hour workday for children, say under the age of fourteen years of age in the State of Alabama, there is nothing which can prevent success."[36] This was an over-optimistic statement, but the possibility of co-operation between organized labor and the upper social groups was demonstrated two years later.

Although the efforts to pass a child labor law in 1898-99 had failed for lack of interest and organized support, the position of labor was somewhat better in the legislature of 1900-1901. There were some labor organizations in the larger industrial centers, and J. H. Leath, who was an employee at the *Daily News* office in Birmingham, a Democrat and a labor union man, was elected to the House of Representatives.[37] The American Federation of Labor urged the locals to press their demands for a child labor law and the regulation of hours of labor. In a circular letter to the Alabama unions, Gompers reminded them of the bill that had been defeated two years before, and urged them to renew their efforts. "You should call upon the members of the Legislature, of both the lower house and the Senate, and appoint committees to wait upon them, and insist upon their support of these measures when they are brought before the Legislature. Such action as this should also be taken while these measures are before the respective committees, so that they will be reported and put upon their passage whenever they come before either the House or Senate."

The motives urged were humanitarian rather than economic. "The result of your action may determine the lives of thousands of the children of the State of Alabama. If any cause appeals to our hearts, our sentiments, our better natures, it is the cause which will protect the health and the lives of the children of our day, the mothers and fathers of future generations."[38]

Gompers at this time took a step which went further than mere advice and encouragement. The existence of child labor on a rather large scale was recognized by the Federation, but the actual extent

[36] Samuel Gompers to G. W. Osborne, May 11, 1898, Letter Book, Vol. XXIII, in office of A. F. of L.

[37] J. H. Leath to Frank Morrison, Jan. 19, 1900, A. F. of L. Letter File, Box 150; J. H. Leath to Gompers, Nov. 19, 1900, A. F. of L. Letter File, Box 212; Owen, *op. cit.*, IV, 1024.

[38] Oct. 18, 1900, in Letter Book, Vol. XXXVII.

of the evils involved was undetermined. There had been no systematic investigations to cover adequately even a limited geographic area, so that it was difficult to make statements of conditions or to meet contradictions with proof. Because of this, and in order to promote the organization of a definite movement for child labor legislation, Gompers, late in 1900, sent a special agent of the Federation to Alabama.

Miss Irene Ashby was a young English woman who had been educated at Westfield College, London. She was interested in social and industrial problems, and had taken some part in social experiments in London, and had organized the girls who worked for Sir Thomas Lipton to protest against their conditions of employment.[39] She came to the United States in 1900 and early in the autumn of that year she was in communication with Samuel Gompers.[40] In October he asked her to come to Washington for an interview with the prospect of becoming an organizer for the American Federation.[41] Although there were some delays[42] the meeting finally took place on November 30, 1900. The result was an agreement that Miss Ashby should be employed, not as a labor organizer, as Gompers had suggested, but for the purpose of promoting child labor legislation. She was provided with a general letter of introduction, and one addressed to the Secretary of the Trades and Labor Council of Montgomery, Alabama. The letters stated that she was "to represent the American Federation of Labor in the effort to secure the passage of a law by the Legislature of the state of Alabama, to restrict and regulate the labor of children and minors in the factories and workshops of Alabama."[43] Miss Ashby was sent directly to Alabama because the legislature was then in session. It had not been definitely decided where the American Federation should concentrate its efforts; there was some consideration at first of the Carolinas.[44]

The new labor member of the House, Leath of Jefferson County, on November 19, 1900, introduced bills to regulate the employment of children in mines and factories and to regulate the hours of labor, but the bills died at the hands of the Committee on Mining and

[39] Irene M. Ashby-Macfadyen, "The Last Stronghold of Infant Mill Slavery," in *Social Service*, IV (1901), 202, editorial note.

[40] Miss Ashby probably began correspondence with Mr. Gompers in September or October, 1900, although the letter is not preserved. The copy of his reply, illegible due to defects of ink and paper, is in Letter Book, Vol. XXXVII.

[41] Gompers to Miss Irene Ashley [sic], Oct. 17, 1900, Letter Book, Vol. XXXVII.

[42] Ibid., Oct. 26, 1900.

[43] Gompers to whom it may concern, and to Secretary of Trades and Labor Council, Montgomery, Ala., Nov. 30, 1900, Letter Book, Vol. XXXVII.

[44] R. Lee Guard to Miss Ashby, Dec. 22, 1900; Gompers to Prince W. Greene, Dec. 27, 1900, Letter Book, Vol. XXXIX.

Manufacturing.[45] It was still early in the session, however, and Leath continued his efforts to arouse the interest of the working people. He made frequent speeches to the new unions,[46] but the extent of his influence was limited by the very nature of his hearers.

The coming of a special agent to work up an anti-child labor feeling aroused the interest not only of the organized workers but of the more progressive and liberal-minded people of the cities. The women's clubs of Birmingham had already discussed child labor and the need for legislation. The Woman's Christian Temperance Union had made legal restriction a part of their platform. But they were ignorant of the fact that a bill had already been introduced that year in the legislature.[47] There had been developed no able or well-defined leadership for the movement.

When Miss Ashby arrived in Montgomery one of the first persons to become interested in her plans was the Reverend Edgar Gardner Murphy, rector of St. John's Episcopal Church. Murphy was a young man hardly past thirty-one. He was born at Fort Smith, Arkansas, August 31, 1869. His early education was received in San Antonio, Texas, and in 1885 he entered the University of the South at Sewanee, Tennessee. After graduation he studied for a year at Columbia University and was ordained as an Episcopal clergyman in San Antonio in 1890. He remained in Texas until 1893 when he went to Chillicothe, Ohio, for a few years and then to Kingston, New York. Returning to the South to become rector of St. John's Church at Montgomery in 1898, he was much impressed by the grave maladjustments in southern society.[48] He took the leading part in organizing the race conferences held in 1900 and wrote and spoke on the subject of race relationships.[49] He was also interested in the problem of education, and in 1901 he resigned his pastorate in order to become the executive secretary of the Southern Education Board.[50] At the time Miss Ashby came to him, the race conferences were over and Murphy was in a position to take an active part in a new cause. He turned to the child labor movement at a time when the leadership of a person of

[45] Ala., *Journal of the House*, 1900-1901, p. 100; also Irene M. Ashby-Macfadyen, "The Fight Against Child Labor in Alabama," in *American Federationist*, VIII, 150.

[46] Leath to Morrison, Jan. 8, 1901, A. F. of L. Letter File, Box 212.

[47] Ashby-Macfadyen, "The Fight Against Child Labor in Alabama," in *American Federationist*, VIII, 150.

[48] Francis G. Caffey's address at the Edgar Gardner Murphy Memorial Meeting, Dec. 7, 1913, MS in possession of Mrs. E. G. Murphy; also Owen, *op. cit.*, IV, 1260.

[49] E. G. Murphy, *The White Man and the Negro at the South*; also *A Southern Conference for the Discussion of Race Problems*; also *An Open Letter on Suffrage Restriction, and Against Certain Proposals of the Platform of the State Convention*.

[50] *Montgomery Advertiser*, Nov. 28, 1901.

ability and influence was needed to bring together the several groups which were interested, and to produce unity of action.

The first persons whom Murphy consulted about the problems of child labor legislation were his fellow clergymen. The Reverend George B. Eager of the Methodist Church, and the Reverend Neal L. Anderson, Presbyterian, were colleagues with whom he had already worked on the race conference committee.[51] These men formed the nucleus of the child labor committee which developed a few months later.

Miss Ashby's presence in Alabama served to reassure the socially élite of Montgomery and the other cities as to their wisdom in advocating a labor measure. She was a person of education and found herself able to meet the conservative classes on their own ground. At the same time the local labor organizations were glad to accept her as the representative of the American Federation. When she succeeded in securing the co-operation of the clergy, some of the unionists were immediately confident of success.[52]

The interval between December 12, 1900, and January 15, 1901, in which the legislature was in recess was used by Miss Ashby in making what was probably the first extensive investigation of child labor in the cotton mills of Alabama, or of any of the southern states. While there were defects in her methods which would make her report scarcely acceptable from the standpoint of investigators of today, her work produced evidence which could be used by the advocates of reform. The publicity which it received also helped to create interest in a problem heretofore rather vague in the minds of the large majority of people. Her method was to ask a uniform set of questions of mill superintendents, managers, and operatives, and people who lived in close contact with the millworkers. From the answers and from her own observations she compiled her report. She declared that she was well treated by all the mill managers except one, "even when they found out, or guessed" her errand.[53]

The report of the investigation made by Miss Ashby to the American Federation listed the mills visited by name, number of employees, children under twelve, and the hours of work per day. The figures are not entirely accurate, but give some idea of conditions. Of 25 mills visited, 10 were operated by northern capital and employed 4,400 operatives, of whom 215 were children under twelve. Thirteen mills were operated by southern capital and employed 1,968

[51] Murphy, *A Southern Conference for the Discussion of Race Problems;* also statement of Mrs. Murphy.

[52] J. A. Shaw to Gompers, Jan. 19, 1901, A. F. of L. Letter File, Box 214.

[53] Ashby-Macfadyen, "The Fight Against Child Labor in Alabama," in *American Federationist,* VIII, 151.

operatives, of whom 115 were children under twelve. The two operated by mixed capital employed 357 people, of whom 40 were under twelve.[54] In an article published in the *Federationist*[55] Miss Ashby stated that the number of children in the northern-owned mills was almost twice as great as the number in those operated by southern capital. According to her own figures, however, the southern-owned mills employed a slightly higher per cent of children. From the figures in her report the average workday was about eleven and a quarter hours. Seven mill managers expressed themselves as against the child labor bill, and one had employed an agent to fight it; fifteen were in favor of the bill; two would favor it if the other southern states had such laws; one declared himself "resigned" to child labor legislation; two believed the state was not ready for it.[56]

Miss Ashby's figures may be compared with those of the census report for 1900. In Alabama there were 45 cotton mills which had a capital of $11,944,398 and total wages of $1,526,759.[57] There was a total of 9,049 mill operatives, of whom 2,747 were children from ten to fifteen years of age.[58] According to the census, therefore, over 30 per cent of the operatives in cotton mills were between the ages of ten and fifteen. According to Miss Ashby's figures 5.5 per cent of the employees were under twelve years of age, and by the law of proportion, there would have been approximately 500 children under twelve employed in the mills of Alabama.

The investigation of the mills brought Miss Ashby directly into contact with the men who opposed child labor legislation and gave her an opportunity to hear their defense and their accusations against labor at first hand. She was told that she was being used as a tool by the American Federation to promote the interests of northern mills by reducing the advantages of the mills in the South. Somewhat disturbed by the charge, she reported it to President Gompers and asked for his explanation. He replied at length, assuring her that the report was false, but that if she believed it she should drop her work at once. The charge of ulterior motives was as old as the first efforts to secure protective legislation in England. The poor widow, dependent on her child for support, was also advanced as an argument against legislation, and Miss Ashby accepted it with concern. Gompers had little patience with such excuses. He wrote, "If you want to

[54] Ashby-Macfadyen, "Cotton Mills in Alabama," A. F. of L. Letter File, Box 252.

[55] "The Fight Against Child Labor in Alabama," VIII, 153.

[56] Ashby, "Cotton Mills in Alabama," A. F. of L. Letter File, Box 252.

[57] U. S. Bureau of the Census, "Manufactures," *Report on Manufactures,* Twelfth Census, 1900, Vol. IX, Pt. III, p. 14.

[58] *Ibid.*, "Occupations," pp. 220-23.

continue in the work to secure a child labor law, I want you to quit
trying to find a way out for the state, for the widows, for the 'worthless or helpless fathers,' or to have your conscience burdened whether
the industries of the south or of any other place are going to be hurt
or disarranged by the passage of such a law.

"You will kindly advise me as promptly as possible whether you
will undertake to work for the passage of the child labor bill and compulsory education bill, without regard to insinuations, suspicions, or
charges of any one made against yourself or the A. F. of L., and upon
the lines indicated both in my conversation with you and in this correspondence."[59]

After this reprimand Miss Ashby was no longer uncertain as to
the attitude she should take toward the arguments of the manufacturers, and her work was from then on entirely satisfactory to the
president of the Federation.[60]

The press approached the question of a child labor bill rather
uncertainly, once it was forced on the attention of the public by the
investigation of the cotton mills. It became known that Leath, whose
bill had been killed early in the season, would introduce another with
the support of both the humanitarians and the labor organizations.
There was at the same time a movement for compulsory school attendance and the *Daily Register* associated the measures together. Commenting editorially on the bills, it said, "The common sense of the
world appears to be enlisted in favor of a reasonable regulation of
child labor. Of course conditions are not everywhere the same. It would
seem that if we are to forbid the employment of all children under a
certain age we should provide some occupation for them if so be
they are idle at their homes. Nothing better than good schooling can
be suggested; and from this we naturally reach the conclusion that
compulsory education will be necessary. We observe that in Great
Britain both the prohibition of child labor and the educational exer-
cises are enforced. In Alabama, however, we confront a very serious
problem when we take up compulsory education, as the thing we
must establish by law. We may very well give it close thought and
take time to discover what is the present ability of the state to provide the education if the acceptance of such education be made compulsory. Moreover, in the absence of schools, it is conceivable that the
factory may serve to some extent as a substitute. Children obtain a
certain sort of training therein, at any rate; and some manufacturers
conduct schools in connection with their factories. In short, in viewing

[59] Gompers to Miss Ashby, Jan. 3, 1901, Letter Book, Vol. XL.
[60] Gompers to Miss Ashby, Feb. 4, 1901, Letter Book, Vol. XL.

the subject advocated by the London missionary [Miss Ashby], we must include a comprehensive survey of local conditions. What is advocated is right, as a general proposition. The question our legislators must ask is, whether it is right as a particular one."[61]

The Alabama labor unions supported compulsory school attendance as well as child labor legislation. The bill which they favored was drawn up by L. C. Jones, who had presented a child labor measure in the legislature of 1898-99. The education bill was sent to Gompers for criticism and he made some suggestions as to the publicity campaign.[62]

The new child labor bill was presented in the House on the first day the Assembly met after the Christmas recess by A. J. Reilly, engineer of the Pratt City mines.[63] Four days later Senator Hugh Morrow presented it in the upper house.[64] The bill provided an age limit of twelve years for the employment of all children except newspaper carriers; exception was made for the children of widowed mothers or disabled fathers, who might be employed at ten. It required an affidavit from the parent or guardian of the employed child as to age, and imposed a fine of from $5.00 to $100 or not more than three months' imprisonment for violation. No child under sixteen should work between the hours of 7:00 P.M. and 6:00 A.M. or more than 60 hours in one week or 11 hours in one day. After March 1, 1902, children employed must be able to read and write, and each employee between the ages of twelve and fourteen was required to file a certificate from his teacher stating that he had completed 12 consecutive weeks of school during the year. A factory inspector should be appointed by the Governor at a salary of $1,500 a year. It should be his duty to inspect the places where women and children were employed and to make annual reports to the Governor. Violations of the law on the part of the employer were subject to a fine of not more than $500.[65] The standards set in this measure were higher than those proposed in the measures previously introduced in Alabama and other southern states. In this the influence of the legislative standards set up by the Federation is apparent.

At about the same time the child labor bill was introduced, its

---

[61] Jan. 18, 1901.

[62] R. Lee Guard to Miss Ashby, Jan. 16, 1901; Gompers to L. C. Jones, Jan. 16, 1901, in Letter Book, Vol. XL.

[63] Ala., *Journal of the House*, 1900-1901, p. 700; Ashby-Macfadyen, "The Fight Against Child Labor in Alabama," *loc. cit.*, p. 154. Reilly was a northern man who had lived in the South only a few years. He was a Democrat. See Owen, *op. cit.*, IV, 1424.

[64] Ala., *Journal of the Senate*, 1900-1901, p. 561. Morrow, a native of Birmingham, was a lawyer and a Democrat. See Owen, *op. cit.*, IV, 1248.

[65] *Daily Register*, Jan. 29, 1901.

companion bill for compulsory school attendance was presented in both houses.[66]

The Reilly-Morrow bill was the first one of its kind to receive any degree of public interest. Miss Ashby reported that petitions favoring the bill came from Birmingham and some of the mill towns. The Ministers' Union of Montgomery, interested through the efforts of Murphy, took the matter up. The leading clubwomen discussed the proposed legislation, and "the society and religious lion lay down with the labor lamb."[67] The State Federation of Women's Clubs appointed for the first time a legislative committee in connection with the publicity campaign. This was the beginning of its active interest in legislation for the protection of women and children.[68]

Efforts were made to secure an early hearing for the child labor bill, but the mill-owning interests had become aroused and began to lobby against the measure. The lobbyists made capital of the fact that Miss Ashby was a foreigner and charged that she was being paid by the eastern and English mills to make trouble in the South and so reduce its competitive power.[69] On February 5, 1901, a joint hearing was held before the committees on Mining and Manufactures to which the bills had been referred. Reilly, the chairman of the House Committee, presided at the discussion. A number of prominent women were present, and Murphy spoke as a representative of the Ministers' Union. The opponents of the measure had an equal amount of time assigned to them to present their arguments. They were represented by an official of the Alabama City mill, a railroad attorney, and a corporation clergyman. The vote of the House Committee stood at nine to four against the bill and that of the Senate Committee was five to two against it. Morrow and Reilly asked that it go up without recommendation, but the committees refused.[70]

An effort to revive the question of child labor was made on the following day when the bill was reintroduced in the House and referred to the Committee on Immigration and Labor.[71] Most of the committee remained away from the hearing and the vote was five

[66] Ala., *Journal of the House*, 1900-1901, p. 761; Ala., *Journal of the Senate*, 1900-1901, p. 510.

[67] Ashby-MacFadyen, "The Fight Against Child Labor in Alabama," *American Federationist*, VIII, 154; also Julia S. Tutwiler, "Reports of State Corresponding Secretaries—Alabama," in *Proceedings*, National Conference of Charities and Correction, Twenty-eighth Session (1901), pp. 37-39.

[68] Lura H. Craighead, "Data Concerning the Alabama Federation of Women's Clubs," MS in Alabama State Dept. of Archives and History.

[69] Ashby-Macfadyen, "The Fight Against Child Labor in Alabama," *American Federationist*, VIII, 155.

[70] *Ibid.*, pp. 155-56; *Advertiser*, Feb. 7, 1901; Tutwiler, *op. cit.*, pp. 37-39.

[71] Ala., *Journal of the House*, 1900-1901, p. 1009.

to three against it. At this hearing Murphy spoke again and was met with the insinuation that the friends of the bill were acting at the instigation of northern capital. He immediately resented the implication as odious and demanded that the speaker substantiate or withdraw the accusation. The millman refused to do either, but at the close of the meeting offered a private apology which was not accepted. Murphy gave his story in a letter to the Birmingham *Age Herald.* He said that it was also asserted that he habitually addressed Negro audiences, which he denied. These trivial incidents served to convince him that his opponents were appealing to prejudices and suspicions that had nothing to do with the real issue.[72]

The compulsory education bill was reported without recommendation and was disposed of by indefinite postponement.[73] Despite the interest of a few prominent people these two measures were not discussed at length by the press. The more prominent papers said little in regard to them, and the only comment of the Mobile *Daily Register* was that the child labor bill was killed because the committees were convinced that the time had not come for such enactment.[74] The Huntsville *Mercury,* representing a locality in which there were a number of mills, defended the defeat of the bill by the manufacturing interests on the ground that such a measure was uncalled for and established a bad precedent for labor legislation which would injure the state. The matter of regulating child labor should be left to the parents. This was a reversal of the position of the *Mercury,* which a short time before had published an editorial in condemnation of child labor and advocating Leath's bill.[75]

The most important outcome of the legislative contest of 1900-1901 was the formation of the Alabama Child Labor Committee. There had not been enough time between the arrival of Miss Ashby in Montgomery and the opening of the legislature after Christmas to organize the demand for legislation, even had its advocates realized that such organization was essential to success. But the nature and strength of the opposition convinced Murphy and his friends that the formation of a committee which would create and direct public opinion so as to bring pressure to bear on the members of the legislature was the only way to secure the enactment of a law. The new committee grew out of the small group of interested clergymen in Montgomery. Neal L. Anderson, one of the first men to associate himself with Murphy in the new movement, wrote, "The original Southern group of Child Labor legislation advocates, was composed

[72] Feb. 16, 1901.
[73] Ala., *Journal of the House,* 1900-1901, pp. 761, 1211, 1241, 1401, 1517, 1528, 1529.   [74] Feb. 8, 1901.
[75] *Age Herald,* Feb. 7, 1901, quoting the *Mercury;* also U. S. Bureau of Labor, *Woman and Child Wage-Earners,* VI, 194-95.

solely of representatives of wealth and aristocracy, and the ministers on the Committee were pastors of large city churches. . . . There was never associated with the Alabama Committee any man or woman, who would be known today as a 'Red.' "[76] Murphy said of the committee that it was composed of "representatives of the Church, the press, the judiciary, the labor unions, and the mercantile and banking interests of the state."[77] Of the men who became members of the committee during the first year several were quite prominent. Besides Murphy and Anderson there were Judge J. B. Gaston, B. J. Baldwin, M.D., former governor and Judge Thomas G. Jones, S. B. Marks, Judge J. W. Thomas, and Father O'Brien of Montgomery; John Craft, Erwin Craighead, editor of the *Daily Register,* and Joseph E. Rich of Mobile; A. J. Reilly, the Reverend John G. Murray, A. T. London, and J. A. Phillips, superintendent of schools of Birmingham.[78] The membership was divided among the capital and the two largest cities of the state, only one of which was an industrial center.

Murphy was convinced that the defeat of the child labor bill in 1901 was the result of the efforts of a representative of the Dwight Mill at Alabama City, which was owned in Massachusetts and had figured in the repeal of the Act of 1887. Feeling that the attitude of New England was critical of the southern mill situation, the Alabama Committee addressed a public appeal to the people and press of New England through the columns of the *Boston Evening Transcript.* The avowed purpose was to awaken public opinion there against the New England men who were doing in the South a thing which they were not allowed to do at home.[79]

On October 31, 1901, J. Howard Nichols, treasurer of the Alabama City Mills, published a reply to the "appeal" in the *Transcript.* He stated that he always protested to his agents against the employment of children under twelve, because it was not only a humanitarian wrong but also an economic loss; but the parents forced the mill managers to accept the children by threatening to leave if they were not employed. Regarding Miss Ashby, he said, "The labor organizations at the North imported from England a very bright and skillful female labor agitator and sent her to Alabama," where she held meetings and appeared before the legislature. The manufacturers resented this outside interference, "knowing the source from which it came. . . . As they recognized that this bill was only an

[76] Neal L. Anderson to the author, Feb. 14, 1930.

[77] *Problems of the Present South,* p. 119.

[78] *Ibid.,* p. 312, n.

[79] *Ibid.,* p. 309. Appendix B, "Appeal to the People and Press of New England," and the resulting correspondence are reproduced in full here. They were published in pamphlet form in several editions and circulated by the Alabama Committee in 1901-2, besides appearing in the newspapers.

entering wedge, they determined that action must come from within the State and not outside." The manufacturers felt that Georgia should act first in the matter of child labor legislation, since she had a larger number of spindles than Alabama. "With these considerations in mind, the manufacturers selected among others our agent, a native Alabamian, to appear before the legislative committee, with the result that the bill was defeated. I think it may be said with truth, that the interference of Northern labor agitators is retarding much needed legislation in all the manufacturing States of the South."[80]

A copy of the *Transcript* reached Murphy on November 2, 1901, and he immediately wrote to the editor in reply to Nichols' arguments. His first point was that the members of the Alabama Committee who had signed the appeal were entirely disinterested, whereas the reply was signed by one man only, who was the treasurer of a mill and obviously not disinterested. In the second place, while Nichols conceded the two fundamental principles of the argument against child labor, social wrong and economic error, yet he sent a representative to oppose legislation which would remedy these evils. Claiming that he did not wish to employ children and did so only because of pressure from the parents, he yet used his influence against legislation that would prevent his being subjected to such necessity. Nichols, himself a northerner, argued that the agitation came from outside the state, but that the remedy should come from within. Murphy paraphrased this to say that the evils might come from without but the remedy must be indigenous.[81] Murphy believed that the whole success of the child labor movement depended on whether or not it was made to appear to the public as a spontaneous development from within the state. While he was himself fully willing to co-operate with the labor organizations in promoting legislation and would have gladly shared with them any credit for the results, he knew the tenor of public feeling well enough to realize that the argument of "outside interference" and "an entering wedge for labor legislation" could be used with enough effect to prevent the success of any bill so stigmatized. For this reason he emphasized the fact that the movement for legislation had not begun with Miss Ashby's arrival, but that a demand had previously been made for it.[82] In a reply to Nichols, he said, "We yield sincere gratitude to the American Federation of Labor for their earnest, creditable and effective co-operation. Our indebtedness to them is very great. Their interest in the situation is entirely legitimate. When the little child is thrust into the labor market in competition with the adult, the adult-wage

[80] *Ibid.*, pp. 309-11.
[81] *Ibid.*, pp. 312-14.
[82] *Ibid.*, pp. 314-15.

is affected throughout the world. But the agent of the Federation of Labor—earnest and devoted woman that she is—has worked under the absolute command of the local forces of this State, she is now in this State upon the explicit invitation of these forces, and the demand for this legislative protection of our little children was made by the Ministers' Union of Montgomery and by the Woman's Christian Temperance Union of Alabama, before she was ever heard of in the South."[83]

Murphy was wise in not wishing the child labor measure to appear before the public as a labor measure. It is not probable that men of political influence would at that time have supported any other form of labor legislation, or even that measure if it had been presented solely as a labor measure. The labor organizations which were growing in the larger cities did support the child labor bill and other labor measures when they were presented. In that sense the proposed law might have been justly considered as an "entering wedge." This in no way detracts from the sincerity of the labor organizations in wishing to put an end to the evils of child labor from a humanitarian standpoint.

The controversy between Murphy and Nichols was taken up by Horace Sears, treasurer of the West Point Manufacturing Company of Langdale, Alabama, another northern-owned mill. His reply to the Alabama Committee was published in the *Transcript* and reprinted in the December *Monthly Leader*. He characterized Murphy's first reply as that of "the professional labor agitator and the well-meaning but ill-advised humanitarian," and advised the members of the committee "to cultivate a calm and judicial mind." He urged them to copy Massachusetts, which had a compulsory education law, although he was willing to advocate one for Alabama only on condition that it should not go into effect until North Carolina, South Carolina, and Georgia had agreed to a similar one.[84]

Sears' criticism called for a still more vigorous reply from Murphy, which he published in the *Monthly Leader*. Sears had stated that he did not believe that any of the members of the Alabama Committee had been present at the legislative session which rejected the child labor bill. Murphy replied by reminding him that the chairman of the House Committee that had considered the bill was a member of the Alabama Committee; that he had presided at the public hearing on the measure; that he had been personally in charge of the compulsory education bill; and that Murphy himself had appeared at both hearings and spoken for the bill. He also indicated that the manufacturers while professing to favor compulsory school

[83] *Advertiser*, Nov. 10, 1901.
[84] Murphy, *Problems of the Present South*, pp. 319-21.

attendance had not been active in the discussion of that bill. While the worst conditions of child labor were not found in the Massachusetts-owned mills, these mills were the ones publicly opposed to reform. Efforts of the good mills to prevent legislation to protect children meant the continuation of the conditions found in the worst mills of the state.[85]

The Nichols-Sears controversy had definitely introduced sectionalism into the child labor issue. Murphy had begun it by an appeal to fair-minded public opinion in New England to coerce its citizens into accepting the same standards in the South that they had at home. Nichols and Sears had responded in a bickering tone and fell back on the argument—traditionally expected from southerners rather than northerners—that the proposals were due to outside interference. Murphy did not hesitate to take advantage of this. He wrote, "New England might find analogies in our situation. Was New England solicitous for the policy of 'non-interference' from outside the State, in relation to the evils of slavery? . . . More than a generation ago it was argued, for the system of slavery, that there were good plantations upon which the slaves were well treated. That statement was true, but the argument was weak. The presence of the good plantation could not offset the perils and evils of the system in itself, any more than the 'good factory' can justify the system of child labor. . . . There can be no 'good' child labor. And this system is monstrous, not only in principle, but in results."[86]

Sears had charged the committee with sectional hatred. Murphy replied, "And which is the more likely to induce that malignant and excuseless passion—the spectacle of the attitude of the South toward the capital of Massachusetts, or the attitude of the capital of Massachusetts toward the little children of the South? The fact that these are white children, and that Massachusetts—always solicitous for the negro—should be largely indifferent to the fate of our white children, does not relieve the situation. Suppose the conditions were reversed, and that the mills of Southern men were full of negro children under twelve—how quickly and how justly New England would ring with denunciation."[87]

This controversy was the beginning of a series of pamphlets written by Murphy and published under the authorization of the Alabama Committee. If a law were to be passed Murphy believed that formation of a favorable public opinion which would demand it was essential. His pamphlets formed the first body of printed material of any considerable extent or value that presented arguments favorable to child labor legislation in the South. There had been

[85] *Ibid.,* pp. 323, 325.
[86] *Ibid.,* p. 325.   [87] *Ibid.,* pp. 327-28.

a few articles published in the *American Federationist*,[88] but its circulation in the South was necessarily small, and the very nature of the magazine would have prevented its having a favorable influence on those it was most desirable to reach. A few articles had appeared in *Gunton's Magazine* and in other periodicals devoted to sociological problems.[89] But they probably had only a small circulation in the South, and had the added handicap of traditional sectional prejudice against them. But the Murphy pamphlets were written by a native southerner, a man belonging by birth and profession to the conservative class. They did not depend on the circulation of little-read periodicals, but were sent directly to persons whom it was considered desirable to interest. Murphy was convinced that this was the best way to create favorable opinion. He wrote, "I think that there is at present no need for an agent from the Federation in Alabama. I think at this time whatever money can be given to the campaign in this State should be expended upon the circulation of literature. People are beginning to take an interest in the subject, and are beginning to read about it. A considerable body of literature could be circulated to all the newspapers of the State, and to such selected addresses as we might gather, at comparatively small expense. I have paid recently for all of this work out of my own pocket."[90]

It is not possible to determine the order in which the pamphlets appeared, but a large number of them were published in 1901-2, sometimes in more than one edition. Following the Nichols-Sears controversy, which was distributed in pamphlet form, the next long publication was a fifty-page pamphlet entitled *The Case Against Child Labor*, which was written in June, 1902, and probably distributed during the following month. The argument was logical and direct. The wiser millowners saw that the employment of children under twelve was not only a moral evil, but an economic loss. The doctrine of freedom of contract loses validity when applied to children. In reply to the argument that compulsory education would keep the children out of the factories, Murphy quoted D. A. Tompkins, prominent cotton manufacturer of North Carolina, as saying that the South could not support more than a three months' school

[88] M. Raphael, "Child Labor," III (1896), 157-59; Samuel Gompers, "The Crime of '94-5," IV (1898), 278; Prince W. Greene, "Southern Textile Workers," VI (1899), 126; Ashby-Macfadyen, "The Fight Against Child Labor in Alabama," VIII (1901), 150-57; Eva M. Valesh, "Three Notable Lines of Child Labor Work," VIII, 457-62.

[89] The following appeared in *Gunton's Magazine*: "Factory Labor in the South," XIV (1898), 217-28; Jerome Dowd, "Cheap Labor in the South," XVIII (1900), 112-21; George Gunton, "What Can Be Done About It?" XVIII, 121-30, and "The South's 'Labor System,'" XVIII, 234-39; Leonora Beck Ellis, "Child Labor Legislation in the South," XXI (1901), 45-53.

[90] Murphy to Mrs. Macfadyen, May 21, 1902, A. F. of L. Letter File, Box 303.

term. This would leave the children nine months to work in the mills, and therefore a compulsory school law was no substitute for child labor legislation. Murphy rejected the plea that the child was better off in the mill than idle on the streets, even though school were not in session. He based his appeal on grounds of common sense.[91]

The publication of this pamphlet brought an immediate reply from the *Manufacturers' Record* of Baltimore, a trade journal and mouthpiece for southern manufacturers. Earlier in the year the *Record* had spoken of the "good-hearted individuals" of Alabama who had "become participants in a social agitation manufactured elsewhere by skilled artificers and trained performers upon sentimentality."[92] It now attacked Murphy's pamphlet with bitterness. "Wandering, as it is, impracticable, radical and unreasonable, the pamphlet, with its appended bill, presents a poor case against child labor. It is an eloquent argument in itself against the interference of enthusiasts in social problems beyond their range." The editorial criticism extended from ridicule of the "imported agitatress" using "Miss Lizzie Barrett's" poem[93] to denunciation of the reformers for following the methods of the abolitionists, and the New England people for endeavoring to cripple the South.[94]

Murphy replied to the *Record's* attack with a new pamphlet, *The South and Her Children.* He quoted the editorial of the *Record* and challenged the editor to take a definite stand on child labor. The editorial was analyzed and its assertions denied. Murphy particularly resented the implication that the millowners were "representative men" of the South and that possibly he and his associates were not. He again made an emphatic denial of the charge of "outside influence": "If there is an 'outside' influence back of this agitation for a child-labor law, I do not know where it is. It is true that outside interest has been awakened, but this legislation was demanded by representative bodies in Alabama long before such interest was aroused. If we have carried this war into New England it has been solely with the request that she would control, not the South, but the New England man, who, in using the labor of our children under twelve, is doing at the South what he cannot and dare not do at home."[95]

The editor of the *Record* continued the controversy on September 18, 1902, although he failed to define his position on the sub-

[91] E. G. Murphy, *The Case Against Child Labor—An Argument,* pp. 4-32.

[92] XLI (Jan. 30, 1902), 17.

[93] The advocates of child labor legislation repeatedly quoted from Elizabeth Barrett Browning's "The Cry of the Children."

[94] *Manufacturers' Record,* XLII (Aug. 28, 1902), 93-95.

[95] *The South and Her Children,* p. 18.

ject of child labor legislation as Murphy had asked him to do.[96] Compared with Murphy's clear logic his reply was ineffective and amounted to nothing more than blustering criticism.

Murphy continued to publish other and shorter pamphlets. They were characterized by logical reasoning and a complete lack of the sentimentality usually attributed to reformers. He did not depict isolated instances of specially bad conditions or relate harrowing stories of mistreated children. He tried instead to give a fair and reasonable presentation of his view. He hoped to win over the more progressive manufacturers to the side of legislative regulation, and there was nothing to be gained by antagonizing them unnecessarily. In *Child Labor and Business,* an eight-page pamphlet, he used United States census figures to show that the South had made no progress in the past twenty years in cutting down the percentage of child labor, and that there was still a much greater proportion of cotton mill operatives under sixteen in the South than elsewhere in the United States. It was bad business to allow the impression to get abroad that the success of southern industry was dependent upon child labor.

In *Child Labor Legislation* Murphy summarized the laws relating to child labor in the states outside the South, and argued that if the northern states could protect children of immigrants the South could do the same for its native-born children.

The proposed remedy of child labor by voluntary agreement among the manufacturers was dealt with in a pamphlet entitled *A Child-Labor Law.* It was produced because of the attitude taken by the president-elect of the Alabama Federation of Women's Clubs, Mrs. Lillian Milner Orr. In an address to club women she advocated leaving the regulation of child labor to the millowners.[97] The experiment of voluntary or "gentlemen's agreements" was at the time being tried in North Carolina and Georgia.[98] Murphy did not refer to Mrs. Orr by name in the pamphlet, but his argument was clearly a reply. First, there was no assurance that all mills would make such an agreement; second, all who signed an agreement might not keep it, thus putting the good mills at a disadvantage; third, such agreements had failed elsewhere; fourth, men who would honestly keep the agreement could have no valid objection to a law covering the same points.[99]

A short leaflet in September, 1902, merely quoted an editorial from the *World's Work.*[100] Another of thirty-one pages was a series

---

[96] XLII, 147-50.
[97] *Manufacturers' Record,* XLII (Sept. 4, 1902), 110.
[98] See chapters relating to Georgia and North Carolina.
[99] *A Child-Labor Law.*   [100] *An Editorial About Child Labor.*

of quotations favorable to child labor legislation from leading southern papers. It quoted from thirty-nine papers in twelve states and
the District of Columbia, and included church papers as well as
daily newspapers. The date of each quotation and the political association of each paper was mentioned, though with the exception
of the denominational periodicals they were all Democratic.[101] It
was part of the policy of the reform advocates to stress the support
of child labor legislation by the Democratic party. The *Montgomery
Advertiser* in October published an editorial ridiculing the Republicans of Alabama for trying to make a political issue of child labor
by claiming to support reform. "Some of the members of the party
are doubtless sincere in their advocacy of a child labor law. But we
suspect that many of them are chiefly interested in the measure because of its obvious strength with the masses of the people." The
Advertiser claimed it as a nonpartisan issue, advocated by leading
Democrats of the state long before the Republican party turned attention to it. This editorial was reprinted as a sort of broadside for
distribution.[102] The claim of nonpartisan interest was justified in
the sense that the child labor movement was not the work of a
single political group. Most of the men who either supported or
opposed it were members of the Democratic party. Although the
bill of 1898 was introduced and supported by a Populist, the Labor
men who proposed the bills of 1900 were Democrats.

In *Child Labor and the Public* Murphy made an appeal for active public interest in legislation. He suggested that persons interested in securing legislation organize local committees, circulate child
labor literature, use their influence with the legislators, and correspond with the central committee.

The Murphy pamphlets were distributed throughout the state
of Alabama and reached some of the editors of papers in other states
as well. Their influence can be traced in the newspapers which took
up the contest for child labor laws, and their arguments very largely
determined the line of reasoning of the opponents of child labor
throughout the South. Murphy estimated that the circulation was
about thirty thousand copies.[103]

While the publication of pamphlets was sponsored by the Alabama Committee, the real burden of work, and largely of expense,
fell on Murphy. When he began the movement he received a contribution of fifty dollars from the American Federation of Labor.[104]
Early in 1902 the Consumers' League asked for copies of the

[101] *Child Labor in the Southern Press.*
[102] *Child Labor and "Politics,"* Oct. 29, 1902.
[103] *Problems of the Present South,* p. 120, n. *Pictures from Child Life—Mill
Children in Alabama* is the name of another of these pamphlets.
[104] Murphy to Gompers, July 1, 1901, A. F. of L. Letter File, Box 252.

pamphlets containing the Nichols-Sears correspondence to use at a national meeting of women's clubs in Los Angeles. Murphy asked President Gompers to help again. "As I defrayed the entire expense of the original edition," he wrote, "I do not feel able to increase my own contribution to this particular piece of work."[105] He had spent about one hundred and fifty dollars on the publication and distribution of this one pamphlet. When he wrote *The Case Against Child Labor* he asked the Federation to help circulate it.[106] Gompers took the matter up with the executive council of the Federation,[107] and after several months' delay was able to send Murphy a hundred dollars.[108] For reasons which will appear later this sum was returned to the Federation.[109]

After the defeat of the Alabama bill of 1901 Gompers had re-called Miss Ashby to Washington.[110] Although he now had complete confidence in her, he was uncertain whether to return her to the South.[111] She settled that question for the time being by deciding to go to England in order to marry a British officer returning from the Boer War. Gompers was disappointed by this turn of events.[112] He so sincerely wished to retain her in the service of the Federation that he wrote to the prospective groom and urged him to allow Miss Ashby to come back to the United States and take up her work in the South again, where she had "created a healthy public sentiment not only among the workers of the South, but among those engaged in other, and what is popularly known, as the higher walks of life."[113]

Before Miss Ashby left for England Gompers secured her promise to return,[114] and he reminded her of it later in the summer, urging that she arrive in the States by the twenty-first of September.[115] By the middle of October she was back in America making plans for her work.[116] It was arranged that she should return to Alabama to co-operate with the Child Labor Committee there, and, in order to make her return appear to be in response to the committee's demand, the organization agreed to extend her a formal invitation to come back to the state. On October 16, 1901, she wired Murphy to "hurry

[105] *Ibid.*, March 15, 1902, A. F. of L. Letter File, Box 303.
[106] *Ibid.*, June 25, 1902, A. F. of L. Letter File, Box 303.
[107] Gompers to Murphy, June 28, 1902, Letter Book, Vol. LVII.
[108] *Ibid.*, October 11, 1902, Letter Book, Vol. LX.
[109] *Ibid.*, Nov. 5, 1902, Letter Book, Vol. LXI.
[110] Gompers to Miss Ashby, Mar. 6, 1901, Telegram, Letter Book, Vol. XLI.
[111] *Ibid.*, Mar. 11, 1901, Letter Book, Vol. XLI.
[112] *Ibid.*, May 6, 1901, Letter Book, Vol. XLI.
[113] Gompers to Alfred McFadden [*sic*], May 4, 1901, Letter Book, Vol. XLIII.
[114] Gompers to Miss Ashby, June 12, 1901, Letter Book, Vol. XLIII.
[115] *Ibid.*, Aug. 28, 1901, Letter Book, Vol. XLVI.
[116] Gompers to Mrs. Irene M. Ashby-Macfadyen, Oct. 14, 1901, Letter Book, Vol. XLVI.

that invitation."[117] It may have already been written, for it was dated several days earlier.[118] Miss Ashby, now Mrs. Macfadyen, left for the South again equipped with a general introduction as a representative of the Federation to work for child labor and compulsory education laws.[119] She stopped in Georgia for a short time and went to Alabama in November, 1901. Her return was announced through the society columns of the *Advertiser*.[120] Arriving as she did in the midst of the Nichols-Sears controversy, her presence may have been somewhat embarrassing to the Child Labor Committee. Murphy sincerely wished to co-operate with the American Federation, but he realized that the popular opposition to organized labor would lead many people to oppose a child labor bill if it appeared either as a labor measure or an innovation from outside the state. He emphasized to the public the fact that Mrs. Macfadyen was working under his direction.[121]

Mrs. Macfadyen divided her time between Georgia and Alabama. When in the latter state she worked with Murphy, mailing out copies of the pamphlets and handling the resulting correspondence. She also met with the women's clubs and representatives of the Montgomery papers. Although the *Advertiser* was still neutral editorially on child labor because of a division of opinion in the management, the society editor gave Mrs. Macfadyen prominence through the social columns. She was popular with the society women of Montgomery, went to teas and card parties, and was a guest in the homes of prominent people.[122]

In December[123] the *Advertiser* published a special article by Mrs. Macfadyen, in which she presented her appeal against the evils of a system which she claimed was permitting twelve hundred children under twelve years of age to work in the mills. Her appeal was emotional, referred to the children as little white slaves, related incidents of the harmful effects of employment, and mentioned the hundreds of little graves filled by mill victims. It was altogether different from the type of propaganda spread by the Murphy pamphlets. It condemned the state legislature for refusing the demand of a "small but strong band of men and women of culture and understanding," and the capitalists for ruining the future supply of skilled labor. On

[117] Letter Book, Vol. XLVII.

[118] Alabama Committee to Mrs. Macfadyen, Oct. 4, 1901, A. F. of L. Letter File, Box 232.

[119] Gompers to whom it may concern, Oct. 19, 1901, Letter Book, Vol. XLVII.

[120] Nov. 3, 1901.

[121] *Advertiser*, Nov. 10, 1901.

[122] Report of Mrs. Macfadyen to Gompers, A. F. of L. Letter File, Box 252; *Advertiser*, Oct. 29, 30, Nov. 3, 17, 28, Dec. 20, 1901.

[123] Dec. 15, 1901.

Christmas Day and again a few days later similar articles were featured in the society section.[124]

Mrs. Macfadyen, through her relationship with the Alabama Committee and the prominent women of Montgomery, made contacts with the leaders of organizations throughout the state. In December she spoke before the State Woman's Christian Temperance Union at Fort Payne, where resolutions favorable to child labor legislation were adopted and a committee appointed to co-operate with the State committee.[125] The State Federation of Women's Clubs was also supposed to be working in co-operation with the committee,[126] in spite of the attitude of its president.

Mrs. Macfadyen addressed public meetings at Tuscaloosa and Mobile, where she met members of the clergy and prominent politicians.[127] She encountered opposition, but her work was satisfactory to the American Federation. She wrote to Gompers about a newspaper reporter who had been arrested at the instigation of mill authorities. He replied that he did not believe that the companies would go so far as to arrest her in Huntsville, where she was planning to visit, but that it would not be bad for publicity purposes if they did. "I know it would be uncomfortable, but perhaps it might be a good thing in the interest of the children for it would certainly create a sensation, and react upon the company as well as do much to awaken the conscience of the people."[128]

There were eleven mills in the vicinity of Huntsville, but Mrs. Macfadyen found the public ignorant of conditions existing among the workers. The editor of the Huntsville *Tribune* opened the columns of his paper to her and she wrote the leading articles for a week. A meeting was arranged for February 2, 1902, at the city hall, where she spoke to a large audience. Not everyone was friendly, however. She was refused admission to the Dallas and Merrimac mills, which were owned by northern capital. John Wallis, a member of the legislature who had been actively opposed to child labor legislation, was still on the side of the opposition, although he refused to meet her in public debate. Several managers of the mills came to the public meeting but none of them undertook to answer her arguments there. It was difficult to get an open response even from those who favored the child labor movement, because of the political situation. Several prominent men promised to advocate child labor legislation openly after the primary elections, but were afraid

[124] Report of Mrs. Macfadyen to Gompers, A. F. of L. Letter File, Box 252; *Advertiser*, Dec. 25, 31, 1901.

[125] Report of Mrs. Macfadyen to Gompers, A. F. of L. Letter File, Box 252.

[126] Lura H. Craighead, *op. cit.*

[127] Report of Mrs. Macfadyen to Gompers, A. F. of L. Letter File, Box 252.

[128] Gompers to Mrs. Macfadyen, Feb. 4, 1902, Letter Book, Vol. LI.

to antagonize the millowners before that time, as they said that the latter had promised to use their influence for certain political ends. Two physicians agreed to bring the subject before the state and local medical associations.[129] When she left Huntsville Mrs. Macfadyen wrote to Gompers that she had had "a gorgeous time" even though she was not arrested.[130]

At Auburn Mrs. Macfadyen spoke to the students at the state polytechnic school and to the local chapter of the Daughters of the American Revolution. Then back in Montgomery she met a final gathering of friends just before leaving the state.[131] She was about to go to South Africa to join her husband, who was an officer in the British army.[132]

The effect of Mrs. Macfadyen's work in the South was to arouse the interest of people who might otherwise have been ignorant or indifferent to child labor. She appealed especially to the women and through them to the voters. The publicity which she gave extreme cases of child labor abuses was a part of the building up of public sentiment in favor of a law. It is doubtful whether she converted to her point of view any people directly interested in the mills. They were undoubtedly annoyed by her type of argument which they characterized as "sickly sentimentalism."[133] Her connection with organized labor was minimized in her public addresses during her second visit to Alabama. Her policy was to present the child labor question apart from the other labor problems, so as to secure the support of "those who are willing at once to help in this matter, but who would need a good deal of education and instruction to make them willing to help in what might be called a general labor movement."[134]

Murphy felt that the opposition to labor movements was so strong that it was unwise to have another representative of the American Federation sent to the state to work for child labor legislation. In the spring of 1902 he was discouraged with the outlook for reform, but his resolution to continue demands for a law was in no way weakened, and he pushed forward the series of pamphlets. His greatest difficulty lay in financial limitations.[135] In November, 1901, he had resigned his pastorate to become the executive secretary of

[129] Mrs. Macfadyen's report to Gompers, A. F. of L. Letter File, Box 252.
[130] Mrs. Macfadyen to Gompers, Feb. 7, 1902, A. F. of L. Letter File, Box 252.
[131] Report of Mrs. Macfadyen to Gompers, A. F. of L. Letter File, Box 252.
[132] Gompers to Mrs. Ashby-Macfadyen, April 4, 1902, Letter Book, Vol. LIV.
[133] Report of Mrs. Macfadyen to A. F. of L., Letter File, Box 252.
[134] Mrs. Macfadyen to Miss Charlotte Kimball, Mar. 28, 1902, A. F. of L. Letter File, Box 303.
[135] Murphy to Mrs. Macfadyen, May 21, 1902, A. F. of L. Letter File, Box 303.

the Southern Education Board.[136] While this association had its advantages it is not probable that it brought a large remuneration. In the contest for child labor legislation he felt that the mill interests had all the advantages of material wealth on their side. He wrote to Mrs. Macfadyen, "Whenever a measure of that sort is referred to a committee, the opposition have the whole situation in the concrete. It is simply a question of influencing, by one means or another, seven or eight men. Argument is of little avail. Now that the Legislature is to meet only once in four years,[137] the man on the average committee is attempting to do the best he can for himself, for the reason that his public record is of little consequence. The next Legislature is four years off, and it presents very distant and intangible attractions.

"The leaven is working, however, and when we win the battle in one State, the other States are pretty sure to fall into line. They are organizing in Louisiana ahead of the cotton mills, and if our other States had followed that example, there would be no particular trouble. I am more and more satisfied that the whole animus of the opposition is the objection of capital to organized labor *per se*."[138]

The Federation of Labor also realized the difficulty of meeting the competition of the millowners, and believed it was chiefly financial. A report to the Federation, presumably from Mrs. Macfadyen, although it is unsigned, quoted a mill treasurer as saying that in the legislature it was simply a question of money. The manufacturers' interests were at stake, and as they had money at their disposal the opponents of child labor would find themselves up against a stone wall.[139]

The Federation wished to follow up the work of its agent in the campaign for the legislature to be elected in 1902. On June 26, 1902, Gompers sent out a circular letter to the locals in Alabama reminding them that the child labor bill had failed in 1901 and that the meeting of the legislature in 1903 would be the last session for four years. He urged the organizations to exact pledges from the candidates that they would aid in passing a child labor law.[140] Murphy feared this would injure the reform program. The day before Gompers sent out the circular Murphy wrote him a letter[141] which he no doubt received after the circular was mailed. But the views Murphy expressed were already familiar to Gompers, since he had been sent a copy of a similar letter to Mrs. Macfadyen the month previous. Murphy asked for financial aid for his publications, but

[136] *Advertiser,* Nov. 28, 1901.
[137] A recent change in the state constitution to take effect after 1903.
[138] Murphy to Mrs. Macfadyen, May 21, 1902, A. F. of L. Letter File, Box 303.
[139] Report to A. F. of L., Letter File, Box 252.
[140] A. F. of L. Letter File, Box 303.   [141] *Ibid.*

again expressed opposition to the presence of a Federation agent. Things were beginning to look more favorable for reform, he believed. The South Carolina Democratic Convention had endorsed it, which would be a good influence on other states. The millmen who opposed reform were playing on the strong prejudices of the southern people against unionism. They charged that the whole movement for reform was due to outside interference and was in the interest of organized labor.

Murphy was right in his belief that the open support of the reform movement by labor unions would prejudice many people against it. Nevertheless, this attitude seemed hard to the labor leaders. Looking at the matter from such different points of view, it is surprising that the Alabama Child Labor Committee and the American Federation of Labor were able to work together with as much harmony as they did. Each regarded itself as having originated the movement for reform and the other as being an able but subordinate assistant. The first organizations to advocate child labor legislation had been the local unions, and the American Federation had paid an agent for several months to develop publicity. Now it was advised that its efforts should be suspended. The question may well have risen as to whether the Alabama Committee was acting in good faith, or whether it would try to take to itself the credit for any success that might be gained, and discredit the labor organizations, which were regarded with distrust by so many people in the state. Murphy tried to reassure Gompers on this point, but he never yielded his belief that publicity for labor's part in the movement was injurious. He wrote, "You may be sure that at the right time both Mrs. Macfadyen and yourself will receive abundant credit for your honorable part in relation to this work."[142] Murphy held no official position and received no pay for his part in relation to the movement. Instead he carried a financial burden on its behalf, and he felt a keen responsibility for its success. In November before the meeting of the legislature he wrote again to Gompers that he had on several occasions expressed publicly his appreciation for the part the Federation took in the movement, and that "at the proper time" he would do so again. "I have now in mind but one supreme idea, and that is the passage of protective legislation for the children. We may fail, but failure will not be so bitter if I can feel that I have done everything in my power to secure the result desired. The committee are well-meaning men, but have left the work almost entirely to myself. Under these circumstances, I have had to thoroughly canvas the situation and to take my course accordingly. I am sure that when I can talk to you privately, you will see that under the circumstances,

[142] July 27, 1902, A. F. of L. Letter File, Box 303.

there is nothing for us to do this year but to adopt the policy which I am attempting to follow."[143]

Murphy could not stop the activity of the labor organizations in Alabama altogether. Some of the members followed Gompers' instructions to secure pledges from candidates for the legislature.[144] The most important publicity work was conducted through the pamphlets sent out by Murphy. Though unwilling for the Federation to send an agent to Alabama, he suggested to President Gompers that it might pay the salary of a clerk to help in handling the distribution of the pamphlets and the resulting correspondence. Such a helper would be useful in November, December, and January before the legislature met. Murphy would only accept this assistance on condition that the man employed should be entirely at his disposal and that the Federation should not figure in the matter at all.[145] The tension between the committee and the Federation reached a crisis at this time, however, and the Federation did not employ an assistant for Murphy. The latter returned to Gompers the hundred dollars which the Council of the Federation had appropriated for the circulation of the pamphlet on *The Case Against Child Labor*.[146]

Both Murphy and Gompers regretted the difficulties that had arisen and wanted to clarify the situation. Murphy did not yield a point of his position toward labor. He firmly believed that the defeat experienced in Georgia[147] resulted from the fact that the measure was handled by representatives of labor. His chief anxiety was to convince Gompers of the wisdom of his position. As he had to make a trip north in the latter part of December he wrote to arrange a conference with Gompers on his way back home.[148] A meeting was arranged to take place in New York on January 10, 1903.[149]

Gompers never distrusted Murphy's sincerity. When a labor member of the legislature wrote to him in December for information as to child labor legislation, Gompers referred him to Murphy for advice.[150] But in the conference Murphy succeeded completely in convincing Gompers of the wisdom of his views, at least for a temporary policy. Letters which Gompers wrote the following week to the secretary of the Birmingham Trades Council and the secretary of the Alabama Federation of Labor are evidence of this feeling. He ex-

[143] Murphy to Gompers, Nov. 10, 1902, A. F. of L. Letter File, Box 303.

[144] F. L. Petru to Gompers [no date], A. F. of L. Letter File, Box 303; *American Federationist*, IX (1902), 719.

[145] Murphy to Gompers, Oct. 18, 1902, A. F. of L. Letter File, Box 303.

[146] Gompers to Murphy, Nov. 5, 1902, Letter Book, Vol. LXI.

[147] See chapter on Georgia.

[148] Murphy to Gompers, Dec. 27, 1902, A. F. of L. Letter File, Box 303.

[149] Murphy to Gompers, Jan. 6, 1903, A. F. of L. Letter File, Box 303; R. Lee Guard to Murphy, Jan. 9, 1903, Letter Book, Vol. LXIV.

[150] Gompers to T. D. [sic] Hall, Dec. 12, 1902, Letter Book, Vol. LXII.

plained to these two local leaders that he had had a conference with Murphy in regard to the situation in Alabama, in which Murphy had made clear to him that the mill corporations were making the question of organized labor the greatest point of antagonism to child labor legislation. He very carefully avoided any implication that Murphy agreed with these views. His explanation was as tactful as a difficult situation made it possible to be. "Mr. Murphy does not share this opinion of the mill corporations at all, but, on the contrary, he is conscious of the fact and is glad to concede that after all, the work is being done in the interests of the children and the people of the South, and to the A. F. of L. and the labor organizations of Alabama will due credit and honor be fully accorded in due course of time. But he is of the opinion that inasmuch as organized labor is not very strong in Alabama compared to the other interests of the state, that it may easily be taken advantage of by the mill owners and the other interests in order to defeat the child labor bill.

"The best work in which the organizations of Alabama can be engaged is to have the unions and the members in their individual capacity also, write to the members of the legislature of their respective districts, and whenever opportunity affords to call upon the members of the legislature even of other districts, and particularly at their homes, rather than at Montgomery.

"I write this to you so that you may be fully aware of the situation, and advise that no publicity be given it. What we aim to do at last is to secure a beneficent child labor law regardless of who gets the credit for having accomplished it. We will be glad to assist to the best of our power, financially and otherwise."[151]

One of the union leaders of Alabama had already drawn up a child labor bill before the advice from Gompers was received. T. J. Hall of Montgomery, a labor Democrat who had been elected to the House, began early in December to plan a child labor measure, and wrote to Gompers for information on child labor legislation.[152] Although Gompers advised the restraint of the labor group, Hall introduced his measure on January 24, 1903.[153] It proposed that children under twelve should not be permitted to work in or "to remain in or about" any manufacturing establishment. Exception should be made for children over ten who were dependent on themselves for support, or whose mothers were widows or abandoned, or whose fathers were totally disabled, and wholly dependent on them. No

[151] Gompers to H. N. Randall, to D. W. Williams, Jan. 17, 1903, Letter Book, Vol. LXIV.

[152] Dec. 9, 1902, A. F. of L. Letter File, Box 303; Gompers to Hall, Dec. 12, 1902, Letter Book, Vol. LXII.

[153] Ala., *Journal of the House*, 1903, p. 179.

child under fourteen should work more than eleven hours in one day, or sixty-four in one week, or between 7:00 P.M. and 6:00 A.M. Violation should be punishable by a fine of from twenty-five to two hundred and fifty dollars.[154]

The Hall bill was given publicity through the press. The *Advertiser*[155] published a statement that Hall would submit it to the reform group and if the Alabama Committee had a better bill he would vote for it. The *Advertiser* had become an advocate of child labor reform and supported it in its editorial columns on the principle that child labor was "not only poor humanity but bad business." The influence of Murphy's pamphlets is clearly evident in its arguments.[156]

The Alabama Committee was fully aware that a child labor measure setting very high standards would have no chance to pass in the face of the organized opposition of the mill interests. It therefore determined to take a half-loaf rather than none. The millowners showed a willingness to yield to part of the demands, in the hope that the matter would then cease to be agitated. A number of them gathered in Montgomery to confer, and Mrs. Lillian Milner Orr, president of the Alabama Federation of Women's Clubs, who had advocated a "gentlemen's agreement" the previous fall, came to meet with them.[157] While no public statement was yet made there were rumors that a compromise would be effected between the committee and the manufacturers. The *Advertiser* endorsed this step as being the easiest way out for the mills. "Our word to the wise is this. There may be no other session of our Legislature for four years. The mills have an opportunity to accept in good faith and with the appreciation of the whole State a conservative and reasonable law; or they have before them the alternative of four long years of aggressive and ever increasing agitation. The mills, if they are wise in their own interest, will know which to choose."[158]

The compromise was agreed upon[159] and on January 28, 1903, was introduced into the House by J. E. Rich, a lawyer from Mobile, and into the Senate by F. L. Blackmon of Anniston, later a Congressman.[160] The bill contained the same age limit as Hall's bill, twelve years, with exceptions for children over ten who were orphans or had dependent parents. No child under thirteen should work between 7:00 P.M. and 6:00 A.M., and no child under sixteen should work more than forty-eight hours in one week at night. No child

[154] House Bill 201, Original Bills 1900-1927, Jan. 24, 1903, Legislative Papers, Alabama State Dept. of Archives and History.
[155] Jan. 16, 1903.
[156] Jan. 16, 17, 22, 28, 30, 1903.   [157] *Advertiser*, Jan. 21, 1903.
[158] Jan. 22, 1903.   [159] *Advertiser*, Jan. 28, 1903.
[160] Ala., *Journal of the House*, 1903, p. 236; *Journal of the Senate*, 1903, p. 151.

under twelve should work more than sixty-six hours a week. No factory or manufacturing establishment should employ a child until there was placed on file in the office of the employer an affidavit signed by the parent or guardian certifying its age and the date of its birth. Penalty for the parent for giving false information was a fine of from five to one hundred dollars or three months in jail. Penalty for the employer who violated the act was a fine of two hundred dollars.[161]

A statement of agreement to the terms of the bill was signed by J. B. Gaston, E. G. Murphy, and Alexander T. London for the Alabama Child Labor Committee; by B. B. Comer, John W. Tullis, and D. T. Goodwin for the manufacturers; and by London as proxy for Mrs. Lillian M. Orr of the Federation of Women's Clubs.[162]

Once the compromise was arranged there was little trouble anticipated for the measure. Although there were a few delays, the House passed it with only one dissenting vote.[163] There was little argument or excitement over the passage of the bill. The Federation of Women's Clubs, which was in session in Montgomery in order to work for reform measures, went to the capitol to hear the vote. The chief interest of the day in the House was in relation to other matters, however.[164]

There was difficulty in securing passage in the Senate. The opposition which the bill met came as a surprise to the makers of the compromise. In bringing up the bill for the third reading, Blackmon stated that his was an agreement between the opposing groups and that it should be passed. Debate began immediately. Opponents argued that the wishes of the parents should be considered; that industry would be crippled; that dangerous precedents would be established; that the measure was undemocratic; and that it was unconstitutional. A motion to table the bill was lost by only two votes. The debate was resumed with the arguments that the measure was class legislation and would discourage outside investment because the South's chief asset was cheap labor. Here the argument that Murphy had feared came up, for one speaker declared that "England . . . had seen how matters stood, how her markets were being destroyed by America and had sent across the Atlantic a woman lobbyist, to align herself with the Women's Clubs of this country and through them to work for so-called child labor reform, and all for a very obvious purpose." The part of the women in the demands for reform was a special grievance to one senator, who remarked that

[161] House Bill 271, Senate Bill 115, Jan. 28, 1903, Original Bills 1900-1927, Legislative Papers, Alabama State Dept. of Archives and History.
[162] *Advertiser*, Jan. 28, 1903.
[163] Ala., *Journal of the House*, 1903, pp. 272, 316, 606, 607, 667, 670, 704, 820, 934.
[164] *Advertiser*, Feb. 13, 1903.

they had no ballot but that they had come near to voting this time, and had apparently hypnotized some of the members of the Senate. The representatives of the millowners contended that any legislation was a step in the wrong direction. After the defeat of another motion to postpone the bill and one to adjourn, the final vote was taken and the measure passed by a vote of seventeen to eleven.[165]

The compromise measure was approved on February 25, 1903.[166] It was not as strong a measure as the one proposed in 1901 for it only limited the hours to sixty-six a week instead of sixty, made no educational requirement and provided for no inspection or enforcement. The weaknesses were quite obvious, and the only persons who appeared to be satisfied with the results were the members of the women's clubs. They credited their president with having brought about a compromise in which they took great satisfaction, and declared that the Federation alone—"acting independently of all organizations—labor and others"—had been able to achieve this success.[167]

[165] Ala., *Journal of the Senate,* 1903, pp. 407-8; *Advertiser,* Feb. 15, 1903.
[166] Ala., *Acts of the General Assembly,* 1903, pp. 68-70.
[167] "Child Labor in Alabama," in *Annals,* American Academy of Political and Social Science, XXI (1903), 179-80.

CHAPTER III

PROPAGANDA AND DEFENSE

THE LEGISLATION in Alabama forms an introduction to the course of child labor legislation in the South. In order to understand the movement it is worth while to trace the development of the criticism of child labor. The existence of this evil was not new. Long before the manufacture of cloth had reached the factory stage, children were used in the textile industry in the homes of laborers. Child labor had appeared as a normal part of the factory system in England and New England and in the ante-bellum South. Its reappearance in the period of postwar mill development was natural and at first caused no comment. The northern industrial states had already adopted child labor laws and the agitation of the question had disappeared by the time child labor became a problem in southern industry.

The growth of child labor in a particular industry and in states where there was no legal prohibition gradually drew the attention of a few thoughtful people. In 1885 a young divinity student at Yale wrote an article in which he described the child labor evil as not being confined to any state or locality, but as following certain industries. But while the trade unions of the eastern and middle states caused some reaction against it there, in the South a rapidly growing number of child operatives in cotton mills was cause for concern. The writer showed some knowledge of conditions in the South, but the special significance of his article was that he did not consider the problem there as peculiar to the section.[1]

A few other writers for northern periodicals touched on child labor in the nation at large, but only occasionally was reference made to conditions in the South. In 1890 an employee of the Federal Bureau of Labor published a long article in which a few pages were devoted to conditions in Georgia. This study appeared in the *Publications of the American Economic Association*[2] and probably had very limited circulation. A more popular article by the same author appeared in the *Century Magazine*.[3] Practically the only articles re-

[1] John F. Crowell, "The Employment of Children," in *Andover Review*, IV (1885), 42-55. Crowell, two years after writing this article, became president of Trinity College, later Duke University, Durham, North Carolina.
[2] Clare de Graffenried, "Child Labor," v (1890), 193-271.
[3] "The Georgia Cracker in the Cotton Mill," XLI (1891), 483-98.

lating to child labor before 1898 were those published in the official organs of the labor unions, particularly in the *American Federationist*. By that time a discussion of the rivalry of the South for New England's textile leadership had begun to gain attention and this brought southern labor conditions into the limelight.

Southern child labor was not generally regarded as a national problem in the nineties. Its existence was too little known. The South itself had not yet become fully conscious of it as a problem calling for solution. The first child labor bills which were introduced in the 1880's drew very little attention, and the thought and interest of progressive people were absorbed by the other more pressing problems of the day. The cotton manufacturers were put upon the defensive by the early bills, however, and began to present arguments in justification of their practice of employing children in the mills. The first objections to legislation reveal the conservatism which was characteristic of the people of the South. It was felt by many that the authority of the parent, particularly of the father, over the family, should not be interfered with by legislation.[4] The law still allowed the head of the family to control his wife and child, and the majority of men, whether mill operatives or millowners, could see no reason for change. The southern mill hand had been a farmer accustomed to poverty but with a considerable degree of independence. Legislation, even where it might ultimately add to his welfare, was a restriction to be resented.[5]

The mill village parents had seen their children work while they still lived on the farm. The employment of small children was not new to them and they failed to make a distinction between farm and mill labor. The advantages of manual labor as a builder of character were firmly believed in by many and the old adage that the devil finds work for idle hands to do had many defenders. Educational standards were not high and the argument that mill labor deprived the child of an opportunity for education could not go very far in the early nineties when the child would probably get very little education even though he did not work. It was not without some justification that the mill managers stated time after time that the parents insisted that their children be given employment.[6] The child labor reformers took this as one of their strongest arguments for restrictive legislation. The lazy drunken father who lived

[4] *Atlanta Constitution*, Sept. 22, 1887; *News and Observer*, Jan. 19, 1887.

[5] Legislative Papers, Petitions, 1895, in North Carolina Historical Commission Archives.

[6] N. C. Bureau of Labor, *First Annual Report*, 1887, pp. 148-50; *Fourth Annual Report*, 1890, pp. 27, 58, 60, 63; *Fifth Annual Report*, 1891, pp. 135, 141, 145; *Eighth Annual Report*, 1894, pp. 65, 69-70; U. S. Industrial Commission, *Report*, VII, 225, 229; *Constitution*, Sept. 23, 1887; *News and Observer*, Jan. 19, 1887.

by the labor of his small children was universally condemned, and one object of legislation was to protect children from such parents.[7]

The mill managers did not attempt to make it appear that all cases of child labor were the result of viciousness on the part of the parents. The other cause to which they attributed child labor was poverty. The farm family had come to the mill because it was poor—frequently because of the incapacitation or loss of the father and the lack of other adult members who could do the heavy work of agriculture. The work of all its members was needed to earn enough to sustain life with any degree of comfort. The idea had been generally accepted that the mill village was a haven for poor widows with children. The adults declared their inability to make a living without the aid of their children, or to keep the children in school if they did not work.[8] The labor advocates of legislation met this argument with the economic principle that the work of children in competition with that of adults tended to lower the standard of wages and to drive out the adults. Child labor was thus a cause of unemployment and poverty, and not a result.[9]

The millowners consistently declared that they did not wish to employ children under the age of twelve, or sometimes thirteen or fourteen. Such labor, they said, was unprofitable because of the carelessness and lack of skill of the children; but the insistence of the parents forced them to take the children into the mills, even when it was the policy of the company not to do so. If a family did not find employment for its children in one mill it would move on to another whose management had no scruples on the subject. The mill manager was apt to represent the employment of children as an act of charity, since it gave a livelihood to people who might otherwise be municipal dependents. This method of caring for the poor was not frowned upon by the large majority of people.[10]

The reformers disagreed with this view. If child labor was actually unprofitable, they asked, why did the millowners so generally yield to the demands of the parents? The greed for profits, and the demand for cheap labor led to the heartless employment of children whose parents were too ignorant or too poor to resist.[11]

[7] *Constitution*, Oct. 26, Dec. 16, 1899; *Biblical Recorder*, May 12, 1897.

[8] N. C. Bureau of Labor, *Fourth Annual Report*, 1890, p. 34; *Fifth Annual Report*, 1891, pp. 167, 169, 172; *Thirteenth Annual Report*, 1899, p. 231; *News and Courier* (Charleston), Jan. 27, 1900; U. S. Bureau of Labor, *Woman and Child Wage-Earners*, VI, 131.

[9] *Daily Register*, Feb. 20, 1887; N. C. Bureau of Labor, *First Annual Report*, p. 152; U. S. Industrial Commission, *Report*, VII, 241; M. Raphael, *op. cit.*, pp. 157-59.

[10] N. C. Bureau of Labor, *First Annual Report*, p. 148; *Fourth Annual Report*, p. 27; *Fifth Annual Report*, p. 141; U. S. Industrial Commission, *Report*, VII, 491, 494, 503, 512, 522, 529, 570.

[11] *Biblical Recorder*, Jan. 6, May 12, 1897; *Constitution*, Nov. 10, 1897, Nov. 13, 1899; U. S. Industrial Commission, *Report*, VII, 225, 229.

The manufacturers took the position that child labor existed as a result of poverty and parental greed; but the majority of them were unwilling to find the remedy for the problem in legislation. All southern mills ran long hours, and the proposed legislation would cut down the number of hours for a large per cent of the operatives, if not all. This regulation, they declared, would be ruinous to the cotton mill industry. Without this advantage the southern mills could not hope to compete with their older rivals in New England. Such laws would shut out capital and close the doors of factories. To limit the hours, they said, would in practice limit the wage of the worker, since he worked by the piece. The operatives had not asked for and did not want such action. If the laws of a state kept its children from working and reduced the wages of the mill people, they would migrate to some other state which had no restrictions and the mills would lose their labor supply.[12] There was nothing more apt to cause concern to the average southern business man than a threat concerning the welfare of the mills. Cotton manufacturing was an important factor in the returning prosperity of the South. People might lack the imagination to foresee the evil results of continuing the child labor system but they could never forget the experience of poverty, or that manufacturing was bringing relief from it. The states wanted more capital to develop their industries and the hope for it lay in the East. They were willing to make concessions in exemption from taxation, and they were also willing to refrain from passing any legislation that would cut down on the attractive cheap labor supply. While this was not an avowed policy it was in the minds of many people that the industry should be built up first and any by-products of evil resulting from it remedied later.[13]

Another objection to child labor legislation was simply the objection to any labor legislation whatsoever. The old idea of freedom of contract, of the right of the employer and employee to make their own terms and settle their problems, was still strongly put forward. There was a widespread distrust and fear of organized labor and the enactment of any labor legislation was regarded as unwise encouragement of trade unionism. Mill operatives, who were almost entirely unorganized, showed no great enthusiasm for labor reform by legislation and the manufacturers seized upon this indifference as an argument against the enactment of labor laws.[14]

[12] News and Observer, Feb. 17, 18, 1893; News and Courier, Jan. 27, 1900; Constitution, Nov. 10, 1897, Dec. 16, 1899.

[13] Daily Register, Feb. 5, 1887; U. S. Industrial Commission, Report, VII, 619; Jerome Dowd, op. cit.

[14] N. C. Bureau of Labor, Ninth Annual Report, 1895, pp. 64, 66, 70-71; Tenth Annual Report, p. 75; Thirteenth Annual Report, p. 249; U. S. Industrial Commission, Report, VII, 756-64; News and Courier, Jan. 27, 1900.

The advocates of child labor reform asked for legislation chiefly on the ground that premature labor did the child great physical and mental harm. The long hours of monotonous indoor work prevented his normal development, stunted his physical growth, and resulted in permanent injury. The child was also deprived of an opportunity for education and had his mental outlook narrowed and his intelligence deadened. The moral influences might also be bad where the child came in contact with all types of workers and it was believed that he frequently developed undesirable habits as a result of such contact. The children who were allowed to grow up under such conditions could not develop into useful citizens.[15]

The reply made by the manufacturers to such arguments was that the child was better off in the mill where he was taught regular habits of work, frequently under his parent's direction, than idle on the street.[16]

A change in the public attitude toward child labor legislation took place at the turn of the century. From being a matter of mere local interest it became a subject of rather widespread national discussion. As early as 1898 *Gunton's Magazine,* a monthly dealing with social problems, opened the discussion with an article on southern factory labor. In commenting on the opposition of the South to factory legislation the author criticized the *Atlanta Constitution* for taking the position that conditions were as bad in New England as in the South and that the interest of other sections in the labor legislation of the South was undesirable meddling.[17] The *Constitution,* like all southern papers in that period, was inclined to resent any criticism or suggestion from a northern source, but the remarks in *Gunton's* were unfortunate, since the *Constitution* was the most outstanding southern paper that championed the cause of child labor reform at that time.

The growth of the cotton manufacturing industry in the South which developed keen competition with New England also brought out comparisons of labor conditions in the two sections. This led quite naturally to criticisms of child labor and assertions that the employment of women and children was responsible for low wage standards.[18] *Gunton's* pressed the question of southern resentment of

[15] *Daily Register,* Feb. 20, 1887; N. C. Bureau of Labor, *Fourth Annual Report,* pp. 48, 50, 51; *Fifth Annual Report,* pp. 137, 145-47, 177; *Tenth Annual Report,* pp. 69, 70, 73; U. S. Bureau of Labor, *Woman and Child Wage-Earners,* VI, 171; *Constitution,* Nov. 15, 19, Dec. 4, 1896; Nov. 13, Dec. 3, 1899; *News and Courier,* Jan. 26, 27, 1900.   [16] *Constitution,* Dec. 16, 1899.

[17] "Factory Labor in the South," in *Gunton's Magazine,* XIV (1898), 222-23. The author's name is not given.

[18] Jerome Dowd, "Textile War Between the North and the South," in *The Forum,* XXV (1898), 438-44; *idem,* "Cheap Labor in the South," and George Gunton,

criticism,[19] and engaged in an editorial controversy with the *Atlanta Journal*, which it charged with distorting *Gunton's* statements.[20] Since the editor of *Gunton's* had made a tour of the industrial sections of the South, he considered himself well informed on the conditions existing there.[21] The suggestion that New England manufacturers had a selfish interest in securing child labor legislation offered a strong and telling ground for opposition, of which the southern manufacturers were not slow to take advantage. It was said that the northern millowner saw the growth of southern mills drawing capital from the North and even causing entire plants to move to the new industrial section. Not wishing to move his establishment, the northern manufacturer sought to remove the chief advantage which the South enjoyed by destroying the possibility of cheap labor through promoting labor legislation. He also encouraged organized labor in the South so that that section would have to encounter the same difficulties as its rival. It was asserted that the northern millowners financed the American Federation of Labor and its agent, Miss Irene Ashby, in their attempt to secure the enactment of child labor laws.[22] When the New England press began to comment on the child labor situation in the South, even the southern editors who were friendly to reform looked with disfavor on this northern interest. They, however, argued from the point of view that the northern mills were opposing child labor legislation so that they might come South to take advantage of the absence of restrictions.[23] The feeling of resentment against northern suggestions as to the conduct of a southern state was only heightened by the frequent use of this argument and resulted in other assertions based largely on prejudice and the popular feeling that the North should be "hands off" with southern affairs.[24]

Murphy first published the *Appeal to the People and Press of New England* in the *Boston Evening Transcript* on October 23, 1901. An editorial in the same issue called the attention of its readers to the appeal and recommended it as a matter worthy of thought. The resulting correspondence was published in the *Transcript's* columns,

"What Can Be Done About It?" in *Gunton's Magazine*, XVIII (1900), 112-30; Prince W. Greene, *op. cit.*, p. 126; Charles B. Spahr, "Child Labor in England and the United States," in *Chautauquan*, XXX (1899), 41-43.

[19] *Atlanta Journal*, Feb. 15, 1900.

[20] George Gunton, "The South's 'Labor System,'" *loc. cit.*

[21] "Dodging the Child Labor Issue," in *Gunton's Magazine*, XXII, 246-52.

[22] *Charlotte Observer*, Aug. 12, 1900; *Constitution*, Nov. 15, 1900, Nov. 29, 1901; *News and Courier*, Jan. 22, 1901; *Manufacturers' Record*, Sept. 18, 1902, pp. 150-51; Aug. 28, 1902, pp. 93-95.

[23] *News and Observer*, Aug. 17, 1902.

[24] *State* (Columbia, S. C.), Jan. 17, 1902; *News and Observer*, Feb. 8, 1903; *Constitution*, Dec. 7, 1902, July 8, 1903.

but passed without editorial comment.[25]   New England was conscious of the struggle in the South, however, and could not regard it
in an altogether disinterested manner.   A Boston subscriber wrote to
the *Transcript,* claiming that the textile workers of Fall River were
the originators of the labor demands in the South, and quoted from
the *Transcript's* account of the meeting of the American Federation
of Textile Operatives in Washington that "the child labor situation
in the South is a menace to Northern operatives quite as much as the
matter of long hours."[26]   In the summer of 1902, when the controversy as to the responsibility of northern capitalists in the matter of
southern child labor was being debated, with one side blaming them
for preventing legislation and the other for promoting it, the *Transcript* no longer withheld its opinion.   The New England mills were
feeling the South's competition.   Although southern progress had
slowed up the growth of New England mills, the *Transcript* would not
concede that it had been stopped or that the advantages offered by
the South were permanent.   "If Northern mill labor is higher, it is
better; if the Southern mills are nearer the cotton, the Northern mills
are nearer the banks.   There are conditions which have not arisen in
the South yet which are sure to arise when Southern labor, feeling
its power, organizes in force enough to secure the better pay and better
environment of the workers of the North."[27]

The *Transcript* also quoted comments from the New York *Evening
Post* on the recognition of the demands for child labor legislation by
the Texas and South Carolina Democratic conventions.[28] In another
connection the *Transcript* referred to the closing of the New Hartford
mills and transfer of their business to the South in order to take
advantage of child labor.   "The idea is repugnant to our humane
and Christian sensibilities," it wrote, "that children should be sacri-
ficed to corporate greed."[29]   Such comments as these substantiated
the southern millowner in his belief that the northern capitalists were
promoting legislation in the South in order to hold their own in the
competition.

Another phase of the opposition to legislation was the belief that
organized labor, which was in itself held to be undesirable, was responsible for the agitation.   While this feeling had appeared as early
as the child labor bills themselves, the very weakness of the labor
movement in the South kept it from gaining much force.   But the
rapid growth of the American Federation of Labor which began about
the end of the nineteenth century paralleled the increase in child
labor and the demands for its regulation. The appearance of union

[25] Oct. 30, Nov. 6, 13, 1901.
[26] Nov. 9, 13, 1901.
[27] July 2, 1902.
[28] July 29, 1902.
[29] Aug. 7, 1902; see also Aug. 15, 1902.

organizers in the South, the organization of workers in some of the urban centers, and the outbreak of a few strikes served to put the cotton manufacturers on their guard and to increase the force of their argument against child labor laws as a form of labor legislation. The employment of a special agent by the American Federation of Labor to work for reform strengthened this argument. If union demands for child labor reform and limitation of hours were met, would not other changes be asked? If an age limit for night work were set, the next legislature would be called upon to move it higher.

Such bills the manufacturers conceived as originating in the unwholesome doctrines of discontent which they claimed the labor unions taught. They were an effort to secure class legislation and to build up a state paternalism that was undesirable for a democratic and independent people. The only result would be to disturb the good relations that had always existed between the laborers and capitalists of the South—good relations due to the lack of evil influences of organizations among workers. The American Federation of Labor was not southern. It had its headquarters at the capital of the nation and its principal strength in northern and eastern industrial areas. The conservatism of the South and its sensitiveness and resentment when it felt that an effort was being made to force it to accept alien ideas and standards of action gave the millowners' arguments undue weight. Such phrases as "an entering wedge for labor" and "outside interference" were applied to the child labor movement with frequency and with telling effect.[30]

The strength of the arguments against New England and the labor unions was great because of the position and influence of the men who made them. The employers of labor had built the cotton mills of the South and had done much to restore prosperity. They were natural leaders, men of ability and property, and they commanded the respect of their communities. Since they had created an industry which gave employment to thousands, they represented themselves as the best friends of the laboring class. Since they had made prosperity, they claimed the right to decide what was for the good of the state. Some of them had built schools and churches which were largely supported by the mills. They had provided recreational centers and libraries and promoted welfare work. They felt themselves to be philanthropists, and having made the mill operatives the object of their attention they resented the assumption that the workers or anyone else should presume to dictate what was for the good of their

[30] *Constitution*, Nov. 15, 20, 28, 1900; Nov. 13, 1901; Nov. 20, Dec. 7, 1902; July 5, 1903; *News and Observer*, Feb. 8, 1901; Feb. 6, 1903; *State*, Jan. 29, 1902; *Advertiser*, Feb. 15, 1903; N. C. Bureau of Labor, *Fourteenth Annual Report*, pp. 194, 196; Murphy, *Problems of the Present South*, pp. 112, 310.

protégés. Surely no one else could be more concerned or more able to decide on the welfare of the people whom they had brought from the abject poverty of the farm to the relative prosperity of the mill village.[31]

The millowners resented the child labor reformers, but the best of them admitted the fundamental truth of their arguments. The theory that the real burden of decision lay with the manufacturer and that he had the right and obligation to plan for the welfare of the operatives was most clearly stated in an editorial in the *Charlotte Observer*, which represented the interests of some of the largest and most progressive corporations in the South. The problem of what to do with the children was one of the gravest responsibilities of the manufacturer. "He might escape some of the burden of this responsibility by simply acquiescing in the public sentiment asking for a restrictive law and being done with it; but he cannot drive from his mind the query, what would become of these children if turned from the mills into the streets? If there were ample school facilities in the South it would be different. The mill operators have not only acquiesced in all propositions to raise taxes for educational purposes, but have by resolution recommended it in order to bring about as quickly as possible that condition in which the children could be, with advantage, excluded from the mills—transferred from the direction and control of the mill superintendent to the school teacher. Many of the operators want the children out of the mills, but have not been willing to arbitrarily force them out as long as there are not schools or other surrounding influences outside the mill more advantageous than the streets."[32]

The argument that compulsory school attendance should come first in order to save the child from an idle and undirected life was offered by the millmen generally.[33] The *Observer* continued its explanation of the attitude of the manufacturers toward reformation. "The abolition of slavery came about by influences outside the South. This fact has encouraged all people who conceive themselves to be reformers to begin their work in this section. The confessed error of slavery, together with the South's effort and failure to perpetuate it, makes it more or less a victim of numerous sorts of experiments and criticisms by outsiders. The experiments forced upon the South by outsiders in social equality, political supremacy, the organization of

[31] *Constitution*, Nov. 15, 1900; May 10, 1903; *News and Courier*, Jan. 1, 21, 1900; Jan. 28, Feb. 4, 1901; *Charlotte Observer*, Jan. 17, 22, 1901; *News and Observer*, Feb. 8, 1901; *State*, Jan. 17, 29, 1902; *Advertiser*, Feb. 15, 1903; *Manufacturers' Record*, Jan. 30, April 10, Sept. 18, 1902.
[32] Aug. 11, 1902.
[33] *News and Courier*, Jan. 7, 1901; *Daily Register*, Jan. 18, 1901; *State*, Jan. 29, 1902; S. C., *Journal of the House*, 1901, p. 179.

the freedman's bureau, the Union League and even much of the educational work in the twenty-five years succeeding the war did irreparable injury to the South. . . . The difference is that these several projects were as wrong in their way as slavery was and failed for the same reason that slavery did—because it was wrong. It may be supposed by those who foster the institution of child labor that the crusade against it will fail as other crusades of the sort just mentioned . . . failed. But not so. . . . This matter of child labor is fundamentally opposed by advancing civilization. It will as surely be swept out of all the United States as slavery was. . . .

"The mill men recognize that civilization is against child labor. They recognize that their own interests are not served by child labor. They are working towards its abolition in a gradual way and in ways that will contribute to the best results in the end. . . . [Since the voluntary regulations have not been lived up to] it stands the mill men in hand to meet the situation in a spirit of fairness, with amiability and conservatism, to the end that they may have some influence in framing the legislation, while the General Assembly should approach the subject in a spirit of moderation and accomplish its purpose without injury to the cotton mill interest and without checking the State's industrial growth."[34]

The other arguments against child labor legislation advanced by cotton manufacturers varied more or less and were sometimes contradictory. The arguments that poor widows and invalid fathers needed the income from the work of their children continued to appear.[35] There were repeated assertions that the operatives did not want labor laws, and that parents objected to interference with their authority and insisted on their children working.[36] Some contended that child labor was not harmful, and presented medical testimony as proof, and it was occasionally asserted that the southern child developed more rapidly than the northern child so that the same standard could not be justly enforced.[37]

Another reason offered against legislation was that the number of children employed was small, and that the child labor evil in the cotton mill industry was not extensive enough to justify legislation. The millmen were remedying the situation, and their volun-

[34] Aug. 11, 1902.

[35] Constitution, Nov. 15, 19, 20, 1900; News and Observer, Jan. 17, 1901; State, Jan. 17, 1902; S. C., Journal of the House, 1901, p. 179.

[36] News and Courier, Jan. 22, 1901; S. C., Journal of the House, 1901, pp. 184-235; Journal of the Senate, 1901, pp. 149-54; Charlotte Observer, Aug. 19, 1900; Constitution, Nov. 15, 28, 1900; Advertiser, Feb. 15, 1903; Manufacturers' Record, Sept. 25, 1902; Murphy, Problems of the Present South, p. 310.

[37] News and Observer, Feb. 15, 1903; State, Jan. 29, 1902; S. C., Journal of the House, 1901, pp. 181, 183, 184, 194-96.

tary agreements made legislation superfluous.[38] It was said by some
that labor legislation was an insult to millowners, since it implied
that they were inhumane in their treatment of operatives, and to
the working people, since it considered them incapable or unwilling
to do what was for the good of their children.[39] The plea that labor
legislation would shackle industry, prevent investments, and drive
laborers into other states continued to appear.[40] Some of the opponents of legislation tried to discourage it by ridicule and sarcasm.
They claimed that the only people demanding child labor laws
were the women, who were supposedly kindhearted but unintelligent
enough to be misled by sentimentalist preachers and people with
whom the reformation of social evils was a paying business. The
implication of all such remarks was that the reformers were either
unintelligent, uninformed, or dishonest.[41]

The arguments made by the reformers in the South were chiefly
humanitarian. Aside from the labor organizations few people considered child labor as an economic problem, and the unions did not
emphasize the economic motive as the primary reason for reform.
The principal argument for legislation was the bad effect of premature labor on children. It did them physical injury and interfered
with their education. The reformers struck one note of popular appeal when they declared that, while the poor white child was forced
to work, the black child was going to school, and the future domina-
tion of the whites was thus jeopardized.[42] Not only was the effect of
child labor bad for the child—it was destructive to the South. By
working children so young,. the future supply of skilled labor would
be ruined, the parents of the next generation injured, and an intelligent citizenship prevented. Furthermore, it was bad publicity
and put the South in ill repute in the nation for it to be said that
the prosperity of the section depended on the employment of children.[43] Such claims as these had been made in earlier years and in
other countries and the actual evil results of factory child labor had

[38] *Constitution*, Nov. 19, 1900; *News and Courier*, Sept. 11, 1901; *Daily Register*,
Sept. 7, 1902; Oct. 31, 1901.

[39] Memorandum in A. F. of L. Letter File, Box 252; *State*, Jan. 29, Feb. 5, 1902.

[40] *Advertiser*, Feb. 15, 1903; S. C., *Journal of the House*, 1901, pp. 179, 180,
182; *Constitution*, Nov. 15, 1900.

[41] *Constitution*, June 30, July 8, 1903; *Manufacturers' Record*, April 10, Aug. 28,
Jan. 30, 1902.

[42] *Constitution*, Nov. 20, 1900; Nov. 29, 1901; *Charlotte Observer*, Feb. 7, 1901,
Jan. 19, 1903; *State*, Jan. 18, 29, 1902; Feb. 5, 1902; *Christian Advocate*, Aug. 13,
1902; *News and Observer*, Jan. 9, 1903; Murphy, *Problems of the Present South*,
p. 118.

[43] *Charlotte Observer*, Aug. 12, 1900; *Advertiser*, Dec. 22, 1901; Jan. 17, 1903;
Register, Aug. 6, 1902; *State*, Aug. 11, 1902; S. C., *Journal of the Senate*, 1903,
pp. 18-19; Murphy, *Problems of the Present South*, p. 116.

been demonstrated, especially in England. Yet the southern reformers seemed hardly aware of this, and their statements were based chiefly on observation of conditions in their midst. Writers in northern periodicals drew the comparison with England,[44] but in the South the local reformers hardly took it into account until the first laws were passed.

The chief cause of the existence of the child labor evil as the reformers saw it was the greed of the capitalists. They were willing to employ children to the detriment of the child and society in order to increase their own gains. This assertion was made often by or ganized labor.[45] In order to hide their real reasons for the employ· ment of children, the manufacturers made specious arguments tha! appealed to prejudices and had no real connection with the matter, said the reformers.

The association with labor unionism being largely harmful to the cause of reform, the nonunionists declared repeatedly that the problem was not primarily one concerned with labor.[46] And even though the labor unions did account the movement their own, why should that affect the attitude of intelligent people, asked the Columbia, South Carolina, *State*. "They know that the labor unions have their selfish interests in the matter and that the cotton manufacturers in turn have their selfish interests to promote. They are willing to concede that one reason, perhaps a prime one, for the labor union agitation is the belief that in proportion as children shall be excluded from the mills adults will be employed, to the immediate wage gain of members of the union. Likewise they know that for every child under 12 years employed in the mills the manufacturers save in wages which would otherwise go to more mature help commanding higher compensation. The people are not fools, and they can discern pretty clearly the motives underlying union employers and union employed. It is not their purpose to be influenced by either. But it is their purpose and they feel it their duty to promise this reform for larger reasons of their own. . . . What do they care what Mr. Samuel Gompers likes or does not like, what he champions or what he opposes!"[47]

[44] Dowd (a southern college professor), "Cheap Labor in the South," in *Gunton's Magazine*, XVIII, 112-21; Gunton, "The South's 'Labor System,'" *Gunton's Magazine*, XVIII, 234-39; Spahr, "Child Labor in England and the United States," in *Chautauquan*, XXX, 41-43; Felix Adler, "The Evil of Child Labor—A Crime Against Humanity," in *Social Service*, VI (1902), 107-15.

[45] *Constitution*, Nov. 24, 1901; July 5, 1903; *Advertiser*, Dec. 22, 1902; Memorandum in A. F. of L. Letter File, Box 252.

[46] *State*, Feb. 5, March 22, 1902; *Constitution*, Nov. 26, 1901; Memorandum in A. F. of L. Letter File, Box 252.

[47] Nov. 5, 1902.

Not only did the reformers contend that the child labor movement was not primarily a labor cause. Murphy maintained that it was a result of demands coming first of all from within the South, and his opinion influenced others throughout the section.[48] It was not until 1903 that the national aspects of child labor were recognized.

After the efforts to satisfy demands for reform by voluntary agreements had been made, the reformers had another effective argument. The agreements, they said, were an admission that child labor evils existed. Such rules were not and could not be binding, and it was admitted that they were not enforced. If good mills were willing to abide by the rules, they could have no legitimate objection to a law covering the case, and the other mills should be coerced.[49] The best mills, where conditions were not bad, and where a great deal of welfare work was done, opposed legislation, and the others with lower standards hid behind their more progressive associates. This was possible because the millmen, even when unorganized, had a sort of unwritten agreement to uphold one another. The number of children employed in the better-class mills might be small, but these mills were the ones represented most frequently in opposing legislation. The reason lay in the feeling that the mills should "stand together" on all matters of legislation.[50]

The final argument for legislation which the newspapers advanced was its expediency. Reform was inevitable. It was better to yield gracefully to small demands than to be forced to yield later to more radical measures.[51] The editors did not admit the point which the manufacturers maintained with some foresight, that a law once passed would not be final, but only a beginning.

The growth of interest in the child labor problem in the South was followed by a wave of national interest. Whereas a mere handful of articles relating to the South had appeared in and before 1900, there were dozens of articles and editorials in all types of magazines and periodicals published in the North and having a national circulation. *Gunton's Magazine,* which had begun the attack on the southern situation in 1898, continued at intervals to take the South to

[48] Murphy, *Problems of the Present South,* p. 314; *State,* Oct. 10, 11, Sept. 29, 1902.

[49] *News and Observer,* Jan. 19, Feb. 7, 1901; Aug. 3, 1902; Feb. 6, 1903; *Constitution,* Nov. 29, 1901; July 8, 1903; *State,* Feb. 4, 1902; *Charlotte Observer,* Jan. 10, 1903; Memorandum, A. F. of L. Letter File, Box 252; Ashby-Macfayden, "Abolish Child Labor," in *American Federationist,* IX (1902), 19-20.

[50] *State,* Jan. 18, Aug. 15, 1902; *News and Courier,* Aug. 23, 1902; Murphy, *Problems of the Present South,* pp. 316, 325-26.

[51] *Charlotte Observer,* Aug. 12, 1900, article by J. A. Baldwin; *State,* Jan. 14, 1902; *Advertiser,* Jan. 22, 1903; *Constitution,* July 23, 1903.

task. *Charities,* a publication devoted to social reform, published accounts of the various efforts and failures to secure legislation in the South. The *American Federationist* had been the first to put the southern problem before its readers. After the Federation had taken a definite step toward investigation, it published articles by Mrs. Macfadyen, Eva McDonald Valesh, and other labor unionists descriptive of conditions in southern mills, as well as continuous editorial comment.[52] The *Outlook* followed rather closely the trends toward legislation in the South. Aside from these there were numbers of articles and editorials in a dozen or more other periodicals of national repute.

The movement for legislation in Alabama had an element of the spectacular about it which attracted rather wide attention. Mrs. Macfadyen's articles appeared not only in the *Federationist,* but in *Social Service*[53] and *World's Work*[54] also. Murphy's *Appeal to . . . New England,* and the controversy which it produced, attracted the attention of the editorial writer of the *Outlook*[55] and the relation of New England to the southern problem gained national attention. The same magazine also gave publicity to some of the pamphlets issued by the Alabama Committee.[56]

The manufacturers' agreements were not fully understood. *Gunton's* quoted the North Carolina agreement at length, then carelessly misread the terms and congratulated the millmen on adopting a ten-hour day—a compliment which it retracted the following month.[57] *Charities* commented on the Georgia agreement in a way which indicates that it was expected to show some binding force.[58]

Much of the criticism of the southern mill system was sensational. Some of the stories written by the people who went into the mill communities to investigate have all the characteristics of the human interest tabloid story of today. The mill children were little slaves chained to machines. The manufacturers were greedy and brutal

---

[52] Ashby-Macfadyen, "The Fight Against Child Labor in Alabama," VIII, 150-57; *idem,* "Abolish Child Labor," IX, 19-20; *idem,* "Child Life vs. Dividends," IX, 215-23; Valesh, "Three Notable Lines of Child Labor Work," VIII, 457-62; *idem,* "Child Labor—A Symposium," X, 339-60; Samuel Gompers, "Children of All Ages Employed," VIII, 277; *idem,* "Child Labor in the South," VIII, 262-63; *idem,* "Subterfuge and Greed in North Carolina," VIII, 163-64; *idem,* "Child Labor Verified by Disaster," X, 576-77; *idem,* "To Abolish Child Labor," X, 835.

[53] Ashby-Macfadyen, "The Last Stronghold of Infant Mill Slavery," IV, 202-5.

[54] *Idem,* "Child Labor in Southern Cotton Mills," II, 1290-95.

[55] "Alabama's Appeal to New England," LXIX (1901), 524; "Child Labor in Alabama," LXIX, 957-58.

[56] "Southern Protest Against Child Labor," *Outlook,* LXXI (1902), 906-8; "Child Labor Reform by 'Voluntary Agreement,'" *ibid.,* LXXII (1902), 144-45.

[57] XX (1901), 253-54, 354.

[58] "Regulating Child Labor," VII (1901), 225.

tyrants coining wealth from the lifeblood of babies. Such articles were written to appeal to public sentiment and they played up to the fullest extent the ever-present emotional appeal of the working child. Such pictures were accredited by the South to sectional hatred. Even Southerners who opposed child labor and were active in working toward reform showed their resentment of the exaggeration and play on emotions practiced by the journalists. Elbert Hubbard published in the *Philistine*[59] a scathing criticism of the South. To a southern manufacturer it was "a second Uncle Tom's Cabin."[60] That such criticism should be resented was natural. It was quoted by *The State,* which pointed out its exaggerations and unjustified generalizations, but commented that it only showed the South how it might appear to outsiders.[61] A similar moral was drawn concerning the article published in *Everybody's Magazine* by Marie Van Vorst. In an editorial entitled "The Lash of Lying," *The State* said that her picture was "not a truthful photograph of facts but a mere caricature of fair analysis and criticism. . . . The south will have to settle its labor and other problems itself. It is able to do so and intends to do so. But the people of this section do not like to be driven by the lash of lying."[62] Mrs. Macfadyen's articles were of the same general nature. What she wrote was apparently the basis of much else that appeared in the press from the pens of other writers.[63] A Columbus, Georgia, mill president, F. B. Gordon, replied to one of Mrs. Macfadyen's articles in *Social Service* with a denial of its truth and a statement quite typical of the objections to legislation offered by the manufacturers.[64]

Not all the articles that appeared in the periodicals were wholly sensational or entirely prejudiced against the mill corporations. If the reformers gained a hearing in the press, so did the manufacturers.

[59] "White Slavery in the South," XIV (May, 1902), 161-78, republished in the *American Federationist,* XII (April, 1905), 205-9, under the title "Slaughter of the Innocents."

[60] "Child Labor in Factories," in *Harper's Weekly,* XLVI (1902), 1280.

[61] May 16, 1902.

[62] Nov. 20, 1902. See also Mrs. John Van Vorst and Marie Van Vorst, *The Woman Who Toils,* pp. 215-305. Miss Van Vorst had come to Columbia and spent a short time working as a mill hand. She and her sister-in-law had similar experiences in northern industries and their book is a narrative of these experiments.

[63] "Child Labor," in the *Independent,* LIV (1902), 2032-33. When the Charleston *News and Courier* denied the truth of Mrs. Macfadyen's reports about Columbia, the *Independent* rose to her defense. See "Child Labor Again," *Independent,* LIV, 2205; Robert Hunter, "Child Labor: A Social Waste," *Independent,* LV (1903), 375-79; B. O. Flower, "Topics of the Times," in the *Arena,* XXVIII (1902), 305-17, quotes Mrs. Macfadyen, also Hubbard in the *Philistine.*

[64] "F. B. Gordon, President Mill, Columbus, Ga., Answers 'The Last Stronghold of Infant Mill Slavery,'" V (1902), 148-49.

Some people who seriously desired to bring about a change in child labor conditions were yet able to see that the mills were not all bad and that the problem involved not so much a change of heart on the part of the employers as a change of understanding. Leonora Beck Ellis published a series of articles in several periodicals. While not minimizing the evils of the child labor system, she reviewed the situation which she believed had produced it in the South. Emerging from the Civil War, the defeated states had sought to restore prosperity by a return to agriculture. When this failed they turned to cotton manufacturing. The new industry had come late to the South, and there was an eagerness to press forward to a greater prosperity. "Absorbed in the rapid development of her new source of wealth, the South is pushing on blindly, drawing to its uses every available tool, refusing to recognize any sacrifice when she consumes the powers and lives of little children for grossly material ends, obstinately forgetting that she can have no future except that founded upon the intelligence of her coming generations."[65]

The same writer praised the social welfare work of the better-class mills, describing in particular the famous Pelzer Mills in South Carolina, where conditions were reputed to be exceptionally good.[66] In another place she denied that the majority of manufacturers opposed legislation as bitterly as a few seemed to do. They were finding child labor unprofitable and the percentage was on the decrease in North Carolina, the only state which had available statistics. The mills were not an unmixed evil. They had brought the poor people from the tenant farms to a better life.[67]

The mills found still other friends to explain if not to excuse conditions. Jesse A. Baldwin, a young Methodist minister in one of the largest centers of manufacturing in the South who had been urging reform for several years, showed great concern over the evil effects of night work, long hours, and poor surroundings on children working in the mills; but he defended the millmen as doing all they could to alleviate conditions.[68] From another source came an article that was at once an accusation and a defense. The *World's Work* was always sympathetic with the South, though its constructive criticism

[65] Ellis, "Child Operatives in Southern Mills," in the *Independent*, LIII (1901), 2637-47. See also, "Child Labor Legislation in the South," in *Gunton's Magazine*, XXI, 45-53, and "The Movement to Restrict Child Labor," in the *Arena*, XXVIII (1902), 370-78, by the same author.

[66] "A Model Factory Town," in the *Forum*, XXXII (1901), 60-65. Compare Richard T. Ely, "An American Industrial Experiment," in *Harper's Monthly Magazine*, CV (1902), 39-45.

[67] Ellis, "A Study of Southern Cotton-Mill Communities," in the *American Journal of Sociology*, VIII (1903), 623-30.

[68] "Evils of Southern Factory Life," in *Gunton's Magazine*, XXII (1902), 326-37.

urged reforms. In 1902 its editor felt that remedy for child labor evils must come from within the South. "Local agitation is the remedy and local agitation is sure to prevail, especially when it is conducted with the vigor and skill that are used by the Executive Committee on Child Labor in Alabama."[69] After the laws of 1903 were passed, the *World's Work* announced them as proof that southern opinion was essentially "humane and sound," and that noninterference with state control was the best way to promote reform.[70] The mill official was more guilty of a misconception of the problem of child labor than of malicious greed. "The day will come when every man who now puts a child of less than twelve to continuous toil will humbly pray God and his fellow-men to forgive him; for they are 'good' men who do this colossal crime, blinded by some economic untruth. Yet it is the blackest sin that men in a democracy have ever committed. A democratic society exists for the nurture of men; that is its aim and that is our boast. God help us in this blindness to the very first lesson in all civilization; for our savage ancestors knew better."[71]

[69] "The Worst Crime of Civilization," IV (1902), 2475-76.
[70] "Progress in Child-Labor Legislation," V (1903), 3264.
[71] "The Worst Crime of Civilization," in *World's Work*, IV (1902), 2475-76. Compare Adler, "The Evil of Child Labor—A Crime Against Humanity," in *Social Service*, VI (1902), 108.

CHAPTER IV

GEORGIA, 1886-1903: LABOR COMPLICATIONS

GEORGIA was the only state in the South to adopt any restrictive legislation before the Civil War regarding the employment of minors. A law, passed in 1854, restricted to daylight hours the work of white persons under twenty-one in cotton and woolen mills and other manufacturing establishments.[1] Such legislation was unimportant and ineffective, however, and with the revival of the mills a movement for child labor legislation began.

In 1886 bills for the establishment of a bureau of labor, for arbitration of labor disputes with manufacturers, for reduction of hours of labor, and for regulation of child labor were introduced. Most of them, including the one on child labor, came from the Augusta District, Richmond County,[2] where there were several factories. These measures were not acted upon at that session of the legislature, but the following year a number of petitions were presented in favor of the child labor and ten-hour bills which were still on the House calendar.[3] The Committee on Labor and Labor Statistics reported favorably on the child labor bill, and favorably by substitute on the ten-hour bill. The child labor bill was not opposed by the argument that it would injure the cotton mill industry, which had not at this time reached very great proportions, but by the arguments that idleness was injurious to children and that the state had no right to encroach upon the authority of the parent. The bill received a majority of votes cast, but not the constitutional majority required for the passage of a law.[4] A motion to revive it was tabled.[5] The ten-hour bill also failed to receive a constitutional majority, and was allowed to die in the committee the following year.

In 1889 the ten-hour bill was again presented. The committee listened to the arguments of several manufacturers who opposed and one laborer who supported it,[6] and gave the bill a favorable report.[7]

---

[1] *Acts and Resolutions of the General Assembly,* 1853-54, p. 37. Hereafter cited as *Acts of the General Assembly.*

[2] Ga., *Journal of the House of Representatives,* 1886, pp. 50, 133, 145, 178, 208, 225. Hereafter cited as *Journal of the House.*

[3] U. S. Bureau of Labor, *Woman and Child Wage-Earners,* VI, 168.

[4] *Atlanta Constitution,* Sept. 22, 1887.

[5] *Ibid.,* Sept. 23, 1887.

[6] U. S. Bureau of Labor, *Woman and Child Wage-Earners,* VI, 169.

[7] Ga., *Journal of the House,* 1889, p. 154.

In the House the chief opposition was on grounds of interference with private rights. Comparison was made with farm labor, which was not regulated. The advocates of the measure based their arguments on the need of defenseless women and children for protection. Conditions were pictured as involving unreasonable hours for large numbers of them. A letter from a mill treasurer was read which pointed out the economic value of a ten-hour day over a longer one.[8] The House passed the ten-hour bill by a vote of ninety-five to thirty-eight, forty-one not voting.[9] In the Senate it was amended to a sixty-six hour week, and passed.[10]

The enactment of this law, which provided that the hours of labor in cotton and woolen mills should not exceed sixty-six hours in a week, nullified the old provision of 1853 that a white minor should not work between sunset and sunrise. The Code of 1895 puts this interpretation on the Act of 1889.[11]

At the same session of the legislature a child labor bill was introduced into the Senate to prohibit the employment of children under ten in manufacturing, mercantile, and mechanical establishments, and under twelve during days school was in session.[12] The committee returned a substitute, that children under twelve should not be employed, and children under seventeen should work only ten hours a day. The bill passed the Senate without opposition but was postponed indefinitely in the House.[13] Another bill in the Senate proposed to limit the hours for minors to ten a day. It differed from other similar bills, however, in that its purpose as defined by its author was to protect country children from overwork in the cotton-picking season. It was referred at his request to the Committee on Agriculture, but was adversely reported.[14]

The bill of 1889 marked the end of all effort to secure legislation for several years. The investigators of the United States Bureau of Labor believed that the bills introduced in the late 1880's had resulted from the influence of the Knights of Labor. There is no certain proof of this, but if true, this influence ceased to exist in Georgia after 1889.[15] Although the number of child workers was rapidly

[8] U. S. Bureau of Labor, *Woman and Child Wage-Earners*, VI, 169.

[9] Ga., *Journal of the House*, 1889, pp. 1176-77.

[10] Ga., *Acts of the General Assembly*, 1888-89, p. 163, and *Journal of the Senate*, 1889, p. 733.

[11] U. S. Bureau of Labor, *Woman and Child Wage-Earners*, VI, 171.

[12] Ga., *Journal of the Senate*, 1889, p. 224; *Constitution*, Aug. 10, 1889.

[13] Ga., *Journal of the House*, 1889, pp. 1485, 1562.

[14] Ga., *Journal of the Senate*, 1889, pp. 60, 211; *Constitution*, July 17, 1889.

[15] U. S. Bureau of Labor, *Woman and Child Wage-Earners*, VI, 172. See also *Constitution*, Nov. 13, 1886, which gives an account of an address made by a member of the Knights of Labor in Atlanta, in which the speaker recommended labor legislation.

increasing as the mills grew, there was as yet no marked feeling against child labor.

The movement for child labor legislation and the limitation of hours of labor for adult workers began in the South at about the same time that the agrarian movement was in full swing and before the Populist party came into being. The Farmers' Alliance, which had rapidly spread in the South, met in 1889 at St. Louis with the Knights of Labor and agreed on a common political platform with that body. The demands made were not primarily labor demands.[16] While in some instances it is quite apparent that the agrarian leaders gave support to demands for factory legislation, as when the Tillman faction in South Carolina passed an eleven-hour-day law, it does not appear that there was any consistent effort on their part to help the labor organizations carry out their program in the South. The early 1890's were hard years in Georgia and the factory town population suffered with the rest. The undue amount of unemployment in such centers of industry as Augusta, Macon, and Columbus[17] caused suffering and created a feeling of unrest which prepared the way for a new labor movement. The strength of the Knights of Labor had declined, and the American Federation of Labor, just rising into a dominant position in the labor world, did not seek union with the farmer class.[18] When the People's party was formed, the American Federation refused to give it official endorsement, although many local unions gave it their support.[19]

The next steps toward labor legislation were taken by the labor unions affiliated with the American Federation of Labor. The movement to organize the South was under way in 1896,[20] and in the years following grew slowly. In 1899 a state federation was formed. In 1896 a child labor bill was again introduced, this time supported by the labor unions, especially the Atlanta Federation of Trades. It was the beginning of a series of such bills that was kept up until success was achieved in 1906.[21]

The bill of 1896 was introduced into the House by Craig of Bibb County, one of the centers of cotton manufacturing.[22] It provided that no child under thirteen years of age should be employed in any manufacturing establishment, factory, laundry, or workshop; it required an affidavit of the age of each child between the ages of thirteen and sixteen who was employed to be filed with the employer; and it empowered any magistrate or peace officer to inspect

[16] Alex Mathews Arnett, *The Populist Movement in Georgia*, pp. 83-84.
[17] *Ibid.*, p. 160.
[18] *Ibid.*, p. 125.   [19] *Ibid.*, p. 175.
[20] *American Federationist*, II (1896), 145.
[21] *Constitution*, Nov. 19, 1896.
[22] Ga., *Journal of the House*, 1896, p. 315.

establishments for violations of these provisions.[23] The Atlanta Federation of Trades used all its influence in behalf of the bill.[24] The Federation held a meeting on November 21, 1896, at which it was announced that nearly every labor organization in the state had taken action against child labor.[25]

At the hearing of the Craig bill before the Committee on Labor and Labor Statistics, the attorney of the Atlanta Federation of Trades, C. T. Ladson, spoke in behalf of the bill, which he was said to have written. He argued that the work did physical injury to the children and prevented them from getting an education. Their employment for wages as low as from nine to twenty-five cents a day benefited no one except the factory owner, who was thus securing labor at one third the price paid to adults. Ninety per cent of the children worked because they were forced to do so by lazy fathers. Attorney Ladson submitted an amendment allowing children over ten years of age who were orphans or the children of widows to be excepted from the provisions of the bill. Several factory presidents from Atlanta and Augusta opposed the bill.[26] The committee gave a unanimous vote in favor of the measure, with the amendment.[27] The bill was not acted upon, however, but was held over until the following year.[28]

When the legislature met in 1897 it was evident that the manufacturers had been busy building up opposition to the child labor bill. There was an extended debate, and an effort was made to defeat the whole purpose of the bill by amendments. The ten-year exception, recommended by the committee, was adopted. A motion that the bill should be amended so as not to apply to cotton mills almost passed before the advocates of the bill realized that it would defeat the aim of the measure. Reid, Craig's colleague from Bibb County, opposed the measure. The opposition declared that it would drive the factories out of the state, that child labor was not injurious to health, and that the measure was an infringement of personal rights. The friends of the bill took the position that they had held before the committee in the previous year.[29] The bill was finally killed, and an effort to revive it by reconsidering the action failed on the day following.[30]

The *Atlanta Constitution*, edited by Clark Howell, gave unquali-

[23] General Assembly, House Bills (a) 1896-97, MS, State Dept. of History, Ga.
[24] *Constitution*, Nov. 19, 1896.
[25] *Ibid.*, Nov. 22, 1896.   [26] *Ibid.*, Dec. 4, 1896.
[27] *Ibid.*; General Assembly, House Bills (a) 1896-97, MS, State Dept. of History, Ga.
[28] Ga., *Journal of the House*, 1896, p. 579.
[29] *Ibid.*, 1897, pp. 327-32; *Constitution*, Nov. 10, 1897.
[30] Ga., *Journal of the House*, 1897, pp. 332, 381, 383.

fied support to the demands for child labor legislation as well as some of the other labor measures. The matter of child labor was allowed to rest in 1898, but in the year following as labor organizations grew stronger the outlook for labor legislation improved. The local labor groups of Georgia joined in a state federation in April.[31] This gave them added strength with which to demand legislation. The only labor law which had been secured in Georgia was the eleven-hour-day law of 1889, which a labor leader declared to be ineffective in most cases because of lack of provision for enforcement. The first step in promoting better conditions he believed to be the creation of a bureau of labor statistics whose commissioner could gather the necessary information as a basis for reform. The other legislation chiefly desired was the reduction of hours of labor and the prohibition of child labor under fourteen years.[32]

When the Assembly met in the latter part of October, Governor Allen D. Candler recognized the demands of the Federation of Labor for a bureau of labor statistics and child labor legislation. He did not clearly recommend action on child labor, but merely called the attention of the legislators to the situation in such a way as to indicate his sympathy with the idea that children needed legal protection.[33]

The *Constitution* announced its support of the bureau of labor statistics and child labor bills which the State Federation of Labor was presenting before the bills were introduced in the legislature. It gave the terms of the child labor bill and commented on it as a moderate measure.[34] The labor organizations also had the pledge of co-operation from the Methodist Ministers' Association of Atlanta,[35] and the endorsement of the State Federation of Women's Clubs. The latter organization met in Macon the first few days of November. While in session they received a request from the Macon Central Union to help secure the passage of the child labor law. The women adopted unanimously resolutions in favor of the measure, and considered what methods should be used to co-operate with the labor unions.[36]

The child labor bill was presented in the Senate on October 31, 1899, by Senator Nesbitt, and referred to the Committee on Immigration and Labor.[37] It provided that children under ten years of age should not be employed under any condition, in factories or mines,

[31] U. S. Industrial Commission, *Report*, VII, 233; *Constitution*, Oct. 29, 1899.

[32] Testimony of J. W. Bridwell, secretary of Atlanta Federation of Trades, U. S. Industrial Commission, *Report*, VII, 235.

[33] *Constitution*, Oct. 26, 1899; Ga., *Journal of the House*, 1899, p. 49.

[34] Oct. 29, 1899.   [35] *Atlanta Journal*, Oct. 30, 1899.

[36] *Constitution*, Nov. 4, 1899; *Atlanta Journal*, Nov. 7, 1899.

[37] Ga., *Journal of the Senate*, 1899, p. 150.

and that children between ten and fourteen should be required to present a certificate from the superintendent of schools that they had
attended school sixteen weeks before they might be employed. The
penalty for violation was a fine of from ten to fifty dollars.[38] The
bill was favorably reported by the committee after a hearing at
which Ladson, now attorney for the State Federation of Labor, and
Garrett, the president of the Federation, spoke.[39] But instead of
acting on the bill the Senate returned it to the committee.[40] The
second hearing brought the millowners and labor unionists again
before the committee, which prepared a substitute, with a twelve-
year age limit and exceptions for children of widowed mothers and
indigent fathers, and omitted educational qualifications.[41] After a
"warm discussion" in the Senate the bill failed to receive a constitutional majority. Its friends secured a reconsideration, and it was
again debated, with Nesbitt, who had introduced it for the Federation, championing it. An amendment to except ginneries, saw mills,
and fruit-packing establishments was adopted. Several men who at
first opposed the bill changed sides. Attempts were made at filibuster-
ing, but a motion was put through to extend the session until the
measure was disposed of. It finally passed the Senate by a vote of
twenty-four to fifteen.[42]

The Nesbitt bill was introduced in the House on November 17,
1899, and referred to the Committee on Labor and Labor Statistics.[43]
Ladson again came before the committee to present his views on
the bill which he had prepared and a number of mill presidents
replied to his arguments. At a second hearing some of the officers
of the Federation of Labor brought in five children between the
ages of eight and eleven that they had picked up as they came out
of the Exposition Mills, an Atlanta corporation whose president frequently appeared in opposition to child labor measures.[44] The labor
men pointed out that the children were barefoot, ragged, and illiterate, and that they worked eleven hours a day for a wage of from
ten to twenty cents. Ladson charged that the millowners were heartless and inhumane. He declared that the bill had the support of
six thousand club women, nearly one hundred thousand working men,
the ministers of Atlanta, and ten thousand citizens who had signed
petitions for its enactment.[45]

[38] General Assembly, Senate Bills, 1898-99, Bill 118, State Dept. of History, Ga.
[39] *Constitution*, Nov. 3, 1899; Ga., *Journal of the Senate*, 1899, p. 176.
[40] Ga., *Journal of the Senate*, 1899, p. 185.
[41] General Assembly, Senate Bills, 1898-99, Bill 118, State Dept. of History, Ga.
[42] *Constitution*, Nov. 15, 16, 17, 1899; Ga., *Journal of the Senate*, 1899, pp.
245-48, 254, 282-83.   [43] Ga., *Journal of the House*, 1899, p. 475.
[44] U. S. Industrial Commission, *Report*, VII, 544.
[45] *Constitution*, Dec. 3, 1899.

The bill was favorably reported in the House,[46] but its consideration was then delayed eleven days. The labor organizations were uneasy because of the apparent influence of the manufacturers over the legislature. Three labor officers representing the carders' and spinners' union in Augusta urged the legislature to send a committee there to investigate. They demanded a hearing for operatives as well as millowners. It was rumored that the mill managers were circulating a petition among the operatives against the bill. The union men represented the bill as "the only redemtion [sic] to save this class of workers from the very grossest Ignorance."[47]

The debate in the House was heated. The Speaker, John D. Little of Muskogee County, which was one of the manufacturing centers of the state, left the chair in order to advocate the measure. He directed his arguments especially against the "dinner toting" fathers who lived on the wages of their children and brought their midday meals to the mill. The old arguments of the moral value of work for the child, the necessity for some children to support their parents, and the danger to industry in tampering with the labor system were rehearsed by the opponents. A discussion arose as to whether the mill operatives favored such a law and a representative from Richmond County read a petition from the employees of one mill to prove that they did not. This was probably the petition to which the labor union officers had referred in their letter to the House. The representative from Oconee replied that the operatives were compelled to sign the petition. The first speaker denied this and claimed that notices had been posted in the mill giving operatives the option of signing or not.[48] The House failed to take any action after this debate, and tabled the bill *sine die* just before adjournment.[49] This was done by its friends to save it from defeat.[50]

Child labor reform in Georgia was clearly allied with the issues of organized labor. The women's organizations and some of the clergy gave their support to the cause, but it was only secondary. The efforts of the national unions to gain a foothold in the South were regarded with suspicion and distrust by most people of political and social prominence. The championship of child labor by the unions did not win friends from among such citizens. The political strength of the working class was growing, but very slowly. In May, 1900, a national convention of textile workers was held in Augusta, Georgia. Delegates from the four leading southern manufacturing states were

[46] Ga., *Journal of the House*, 1899, pp. 895, 917.
[47] W. T. Hanley, W. L. Keel, and G. B. McCrackan to the House, Dec. 6, 1899, attached to House Bill 118, in Senate Bills, 1898-99, State Dept. of History, Ga.
[48] *Constitution*, Dec. 16, 1899.
[49] Ga., *Journal of the House*, 1899, p. 1291.
[50] *Atlanta Journal*, Dec. 15, 1899.

present as well as those from the North. This convention passed
resolutions condemning child labor in the southern states as interfering with the wages and employment of adults, and recommending
a law prohibiting the employment of children under fourteen years
of age in all manufacturing, mining, and railroad industries. It also
recommended a compulsory education law.[51] These resolutions did
not represent the will of the large majority of textile mill employees,
however, for most of them were not organized. Of all the trades,
textile workers were the most difficult to bring into unions and the
southern workers were exceptionally so.[52]

The laborers were successful in electing a number of representatives to the legislature in 1900 from Columbus, Macon, Augusta, and
Atlanta.[53] These men and the leaders of the Georgia Federation of
Labor wished to press the matter of child labor legislation, and they
looked to the National Federation for advice.[54] The Executive Board
of the Georgia Federation met just before the opening of the Assembly and urged that the issue be made paramount.[55]

There were two measures introduced in the House on October 26,
1900. C. C. Houston, editor of the *Journal of Labor* of Atlanta,
and member for Fulton County, presented a child labor bill. It set
a twelve-year age limit for factories and mines; required that children
between twelve and fourteen should be able to read and write simple
sentences in English before they were eligible for employment; forbade
the employment of boys under sixteen and girls under eighteen for
more than sixty hours a week; and required that thirty minutes be
allowed for the noon meal in factories.[56] Houston also introduced
a bill for a bureau of labor statistics.[57] Another child labor bill was
presented immediately after the Houston bill by Seaborn Wright of
Floyd County. Wright had been active in Georgia politics for several
years, and in 1896 had made an unsuccessful race for the governorship
on the Populist ticket. He was also known as an advocate of prohibition reform.[58] The Wright bill was directed solely against child
labor in the textile industry. Children under ten should be prohibited entirely from working in the mills. Between ten and fourteen
they should be required to attend school two months out of six.
Children between ten and twelve should be employed for half time

[51] *American Federationist*, VII (1900), 169.
[52] U. S. Industrial Commission, *Report*, VII, 565-66.
[53] W. H. Winn to Gompers, May 18, 1900, A. F. of L. Letter File, Box 186.
[54] G. B. McCrackan to Gompers, July 11, 1900, A. F. of L. Letter File, Box 186.
[55] *Constitution*, Oct. 22, 1900.
[56] General Assembly, House Bills (a) 1900-1901, Bill 9, State Dept. of History, Ga.; *Constitution*, Oct. 27, 1900; Ga., *Journal of the House*, 1900, p. 112.
[57] Ga., *Journal of the House*, 1900, p. 202.
[58] L. L. Knight, *A Standard History of Georgia and Georgians*, II, 1000.

only. Two physicians, one of them the county health officer, should be appointed by the judge of the superior court to visit the factories twice a year for the purpose of investigating sanitary conditions in order to report to the grand juries.[59]

Both bills were referred to the Committee on Labor and Labor Statistics, which held extensive hearings. At the first of these the principal speaker was Jack J. Spalding, an Atlanta lawyer who was active in state politics. He was an attorney for the cotton mill owners and for a number of years he represented their interests in the matter of legislation. In a long address he presented the arguments of the manufacturers in opposition to restrictive legislation. First, the demands for labor legislation were inspired by New England mill-owners, who, not wanting to move their factories South, sought to weaken the competition of southern manufacturers. As proof of this he pointed to the advertisement which had run in the *Constitution* a few months before for mill operatives for New England, and an article in the Boston *Journal of Commerce and Textile Industries* which prophesied that the South would have laws regulating woman and child labor. A man from Massachusetts had urged the textile workers in Augusta to strike if a ten-hour day were not granted them, and he inferred from this that the man was paid by the New England mill interests. His second argument was that no other southern state had child labor legislation, and to enact such laws in Georgia would be an injustice to the cotton manufacturing industry. Third, parental authority should not be interfered with. In the fourth place, the bill required that all children should be able to write correctly in order to hold a job, which was a qualification not even required of voters. The limitation of hours was unfair, as it did not apply to farmers. It would injure industry by causing mill families to move into neighboring states. Children who had dependent, widowed mothers and children of drunken fathers would have no means of support if they were not allowed to work. The danger to the child was not in work, but in idleness which led to vice and crime. The arguments of the would-be reformers were nothing more than maudlin sentiment. The millowners were Georgia men, representing large investments of capital. They were the friends of the operatives and provided them with churches, schools, and other benefits. They would not do anything to brutalize the employees or to wrong labor. Yet they protested against such legislation.[60] This speech embodied practically all the arguments which had been offered against child labor legislation up to this time.

[59] General Assembly, House Bills (a) 1900-01, Bill 10, State Dept. of History, Ga.; Ga., *Journal of the House*, 1900, p. 111.

[60] *Constitution*, Nov. 15, 1900. A number of other speakers appeared on both sides. See *ibid.*, Nov. 20, 1900.

As an outcome of the hearings, a substitute bill which Wright and Houston helped to prepare was recommended.[61]   It provided that no children under twelve should be employed, except the children of widows who could prove that they were physically unable to work and had no other means of support.   The ability to read and write was required of children between twelve and fourteen who were employed.   The sixty-hour week was dropped.[62]   Since it was apparent that the child labor advocates had yielded on some points, it was believed that the substitute measure would be acceptable to the manufacturers, and the *Constitution* made a statement to the effect that opposition was not to be expected.[63] This was immediately challenged by Spalding, who declared that the bill would be vigorously opposed.   The *Constitution* published his statement, but claimed that its assertion had been based on information coming indirectly from Spalding.[64]

Interest in the child labor bill was so aroused that a large crowd of visitors came to hear the debate in the House.   The speakers were limited to five minutes each.   The same arguments were rehearsed that had been presented to the committee. When the vote was taken, the measure was defeated by fifty-six to one hundred and four.   This defeat was so overwhelming that no effort was made to reconsider it. The argument which apparently carried the most weight was that the bill was the work of labor agitators employed by New England millmen.[65]   Although Wright introduced another bill a few days later, it was dropped.[66]

The consistent demands made by the labor unions for a child labor law, while not successful, were strong enough to make the cotton manufacturers realize that some regulation of the problem must be attempted.   The investigations held in the spring of 1900 by the United States Industrial Commission had included the testimony of a number of manufacturers in and about Atlanta, as well as that of several of the labor leaders. The general trend of the views of the former was that the mills did not as a rule employ children under twelve, except at the urgent demand of their parents, because it was economically unprofitable.[67]   The labor leaders claimed that about 10 per cent of the children employed were under twelve, and that the reason one Atlanta mill had adopted the policy of excluding such children was the pressure brought to bear on that mill by the

[61] *Constitution*, Nov. 20, 1900.

[62] General Assembly, House Bills (a) 1900-01, Bill 10, Substitute attached, State Dept. of History, Ga.

[63] Nov. 22, 1900.   [64] Nov. 23, 1900.

[65] Ga., *Journal of the House*, 1900, pp. 464-66; *Constitution*, Nov. 28, 1900.

[66] Ga., *Journal of the House*, 1900, p. 549.

[67] U. S. Industrial Commission, *Report*, VII, 512-13, 522, 529, 540, 570.

Journal of Labor.[68] The manufacturers found it necessary to meet the attacks made upon them by the unions, the women's clubs, and some of the clergy. In December, 1900, following the defeat of the child labor bill, they formed a rather loosely organized industrial association and adopted a set of regulations for child labor by voluntary agreement. The terms were that no child under twelve should work at night; parents should be compelled to alternate their children in the mills, that is, send one to school while the other worked. As far as possible parents would be required to keep children out of the mills except when it was necessary for them to earn a living. The mills would refuse employment to those whose fathers were able to support them.[69] The terms of this agreement were no more than the avowed policy of the leading mills around Atlanta, as shown in the testimony before the Industrial Commission. They did not set a definite age limit for day work or include the provisions for educational tests that the several child labor bills had contained. They offered no guarantee that the agreement would be enforced, and were so general that it would be difficult to say when they were not being observed.

Up to this time the labor organizations in Georgia had conducted their campaign for child labor legislation with the approval, but not the direct assistance, of the national organization. Local support of non-labor people in Georgia had not been well organized and had played only a small part in the legislative contests. The bill of 1900 had just been defeated when the American Federation of Labor sent Miss Ashby to Alabama to work for child labor reform. The way in which she had been received by the prominent clergy and some of the society women in Alabama caused the non-labor advocates of legislation in Georgia to hope that her visit to Atlanta would help solidify public opinion in favor of a child labor law. The *Atlanta Constitution* announced her arrival with an appeal to the "conservative people." In the spring of 1901 Miss Ashby came to Atlanta and held a conference with the "conservatives," who were interested in child labor from purely humanitarian motives. This led to the formation of a central committee modeled on the same lines as the Alabama Child Labor Committee.[70] The labor organizations had proposed bill after bill, but the prospect for the enactment of a law through their support alone was very poor. The only hope lay in a working combination of the labor unions and the disinterested humanitarian group which included many of the politically and socially prominent. It was this *rapprochement* which Miss Ashby, now Mrs. Macfadyen, hoped to bring about.

[68] *Ibid.*, pp. 544, 550-51, 565-66.
[69] *Atlanta Journal*, Dec. 6, 1900.   [70] *Constitution*, Oct. 30, 1901.

The membership of the Georgia Central Committee included Judge Henry B. Tompkins, the chairman; General and former Governor John B. Gordon; the Reverend W. W. Landrum, Burton Smith, and Hooper Alexander, attorneys of Atlanta; the Reverend C. B. Wilmer, Episcopal clergyman; Clark Howell, editor of the *Atlanta Constitution* and member of the legislature; Bishop Nelson and Bishop Chandler of the Episcopal and Methodist churches; and Mrs. J. K. Ottley and Mrs. Lindsay Johnson, prominent officers of the Federation of Women's Clubs.[71] While some of the members gave good support to the reform movement, and the *Atlanta Constitution* was untiring in its demands, there was no single leader who made the cause his own so wholeheartedly and so ably as Murphy was doing in Alabama.

Mrs. Macfadyen was invited by Wilmer to stop in Atlanta on her way back to Alabama in the fall of 1901. She arrived on the day that Houston introduced the child labor and bureau of labor bills into the House. She immediately conferred with Houston, Jerome Jones, of the *Journal of Labor,* and Wilmer. There was already some friction between the labor men and the committee, for Wilmer had understood Houston to promise that he would hold back his bill "in favor of one presented as a public and not a labor measure." The committee was undecided whether to support Houston's bill, which was associated with the other labor measure, or to introduce one of its own. Mrs. Macfadyen saw the danger in continuing Houston's policy, but there were already two bills before the House.[72] She persuaded the Central Committee to put its influence back of the Houston measure.[73] This action met with the approval of Gompers, under whose direction Mrs. Macfadyen worked. He said they could not afford to have their "fellow-unionists of Georgia feel as though they had been snubbed; for after all, the agitation is initiated by the organized labor movement, of which the Georgia trade unionists are a part."[74] After having interviewed some of the members of the women's clubs of Atlanta and obtained their promise of support, Mrs. Macfadyen left for Alabama.[75]

The first child labor bill of 1901 was presented by the representative from Richmond, one of the manufacturing counties, five days before the Houston bill. It set an age limit of ten years with an educational requirement for children ten to fourteen, unless they had dependent parents.[76] The Houston bill providing for a twelve-

---

[71] Report to A. F. of L., Letter File, Box 252.

[72] Ga., *Journal of the House,* 1901, pp. 71, 151.

[73] Report of Mrs. Macfadyen to Gompers, A. F. of L. Letter File, Box 252.

[74] Gompers to Mrs. Macfadyen, Nov. 12, 1901, Letter Book, Vol. XLVIII.

[75] Mrs. Macfadyen's report to Gompers, A. F. of L. Letter File, Box 252.

[76] General Assembly, House Bills (a) 1900-01, State Dept. of History, Ga.

year age limit was introduced on October 28, 1901.[77] The bills were referred to the Committee on Labor and Labor Statistics, which, after the usual hearings at which Spalding again appeared, recommended a substitute. This provided a twelve-year age limit with exceptions for children of widows who were dependent on them for support. Night work under fourteen was forbidden, and children under fourteen were required to be able to read and write in order to secure employment. A minority report against the bill declared that the House in its previous session had sustained the minority by refusing to pass a child labor law. The persistent agitation for a law tended to deprive the owners of the mills of their control over them and to put them under the influence of the "walking delegates."[78]

The minority report was printed by the manufacturers and a copy presented to every member of the legislature. The manufacturers also published a pamphlet containing the speeches of the lawyers and millmen who opposed the bill. The Georgia Central Committee replied with a pamphlet written by Wilmer and Mrs. Macfadyen, who had just returned, and signed by every member of the committee.[79] They undertook to refute the charges that the bill was advocated by no one except labor agitators, opponents of industry, and club women. The opponents were challenged to name the persons sent by the eastern mills to promote the legislation. References were made to the *Appeal to the People and Press of New England,* which had just precipitated the Nichols-Sears controversy. The committee members denied that they were sentimental women or labor agitators, or paid by the New England capitalists. The attack, they said, would be amusing if it were not so important. "We can account for this only on the theory that the best way to advocate a bad cause is to abuse the plaintiff. May we inquire who, besides those financially interested in defeating the bill, are opposing it?"[80] The legislative committee of the Atlanta Federation of Trades also issued a statement answering the minority report.[81] The *Constitution* commented editorially on the bill, using arguments put forward by Murphy in his pamphlets.[82]

The Georgia Committee, under the influence of Mrs. Macfadyen, planned a mass meeting to present child labor legislation to the public. Houston obtained the use of the hall of the House of Representatives for November 26, 1901, and it was announced through the papers that Governor Candler, Hoke Smith, several members of the Georgia Committee, and Mrs. Macfadyen would speak.[83] The

[77] Ga., *Journal of the House,* 1901, p. 151.
[78] *Constitution,* Nov. 12, 1901; Ga., *Journal of the House,* 1901, p. 397.
[79] Report of Mrs. Macfadyen to Gompers, A. F. of L. Letter File, Box 252.
[80] *Constitution,* Nov. 29, 1901.   [81] *Ibid.,* Nov. 24, 1901.
[82] Nov. 15, 1901.   [83] *Constitution,* Nov. 25, 1901.

meeting drew a large crowd, but there were noticeably few members of the legislature present. Governor Candler failed to appear but Hoke Smith, Judge Tompkins, Wilmer, Mrs. Macfadyen, and others spoke.[84] The main object of the meeting was to appeal to non-labor support, and since the speech of a labor man would not have helped to do so, Houston did not appear on the program.[85]

As an aid to legislation the meeting was a failure. The House refused to pass the measure.[86] The continued appeal made by the Alabama reformers and echoed in the Georgia press for New England capitalists to use their influence against child labor finally brought a declaration in favor of legislation in the South from Seth Low, the reform mayor-elect of Greater New York.[87] The message was given publicity, but it came too late to have any influence in 1901.

The defeat left discordant feelings among the reformers. The Central Committee, or a part of it, and Seaborn Wright, author of one of the bills, attributed the defeat of the measure to its association with organized labor. Houston's bill was definitely aligned with the Bureau of Labor Statistics bill as a labor measure. Houston resented Mrs. Macfadyen's activities. He opposed having her speak in the cities throughout the state, but in this she followed the advice of the Central Committee.[88] She was not as successful in winning the confidence of the club women as she had been in Alabama. The president of the Federation of Women's Clubs distrusted her on her first visit to Georgia in the spring of 1901, and wrote a critical letter to President Gompers. He sent the letter to Miss Ashby with his assurance of confidence.[89] With this situation it is natural that the club women took no part in the movement in 1901. Although Mrs. Macfadyen was in the pay of the American Federation, the Georgia Committee seemed to overlook the fact. It lacked the tact that Murphy used in keeping labor in the background without giving undue offense. But the labor organizations in Georgia had gone much further in their work for legislation than the Alabama unions, so that the situation was more difficult to handle. After she left the South, Mrs. Macfadyen wrote to Wilmer reminding him that while the American Federation considered child labor a public problem, it had done more toward a solution in Georgia than any other

[84] *Ibid.*, Nov. 27, 1901.

[85] Report of Mrs. Macfadyen to Gompers, A. F. of L. Letter File, Box 252.

[86] Ga., *Journal of the House*, 1901, p. 477.

[87] Murphy, *Problems of the Present South*, pp. 328-29; Report of Mrs. Macfadyen, A. F. of L. Letter File, Box 252.

[88] Report of Mrs. Macfadyen, A. F. of L. Letter File, Box 252.

[89] Gompers to Miss Ashby, June 5, 12, 1901; Gompers to Mrs. J. Lindsay Johnson, June 12, 1901, Letter Book, Vol. XLIII.

agency.[90] Wilmer regarded labor support as a hindrance rather than an aid in the long contest, and clearly admitted his distrust of it. Four years later he said that Mrs. Macfadyen's presence in Georgia as a paid representative of the American Federation "made it more difficult for us to win . . . because it puts us up against the claim made by the other side that this movement was all in the interest of the laboring classes, and there was a considerable degree of plausibility in the contention made for a while that only a few sentimental preachers and a few women and labor agitators and paid emissaries of the northern mills were in favor of this movement."[91]

In 1902 Houston again took up the movement for a child labor law. On October 27 he introduced a bill which was practically the same as the bill of the previous year. It set the twelve-year age limit with the ten-year exception, and authorized the grand jury to investigate violations. The judges of the circuit and criminal courts were to charge the juries to do so each term. The bill was referred as in previous years to the Committee on Labor and Labor Statistics of which Houston was chairman.[92] A few days later Houston took an unexpected step when he asked the unanimous consent of the House to have the bill withdrawn from this committee and referred to the Committee on Education. When a small minority of the members voted against the change, Houston resigned from the Committee on Labor and Labor Statistics. The speaker then designated the vice-chairman of the committee, Kilburn, who was also a labor representative, as chairman. Kilburn refused to serve and withdrew from the committee. A third man was then appointed, and the child labor bill was transferred to the Committee on Education.[93] Houston gave no reason for his action on the floor of the House, but in a later interview he stated his belief that the Labor Committee, which had on former occasions given favorable reports, had been packed so as to give an adverse report, which he as chairman would have had to carry back to the House against his own bill. He claimed that fifteen of the twenty-two members would have opposed the Child Labor bill.[94]

The Committee on Education held meetings to hear evidence on the bill. A number of cotton manufacturers and Spalding again spoke against it, and Ladson and Wilmer in its behalf. The chief arguments used against the bill were the "entering wedge," the senti-

[90] Mrs. Macfadyen to Wilmer, April 5, 1902, A. F. of L. Letter File, Box 252.

[91] "Reports from State and Local Child Labor Committees and Consumers' Leagues," in *Annals*, XXIX (Dec., 1906), 20.

[92] General Assembly, House Bills (a) 1902-1903-1904, Bill 37.

[93] Ga., *Journal of the House*, 1902, p. 217.

[94] *Constitution*, Nov. 6, 1902.

mentalist women and preachers, and the value of industrial training for idle children. After a long session for hearing debate, the committee gave a favorable report.[95] When the bill came up for consideration in the House, a bare quorum was present, and as there were not enough members to insure its passage, its friends tabled the bill.[96] It was not taken up again in 1902.

The new defeat was again associated with the fact that child labor was regarded as a labor issue. When a bill for a ten-hour day for mill labor was under consideration before the Senate Committee on Immigration and Labor, Spalding made this association the basis of his argument against the bill. He referred to what he had said in 1900 when he declared that child labor legislation was the first round of the ladder of labor legislation. The next, he said, would be to diminish the hours of labor, then to create a labor bureau, and finally to cut down on the hours and advance the age limit more and to forbid the employment of women under eighteen. He then came to the point which none of the speakers in opposition to labor legislation could allow to pass without mention—an attack on Mrs. Macfadyen as a labor agent. He claimed to have discovered that she was paid by the American Federation of Labor, although this fact had been generally known since her first trip to the South. In a manner intended to be sarcastic he described the way in which she had been welcomed by leading women. "She was a very charming lady, as I said, but she was nothing in the world but a hired emissary from Great Britain, brought here by the Federation of Labor, and paid for her job."[97]

Spalding was not disinterested, and his opponents might have accused him also of receiving "hire." But the friends of child labor reform from among the conservative and wealthy did not manifest much interest in legislation during 1902. The emphasis placed on it as a labor problem led them to feel that a law would be rejected. Although the Federation of Women's Clubs showed some interest in a general way, it did not take any active part in promoting legislation in this year.[98] Wilmer spoke before the Committee on Education, but the Central Committee made no active effort to build up public opinion.

The year 1903 saw a crisis reached in the movement for legislation in the four manufacturing states of the South. In Alabama, North Carolina, South Carolina, and Virginia laws were passed prohibiting labor under twelve. Georgia alone failed to yield to the demand for such a law. Yet in Georgia the movement had been car-

[95] *Constitution*, Nov. 20, 1902; Ga., *Journal of the House*, 1902, p. 438.
[96] Ga., *Journal of the House*, 1902, p. 556; *Constitution*, Nov. 27, 1902.
[97] *Constitution*, Dec. 7, 1902.   [98] *Ibid.*, Nov. 7, 1902.

ried on consistently for a longer time than in either of the other states. The labor unions, supported by the *Constitution,* returned to the attack in 1903. The Georgia Federation of Labor held its fifth annual convention in Macon a few days before the opening of the Assembly in July. Kilburn was president of the Federation and Houston was secretary-treasurer. The president of the Chamber of Commerce, who was financially interested in a number of mills, warmly expressed his sympathy with the child labor law movement.[99] The Federation of Women's Clubs sent a telegram to the convention endorsing Houston's bill, and stating that it was working through circular letters, pamphlets, and special editions of their official magazine to promote a sentiment favorable to legislation.[100] Kilburn officially expressed thanks to the club women and to Ladson, the attorney of the Federation, who had "worked almost unceasingly, day and night sessions," for the labor bills, without pay.[101]

Interest in child labor received impetus from the meeting of the National Conference of Charities and Corrections which was held in Atlanta in May. The program was centered chiefly on child labor and an effort was made to bring about an open discussion of the problem. The results were disappointing to the members of the conference, who reported that it was lacking in local color. A special invitation was given to some of the industrial leaders of the South to be present and to present their views on child labor. The attorney for the Cotton Manufacturers' Association, Spalding, declined to appear, and the president had business engagements which kept him away. The only ones who allowed their names on the program were D. A. Tompkins of Charlotte, North Carolina, and Major J. F. Hanson of Georgia. The latter was ill and had to remain away.[102] Tompkins made a speech describing mill village life but he avoided any discussion of child labor.[103]

The Georgia reformers were represented at the conference by Wilmer of the Central Committee, Hoke Smith, who was prominent in politics as a former member of Cleveland's cabinet and an ardent silver Democrat, and others.[104] But the outstanding address of the conference was made by Edgar Gardner Murphy. A child labor law which was a compromise measure and which he regarded as inefficient had just been adopted in his own state. The idea of a national organization to promote uniform legislation was probably already in his mind, for he chose to speak on child labor as a national prob-

[99] Ga. Federation of Labor, *Proceedings,* Fifth Annual Convention, p. 9.
[100] *Ibid.,* p. 28.   [101] *Ibid.,* p. 14.
[102] *Charities,* X (1903), 491-508, 551-62.
[103] "The Sociological Work of the Cotton Mill Owners," in *Proceedings,* Thirteenth National Conference of Charities and Corrections, pp. 157-66.
[104] *Ibid.,* pp. 166-80, 188-91.

lem.[105] He did not use the word national in a political sense, for he never advocated a national child labor law, but in the sense that the problem existed in every section. His address was an able reply to the arguments of the manufacturers.

The National Conference felt that it was coldly received in Georgia and that there was a lack of enthusiasm for the things it represented. But the people of the South in reality knew nothing of the organization. Out of several hundred members in 1902 the conference had only a dozen from the four states under consideration, and, of these, seven were in Alabama, leaving two for Georgia, two for North Carolina, and one for South Carolina.[106] The meeting in Atlanta in 1903 caused an increase but even then there were very few people interested enough to become active members.[107] The South's interest in social problems had been held by the two great questions of what to do with the Negro and what to do about education; it had not yet come to the consideration of other problems perhaps no less important, but apparently less pressing for immediate solution. Neither had the South yet begun to think of the solution of its problems as a part of a national program; they were considered as peculiar to the section, and were to be settled without help or interference from the critical North. The labor organizations alone were a part of a national movement, and they maintained an interest in the problems which immediately concerned them. But in the South they had no great strength in numbers and almost no financial backing. In 1903 the secretary of the Federation in Georgia reported $67.75 spent for printing and circulating material relating to child labor. The local labor organizations contributing to this fund were practically all in Atlanta, Macon, and Savannah.[108] There were at that time eighty-four locals in Georgia, only one of which was a textile union.[109] The long and unsuccessful strike of the cotton mill operatives in Augusta in 1902[110] weakened the textile organizations and probably increased the opposition of the millowners to labor legislation.

The opponents of labor legislation, in spite of the laws passed in other states, determined to hold their ground. Major Hanson, who had failed to speak on the program of the Conference of Charities

[105] E. G. Murphy, "Child Labor as a National Problem; with Especial Reference to the Southern States," in *Proceedings*, Thirteenth National Conference of Charities and Corrections, pp. 121-34.

[106] National Conference of Charities and Corrections, *Proceedings*, Twelfth National Conference, pp. 541-63.

[107] *Ibid.*, Thirteenth National Conference, pp. 42, 594-621.

[108] Ga. Federation of Labor, *Proceedings*, Fifth Annual Convention, pp. 17-18.

[109] *Ibid.*, pp. 42-44.

[110] *The South in the Building of the Nation*, VI, 37.

and Corrections, addressed a mass meeting in the hall of the House of Representatives.[111] When the legislature opened, a resolution was introduced to investigate through a commission the conditions in the cotton mills in the state. The friends of the child labor bill opposed this because it would put the millmen on guard and would also delay action, possibly until another session.[112]

Both parties published long statements in the papers. The Georgia Industrial Association attacked Houston, calling him a labor organizer and a walking delegate, which it considered as terms of great opprobrium. It accused him of gross misstatements of fact and charged the labor unions with encouraging socialism.[113] The unions replied to the Industrial Association and to Major Hanson. Their statement was more logical and straightforward than their opponents', and was free of the bitter personal attacks indulged in by some of the millmen.

The reformers arranged a public meeting at which Thomas E. Watson, Hoke Smith, and Seaborn Wright were the principal speakers. Watson, who had left the Democratic party to become a Populist and who was to run on that ticket for President of the United States the following year, was advertised as the special attraction. It was announced that this would be the first time in ten years that the legislature would have the opportunity of hearing him.[114] This meeting was also held in the hall of the House of Representatives. The speakers used the same line of argument that had been developed in the newspapers. Much of the attack was centered on Hanson, who had made harsh charges against the labor leaders. Watson declared that Hanson was a Republican and that the manufacturers were abusing their opponents through him.[115] Child labor reform thus appears to have had Populist support, although the real division on the question was no more along lines of the recognized political parties than in Alabama.

The Houston bill was taken up in the House on the day following the mass meeting and ordered printed.[116] The debate lasted two days. It reviewed all the former discussions of both sides. When an opponent claimed that socialists and anarchists had been brought to the state to speak for the bill, Houston objected and forced the speaker to say that he was referring to Mrs. Macfadyen.[117] Some discussion of the political affiliations of individual members of the House was indulged in as a result of Watson's attack on Hanson as

[111] *Constitution*, June 30, 1903. [112] *Ibid.*, July 1, 1903.
[113] *Ibid.*, July 5, 1903. [114] *Ibid.*, July 4, 6, 1903.
[115] *Ibid.*, July 7, 1903. J. F. Hanson was interested in the Bibb cotton factories, and was the president of the Central of Georgia Railroad, as well as a director in other roads. See Knight, *op. cit.*, VI, 2948.
[116] Ga., *Journal of the House*, 1903, p. 177.
[117] *Constitution*, July 8, 1903.

a Republican.[118] Several amendments were adopted, all of which tended to lower the standard, in the hope that this would facilitate the passage of the measure. The final vote was seventy-five to eighty-nine against passage, and a motion to reconsider was refused.[119]

Georgia failed to fall into line with the other southern states in 1903. The labor unions had put forth their best efforts and had not secured any of the measures they had advocated. The crisis had passed and a falling off in popular interest was to be expected. The reformers were to return to their demands for legislation at a later day, but the predominant leadership was no longer to be from organized labor.

[118] *Ibid.*, July 9, 1903.
[119] Ga., *Journal of the House*, 1903, pp. 182-85.

CHAPTER V

SOUTH CAROLINA, 1884-1903: A LABOR VICTORY

THE FIRST child labor bill in South Carolina was introduced in the House of Representatives by M. F. Kennedy of Charleston in 1884.[1] Kennedy was a real estate insurance agent, a member of the Catholic Church, and very active as a member and officer of several fraternal organizations.[2] The bill set an age limit of ten years and a penalty of one hundred dollars' fine or thirty days' imprisonment for violation.[3] Although unfavorably reported by the Judiciary Committee, the bill passed the House. It was killed in the Senate.[4] In 1887 F. M. Davenport of Greenville County introduced a ten-hour-day bill in the House, and an amendment was proposed to make it a misdemeanor to work any child under twelve years of age more than ten hours a day. This bill was debated and finally postponed indefinitely by a large majority.[5] Again in 1889 K. S. Tupper of Charleston introduced a bill in the House prohibiting labor in manufacturing establishments by children under fourteen years of age, but it was unfavorably reported and tabled.[6]

Demands for regulation of hours of labor rather than absolute prohibition of child labor were made in the early 1890's. One proposal was made by Stanyarne Wilson of Spartanburg County to regulate hours for children under sixteen and for women.[7] Another by G. B. Fowler of Union County limited hours of labor and prohibited employment under ten years of age. The second bill was tabled.[8] The first was considered by the Judiciary Committee, and a group of manufacturers appeared to oppose it. The result was a compromise bill which provided that children under sixteen and women should not work more than sixty-six hours a week in cotton or woolen mills, except to make up for lost time to the extent of one

[1] S. C., *Journal of the House of Representatives*, 1884, p. 98. Hereafter cited as *Journal of the House*.

[2] Yates Snowden (ed.), *History of South Carolina*, v, 203.

[3] *News and Courier*, Dec. 3, 1884.

[4] S. C., *Journal of the House*, 1884, pp. 114, 241, 312; *Journal of the Senate*, 1884, p. 257.

[5] S. C., *Journal of the House*, 1887, pp. 68, 175, 198; *News and Courier*, Dec. 7, 1887.

[6] S. C., *Journal of the House*, 1889, pp. 12, 20, 241, 391.

[7] *Ibid.*, 1890, pp. 41, 60, 344.   [8] *Ibid.*, pp. 47, 323.

hundred and ten hours in a year.[9] The substitute passed the House, but was reported unfavorably and defeated in the Senate.[10] Petitions in behalf of the ten-hour bill were sent by operatives in the mills in Aiken, Spartanburg, and Newberry counties, and were presented by Wilson and by John Gary Evans and Cole L. Blease, followers of B. R. Tillman.[11]

The ten-hour day for all operatives was again demanded in 1892, and opposed by the manufacturers with a resulting compromise on eleven hours. In spite of opposition this measure passed the House.[12] It was passed in the Senate after limiting the amount of overtime allowed to seventy hours instead of one hundred and ten.[13] The new law limited the hours in cotton and woolen mills to sixty-six a week for all operatives.[14] The eleven-hour law was championed by the Tillman group which had come into power in 1890. "Citizen Josh" Ashley, a well-known illiterate from Anderson County who had become a follower of the Farmers' Movement, introduced and pushed through the bill. Tillman's interest was not in the factory class, which he despised, but in opposing James L. Orr, who was prominent both as a manufacturer and as a political opponent of the new administration.[15] Yet the passage of the eleven-hour law is significant in that it points to the growing importance of the mill population.

An effort to modify this law was made in the Senate in 1896, but though it received a favorable report the bill was dropped after the second reading.[16] In 1897 a similar effort failed in the House.[17]

Both the child labor bills of 1884 and 1889 were presented by men from Charleston, a county in which there were no cotton mills. On the other hand, the bills intended primarily for the limitation of hours of labor came from Greenville, Union, and Spartanburg, three centers of manufacturing, and were supported by Newberry and Aiken, mill counties. The interest in labor legislation from these sections is indicative of the influence of some early efforts at organization, however ineffective they were, which probably came from the Knights of Labor.[18] The trade unions began an attempt to get a foothold in South Carolina at the same time that they did in Georgia, although their progress was slow and difficult. The organizer of the

[9] *News and Courier*, Dec. 6, 1890.
[10] S. C., *Journal of the Senate*, 1890, pp. 382-83.
[11] S. C., *Journal of the House*, 1890, pp. 58-59.
[12] *Ibid.*, 1892, pp. 357, 378.
[13] S. C., *Journal of the Senate*, 1892, pp. 291, 298, 387, 414, 496.
[14] S. C., *Acts of the General Assembly*, 1892, pp. 90-91.
[15] Francis Butler Simkins, *The Tillman Movement in South Carolina*, pp. 176-77.
[16] S. C., *Journal of the Senate*, 1896, pp. 153, 231, 300.
[17] S. C., *Journal of the House*, 1896, pp. 173, 322.
[18] Robert W. Dunn and Jack Hardy, *Labor and Textiles*, p. 178.

American Federation of Labor was busy in the state at the end of the century,[19] and child labor legislation was made a part of the program of the new unions.

Early in the session of 1900 a child labor bill was introduced in both houses. The bill by W. F. Stevenson of Chesterfield County in the House was referred to the Judiciary Committee.[20] In the Senate a bill by J. Q. Marshall of Richland was given over to the consideration of the Committee on Education.[21] There were no labor committees to consider such measures. The bills forbade the employment of children under twelve in factories and mines, and provided for inspectors in each district to be appointed by the governor without salary. The inspectors were to report annually to the governor.[22]

A bill for compulsory school attendance eight weeks a year was presented just before the child labor bill in the Senate.[23] It had the support of the King's Daughters of Columbia, who were concerned because the mill children were deprived of educational opportunities.[24] The same organization also supported Marshall's bill against child labor, having asked him to introduce it.[25] The Marshall bill was reported without recommendation from the committee, and was the subject of a long debate on January 26, 1900. As the *News and Courier* of Charleston stated the case, "The debate consumed all day, but was interesting and had its sentimental as well as practical side. The Senate took the practical view of the question and the bill was rejected by a vote of 29 to 8."[26] The bill had its origin in the fact that some of the members of the King's Daughters Circle in Columbia went to the mill district to teach the children to read and write, but found it impossible to get them in classes because they worked in the mills. The opponents relied chiefly on the argument that the parents frequently needed the help of the children and that while the employment of children did not pay the mill it was sometimes necessary for the support of the families. The state, they declared, did not have the right so to interfere with parents. The friends of the bill were few, and there was apparently no support from other organizations than the King's Daughters.[27]

[19] J. E. Couch to Gompers, Oct. 12, 1899, A. F. of L. Letter File, Box 153; L. H. McAteer to Gompers, May 30, 1900, A. F. of L. Letter File, Box 187.

[20] S. C., *Journal of the House*, 1900, p. 88.

[21] S. C., *Journal of the Senate*, 1900, pp. 74-75.

[22] *News and Courier*, Jan. 13, 1900.

[23] S. C., *Journal of the Senate*, 1900, pp. 75, 119.

[24] *News and Courier*, Jan. 26, 1900. The King's Daughters was a nonsectarian religious organization doing social work.

[25] *Ibid.*, Jan. 27, 1900.   [26] *Ibid.*

[27] S. C., *Journal of the Senate*, 1900, pp. 166, 206; *News and Courier*, Jan. 27, 1900.

Compulsory education was closely associated with the idea of child labor legislation in South Carolina. The state superintendent of education, J. J. McMahon, gathered some statistics from the mill-men on the conditions of literacy in the mill communities. The *News and Courier* on January 1, 1901, quoted from the report of the superintendent to show that conditions were good and that the mills were contributing largely to the welfare of the people. The chief illustrations were drawn from the Pelzer Mills and Lewis W. Parker's mills at Greer, and the mill at Pacolet. These were the show mills of the state, and presented the most favorable conditions. The well-known contract of the Pelzer Mills in which the employee was required to send all his children between the ages of five and twelve to the company school every day it was in session, and to send all children over twelve to work in the mills regularly was quoted. The *News and Courier* consistently upheld the argument of the manufacturers that the real problem was to educate the children. "The cotton mill people do not want to employ little children any more than some people want to keep them out of the factories. If some way could be devised to make these and other children go to school when kept out of the mills a decided step forward would be taken. The chief point is rather to have the children go to school than to keep them out of factories."[28]

The governor, Miles B. McSweeney, a representative of the Farmers' Movement, but not an extremist of the Tillman type, did not commit himself on the subject of child labor in 1901. He said in his message to the Assembly that employment was dangerous to young children, but that it was also dangerous to interfere with the government of the family, and that it would be bad to force children out of the mills into idleness. He recommended a law to require mill children from seven to thirteen to attend school and suggested that they might then relieve the older children in the factories during vacation. But in the end he concluded that it would be better to end child labor by legislation than to do nothing.[29]

On the first day of the session in 1901, Marshall again introduced a child labor bill with a twelve-year age limit.[30] Nine days later two bills were introduced in the House, one to require children from seven to twelve years of age to attend school,[31] and the other to regulate the employment of minors.[32] The latter bill provided for a ten-year age limit in 1901 and a twelve-year age limit after 1904. The contest over child labor began to assume the same proportions

[28] *News and Courier*, Jan. 7, 1901.
[29] S. C., *Journal of the Senate*, 1901, pp. 11-12.
[30] *Ibid.*, p. 19.
[31] S. C., *Journal of the House*, 1901, p. 101.
[32] *Ibid.*, p. 102; *News and Courier*, Jan. 21, 1901.

that it was taking in Georgia when the opponents of legislation took up the argument against outside agitators. August Kohn, a special reporter for the *News and Courier,* who later wrote a number of articles on the cotton industry, assumed that the prosperity of the state depended upon the millowners, men who were loyal South Carolinians. They, rather than the "agitators," knew what was good for the state. He was entirely correct in his belief that the Assembly would respond to their wishes. The failure of the bills to provide compulsory education was the chief objection made by Kohn and other representatives of mill interests.[33]

On January 21, 1901, a joint committee meeting was held to hear arguments on the child labor bills, although an effort was made to postpone it because some of the manufacturers who expected to come were not able to be present. Marshall, who had introduced the bill the year before at the request of the King's Daughters, now appeared in behalf of his new bill, saying that he was more than ever convinced of the need for such a law. The millowners were represented by S. S. Gregory and James L. Orr. Orr's arguments reflect those being made at the same time in other states: the neighboring states had no such law; the mills were helping the people; the Federation of Labor did not represent 2 per cent of the employees; 95 per cent of the operatives opposed the law; New England was the example of the bad conditions produced by organized labor, and New England was promoting the movement in the South. There were some mill operatives present who undertook to reply to Orr, but they were at a natural disadvantage in such an assembly. One workman from Graniteville said that the operatives were afraid to support the legislation for fear of losing their places.[34]

The discussion of the attitude of employees was followed by a flood of petitions in the House. On January 22, 1901, and for several days thereafter, petitions from mills in all the manufacturing sections of the state were presented. Those in opposition to legislation bore in all over fifty-two hundred names, and came from all the important manufacturing counties, while the ones in favor of legislation were signed by about eight hundred and thirty and came chiefly from Aiken County and from Glendale in Spartanburg County. Most of the signers were mill operatives.[35] The petitions asking for legislation came from labor union members, and the Aiken County operatives, together with those in Augusta, Georgia, just across the river, were rather strongly affected by the movement toward unionism at this time. The House was asked to pass the bill "as proposed by the South Carolina Federation of Labor, to prevent chil-

[33] *News and Courier,* Jan. 21, 1901.   [34] *Ibid.,* Jan. 22, 1901.
[35] S. C., *Journal of the House,* 1901, pp. 127-57, 184-201, 231-35.

dren of less than twelve years of age from being employed in Cotton
or Woolen Mills, Work-shops, etc."[36] Among the petitions against
the law was one from the famous Pelzer Mills, which began, "We,
the widows of Pelzer and the employees of the Pelzer Cotton Mills,"
and which made the following prayer, "We found we could not
make a living on the farm. . . . Our lot in life is hard enough as it
is and we beseech you to let us alone." It was signed by twenty-six
women and fifteen men.[37]

In addition to these appeals there were presented statements from
three physicians of Piedmont, South Carolina, as to the effect of
cotton mill life on the health of the people. One man found that
"the health of the people at the cotton mills is better and the mor-
tality less than in the country." Another said, "I know that children
who were born and have spent all their lives virtually in the cotton
mill, are as good specimens of physical man and womanhood as can
be found anywhere."[38]

James L. Orr presented a petition of his own against the proposed law. He declared that the manufacturers were concerned over
education and that they would be "gratified beyond expression" if
a compulsory school law requiring children from seven to ten years
of age to attend school four months a year were passed. If that were
done there would be no dissenting voice to prohibiting children under ten from working, "even though it worked hardship on some
mills or parents." Much less harm would come to the children from
working in the mills than from being idle on the streets. It was a
practical necessity for some children to work in order to obtain food
and clothing. "It is therefore an actual condition, and not a humanitarian theory you are to deal with. Hasty legislation, aimed only
at the mills, may transfer a large percentage of our workers to
adjoining states and check our industrial progress, by crippling the
mills now running and preventing others from coming."[39]

The minority report of the Georgia Committee on the bill recently rejected there was inserted in the *Journal* as evidence. It was
declared that the evils which the bill was designed to remedy were
nonexistent among the class that the bill touched. The objections
were practically the same as those offered by Orr.[40]

In the Senate some petitions were introduced, which may have
duplicated those in the House.[41] Workers in one cotton mill asked
that "no laws be passed interfering with this industry, but that we
be permitted, as others are, to make our own contracts, control our

[36] *Ibid.*, pp. 127, 141, 142-44, 152-55.
[37] *Ibid.*, pp. 233-34.   [38] *Ibid.*, pp. 183-84.
[39] S. C., *Journal of the House*, 1901, pp. 179-81.
[40] *Ibid.*, pp. 181-83.   [41] *Ibid.*, pp. 115, 148-50, 154.

own families, and pursue our chosen calling as we consider best for our interest."[42] Another group protested against the twelve-year age limit because the work of children was easy and aided "widows and crippled parents to make an honest living."[43]

Another committee, meeting on January 23, 1901, went over the same ground. S. J. Thompson of Bath, a mill town in Aiken County, read letters and telegrams from millworkers favoring the passage of the bill, although he withheld the names of the senders for fear they would lose their positions. One worker advocating the measure declared that while the manufacturers now based their objection to child labor legislation on its support by labor, they had opposed the same measure before when it only had the backing of the King's Daughters. The opponents of the bill presented more physicians' certificates and the testimony of a clergyman. One manufacturer admitted that the mills wanted child labor when he said that 30 per cent of the spinners in his mill were children under twelve and their removal would ruin the mill.[44]

The mill interests had command of the situation, and the child labor bill had no chance. The legislative correspondent of the *News and Courier* who had prophesied that nothing would be done contrary to the wishes of the millmen, now said, "There is not now any good reason to change the opinion that has been frequently expressed in this correspondence, which is that nothing whatever would be done that would seem to affect the cotton mill interests of the State or that would be seriously objected to by the representatives of the cotton mill interests."[45] Even an effort to secure the appointment of a joint committee of the houses to investigate child labor conditions failed.[46] Certain friends of the proposed legislation opposed this, as they considered it useless. One man said that it would do no good, for a committee would listen only to millowners and not to operatives, and that James L. Orr "would again come and speak of a member as the paid minion of organized labor." The other child labor bills were killed.[47]

The struggle over child labor in the legislature of 1901 clearly showed the effect of the efforts which were being made by the United Textile Workers to organize unions in the mill centers of the South.[48] This organization, which was affiliated with the American Federation, gained followers for a time in the Carolina and Georgia mill vil-

[42] S. C., *Journal of the Senate*, 1901, p. 150.

[43] *Ibid.*, p. 149.

[44] *News and Courier*, Jan. 24, 1901.   [45] Jan. 28, 1901.

[46] S. C., *Journal of the Senate*, 1901, pp. 214, 276; *Journal of the House*, 1901, pp. 329, 367, 692.

[47] *News and Courier*, Feb. 2, 1901.   [48] Dunn and Hardy, *op. cit.*, p. 184.

lages, and it was from these local unions that the demands for reform came.

South Carolina was profiting by the development of the cotton mill industry. Anything that seemed to threaten the new prosperity would meet with opposition. The fact that reform legislation had been advocated first by women, who were generally conceded to be sentimentalists and lacking in business sense, and then by organized labor, which the conservatives regarded with distrust and dislike, made it easy to convince the legislators that the millowners were the natural protectors of the interests of their workers and that their decisions were best. The *News and Courier*, appealing to this class of investors,[49] supported this view editorially. Let the South develop its industries to the fullest extent first, and then let it correct any evils that might have been created as a by-product of prosperity. It would be soon enough to adopt the legislative restrictions of the New England States when the South had as many spindles running as there were in the North.[50]

It was at this time that Mrs. Macfadyen was at work in Alabama and Georgia. The American Federation expected her to have some influence in South Carolina, and at one time considered making the Carolinas her chief field of labor.[51]   She had some correspondence with Mr. Baldwin of Columbia and with the senator who had introduced the bills in 1900 and 1901.[52]   Her efforts to co-operate with the South Carolinians prior to the session of 1902 were unsuccessful, however.   In reporting her actions to the Federation she said, "I wrote to that state until I was ashamed to write more.   The labor forces took no notice, whatever, of my letters, except Geo. B. McCracken, who in October urged my coming to Columbia.   The ladies who were assisting to get the bill through, feared me as a representative of organized labor and did not wish to change the cumbersome bill they were backing for the simple one suggested.   I did not wish to seem to interfere, and refrained from going to that state."[53]

In his opening message to the legislature of 1902, Governor McSweeney expressed himself more strongly on the subject of child labor

[49] Charleston capital was invested in upcountry mills. The most prominent example of this was the Pelzer Manufacturing Company in Anderson County. This mill, widely advertised as a model, was built by F. J. Pelzer, William Lebby, and Ellison Smyth, three Charleston business men, in 1882. See Louise A. Vandiver, *Traditions and History of Anderson County*, p. 292.

[50] *News and Courier*, Feb. 4, 1901.

[51] R. Lee Guard to Miss Ashby, Dec. 22, 1900; Gompers to Prince W. Greene, Dec. 27, 1900; Gompers to G. B. McCracken, Dec. 27, 1900, Letter Book, Vol. xxxix.

[52] Report of Mrs. Macfadyen to Gompers, A. F. of L. Letter File, Box 252.

[53] *Ibid.*

than he had in the previous year, although there was still a note of reservation. He had by this time concluded that an immediate solution of the child labor problem was necessary and that the state might intervene on behalf of the child if the parent would not do so.[54] *The State* on the opening day urged that the legislation begun in the previous session be completed. It was better to accept a mild measure than to have a rigorous one forced upon the manufacturers. "There are too many forces already behind this movement for it to fail. The fight for the little children of the mills is being made in the homes and in the schools of the State, and the forces of sentiment—sentiment as wise as it is humane—infallibly prevail against all considerations of selfish greed, whether individual or corporate."[55]

The millowners were not yet ready to give up their position. At a meeting of the textile manufacturers of the state held in Greenville on September 10, 1901, resolutions were adopted appointing a committee of five to draw up an open letter to the legislature on conditions in the mill villages and what the corporations were doing for the advancement of the people. The letter was to discourage any legislation on the child labor question as unnecessary. The committee was instructed to appear before the legislature on behalf of the mills. But if the legislature felt that it should pass a law, it was to be asked to establish a ten- instead of twelve-year age limit, and to fix a twelve-year limit for night work after ten o'clock. The committee should "urge most emphatically upon the legislature the necessity of compulsory education in this State." The objections to child labor legislation were based principally on the feeling that legislation interfered with rather than helped the improvement of conditions which the mill corporations were bringing about, and that any child labor law would be recognition of labor unions.[56] New England, hampered by labor legislation, wished to see the South similarly embarrassed. "A few years ago her representatives in congress endeavored to enact an amendment to the constitution of the United States for the avowed purpose of hampering southern labor, which, free from shackling laws and tyrannical unions, is undermining her supremacy in cotton manufacturing."[57] *The State* said of this letter that the only importance it had was "the very respectable signatures attached to it," for the system of child labor was indefensible, and the logic of its opponents weak.[58] In an editorial the editor pointed out these weaknesses, not the least of which was that the five men who signed the letter, James L. Orr, Ellison Smyth, J. H. Montgomery, J. B. Cleveland, and Lewis W. Parker represented conditions as they existed

[54] S. C., *Journal of the House*, 1902, pp. 25-27.

[55] Jan. 14, 1902.   [56] *State*, Jan. 17, 1902.

[57] *Ibid*.   [58] Jan. 17, 1902.

in their own mills, which were the best in the state, and not in the others that offered fewer attractions.[59]

In spite of the declarations of the mills in favor of compulsory education, a bill requiring children from eight to fourteen to attend school eight weeks a year was killed in the Senate after being favorably recommended by the Committee on Education.[60]   The Tillman faction, which was still in control of state politics, opposed compulsory education because it would involve sending Negro children to school as well as whites.   The child labor bill which had remained on the calendar since 1901 was reintroduced on January 24, 1902, by the Aiken delegation.[61]   Four days later the Committee on Commerce and Manufacturing held a meeting to hear arguments for and against it.   There were a number of people present, millowners, King's Daughters, and factory workers.   Each side was allowed an hour for discussion.   The bill considered was Marshall's, which provided for a ten-year age limit the first year, eleven the second, and twelve thereafter.   After some parleying as to who should speak first, the friends of the bill were heard.   The mill operatives were timid in expressing their views, but they were championed by Ellis G. Graydon of Greenwood.   His one point was the question whether it was advisable to have children work sixty-six hours a week or twelve hours a day except Saturday.   As on previous occasions Smyth and Orr represented the manufacturers.   Orr's temper was bad and his manner toward Graydon was particularly offensive.[62]

The committee after this hearing met again the day following and compromised by reporting the bill favorably with modifications. No child under ten should work after May 1, 1902, or under eleven after May 1, 1903, and after May 1, 1902, no child should work from 8:00 P.M. to 6:00 A.M. Children eleven or over could be employed if they attended school three months a year.[63]   *The State* regretted this concession to mill influence, declaring that a question was never settled until it was settled right.   "The only way to keep the child labor question out of next summer's campaign, where it would be most embarrassing to members under cotton mill influence, is to pass a reformatory measure at the present session."[64]   Pointing to the manufacturers' agreement of North Carolina and Georgia, *The State* declared that while an agreement could never have the force of law, the South Carolina manufacturers were not even organized and offered nothing "but bad logic and illusive statistics" to justify their position.[65]

[59] *State*, Jan. 18, 1902.
[60] S. C., *Journal of the Senate*, pp. 53, 130, 212; *State*, Jan. 16, Feb. 1, 1902.
[61] S. C., *Journal of the House*, 1902, p. 56.
[62] *State*, Jan. 29, 1902.   [63] *Ibid.*, Jan. 30, 1902.
[64] Jan. 31, 1902.   [65] Feb. 4, 1902.

The debate on the bill in the House was heated and long. Among the opponents was "Josh" W. Ashley, of Anderson County, who had been influential ten years earlier in securing the passage of the eleven-hour-day law. The Aiken representatives led the debate in defense of the measure. It almost degenerated into a row when a supporter of the mill group called a reform advocate a liar for saying that Anderson County's position on labor questions was notorious and a scandal. The young "reformer" member retorted that he had respect for the grey hair of his opponent, and for nothing else about him.[66] The bill was killed by a vote to postpone it indefinitely, passed by a majority of only two.[67] *The State* would not admit complete defeat and urged that the standard be raised for the next bill to twelve and that the matter be made an issue in the coming election.[68]

Mrs. Macfadyen stopped in South Carolina for a time after the defeat of the bill of 1902. She visited Columbia, where she talked with the leaders of the King's Daughters and M. C. Wallace, the president of the South Carolina Federation of Labor. She found Bishop Ellison Capers of the Episcopal Church and Superintendent McMahon of the public schools favorable toward legislation. Wallace agreed with her that it was inadvisable to make the question a labor issue. She discussed with these and other leaders the idea of forming a central committee such as there was in Alabama and Georgia, to counteract the belief that the movement was backed only by labor agitation. She believed that N. G. Gonzales, who would not adopt the cause of organized labor as such, but who was untiring in his championship of the child labor bill through *The State,* would do more than any man in the state to bring success to the cause.[69] *The State* published an interview with Mrs. Macfadyen in which she gave her estimate that there were twenty thousand children under fourteen in southern mills. This issue, she said, was not primarily a labor question. The working people had a right to look to their own interests, but they had no right to tie the child labor question to their cause, and thus insure opposition from certain sources. Making it appear as a labor question was a trick of the manufacturers to defeat the bill.[70] Mrs. Macfadyen visited the Columbia mills and reported her findings briefly to the American Federation of Labor.[71]

In accordance with *The State's* prophecy, the child labor issue was taken up in the political discussions of the summer of 1902. At the State Democratic Convention held in May the only subjects debated

[66] Feb. 5, 1902.
[67] S. C., *Journal of the House,* 1902, pp. 336-337.
[68] Feb. 5, 6, 1902.
[69] Report of Mrs. Macfadyen to Gompers, A. F. of L. Letter File, Box 252.
[70] March 22, 1902.   [71] A. F. of L. Letter File, Box 252.

were in relation to labor. G. W. Croft, of Aiken, a leader in politics and one of the state's most prominent lawyers, offered a resolution that the Assembly should prohibit the employment of children of "tender years" in manufacturing. Thurmond of Edgefield added that the twelve-year age limit should be adopted.[72] *The State* supported the cause editorially in a most able manner, taking its strongest stand on the position that child labor reform was not a labor problem and that it had not originated outside of the state.[73]

The beginning of 1903 saw the child labor contest revived in both of the Carolinas at almost the same time. On January 12, 1903, *The State* quoted the message of Governor C. B. Aycock of North Carolina on child labor, commending his attitude. On the day following, Governor McSweeney took a stronger stand than he had ever done before. Advocating compulsory education as a necessary complement to the child labor law, he reviewed the progress made in other countries and states and pointed to the passage of restrictive laws as the duty of the South. His practical argument was that, in order to meet competition, skilled and intelligent labor was demanded. This could only come from educating the children of the present, an impossibility as long as they worked in the mills. Statistics showed that the actual per cent of children employed in factories between 1880 and 1900 had increased, in a period when the manufacturers had uninterrupted control, whereas the per cent of children employed in factories outside the South had been cut in half. He closed with the warning that postponement of legislation might lead to regret.[74]

The Senate having organized, Marshall immediately introduced a child labor bill.[75] It was followed by a bill for compulsory school attendance eight weeks a year.[76] In the House a bill to regulate the employment of children in factories was introduced on January 15, 1903, another on January 16th, and two more later in the session. Each of these was tabled after the final passage of a child labor law.[77] Two compulsory education bills were introduced but were also tabled.[78]

On the third day of the session the child labor bill lost its most zealous advocate when N. G. Gonzales was shot by James Tillman.[79] As editor of *The State*, Gonzales had fought the candidacy of Tillman for governor in the election of 1902. He had been unsparing in bitter invective against him, and Tillman attributed his defeat to this cause.

[72] *State*, May 22, 1902. Croft was the leading council for James Tillman in his trial for killing N. G. Gonzales. See Snowden, *op. cit.*, v, 203.
[73] Aug. 11, 13, Sept. 29, 1902.
[74] S. C., *Journal of the Senate*, 1903, pp. 18-20.
[75] *Ibid.*, p. 26.   [76] *Ibid.*, p. 60.
[77] S. C., *Journal of the House*, 1903, pp. 58, 76, 114, 217, 406.
[78] *Ibid.*, pp. 77, 278, 316, 359, 496, 497.   [79] *State*, Jan. 16, 1903.

The death of Gonzales put a stop to the sharp editorial attacks on child labor in *The State* but the opinion which he had helped to create continued to be effective long enough to secure the passage of a law.

Marshall's bill was reported from the committee without recommendation and made special order for January 28, 1903.[80] When it came up, an effort was immediately made to kill it. Marshall declared that every Senator had already made up his mind how he would vote, so that a debate was unnecessary. The vote on the motion to kill the bill was lost and the bill was read a second time and placed on the calendar for the day following.[81] It passed then and was sent to the House.[82]

Unlike the rapid handling the Senate had given the bill, the House went into prolonged debate. Carey, a labor member from Charleston, argued that child labor was cheap labor, which was a curse to any country, and that if the fathers were paid a fair wage, children would not need to work. This argument had not heretofore been given much prominence, either because of the weakness of the labor group in South Carolina or because of its acceptance of the policy advocated by Mrs. Macfadyen not to make the child labor bill appear as a labor measure. McMaster of Columbia reminded the legislators that the Democratic Convention of the previous year had adopted a child labor plank in its platform and that both Ashley and Robinson of Anderson were present and had not fought it.[83] On the following day the labor members introduced a small mill boy as evidence of the bad effects of child labor. The discussion became so prolonged that a filibuster threatened.[84] On the day following, the bill was read again and passed without a struggle. The other four child labor bills before the House were then tabled.[85] On February 11, 1903, the bill was ratified and became a law. It provided a twelve-year age limit after 1905 with exceptions for orphans and children of dependent parents, and forbade such children to work at night between 8:00 P.M. and 6:00 A.M.[86]

The State welcomed the end of the fight. It had predicted victory, for the last round of the battle had really been fought in the previous summer.[87]

[80] S. C., *Journal of the Senate*, 1903, pp. 83, 144.

[81] *Ibid.*, p. 164; *State*, Jan. 29, 1903.

[82] *State*, Jan. 30, 1903; S. C., *Journal of the Senate*, 1903, pp. 185-86.

[83] *State*, Feb. 6, 1903.   [84] *Ibid.*, Feb. 7, 1903.

[85] *Ibid.*; S. C., *Journal of the House*, 1903, pp. 387, 388, 389, 394.

[86] S. C., *Journal of the Senate*, 1903, p. 325; S. C., *Acts of the General Assembly*, 1903, pp. 113-16.   [87] Feb. 9, 1903.

CHAPTER VI

NORTH CAROLINA, 1883-1903: A LONG SKIRMISH

THE FIRST attempts at labor legislation in North Carolina were toward the establishment of a ten-hour day. A bill for this purpose was introduced by H. H. Covington of Richmond County in 1883, but was speedily tabled.[1] In 1887 a bill introduced in the House by S. P. Swain of Brunswick County, proposing to regulate the hours of labor in manufacturing establishments where women and children were employed, was placed on the calendar.[2] Another bill to prohibit the employment of minors without the consent of their parents or guardians was proposed by J. W. Halstead of Camden County.[3] In the same session of the House a bill for a ten-hour day was left on the calendar.[4] A bill introduced in the Senate by C. P. Lockey of Wilmington, Brunswick County, to prohibit the employment of children under fifteen in workshops, mines, and factories was referred to the Committee on Agriculture, Mechanics, and Mining. It was unfavorably reported, whereupon the author had the age limit lowered to thirteen. On second consideration the committee gave it a favorable report, but it was tabled.[5] The wording of the titles of the Lockey bill and a bill for creating a bureau of labor statistics was similar to that used in the platform of the Knights of Labor. This suggests a connection between the Knights and the movement for labor legislation in North Carolina,[6] although there is no direct evidence of such a relationship. If the bills were proposed at the instigation of any labor groups it is not probable that textile workers were included because the men who introduced the bills of 1887 represented eastern nonmanufacturing counties.

A Bureau of Labor Statistics in the Department of Agriculture, Immigration, and Statistics was established in 1887. The commissioner of the bureau was appointed by the Governor for a term of

[1] N. C. Legislative Papers, 1883, Bills, Petitions, etc., Bill for Ten-Hour Law; in N. C. Historical Commission Office.

[2] N. C., *Journal of the House*, 1887, p. 208.

[3] *Ibid.*, p. 276.

[4] N. C. Legislative Papers, 1887, House Bills left on Calendar.

[5] N. C., *Journal of the Senate*, 1887, pp. 21, 52, 62, 73, 77; *News and Observer*, Jan. 19, 1887.

[6] U. S. Bureau of Labor, *Woman and Child Wage-Earners*, VI, 131. Compare Carroll D. Wright, "An Historical Sketch of the Knights of Labor," in *Quarterly Journal of Economics*, I (1887), 158.

two years at a salary of $1,500 a year. His duties were to "collect information upon the Subject of labor, its relation to capital, the hours of labor, the earnings of laboring men and women, their educational moral and financial condition, and the best means of promoting their mental, material, social and moral prosperity."[7] The total expenditures of the bureau, including the salary of an assistant for the commissioner, were not to exceed $5,000 for the first two years or $2,000 a year thereafter. An annual report was to be published, copies of which should be distributed to members of the Assembly, other officials, and citizens who applied for them.[8] This was the first bureau of its kind in any of the four leading manufacturing states of the South, and the only one until well into the twentieth century. It provided North Carolina with statistics not available elsewhere.

The first commissioner of labor appointed in North Carolina was W. N. Jones. He devoted a considerable portion of the first annual report to the consideration of the cotton mill industry. Questionnaires were sent to the various cotton mills, only thirty-one of which reported at all, and some of these only partially. Jones attributed this neglect to the fact that "they did not understand the purposes for which the information sought was to be used, and others doubtless . . . did not sympathise with the objects of the Bureau as they understood them."[9] One reason for the lack of sympathy of the mill managers was the attempt of the questionnaire to gather statistics on the number of children employed and the hours of labor. The first annual report published the statements of a number of both employers and employees on conditions in their mills, although the men who did not reply may have held very different views. The manufacturers emphasized the advantages which the mills offered in the way of education, churches, and good moral environment. A number avoided making any statement on the question of child labor. An employer in Alamance County said that he preferred not to employ children under fourteen because they did not work well, but that parents threatened to leave the mill if employment were not given children. He had forty-eight "youths and children" in his employ eleven hours a day, as compared with forty-two men and fifty-five women.[10] Another employer would take no children under twelve who could not read and write.[11] In Durham, where a manufacturer reported that his operatives were satisfied with conditions, an employee stated that about a hundred of the two hundred and twenty-five or fifty hands were children, many of them under twelve; that

[7] N. C. Legislative Papers, 1887, Bill for Bureau of Labor Statistics.
[8] *Ibid.*
[9] N. C. Bureau of Labor Statistics, *First Annual Report*, 1887, p. 139.
[10] *Ibid.*, p. 148.   [11] *Ibid.*, p. 149.

wages were not paid in cash; and that the workday was twelve hours.[12] An employee in Randolph County said that the mills hired "many children who are too small to work," but added that "the parents are more to blame than the mill owners."[13] In Gaston County a manufacturer reported thirty men, thirty women, and fifteen children in his employ, while an employee spoke of the mill running day and night, with pay in trade checks and long hours which destroyed the health of the young women. Also he said, "The employment of children in our mills at low wages keeps a great many men out of employment."[14]

For a number of years the Bureau of Labor Statistics continued to send queries to the manufacturers relating to the conditions of labor, and to publish replies in the annual report, although only 15 per cent of the mill officials replied.[15] The opinions offered on the question of the employment of children varied to include every possible solution, although the general trend was for the millmen to assert their disapproval of the employment of children in theory but their inability to avoid it in practice because of the attitude of the parents. Likewise a number of them declared their approval of a ten-hour day, although their own mills operated eleven or twelve hours a day. The attitude of a Catawba County employer is typical of a fairly frequent recognition of a problem for which the best solution had not been reached. "In regard to your inquiries about the age of children to work in factories, and the effect on their health, I am not prepared to say; I know that children working in cotton factories generally look pale and bad. But such is the condition of the country that poor men with large families cannot make their living by farming; so they go to the factories, as factory men can give better prices than farmers."[16]

Another millowner said, "Over fifteen years don't hurt; under fourteen should not be allowed, it stunts and deforms the child mentally, morally and physically. Ten hours should be law; too many mills are working women and children twelve to fourteen hours a day."[17] Another declared himself in favor of a law prohibiting the employment of children under twelve, requiring school attendance, and limiting hours for women and children to eleven a day, although he employed five children under twelve and was forced by the competition of other mills to run his own on a twelve-hour basis.[18] Still another who expressed opposition to the employment of children was the employer of fifteen who were under twelve and eighteen

---

[12] *Ibid.*, pp. 149-50.
[13] *Ibid.*, p. 150.   [14] *Ibid.*, p. 152.
[15] *Ibid., Ninth Annual Report*, 1895, p. 60.
[16] *Ibid., Fourth Annual Report*, 1890, p. 34.
[17] *Ibid.*, p. 48.   [18] *Ibid.*, p. 50.

under fourteen for eleven and a half hours a day.[19] A millowner of New Hanover County advocated compulsory education for half the day up to fourteen years, a ten-hour law at least for women and young people under eighteen and mill inspectors to enforce this law, as well as sanitary regulations, and protection from fire and dangerous machinery.[20]

Other employers differed from these in their views. One expressed the hope that children under fifteen would be excluded by law from the mills because their labor was unprofitable to the owners and forced on them by parents; but he did not believe children in the mills were any more unhealthy than those in the surrounding country.[21]

Queries sent to employees brought the same general criticisms as to the bad effects of long hours on children. Especially overseers or workers in charge of a room pointed out the evils of employment at too young an age.[22] Some of the workers complained that poverty of the family made the work of the children a necessity. One widow stated that the combined earnings of herself and two children were two hundred and thirty dollars a year.[23]

The investigations thus made reached only a small per cent of the factories and caused some uneasiness on the part of the mill-owners.[24] The opinions published are those of men who were kindly enough disposed toward the commissioner to report in response to his questionnaires. The large majority did not do so. The responses made in 1894 were somewhat more general, as a part at least of the statistics was collected through personal interviews of an agent of the commissioner with the millowners. The agent, Walter L. Womble, had some difficulty at times in persuading the mill officials to give him the information he desired, although his report presented the case in the same light the employers usually threw upon it. Although it was reported that children as young as six were working as much as twelve and a half hours a day, the millowners generally were humane men who did not expect children to do an adult's work for child's wages. But thriftless fathers forced the children into the mills in opposition to the wishes of the owners. A number of the mills were doing away with child labor. There was protest against the ten-hour day because of the fear that it would cause many of the mills to close and would lead to a corresponding reduction in wages. A compulsory education law was recommended as a sort of

[19] *Ibid.*, p. 51.   [20] *Ibid.*, p. 53.
[21] *Ibid., Fifth Annual Report*, p. 141.
[22] *Ibid., Fourth Annual Report*, pp. 82, 83, 89; *Fifth Annual Report*, pp. 174, 180, 181, 186.
[23] *Ibid., Fifth Annual Report*, pp. 167, 169, 172.
[24] *Ibid., Fourth Annual Report*, pp. 17-19; *Fifth Annual Report*, p. 123.

panacea.[25] In answer to the question as to whether or not they favored a ten-hour day, 175 employers answered in the affirmative, 165 in the negative, and 30 did not reply. As to whether this should be fixed by law, 109 replied in the affirmative, 188 in the negative, and 71 made no reply. When asked at what age children should work full time the following distribution of answers was received:

YEARS OF AGE	EMPLOYERS FAVORING
10	3
12	51
13	4
14	56
15	44
16	9
17	2
18	1
No age given	198

Only 87 approved fixing an age limit by law.[26] Fifty-seven per cent of the North Carolina mills reported in this census, showing that they employed 1,340 boys and 1,000 girls under fourteen.[27] According to this estimate there would have been proportionally over 4,000 children under fourteen in the mills of the state, even supposing that the mills making no report were no greater offenders than the ones that reported.

In spite of their evident realization of the evil of child labor and the problems created by it, many of the millowners were reluctant to have it made the subject of legislation. This was partially for fear of any interference between labor and capital. One secretary-treasurer said in 1895, "Don't meddle with mill employees and employers, but if you must, then pass a law prohibiting children under 14 years from working in Cotton and Woolen Mills and *all other* manufacturing establishments."[28] From another source came the opinion that the laborers did not need or ask for any legislation, and that most of the criticism of conditions came from "the self-constituted champion of the 'poor down trodden' mill hand, the little aspiring politician, and others of his ilk, who, in the absence of honest labor for themselves, undertake to run the affairs of others."[29] A more moderate but equally frank statement came from an employer in Raleigh: "We think all the mills should run not over eleven hours a day and avoid, if possible, taking children under twelve or thirteen years, but we deem legislation on the subject bad policy; let the employer and employee settle these things, this is a free country for all."[30]

[25] *Ibid., Eighth Annual Report,* pp. 67-72.
[26] *Ibid.,* pp. 4-51.
[27] *Ibid.,* p. 58.   [28] *Ibid., Ninth Annual Report,* p. 64.
[29] *Ibid.,* p. 66.   [30] *Ibid.,* p. 71.

During the years in which the commissioner of labor was trying to build up a feeling favorable to child labor legislation and a ten-hour day there were continued efforts to secure legislation on the subject. None of the bills had sufficient backing by public opinion or the support from any organized group necessary to push them through the legislature. In 1889 a bill for a ten-hour day presented by I. H. Pugh of Randolph County was combined with a provision to prohibit the employment of children under twelve years of age,[31] but it was postponed indefinitely.[32] In 1891 the bills again combined the idea of regulation of child labor and the hours of labor in the same measure. On February 11, 1891, a bill was introduced by request into the House by J. W. Hood of Mecklenburg County providing that no woman and no child under sixteen should work as an operative in a cotton or woolen manufacturing establishment for more than sixty hours a week or an average of ten a day. It was referred to the Committee on Judiciary which recommended that it should not pass.[33] In the Senate a bill to make ten hours a legal working day in factories and shops, to require that salaries be paid in lawful money as often as twice a month, and to prevent the employment of children under twelve in factories and shops was introduced in March. This bill embodies three of the demands made by employees as stated in the annual reports of the Bureau of Labor. It was referred to the Committee on Propositions and Grievances and unfavorably reported.[34]

In 1893 similar bills were introduced in the House. On January 18, 1893, F. L. Fuller of Durham introduced a bill to regulate the hours of labor in manufacturing industries where children under eighteen and women were employed. Any employer who permitted a child under fourteen to work in a factory or workshop more than ten hours a day should be subject to a fine of fifty dollars or thirty days' imprisonment.[35] A similar bill introduced by Hugh W. Harris of Charlotte to prohibit the employment of women and minors more than eleven hours a day in cotton and woolen mills was referred to the Committee on Judiciary, and favorably reported.[36] The Fuller bill was then unfavorably reported, with the consent of the author, in order to give way to the Harris bill.[37] Another bill declaring that no person under twenty-one should be compelled to work in a fac-

[31] N. C., *Journal of the House*, 1889, pp. 321, 333.

[32] *Ibid.*, p. 625.

[33] N. C. Legislative Papers, 1891, Bills left on Calendar; N. C., *Journal of the House*, 1891, p. 342.

[34] N. C. Legislative Papers, 1891, Bills left on the Calendar, Senate; N. C., *Journal of the Senate*, 1891, pp. 724, 794.

[35] N. C. Legislative Papers, 1893; N. C., *Journal of the House*, 1893, p. 125.

[36] N. C., *Journal of the House*, 1893, p. 201; Legislative Papers, 1893.

[37] N. C., *Journal of the House*, 1893, p. 301; Legislative Papers, 1893.

tory more than ten hours a day, but that persons over fifteen might work over that time if the employer entered into contract with their parents or guardians, was introduced but was unfavorably reported by the Committee on Propositions and Grievances, and was tabled on the same day as the Fuller bill.[38]

The Harris bill was delayed from week to week, and received the opposition of the manufacturers, or a part of them; a petition against it was presented on February 16, 1893. It declared that the bill was against the interests of both the owners and operatives of manufacturing enterprises. It was signed by thirty-four names, most of them operatives in a mill run by J. H. McDowell.[39] Other people argued that to exclude women and children from labor was worse than allowing them to be overworked and paid well. To pass the bill would shut out capital and close the doors of factories.[40] The opposition attempted several amendments and the bill was voted down by a ballot of thirty-six to fifty-three.[41]

In 1895 the legislative contest was reopened. In the House, Virgil S. Lusk, a Republican from Charlotte and former district attorney for the Western District of North Carolina, presented a bill to regulate hours for women, children, and others in factories.[42] In the Senate, Warren Carver of Fayetteville presented a bill to regulate the hours in cotton mills.[43] When it became evident that the Senate bill would not pass,[44] Carver introduced a second bill which was referred to another committee. But it was unfavorably reported and was tabled by a tie vote.[45] A petition was presented in the House from the operatives of the Mooresville Cotton Mills, protesting against the Lusk bill, "or any other bill that interferes with the present conditions of operatives and do earnestly and humbly ask your Hon. Body not to pass such law." It was signed by sixty-three people and brought up in the House by A. D. Sharp of Iredell County.[46]

What appears to be a counter petition was presented by Lusk: "We the undersigned do petition your honorable body not to be governed by any petitions Sent you from the Cotton Mills of Charlotte 'asking that you will not interfere with the working of the Cotton Mill.' It is a fact and can be proven beyond all contradiction that at least one Cotton Mill in Charlotte is Circulating and having Signed, by ignorant opperatiors (Such a petition) & who are not

[38] N. C. Legislative Papers, House Bills 500-762, Failed to Pass.
[39] Ibid., 1893, Petitions; N. C., Journal of the House, 1893, p. 475.
[40] News and Observer, Feb. 17, 1893.
[41] N. C., Journal of the House, 1893, pp. 498-501; News and Observer, Feb. 18, 1893.
[42] N. C., Journal of the House, 1895, p. 116.
[43] N. C., Journal of the Senate, 1895, p. 85.
[44] Ibid., pp. 93, 129, 142.   [45] Ibid., pp. 186, 473, 502.
[46] N. C. Legislative Papers, 1895, Petitions.

fully aware of what they are Signing Some of whom say they signed
for Shorter hours not reading the paper Signed. The officers of Said
Mill are actually offering money to those of the opperatives who are
not willing to sign their petition.

"Nine tenths of the Cotton Mill hands are in favor of Shorter
hours of work and those who have signed the petition did So by
intimidation, and for fear of loosing their job—and many who signed
did so under protest.

"These are facts and can be proven We could furnish the signatures of a large majority of the hands if they were not afraid of being
turned off & loosing their job.

"We would like you would Send a Committee to examine into
this matter which will prove the correctness of our Statement."[47]

This petition was signed by five men only and the Committee on
Propositions and Grievances to which it was referred gave it an unfavorable report.[48] The Lusk bill failed to pass.

Another bill combining the eleven-hour day with a prohibition
of employment of children under twelve in mechanical or manufacturing establishments was introduced, but unfavorably reported. A
minority of two members on the committee sent in a report recommending the passage of the bill. "We think it justice to the employes
in Said establishments that children under the age of 12 years Should
not be employed unless in very light work. Second, As the hands
are required to work in Some of these establishments, from to 10
hours to 12 and 15 hours for a days work, therefore we ask that 11
hours be established as a legal days work and that children under 12
years Should not be employed."[49]

The two issues of child labor and a shorter working day were
combined in almost every bill presented in the legislature and they
were joined in any discussion of the labor problem. The consideration was quite frequently not to exclude child labor from the mills
altogether but to shorten the hours so as to make the burden of the
work lighter.[50] The mill officials continued to take the attitude that
they did not approve of child labor under fourteen but that the
parents forced it upon them, and that compulsory education was the
real need of the day. The general trend of opinion was in opposition to legislation touching any labor problem. The relationship of
employer and employee was a personal one in which any laws endeavoring to regulate it would be unjustifiable interference.[51] A
manufacturer advised the state to let the mills alone, and help the

[47] Ibid.   [48] Ibid.
[49] N. C. Legislative Papers, House Bills, Failed to Pass, 1895.
[50] N. C. Bureau of Labor, Tenth Annual Report, 1896, pp. 74, 75, 79, 194,
196, 197.
[51] Ibid., pp. 69-78; Thirteenth Annual Report, pp. 231, 232, 233, 245, 248, 249.

people who needed it, instead of "our well-dressed and well-fed young ladies and gentlemen in our cotton mills."[52]

While there were some of the laboring class who saw the bad effects of employment on small children and who expressed themselves in opposition to it, there were also many who showed utter indifference or hostility to a change. The agent of the labor commissioner reported that, while a number of mills voluntarily set fourteen as the minimum age at which they would employ children, many parents would make false statements as to the ages of their children in order to secure them employment. They argued that if they raised the children to the age of ten or twelve they should begin to get money back on their investment. If the children went to school they would probably marry before going to work and the parent would lose all he had spent.[53]

Labor unions had only a slight hold on North Carolina, but their views on child labor had apparently spread to a portion of the laboring population. A few people from the upper classes were also beginning to interest themselves in the welfare of the industrial laborers. This humanitarian element began to gain ground in the nineties. Early in 1897 J. W. Bailey, then editor of the Baptist *Biblical Recorder,* condemned existing conditions. He wrote: "The factory stands closely related to this school question. It is more important that the children be educated than that they be dwarfed in body and in mind for the purpose of helping a drinking father or even increasing the value of shares in a mill. When a resident of Raleigh I tried to get a bill through the Legislature restricting the hours of labor to ten each day for women and children, and well do I remember how so humane a bill was opposed by one who has since bloomed out a professional friend of the people. I could not understand his opposition, but soon learned that he was a stockholder in a mill and was determined to make it pay though the life of the children be squeezed out to do it."[54]

Even the would-be reformers had not yet come around to a position demanding the complete abolition of child labor. The same editorial continues, "In the first place, factories ought not to be allowed to employ very young children; and in the next place, the school house and the factory should be close together and all children under fifteen years of age allowed to work four hours per day only and compelled to put four hours in school. Such a system would save greed, grasp, gain, gold and selfishness from making capital out

[52] *Ibid., Thirteenth Annual Report,* p. 249.

[53] *Ibid., Tenth Annual Report,* pp. 61-62.

[54] Jan. 6, 1897. Bailey was elected to the United States Senate in 1930, after a number of active years in state affairs.

of the lives of children, while it would afford some manual training to the young and not neglect their mind."

Bailey condemned the father who moved to town to put his children to work in the factories and the millowner who made it possible for him to do so. "Compulsory education is the remedy for this; but if that is impossible, all the manhood and womanhood of North Carolina should demand that the State protect her children with proper laws."[55]

Not only the child labor evil but the general conditions of poverty, ignorance, and lack of wholesome environment began to cause concern to other thoughtful people. In 1898 J. A. Baldwin, the young pastor of two small churches in cotton mill communities in Charlotte, began to give the matter much thought and to write articles which were published in the *Charlotte Observer* through the influence of the ministers' association of that city.[56] A year later the *Presbyterian Standard*, always conservative in its attitude on secular matters, began to take an interest in the problem. The Reverend Alexander J. McKelway, afterward prominent as the agent of the National Child Labor Committee, was the editor of this paper. He was also interested in the conditions in Charlotte, and conferred with Baldwin on the details of a bill which the latter wished to have presented in the legislature.[57] Although the *Standard* did not begin to publish editorials dealing directly with child labor conditions in the South until after the Murphy campaign began in Alabama, it did take a general stand in favor of legislation. "Would it not be better for the pressure of public opinion to be brought to bear on our law-makers, whereby the principle could be put into law that life is more sacred than luxury, and the convenience of the many shall not be purchased by the sufferings of the few."[58]

The awakening of a keener interest on the part of the disinterested humanitarians led to some extent to a separation of the idea of child labor legislation from the regulation of hours of labor and instead associated it more closely with compulsory education. In 1897 there was an effort to put through a bill to regulate hours in factories, but it got no further than its predecessors.[59] One step in progress was made when an act to provide for the regulation of mines was passed. It contained a provision forbidding the employ-

[55] May 12, 1897.

[56] Statement made by Mr. Baldwin to the author.

[57] Memorandum of the Work of the National Child Labor Committee in the South, March 25 to April 15, Board Meeting, May 12, 1909, Appendix 1, Memorandum as to the co-operation with the cotton manufacturers in the South, by A. J. McKelway.—National Child Labor Committee Minute Books. Hereafter cited as N. C. L. C. Minutes.

[58] Sept. 28, 1899.   [59] N. C., *Journal of the Senate*, 1897, pp. 139, 211.

ment of boys under twelve.[60] This phase of the child labor problem never assumed great importance in the South, however, since children were not employed to a great extent in the southern mines and the mining companies did not fight legislation on the subject.

Political events in North Carolina took a new turn in 1897 when a fusion of the Republicans and Populists brought the Democratic power to an end for a term, and the factional issues and problems of the years preceding received scant attention, as the new government had other interests. A change was made in the Bureau of Labor in 1899 when a new law provided for a Commissioner of Labor and Printing whose duties were to gather statistics in relation to capital, hours of labor, earnings of laborers, and conditions in mining, manufacturing, and milling industries.[61] The new commissioner under this act reported in 1899 that the number of children in the mills was decreasing and the number of men increasing. The growing sentiment in favor of compulsory education and the voluntary adoption of a twelve-year age limit by some mills was pointed out as an indication of improvement.[62] The figures showing statistics in these reports can scarcely be considered accurate because they were never complete. There were only two men to do this work, and their financial resources were scant. The manufacturers who did not co-operate in the collection of statistics were left out of the count.

The feeling that child labor should not be made the subject of legislation was associated in the minds of the millowners with the hostility to organized labor. This was as marked in North Carolina as in the other industrial states and it was exceedingly difficult for operatives in any of the manufacturing industries to form unions and keep them running successfully. There were people in the state who were interested in promoting such organization, and as early as 1897 a labor paper, the *Asheville New Era,* was reported to have been established.[63] But when laborers organized they met opposition and possibly lockouts from the employers, as had occurred in Salisbury.[64] When some of the operatives of the Erwin Cotton Mills in Durham formed a union, it was reported that the officials announced that the union employees would lose their places at the end of two weeks although they made no demands as to wages or hours.[65] In Alamance County the mills announced that they would not employ union

[60] N. C., *Acts of the General Assembly*, 1897, p. 428.

[61] N. C. Legislative Papers, Bills, 1899.

[62] N. C. Bureau of Labor, *Thirteenth Annual Report*, p. 211.

[63] W. W. Jones to Aug. McCraith [no date, about 1897], A. F. of L. Letter File, Box 51.

[64] A. W. Rounds to Morrison, Jan. 31, 1899, A. F. of L. Letter File, Box 153; C. P. Davis to Gompers, June 11, 1901, A. F. of L. Letter File, Box 236.

[65] *Charlotte Daily Observer*, Aug. 12, 1900.

labor and that all workers must either withdraw from the union or quit work and give up their houses.[66] In Gaston County there were twenty-eight mills and the owners all boycotted union labor.[67] These difficulties seemed insurmountable for the time being. W. H. Winn, one of the most active organizers of the American Federation of Labor in the South, wrote President Gompers that the situation in the Carolinas was unique in that there were so many isolated mills. He was of the opinion that the people were not yet ready to receive organized labor.[68] Because of these circumstances the movement for child labor reform, while having without doubt the approval of many union members or people who would have liked to have been members of unions, did not have the open support of a state labor organization or even of any strong local union. The millowners of North Carolina had less reason to complain that the demands for child labor legislation were being made as a step to other labor laws than had their neighbors in Georgia. Some people turned to the millmen in the expectation that they would see and grasp the opportunity to frame a law with provisions to their liking that would satisfy the growing popular demand for reform, and thereby strengthen their own leadership.

One of the advocates of reform wrote, "I believe that the time has come when remedial legislation should no longer be considered as a scheme to hurt those who are making the South great materially, but when the owners with the operatives and those who have no personal interest except the well-being of both should get together and decide upon a bill that will meet the demands of the time. . . . The operatives and philanthropists are not well enough organized to secure the passage of this law if the mill owners solidly unite against it. It is perfectly useless to say that the operatives don't want it. There are only two classes of operatives that would oppose it— those who want to work their little children, and those who are under the influence of higher authorities who may be opposed to it, and are overpersuaded by them. . . . Nothing could be done that would be so effective in maintaining the pleasant relationship that now exists between owner and operative as for a mill owner to propose an acceptable bill, and for the others to acquiesce. A start was made two years ago but the time was not ripe. It is not an easy matter to formulate a bill that will do what you want done, and not do too much."[69]

[66] C. P. Davis to Gompers, Oct. 6, 1900, A. F. of L. Letter File, Box 223.

[67] J. Milton Howard to Morrison, June 12, 1900, A. F. of L. Letter File, Box 168.

[68] W. H. Winn to Gompers, Jan. 26, 1899, A. F. of L. Letter File, Box 150.

[69] J. A. Baldwin, "New England and the South," in *Charlotte Daily Observer*, Aug. 12, 1900.

In the same spirit the Raleigh *News and Observer*, edited by Josephus Daniels, said, "It would be short-sighted policy for the mill men to fight against proper legislation, and it is gratifying that many of them see that it is necessary and proper. If they will lead the way, wise and conservative laws will be enacted that will help the great industry which they represent."[70]

The *Charlotte Observer*, in the center of the textile manufacturing region of the Carolinas, reflected the feelings and opinions of the mill-owning classes. In 1900 it shifted the responsibility for opposing child labor legislation to the parents of the children employed, saying that it did not believe the manufacturers would object to a law forbidding the employment of children under twelve, but that such an act would make the legislators who voted for it as unpopular as if they had voted to tax every man's dog.[71]

In 1901 the Democrats regained control of the government of North Carolina. This meant that the white people of the state would eliminate Negro suffrage. Charles B. Aycock was elected governor. He was one of the group of educational reformers of which Charles D. McIver and James Y. Joyner were also members. One of his campaign pledges was to promote a system of public school education throughout the state for both Negroes and whites. This was a program which would inevitably meet much opposition, but the Governor lost no time in urging legislation along this line. The child labor agitation that had continued since the last session of the legislature became stronger, and with the opening of the session of 1901 a bill to regulate labor was again introduced into the House of Representatives.[72] The manufacturers of the state felt that some action was necessary. It was evident that a great many of them opposed legislation and yet they could not fail to take some notice of the popular clamor. A meeting to consider the problem of labor and the proposed law was decided on, and it was announced that it would be held on January 16, 1901, at Greensboro. This plan was announced through the papers at the time the legislature opened.[73]

When the meeting took place, J. W. Fries of Winston-Salem presided. Although the *News and Observer* reported that from "the utterances of the manufacturers it was evident that they were not opposed to wise, conservative legislation along this line," they failed to recommend such laws, saying that they would work a greater hardship on the employees than on the owners.[74] Instead they drew up an agreement which they proposed to put into effect voluntarily if the legislature would not pass a child labor law. The agreement

[70] Jan. 11, 1901.   [71] Aug. 19, 1900.
[72] N. C., *Journal of the House*, 1901, p. 19.
[73] *News and Observer*, Jan. 10, 11, 1901.
[74] *Ibid.*, Jan. 17, 1901.

was as follows: "We, the undersigned cotton mill owners and managers agree to the following, taking effect March 1st, 1901:

" (1) That one week's work shall not exceed sixty-six hours.

" (2) That no child less than 12 years old shall work in a cotton mill during the term of an available public school.

"Provided this shall not apply to children of widows or physically disabled parents. Provided further, that ten years shall be the lowest limit at which children may be worked under any circumstances.

" (3) That we will co-operate with any feasible plan to promote the education of the working people in the State and will cheerfully submit to our part of the burdens and labors to advance the cause of general education.

" (4) On the basis of the above agreements of the cotton mill owners and managers we hereby petition the legislature not to pass any labor laws at this session of the legislature."[75]

This petition had the names of over one hundred and twenty-five men representing more than one hundred and seventy mills. The terms were distinctly a compromise. Instead of the ten-hour day demanded by some reformers was an offer of eleven hours. The twelve-year age limit was set up only during the period when school was in session, which was only a few months in many places, and with an exemption clause that would include many children down to ten years.

The weaknesses of the agreement were immediately apparent. The *News and Observer* regretted this attitude of the millowners because it did not believe the agreement would be effective, no matter how good the intentions of the men who made it. The men opposed to child labor could not refuse to employ young children without running the risk of losing some of their labor; those with good intentions could not speak for the others.[76] While citing the fact that the terms of the agreement or even better ones had been in force at some of the mills, notably the Erwin Mills at Durham, for several years, this was no guarantee for the others, and a private agreement was a mere "rope of sand."[77]

The child labor bill before the House was considered by the Committee on Propositions and Grievances at a hearing on February 7, 1901. Wright of Rowan County, the author of the bill, and Collins, chief of police at Randleman, spoke in favor of it, using as their principal arguments the bad effects of child labor on the children. The opposition to the bill was represented by the officials of two mills and by James H. Pou, the attorney for the millmen interested in the matter. Pou stated that since four fifths of the mills had

[75] N. C. Legislative Papers, Bills and Petitions, 1901.
[76] Jan. 19, 1901.　　　　　　　　　　[77] *News and Observer*, Jan. 22, 1901.

signed the agreement there was no need for legislation. The manufacturers stressed the social welfare work of the mills, the danger of disturbing the relationship between employer and employee, and the fact that the operatives did not demand the law. The two advocates of the bill then agreed to give the millmen a chance to remedy the situation without legislation, so a motion was made and carried to suspend consideration of the matter until the agreement could be generally signed.[78]

The fact that the agreement was accepted in lieu of legislation in 1901 did not settle the matter. There were many people still dissatisfied. Although the *Manufacturers' Record* considered the agreement as a step in the gradual solution of the child labor problem by the manufacturers themselves,[79] there were others not so well pleased. The American Federation of Labor, although not able to take an active part in the North Carolina contest, was an interested bystander. It analyzed the agreement and pointed to its weaknesses and loopholes.[80] When the child labor bill came up in 1903, Gompers appointed an agent of the Federation to work for the passage of a child labor law in North Carolina.[81] The labor element was becoming more strongly aroused to the necessity for legislation, possibly through contagion of interest in the neighboring states. A labor paper, *The Industrial Journal*, was published in Charlotte as the official organ of the North Carolina Federation of Labor. On June 7, 1902, a special edition was devoted to the subject of child labor in southern cotton mills and a series of articles on the subject was printed. Mrs. Macfadyen's article, "Child Labor vs. Dividends," was reprinted from the *American Federationist,* as well as an article by Gompers from the same journal. The articles by union members displayed considerable bitterness toward the millowners as a class. J. L. Rodier, a member of a Washington, D. C., typographical union, in speaking of the effort then being made to secure the passage of a law in Georgia, said that the "portly presidents and smug managers of cotton mills argued with pious fervency that they (the presidents and managers aforesaid) employed the tots of from eight to twelve years (certain of which, by the way, had been placed on file as exhibits) as an act of charity and in a spirit of generosity toward the lowly labor of the South."

He criticized the opportunist clergymen who waited until labor aroused public sentiment to take up the cause and get the credit.[82] While the churches as organizations had not taken any stand on

---

[78] *Ibid.,* Feb. 8, 1901.   [79] Jan. 24, 1901.
[80] *American Federationist,* VIII (1901), 163-64.
[81] Gompers to O. R. Jarett [*sic*], Jan. 17, 1903, Letter Book, Vol. LXIV.
[82] J. L. Rodier, "The Times, their Trend, Child Labor," in *Industrial Journal,* June 7, 1906,

child labor, the strongest non-labor friends the child labor cause had were from among the clergy, so that this attitude of the labor unionists was somewhat unfair. This spirit was also reflected in the article by Elbert Hubbard quoted from the *Philistine*,[83] and in the article of a workingman of Salisbury, who wrote, "The laboring man of the South turns with disgust from the preacher or priest who would tell him that his misfortunes were ordained of God. They know theirs is a local ailment and they contemplate a local remedy."[84]

The demands of labor went beyond child labor legislation, where many of the advocates of this reform were not able to follow. "Instead of free libraries, give them free schools; instead of bath tubs, give them time; instead of free lunch at midnight, give them enough for their work to buy themselves a dinner at mid-day; instead of windy speeches, give them what by right belongs to them and soon the land will be a wonder."[85]

The aroused interest of a part of the laboring class in the matter of reforms was similar to that which had displayed itself in South Carolina the year before. While the influence of unions was destined to be short-lived at this time in the Carolinas, it increased the fear of the manufacturers for labor legislation of all kinds.

The members of the clergy, whether welcomed by the laboring organizations or not, were becoming more interested in child labor problems and other phases of social welfare of the mill class. The center of this interest was quite naturally in Charlotte, which was the central point in the manufacturing area of the Carolinas. J. A. Baldwin, who had begun to work for reforms in 1898, continued his activities and his articles spread from the local papers to his church periodicals and *Gunton's Magazine*. In the *Methodist Review of Missions* he published an article on the conditions prevailing in the cotton mills.[86] In *Gunton's* he expressed his theories for a co-operative plan of education and industry for the child, for which he was criticised by the *Manufacturers' Record* for being a sentimentalist.[87] Baldwin never considered the child labor question as a thing which could be settled apart from the general conditions of physical and moral welfare of cotton mill workers, as his own efforts showed.

The *Raleigh Christian Advocate*, a Methodist periodical, declared its position in an article on "Our Waste of Child Life." The cause of this waste was the idea that "children live for the benefit of the parent, not that parents live for the welfare of the children. Hence the widespread belief that a child is worth more in the cornfield,

[83] *Ibid.*

[84] E. B. Melton, "We Will Be Freed from Capital's Clutches," in *Industrial Journal*, June 7, 1902.   [85] *Ibid.*

[86] "Southern Cotton Mill Workers: Their Spiritual Condition and Need," XXII (1901), 194-95.   [87] April 10, 1902.

shop, and factory, than in the school room. Thus children are wasted among the wheels of an ever-grinding 'bread and butter' machine." While not fixing the blame on any agency the *Advocate* declared that the waste must end. "This is the great duty of the hour. It rises in importance above many other great problems which seem to receive the exclusive attention of Church and State. In saving the children we save the world."[88]

The denominational periodical which most determinedly took up the fight against child labor was the *Presbyterian Standard,* of which A. J. McKelway was the editor. McKelway said that he began to consider the problem seriously and to write editorials after he had seen some of the pamphlets which Murphy in Alabama was at this time publishing.[89] He answered an article in the *Central Presbyterian* which opposed a general child labor law,[90] and he placed the blame for conditions to some extent on New England investors in the South.[91] An editorial, "Child Slavery," likened the northern overseers found in some southern mills to the northern slave drivers of ante-bellum days in the South.[92] Such an editorial was sure to call forth comment from the millowners. An open letter from E. B. Neave to the editor protested against the article as unfair; it misused the word slavery which did not apply to child workers, as they could withdraw from employment when they chose. It implied that children were abused in that they were underpaid and overworked. Neave maintained that children were paid the same wages for the same work as an adult, and that the mills only ran eleven hours by agreement. In answer to this letter McKelway referred to the Murphy pamphlets concerning wages of children, and to the statement of Parker in South Carolina that there were 22,000 children under fourteen and 10,000 under twelve in the mills. Murphy estimated that there were 12,000 children under twelve, many of them as young as eight or nine, and some five or six. While McKelway held the parents more responsible for child labor than the millowners, he declared that the latter should advocate legislation to protect both themselves and the children.[93] In "The Truth About Child Labor" he replied to the criticisms of the *Tradesman,* which demanded specific figures to back up accusations. He quoted figures from that paper's own reports. While he advocated reform, McKelway still saw it as a southern problem, in which it was not desirable to have any "out-

[88] Aug. 13, 1902.
[89] Memorandum as to co-operation with cotton manufacturers in the South, by A. J. McKelway.—N. C. L. C. Minutes, May 12, 1909, Appendix I.
[90] Aug. 13, 1902.
[91] *Presbyterian Standard,* Sept. 3, 1902.
[92] *Ibid.*
[93] *Ibid.,* Sept. 17, 1902.

side interference." "It is a Southern problem that confronts us and Southern legislatures are to deal with it."[94]

With the approach of the legislative session of 1903 it became evident that the child labor problem would be fought out again. The advocates of legislation maintained that the manufacturers' agreement of 1901 had not been successfully enforced. A decision of the state supreme court, rendered by Chief Justice Walter Clark, ruled that contributory negligence in cases of accident to children could not be pled for children under fourteen years of age in the absence of any legal prohibition of the employment of children. This helped bring the manufacturers to the acceptance of legislation.[95] A large number of millmen were not willing to accept this solution, however.

A new champion of child labor reform appeared in Governor Aycock. Interested primarily in building an efficient public school system in the state, he saw that child labor legislation was naturally related to the success of such a plan. In his message to the legislature of 1903 he clearly advocated a law which would prevent the employment of children under twelve entirely; under fourteen at night, and, after 1905, under fourteen unless they could read and write. He favored no exceptions for orphans or the children of widows or disabled parents, declaring that the community should provide for such cases and see that the child did not suffer. His interest in child labor was from an educational standpoint and he did not express so forcefully his opinions on other labor problems. "The controversy, if there is any, between capital and labor has nothing to do with this question."[96] With his views the *News and Observer* heartily agreed,[97] and the *Charlotte Observer* felt constrained to express approval. "Cotton mill men are agreed, we think, on the proposition that it is not profitable to work children under twelve; they would rather not have them; and this being the case, and they having bound themselves in a pledge two years ago not to employ such children, there can be no substantial objection to a law governing the matter. It would, in fact, be a protection for the operators."[98]

The first child labor bill of 1903 was introduced in the House on January 12 by H. B. Parker of Wayne County and referred to the Committee on Manufacturing and Labor.[99] The bill set the twelve-year age limit with exceptions for children of ten or over who were orphans or who had dependent parents; required affidavit of age from the parent for the child; and forbade night work and work for more than eleven hours a day and sixty-six hours a week for children under

[94] *Ibid.*, Oct. 8, 1902.
[95] N. C. L. C. Minutes, May 12, 1909, Appendix I.
[96] *News and Observer*, Jan. 9, 1903.
[97] *Ibid.*   [98] Jan. 10, 1903.
[99] N. C., *Journal of the House*, 1903, pp. 31-32.

sixteen years. It also forbade employment to any child under fourteen who could not read and write and who did not attend school nine weeks a year. A similar bill introduced by A. Settle Dockery of Rockingham[100] made the maximum week's work in factories sixty hours, with not more than twelve hours a day. Both bills provided penalties for violation but no system for enforcement.[101]

On January 21, 1903, a bill was introduced in the Senate by Donnell Gilliam of Tarboro and was referred to the Committee on Manufactures.[102] It was at about this time that President Gompers of the American Federation appointed O. R. Jarrett to represent the Federation in securing legislation, and he arrived in Raleigh late in January to work for the passage of certain laws.[103]

When the matter of legislation came before the committees it was found that the manufacturers still opposed it. There were four separate bills, which indicates a lack of unity on the part of the advocates of reform. Besides the bills already mentioned there was one which would forbid employment under twelve during the school term and to any minor who could not read and write unless he had attended school for a certain period each year.[104]

The millowners argued that support of the child labor bill was a bid of politicians for the labor vote. The reformers claimed that the agreement had not been kept at all, and that if the manufacturers were willing to abide by its terms they could not object to a law embodying them.[105] The *News and Observer* came out in an editorial strongly in favor of legislation. It declared that the agreement had not been kept by all who signed it; the report of the commissioner of labor was evidence of this. But the agreement did not go far enough. It only prohibited working children during the school term and made no provision for the rest of the year. The editor regretted the fight made against the bill by the millowners. "In their opposition to the prohibition of child labor, these gentlemen are standing against the inevitable. As certain as day follows night, legislation of this character will be adopted."[106]

The hostility to supposed northern influence was not absent in this contest, although it did not appear as strongly as elsewhere. In the hearing before the committee the manufacturers referred to the legislation as "Yankee doings,"[107] while the author of a letter to the

[100] *Ibid.*, pp. 32, 471.
[101] *News and Observer*, Jan. 13, 1903.
[102] N. C., *Journal of the Senate*, 1903, p. 81.
[103] *News and Observer*, Jan. 28, 1903.
[104] *Ibid.*, Feb. 6, 1903.   [105] *Ibid.*
[106] *Ibid.*   [107] *Ibid.*

News and Observer declared that "the agitation is simply a 'Yankee trick' and started in New England, the home of 'Uncle Tom's Cabin,' and all the abolition deviltry."[108]

After much discussion between the opposing factions a compromise bill was agreed on by a committee of the manufacturers and the committee of the Assembly.[109] The substitute was based on the Gilliam bill. The manufacturers agreed to the age limit with no difficulty, but debated at length before accepting the sixty-six hour week for employees under eighteen. The clause forbidding any child under fourteen working at night was opposed because the doffers were needed then; they were usually small boys. This clause was stricken out. The date for the law to go into effect was changed from July 1, 1903, to January 1, 1904.[110]

In both houses there was some debate over the bill as it had been agreed on by the committee, and efforts were made to amend it. This called forth a strong statement from Governor Aycock, who lost patience with the delays. "After the child labor bill had been introduced," says McKelway, "the manufacturers attempted by amendments, to nullify any good results, and Governor Aycock told the committee of manufacturers, as he had stated to me that if they persisted in the amendments, he would stump the state himself, in the interest of the child labor law, in the next session of the legislature. Thereupon, they agreed to the twelve year age limit with the 66 hour week for children under 18."[111]

The bill passed the Senate, and on March 5, 1903, went through the House and became a law.[112] Although forced into agreeing to this law, the general trend of opinion expressed by the manufacturers in the seventeenth annual report of the labor commissioner was that they were satisfied with it. Their only wish was that it might be the last one.[113]

[108] Feb. 8, 1903.

[109] *News and Observer*, Feb. 12, 1903.

[110] *Ibid.*, Feb. 13, 1903.

[111] N. C. L. C. Minutes, May 12, 1909, Appendix I.

[112] N. C., *Journal of the House*, 1903, pp. 1217, 1286; *News and Observer*, Feb. 21, 1903; *Public Laws and Resolutions of the State of North Carolina*, 1903, pp. 819-20.

[113] N. C. Bureau of Labor, *Seventeenth Annual Report*, pp. 124-41.

CHAPTER VII

THE FIRST EIGHT YEARS OF THE NATIONAL CHILD LABOR COMMITTEE

BEFORE 1903 the movement to secure child labor legislation in the South had been separate and distinct in each state. The American Federation of Labor had furnished the inspiration for a part of the agitation for reform, but its activity had not been evenly distributed, for it scarcely touched the Carolinas. The Murphy pamphlets had influenced the arguments used by the reformers in the other states in 1902 and 1903, but there was no other connection between the several reforms. The fact that the same line of reasoning was followed by partisans of either side in all the states concerned was due more to the similarity of conditions and background than to interchange of ideas.

The criticism of the southern mill situation which had come so freely from the North and which had aroused the old antagonism against any suggestions from that direction had been the result of investigations by a few reformers, such as Mrs. Macfadyen and Mrs. Van Vorst, who had no connection with one another, but who told similar vivid stories of evil conditions existing in the cotton mill communities. From each such investigation a number of articles resulted, if not by the original investigators, by some other person who rehashed their ideas and gave greater publicity to the southern situation. No agency existed which undertook to direct a uniform campaign of propaganda against the evils of cotton mill child labor.

After 1903 child labor reform took on a different aspect. When Alabama passed a law providing for the twelve-year age limit, the *Outlook* declared that the Alabama Committee had lighted a fire in the nation, which now cried out for the reform of industrial abuses. At almost the same time New York had organized a child labor committee to remedy the evils existing there, and four northern governors had urged their legislatures to pass new child labor laws.[1] The idea that child labor was a national problem involving the welfare of all states in the Union, and that it could only be solved by a nationwide protest against its evils and a united demand for effective legislation originated with Edgar Gardner Murphy. A few weeks after the pas-

[1] *Outlook*, LXXIII (Feb. 14, 1903), 373-74.

sage of the twelve-year laws in Alabama and the Carolinas, Murphy made a speech before the National Conference on Charities and Corrections at Atlanta, which one of his colleagues called the greatest speech against child labor ever delivered in America.[2] In this able address he spoke of the national problem of child labor. He used the word "national" in a geographic rather than a political sense. The problem was national in that it existed in every place where manufacturing had gone in proportion to the industrial development of each section, which resulted in the number of children employed being much greater in a single large industrial state of the North than in all the South.[3]

When Murphy addressed the National Conference he did not discuss the formation of a National Committee directly, although it is probable that he was already developing a plan for such an organization. In the course of the next few months he was in New York and discussed the possibility of the formation of such a committee with Dr. Felix Adler, head of the Ethical Culture Society and professor of political and social ethics at Columbia University. In October, 1903, the New York Child Labor Committee appointed Adler, W. H. Baldwin, Jr., and Mrs. Florence Kelley, secretary of the National Consumers' League, as a committee to consider the formation of a national organization. This group agreed with Murphy as to the policies to be followed and sent out letters to a list of people who were known to be interested in social reforms. Practically all of them responded favorably to the idea of organizing a National Child Labor Committee.[4] This group, acting as a nucleus for the proposed organization, sent out a leaflet to still others, briefly reviewing the recent movement for reform, and suggesting needed legislation. The function of the proposed national committee was explained. It might be composed of twenty-five members from states where conditions were either of the best or the worst. The details of its work could be left to an executive committee of nine members within easy reach of New York. Before formal organization could take place it would be necessary to raise about twenty thousand dollars, as an executive secretary and two assistants would be needed for effective work. The names signed to this statement were Felix Adler, Jane Addams, Stanley McCormick, John W. Wood, William H. Bald-

[2] A. J. McKelway, an address at the Edgar Gardner Murphy Memorial Meeting, New York City, Dec. 7, 1913.

[3] "Child Labor as a National Problem; with Especial Reference to the Southern States," in *Proceedings*, Thirteenth National Conference of Charities and Corrections, pp. 121-34.

[4] Statement made by Mrs. E. G. Murphy, Sept. 25, 1931; N. C. L. C. Minutes, April 15, 1904; *Charities*, XII (April 23, 1904), p. 409.

win, Jr., V. Everit Macy, Lillian D. Wald, Florence Kelley and Edgar Gardner Murphy.[5]

Formal organization of the National Child Labor Committee took place on April 15, 1904, in New York City. The response from people of prominence to the appeal sent out by the original group was good, for a long list of names, including many of national importance, appeared on the membership roll.[6] A number of them were well-known southerners, such as Neal L. Anderson, N. B. Feagin, and Judge Gaston of Alabama, who had been members of the Alabama Committee; Clark Howell and Hoke Smith of Georgia; Ben R. Tillman of South Carolina; and James H. Kirkland, chancellor of Vanderbilt University at Nashville.

The objective stated by the members of the committee was to promote the welfare of society with respect to the employment of children in gainful occupations.   This end was to be achieved by investigations to determine the facts concerning child labor, publicity which would arouse public opinion and create a sense of parental responsibility, and legislation which would give protection against premature or otherwise injurious employment and insure educational opportunity.   The committee expected to act as an agency to co-ordinate and supplement the work of state and local child labor committees and to encourage the formation of such committees where they did not exist.[7]

The committee was incorporated three years later by an act of Congress, with an organization practically the same as that adopted in the beginning.   The original corporate members formed the board, which was the real ruling body of the committee.   All officers

[5] *The National Child Labor Committee* (A Suggested Organization), Leaflet [1903].

[6] The membership included, besides those already named, Neal L. Anderson, Montgomery, Ala.; the Reverend John G. Anderson, Tampa, Fla.; Mrs. Emmons Blaine, Chicago; John Graham Brooks, Cambridge, Mass.; A. J. Cassatt, Haverford, Penn.; Edgar E. Clark, Cedar Rapids, Iowa; Grover Cleveland; Robert W. De-Forest, New York; Edward T. Devine, New York; Mrs. Sara Platt Decker, Denver; Charles W. Eliot, Harvard; Arthur F. Estabrook, Boston; N. B. Feagin, Birmingham, Ala.; Homer Folks, New York; Hugh F. Fox, Plainfield, N. J.; Edward W. Frost, Milwaukee, Wis.; Cardinal Gibbons, Baltimore; the Right Reverend David H. Grice, New York; J. B. Gaston, Montgomery, Ala.; William E. Harmon, New York; Clark Howell, Atlanta, Ga.; Robert Hunter, New York; John S. Huyler, New York; James H. Kirkland, Nashville, Tenn.; Ben B. Lindsey, Denver, Colo.; Beverly B. Munford, Richmond, Va.; Adolph S. Ochs, New York; Gifford Pinchot; Isaac N. Seligman, New York; Hoke Smith, Atlanta, Ga.; Samuel Spencer, president of Southern Railroad; J. W. Sullivan, New York; Graham Taylor, Chicago; B. R. Tillman, South Carolina; Paul Warburg, New York; Talcot Williams, Philadelphia; and C. B. Wilmer, Atlanta, Ga.   See N. C. L. C. Leaflet No. 1; also N. C. L. C. Minutes, April 15, 1904.

[7] *Objects of the Committee,* N. C. L. C. Leaflet (April, 1904).

except the executive secretary were chosen annually. The secretary served at the pleasure of the board which appointed him. Noncorporate members fell into three classes: the guarantors, who contributed $100 annually; sustaining members, who contributed $25 each year; and the associate members, who contributed $2.00 or more.[8]

It was generally conceded that the origin of the committee was due to Murphy. There was no one better suited to mould its policies than he, for he understood the reasons for the existence of factory child labor and the problems involved in remedying it as well or better than any one else. He recognized the problem as one of both economics and sociology, and he saw in the industrial development of the South merely a repetition of what had happened in other localities when similar conditions of industrialization and change from home to factory work had presented themselves. He was not deceived into the idea, like so many of the more emotional reformers, that the employer of child labor was a personal tyrant or cruel barbarian. The cruelty involved belonged to a system and was not personal. The remedy therefore lay in legislation, to secure which it was necessary to overcome the opposition of the "good" manufacturer, who, because his own mill represented few evil conditions, opposed social legislation of all kinds. "The trouble is to get him to realize his responsibility for the social relations and conditions in which his life is inevitably involved. . . . It is the good factory that steps in between the social conscience and the bad factory and protects the bad one." But legislation and inspection alone were not enough. "Inspection is very well, but there are not enough inspectors in all the states of our Union put together, to enforce the laws of any one State, if the people of that State will not individually co-operate with the law." The prime necessity, then, was to build up in the mass of citizens a feeling of personal responsibility for the welfare of the children whom the laws were designed to protect.[9]

Murphy's other obligations prevented him from keeping the leadership of the National Committee, once it had been formed. The first executive secretary was Samuel McCune Lindsay, a professor of sociology at the University of Pennsylvania, and, at the time of his election, Commissioner of Education in Porto Rico.[10] The Executive Board appointed Lindsay, Murphy, and Folks to select a man for assistant secretary. It was considered wisest to appoint a southern man to this

[8] *Constitution of the National Child Labor Committee,* N. C. L. C. Pamphlet No. 148 (1907).

[9] E. G. Murphy, "Child Labor in the United States," an address delivered at Carnegie Hall, March 20, 1904, before the Society of Ethical Culture.—MS, Murphy Papers. Murphy's book, *Problems of the Present South,* appeared about this time.

[10] *Charities,* XII (July 23, 1904), 754.

position, so Murphy recommended Alexander Jeffrey McKelway.[11] He was elected by the board and accepted the position when it was offered to him a second time. Owen R. Lovejoy was selected as an assistant for the northern states.[12]

McKelway was a Presbyterian minister of Charlotte, North Carolina. He was born in Sadsburyville, Pennsylvania, in 1866, and in 1867 his father, who was also a clergyman, brought his family to Charlotte County, Virginia. McKelway was educated at Hampden-Sidney College, where he graduated in 1886, and at the Union Theological Seminary in Richmond, from which he was ordained to the ministry in 1891. He then went to North Carolina, first as a minister in Fayetteville and later as editor of the *Presbyterian Standard* in Charlotte. He also edited the Charlotte *News,* in 1903-4, a small daily paper.[13] It was while editing the *Standard* that he first developed an interest in the child labor situation. He was influenced by Murphy's pamphlets which came to his attention in 1902, and helped to form his arguments against child labor. The first invitation to become a member of the National Committee he declined, but when he was offered the position as secretary for the southern states he gave up his newspaper work and accepted.[14] He was at the time thirty-eight years of age.

In order to be in a position to make intelligent comparisons and to find out the results of child labor laws in force, McKelway began his work for the South by making a tour of some of the more important New England mill towns. Accompanied by Lovejoy, he visited Lowell, New Bedford, and Fall River, Massachusetts, before returning to his home in Charlotte, which was in the center of the greatest textile area of the South.[15]

The situation in the South which confronted the National Committee was filled with difficulties. In three of the four leading manufacturing states laws had been passed limiting the age at which children might legally work, except under certain conditions, to twelve years. None of them was provided with means of enforcement. Although these laws were of almost no practical value in restraining the employment of children, they had set a precedent for state action. McKelway at once began plans to work in the Carolinas and Georgia before the next session of their legislatures so as to arouse public

[11] Homer Folks to E. G. Murphy, Sept. 2, 1904, Murphy Papers.

[12] N. C. L. C. Minutes, Oct. 3, Nov. 10, 1904.

[13] "Sketch of Dr. McKelway for the National Cyclopedia of Biography," McKelway Papers.

[14] An unpublished account of McKelway's activities in the South in behalf of child labor legislation, hereafter referred to as "McKelway's Account," McKelway Papers.

[15] *Ibid.;* N. C. L. C. Minutes, Nov. 10, 1904.

sentiment to a demand for reform and win the legislators over to support the committee's program. He was still indebted to Murphy for sound advice as to how to meet the arguments of his opponents,[16] but the results of his first efforts were disappointing, even though this might have been expected. It was no easy task to convert the manufacturers from their belief that child labor legislation was economically and socially undesirable and even unjustifiable.

The National Committee undertook thorough investigations of child-employing industries in order to be able to show the need for legislation with concrete proof that evils existed. In the South the chief industry employing children and practically the only one which had attracted attention in 1905 was the textile industry. The methods of the committee were to carry on an extensive correspondence with welfare organizations and labor officials so as to win their interest and sympathy, and to send investigators to the manufacturing communities to go into the mills and ask questions of the owners and operators and other people who knew the mill population, and to take photographs and collect statistics illustrative of the conditions found to exist.[17] The results were given publicity through a series of pamphlets issued from time to time by the National Committee, and through magazines of all kinds as well as the newspaper press. The reports made at the annual conference held by the Child Labor Committee were for a number of years published in the *Annals of the American Academy of Political and Social Science,* as well as in separate volumes issued by the committee. They later appeared in the *Child Labor Bulletin* and the *American Child,* published by the committee.

The investigations sometimes brought the agents of the committee into unpleasant situations. Such studies of social conditions were then a new field of endeavor and methods were a bit crude. "There was no means of measuring the exact effects of child labor, its effects upon health, upon education, upon character. These means had to be worked out, nor could they be worked out in an academic way, aloof from the actual problems. They were worked out in the stress and strain of trying to accomplish a purpose."[18] The investigations began to be made more systematically about 1908 when a photographer was employed to work under McKelway's direction. Photographs of mills and of workers were taken. These methods antagonized mill officials in some cases. Admission to a mill might be refused or grudgingly allowed. If pictures could be obtained no other way,

[16] Murphy to McKelway, Jan. 23, 1905, Murphy Papers.

[17] Accounts of the investigations are given in the chapters dealing with the several states.

[18] Agnes E. Benedict, "History of the National Child Labor Committee," MS in N. C. L. C. Library.

flashlights after dark were resorted to.[19]   If millowners objected, it is not surprising.   The investigators had no legal authority and they used their findings in criticism of the mill system.

Another means of securing publicity was through use of the lecture platform.   McKelway spoke repeatedly to a variety of audiences scattered over a wide area.   He also interviewed every public man in both state and national politics who would give him a hearing. An idea of his activity may be drawn from one example.   On February 16, 1905, he addressed an audience at the Cooper Union in New York, speaking on "Child Labor in Southern Industry."   On his way South he stopped in Washington and interviewed some of the southern members of the House and Senate district committees on the subject of passing a law to prohibit child labor in the District of Columbia.   He also talked to President Gompers of the American Federation of Labor.   Returning South he took measures to organize state committees in the Carolinas and consulted with his friend, former governor Aycock.   He then visited Atlanta and Rome, Georgia, interviewed members of the state legislature and of the child labor committee, planned a drive for a new law in Georgia, spoke to women's clubs, visited a number of mills, and wrote a pamphlet for publication, all in the course of a little more than a month's time.[20]

The same criticisms were made against the National Committee that had appeared a few years earlier in the case of the agent of the American Federation of Labor.   In spite of the large part played by Murphy in organizing the committee and the number of prominent southern men listed as members, it was stigmatized almost immediately as an organization supported by northern capital, an agency of New England millowners to destroy the competition of the South, a channel for emotionalist reformers to give vent to their feelings, and a means of livelihood for men who preferred agitation to making an honest living.[21]   Such articles as Elbert Hubbard's "Slaughter of the Innocents," which depicted child labor as worse than slavery and professed the belief that children in the mills only lived about four years, aggravated the hostility to the committee, though the committee might not be responsible for them.[22]   The same thing was

[19] L. W. Hine, "Report of a Photographic Investigation of Child Labor Conditions in North and South Carolina, 1908"; *idem*, "A Photographic Investigation of Child Labor Conditions in the Cotton Mills of Georgia," 1908; A. E. Seddon, "Investigation of Conditions of Child Labor in Georgia Cotton Mills," 1908.—MSS in N. C. L. C. Library.

[20] N. C. L. C. Minutes, March 23, 1905.

[21] N. C. L. C. Minutes, Appendix I, May 12, 1909; George T. Winston, *A Builder of the New South*, p. 265; *Charities*, XII (Feb. 11, 1905), pp. 461-62; *Manufacturers' Record*, Jan. 26, Feb. 16, 23, 1905, June 21, 1906; *American Cotton Manufacturer*, Nov. 29, 1906.

[22] *American Federation*, XII (April, 1905), 205-9, reprinted from the *Philistine*.

true of the interest displayed by some northerners engaged in state politics, such as Curtis Guild, Jr., of Massachusetts. Southern manufacturers felt that they favored reforms in the South so as to gain the political support of the manufacturers in their states.[23]   An address made by Guild in 1910 somewhat justifies this viewpoint, for he declared that national child labor legislation was the only way to prevent the capital of the states in his section being drained into others where there were no restrictions on the employment of children.[24]   The bitterest criticism that the committee received came from the *Charlotte Observer* and the textile journals published in Charlotte, and from the *Manufacturers' Record.*

The efforts of the National Committee in the first three years of its existence to secure state legislation met with very little success.   McKelway organized state committees in the Carolinas and reorganized the Georgia Committee on a fairly effective basis.[25]   In North Carolina he undertook to secure the passage of a bill raising the standard in several respects above that of the law of 1903.   It was an inopportune moment, and having no support, he met with complete defeat.[26]   In South Carolina no law was passed.   In 1906 McKelway made his headquarters in Atlanta, establishing a sort of branch office there, and devoted most of his time to co-operation with the local committee in a campaign for the law of 1906.   The enactment of the Georgia law was the first success to which the National Committee could lay claim in the South.[27]   In the fall of 1906 the Alabama Committee was reorganized in preparation for the 1907 legislature, the first in four years.[28]

The National Committee failed to gain a strong foothold in the South in either membership or legislation. The financial report of the secretary in October, 1906, showed that of seven hundred and thirty-four subscriptions from contributors in forty states only thirty-six came from the South.   Of these Alabama had eight, Georgia six, North Carolina four, and South Carolina none.[29]   The fact that the committee had its origin in the South did not help to arouse interest in it there.   Of fifteen organizations of various kinds affiliated with the National Committee only one was in the South.[30]

It may have been partially due to the indifference of the southern people to the National Committee, partially because of the committee's failure to secure reform legislation in the states, that it

[23] *Manufacturers' Record,* June 1, Nov. 9, 1905.
[24] *Address Before the Child Labor Convention* [leaflet], Jan. 15, 1910.
[25] N. C. L. C. Minutes, March 23, 1905.
[26] *Ibid.,* Feb. 15, 1905.   [27] *Ibid.,* Oct. 12, 1905, Jan. 25, 1906.
[28] A. J. McKelway, "Report to Board of Trustees," Oct. 1, 1906, MS in N. C. L. C. Library.
[29] N. C. L. C. Minutes, Oct. 4, 1906.   [30] *Ibid.,* Sept. 31, 1906.

adopted a completely new policy in the winter of 1906-7. On November 22, 1906, formal notice was sent out of a meeting of the Board of Trustees of the committee to be held on the day following to consider the program for the next annual meeting and to discuss the text of a child labor bill which Senator Albert Beveridge was planning to introduce in Congress, and which he wished the committee to endorse.[31] Murphy was in New Haven, Connecticut,[32] and was unable to come to this meeting. Nine members of the board were present and discussed the bill which Beveridge presented. There was such difference of opinion as to the wisdom of federal legislation that after a full evening of consideration the board decided to postpone for two weeks decision as to the attitude it should adopt.[33] The bill forbade the carriers of interstate commerce to handle the products of any factory or mine in which children under fourteen were employed. The carrier was made responsible for securing from the company an affidavit that no such children had been employed. Affidavits were to be filed every six months, and any carrier that knowingly violated the provisions of the act incurred a penalty of a fine of five to twenty thousand dollars or from three to twelve months in prison.[34]

The executive secretary sent a copy of the bill and a circular letter to the members of the committee, asking for an expression of opinion as to the advisability of national legislation.[35] When the discussion was resumed at the board meeting of December 6, 1906, Senator Beveridge was present and explained the purpose of his bill. He then withdrew and a debate took place in which practically every one present took part, and a number of letters from absent members, including one from Murphy, were read and considered.[36] It was no doubt well understood before the meeting that the southern members of the committee opposed federal legislation. Murphy had never favored anything tending in that direction, and he was fully aware of the light in which such action would be regarded in the South. Francis G. Caffey of Alabama held the same opinions and had expressed them at the first consideration of the Beveridge bill. He wrote Murphy late in November, "I think Dr. Adler agrees with us on the ground that it is wrong to extend federal power in this way. He is also doubtful about the policy so far as it affects the work being done by our friends in the South. . . . Mr. Seligman seemed in doubt about the practicability of a measure placing so great a burden

[31] S. M. Lindsay to Murphy, Nov. 22, 1906, Murphy Papers.

[32] *Ibid.* (a second letter), Murphy Papers.

[33] N. C. L. C. Minutes, Nov. 23, 1906; Lindsay to Murphy, Nov. 24, 1906, Murphy Papers.

[34] N. C. L. C. Minutes, Nov. 23, 1906, copy of bill attached.

[35] Lindsay to Murphy, Nov. 26, 1906, Murphy Papers.

[36] N. C. L. C. Minutes, Dec. 6, 1906.

upon the carriers and producers, but at a meeting with Senator Beveridge on Wednesday last, he seemed more or less satisfied with the Senator's statement as to the ease with which the scheme would work. Senator Beveridge . . . did not convince me on any one of the three grounds of objection which I raised at the last meeting of the committee; first, the bill is of doubtful constitutionality; second, it would be complicated in execution and of doubtful efficiency and third, it would be bad tactics for the committee to support the bill because it might embarrass our own friends who are now accomplishing so much for state regulation and might make enemies for our cause of those who are now our friends but are opposed on principle to the extension of federal regulation in general."[37]

Robert W. DeForest, in his letter asking that his vote be recorded against the Beveridge bill, took the same position as the leading southern members. The field in which the committee wished to lay the chief emphasis was the South, where it felt that public opinion could not be relied upon so much as in other sections to produce state legislation. "We have sought to dissipate Southern prejudice against our organization, in which Northern influence predominates, but by some measure of assurance that we would not attempt to secure Federal legislation to directly affect state action. I think our influence in the South would be seriously impaired by giving our official approval to a measure which many Southerners will think of the Force Bill variety."[38]

DeForest said that his objection would be removed if the southern members of the board were of a different opinion. Another objection raised was on grounds of constitutionality. He did not believe the measure to be constitutional, and to support a bill of doubtful constitutionality would weaken the influence of the committee. Furthermore, he was convinced that in practice such a law without federal inspection would prove ineffectual. He advised that the committee support the bill for a federal children's bureau which President Roosevelt had approved, and maintain a strict neutrality on any other proposed federal legislation. This would not be opposing Senator Beveridge's bill; it would merely be an avoidance of antagonizing those who did oppose it. "We have all the sentimentalists of the country with us. We want the support of practical business men. It will tend to alienate that support to have us tie our fortunes to a particular bill so open to constitutional and home rule objections and so futile in any promise of practical accomplishment. We have ample justification for neutrality in the degree of assurance we have given

[37] Nov. 30, 1906, Murphy Papers.

[38] Robert W. DeForest to N. C. L. C. Board, Dec. 6, 1906, in Minutes, Appendix A, Dec. 6, 1906.

to those who have joined our movement on the faith of our declaration against Federal interference with [what] most people consider state issues."[39]

Following the discussion in which the views of DeForest and others were presented, Edward T. Devine offered a resolution stating that while the committee was not ready to endorse any pending bill for federal regulation of child labor, it was glad to find the subject was receiving the attention of the President and Congress, and resolving that "the officers and individual members of the Committee are expected and requested to give such attention to these measures as they may find possible, and to aid in any way in which they can consistently with their personal convictions to secure well-considered, constitutional and effective legislation."[40]

This resolution was defeated. It was then moved and carried that the board should take some action on the bill before adjournment. Those who wished to endorse the bill probably felt that further postponement would throw the discussion so late that the measure would already be before Congress before action was taken. Isaac N. Seligman then proposed a resolution that the committee endorse the Beveridge bill, "believing that it will establish a National standard to correct the evils of child labor in their important National aspects, especially in the deterioration of our racial stock, and will tend to establish equality of economic competition, without minimizing State responsibility."[41] It was on such phrases as "to establish equality of economic competition" that opponents of the committee were able to base their claim that it wished to reduce the advantages which the South held over New England in manufacturing.

The National Committee did not consider that in supporting federal legislation it was giving up the effort to secure state laws. It had several state campaigns in progress when the Beveridge bill was under discussion in Congress. But the executive secretary and some others felt that the efforts to enforce state laws were a failure in both North and South because of the opposition of manufacturers who feared interstate competition, and because of the lack of necessary provisions for state inspection. Although centralization of power in the federal government might diminish state activities in general, in this instance a federal law would, they believed, increase state activity.[42]

Murphy was irrevocably opposed to federal legislation on child labor, for he considered that the committee had at the time of its organization pledged itself against supporting such measures. He

[39] Ibid.
[40] N. C. L. C. Minutes, Dec. 6, 1906.   [41] Ibid.
[42] Lindsay to George F. Peabody, Jan. 25, 1907, Murphy Papers.

sent in his resignation as a member of both the board and the committee, saying, "The very fact that there were protests at first against
our exclusion of federal legislation from our aims and yet that the
document recording this exclusion was after deliberation signed by all
parties, including the protestants themselves, convinces me that the
Board has departed from a compact which I regarded as inviolable."

Aside from this objection, however, he considered the policy bad
for the same reasons that Caffey and DeForest did. "The questions
at, issue are . . . so vital and my own convictions are so increasingly
clear, that my position in the Committee becomes inconsistent and
untenable. . . . The Beveridge-Lodge proposals may be temporarily
successful and effective, but I would have regard, first of all, to their
permanent and ultimate effect upon those social forces which determine the vitality of all laws and upon which we must at last
depend both for legislation and administration."[43]

Although Lindsay strongly advocated supporting the principle of
federal legislation, he sincerely regretted to see Murphy leave the
committee. He wrote, "I have always felt that in so many ways you
were a tower of strength to this work, and somehow it does not seem
quite like the National Committee, which you organized and created,
without your name."[44]

Murphy felt it his duty not only to resign from the committee
but to oppose publicly the principle for which it had declared itself.
It was the only way to prove to southern people who held federal legislation of such a nature to be unjustifiable that his position was sincere. He announced his resignation in the *Montgomery Advertiser*
on January 13, 1907, before it had been accepted by the committee.
He also included Judge Gaston, Neal L. Anderson, and Francis Caffey
in his statements of disagreement with the committee. His arguments were published again in the New York *Evening Post* on March
8, and were expanded into a pamphlet entitled *The Federal Regulation of Child Labor*. No more able statement of the objections to
federal child labor legislation has ever been made. The reasons he
offered for opposing federal legislation followed the line of argument
that the state is the channel through which the nation acts and
through which the people exercise their most comprehensive func-
tions of sovereignty. The states were active on the subject of child
labor legislation and tended to become more so, if not checked by
mistaken federal action. The advocates of federal legislation said that
state laws were violated. But that was no reason why the police
power should be turned over to the federal government. To do so
would be contrary to the principles of democracy and there was no

[43] Murphy to Adler, read at Board meeting, N. C. L. C. Minutes, Jan. 29, 1907.
[44] Lindsay to Murphy, Jan. 10, 1907, Murphy Papers.

reason to assume that federal administration would be more efficient than state administration. The method proposed by the Beveridge bill was indirect and did not bid fair to work well. It merely fixed an age limit, whereas any good law depended on a provision for inspection and enforcement. Beveridge claimed that uniformity was essential, but in reality it did not exist and it was impossible for Congress to create such a condition. The menace of federal intervention was harming the cause of reform, since it aroused for its opponents a "popular sympathy they had almost wholly forfeited." Finally there was no sound constitutional basis for such a law.[45]

The members and associates of the National Committee were formally notified in January that the board had endorsed the principle of the Beveridge-Parsons bill. They were urged to support the proposal, if they could conscientiously do so, by writing to representatives and senators. Letters were sent to about ten thousand clergymen asking them to observe January 26 or 27 as child labor day and to preach on this topic.[46]

Having endorsed the Beveridge bill the National Committee sent McKelway to Washington to work for it. He entered enthusiastically into conferences with southern senators and congressmen on the subject, for he was heartily in favor of national legislation.[47] He believed the proposal was justifiable on the same grounds as the federal pure food laws, railroad rate law, or the Louisiana lottery law. The child labor evil, he claimed, was worse in the South than in any other part of the civilized world, due, not to any fault of the section as a whole, but to one industry. Public opinion was putting an end to the employment of children six and seven years old and the better-class mills tried to observe the state laws; but the other mills evaded them. Therefore the South should welcome the assistance of the nation in ridding itself of this evil.[48]

On January 23, 1907, Senator Beveridge launched his three-day speech in behalf of the child labor bill. He began with the figures of the United States Census and went from there to the mass of material which had recently appeared in magazines and book form, much of it written in a highly emotional vein. He produced sworn statements from such people as John Spargo,[49] Mrs. Florence Kelley,[50] and Owen R. Lovejoy[51] that the articles and books written

[45] E. G. Murphy, *The Federal Regulation of Child Labor*, Alabama Child Labor Committee, pamphlet, 1907. There were at least two editions, and probably more.
[46] Lindsay to Members and Associates of N. C. L. C., Jan. 17, 1907, circular letter, Murphy Papers. [47] N. C. L. C. Minutes, Jan. 29, 1907.
[48] A. J. McKelway, "The Evil of Child Labor," in *Outlook*, LXXXV (Feb. 16, 1907), 360-64. [49] *The Bitter Cry of the Children.*
[50] Secretary of the National Consumers' League.
[51] "Schoolhouse or Breaker," in *Outlook*, Vol. LXXX (Aug. 26, 1905).

by them were correct. His attacks were chiefly on the coal and glass industry in the North and East and the cotton textile industry in the South. The South he declared to be in a worse condition than any other section. He quoted from articles by Mrs. Macfadyen and Mrs. Van Vorst. When he asserted that the Georgia law, recently passed and in effect less than a month, was worthless, Senator A. O. Bacon of Georgia challenged his statement. Beveridge asserted that three thousand applications for permits to allow children to work had been received in one Georgia county since the law went into effect. Bacon wired home for proof that this was a gross exaggeration of fact, and received the reply that only ten permits had been issued in the county concerned.[52] Tillman of South Carolina also exchanged words with Beveridge. He opposed the bill on grounds of constitutionality, acknowledging the existence of a great child labor evil in his own state in such a way as to cause his political opponents at home to charge him with allowing Beveridge to stigmatize South Carolina without sufficiently resenting it.[53] Overman of North Carolina also disputed the truth of Beveridge's statements about conditions in Salisbury, North Carolina. The final phases of the debate centered on constitutionality.[54]

Congress did not act on the Beveridge bill. Early in February Murphy wrote to President Theodore Roosevelt asking that six months be allowed to elapse before the passage of the bill was pressed by the administration, because the measure was a radical departure from established custom and the country as a whole had had no preparation for consideration of it. If the bill proved to be sound, he wisely added, it would gain by the delay; if unsound, the delay would save Congress from making a serious mistake.[55] Meanwhile there was discontent among the members of the National Committee as to the action taken in supporting the Beveridge bill. Murphy was conducting an active drive against it and he had the support of some of the members of the National Committee. DeForest sent him fifty dollars in response to a circular letter announcing an anti-Beveridge bill campaign and assured Murphy that he agreed with his views.[56]

Charles W. Eliot wired Murphy that he might use his name against the Beveridge bill as he saw fit.[57] Murphy, although no longer a member of the committee, still tried to bring the members to an understanding of the feeling in the South. Finding it difficult to discuss such a controversial subject with McKelway in an impersonal way, he wrote to Adler that he wanted a frank discussion of the issue

[52] *Congressional Record*, XLI, 2214-16; *Constitution*, Jan. 29, 30, 1907.
[53] *State*, Jan. 31, 1907.
[54] *Congressional Record*, XLI, 1552-1884, *passim.*
[55] Feb. 4, 1907, Murphy Papers.
[56] May 28, 1907, Murphy Papers.   [57] Jan. 18, 1907, Murphy Papers.

between the committee and himself. "The Board of Trustees voted on the Bill under the impression that Tillman was for it. I wonder how this impression arose? Are full reports being made to the Committee as to the effect of the Bill . . . at the South? Has the attitude of the Maryland Child Labor Committee been reported? How far is it known to the Committee that the co-operation of the National Committee could not be entertained in Alabama except after due notice to McKelway (not given or inspired by myself, for I was in Texas) that all reference to the Beveridge bill must be suppressed. If . . . the Committee knows these facts, and knows the present condition of the campaign of the N. C. L. C. at the South—are such editorials (evidently inspired) as recently appeared in the *Outlook* fair? How far am I justified in silently permitting these public statements to continue uncorrected, when their evident purport and effect is to show that I have misrepresented the real situation at the South."[58]

Aside from the question of the probable effect of the Beveridge bill on the attitude of the South toward the committee, Murphy reiterated the principle that coercion was not a permissible remedy in a democracy for anything short of rebellion. "A government, no matter how large the majority in a democracy, or how sacred the interests the majority may espouse, must keep faith with its own processes. This simply raises the question of constitutionality, which is not 'technical' or superficial as Beveridge assumes, but fundamentally legal and therefore moral."[59]

While this matter was still causing grave concern to some of the members of the committee, Congress passed another bill which appropriated $150,000 for an investigation of the condition of women and child workers in the United States to be made under the direction of the Commissioner of Labor.[60] The Department of Labor also prepared a special report compiled from unpublished information gathered in the Census of 1900 which related to the employment of children in the United States, and which laid special emphasis on the employment of children in the textile industry in the South.[61]

At the October meeting of the committee, DeForest presented a resolution which stated that since members of the committee disagreed as to the support of the Beveridge bill, the board should withdraw its approval, and allow each member individually to take such a position as he saw fit.[62] After a discussion of this proposal, a substitute was drafted. It stated that since there was disagreement as to the desirability of federal regulation, and since an investigation had been

[58] May 27, 1907, Murphy Papers.   [59] *Ibid.*
[60] N. C. L. C. Minutes, Oct. 1, 1907.   [61] *Census Bulletin No. 69*, pp. 7, 42.
[62] N. C. L. C. Minutes, Oct. 25, 1907. A copy of the resolution appears among the Murphy Papers. It is possible that Murphy may have had a part in framing it.

authorized, the committee should take no further action until the results of the investigation were available. Its attention should be concentrated on improving state laws and securing the establishment of a federal children's bureau. This did not imply disapproval of the principle of the Beveridge bill, but allowed every member to take what stand he saw fit. Adler, Caffey, DeForest, and Devine were among those who voted for this resolution.[63] As only eleven members were present, final action was postponed until November, when those who were unable to vote in person did so by letter. Among others favoring it were Charles W. Eliot, Clark Howell, Chancellor Kirkland, and Hoke Smith. A total of eighteen approved and ten opposed.[64]

The Beveridge bill was a disappointment to the committee. It had not been well received in Congress or by the country at large. Lindsay, who had strongly advocated it, resigned as secretary because of his university duties, and the new acting secretary, Owen R. Lovejoy, wrote to Murphy in January, 1908, that so far as the committee was concerned the Beveridge bill was dead, and he seemed to be glad to be rid of it. "My own feeling is that the less said about this matter of our relation to Federal legislation, the better, and I regret some of the things the newspapers are publishing on the subject." DeForest expressed the hope that Murphy would come back to the committee. The Beveridge bill was dead, even before the resolution against supporting it passed, and the committee would certainly not support another. "You have won out," he wrote to Murphy, "and there are no 'feelings to swallow.' "[65]

Murphy and DeForest were correct in their belief that sponsoring the Beveridge bill would cause the South to react unfavorably to the National Committee. The bitter feeling against the North for its part in giving publicity to the child labor movement in the early years of the decade was revived when the activities of the National Committee began to draw unfavorable public notice to the South again. Southern manufacturing publications were unreasonable in the bitterness and ridicule with which they sought to counteract the influence

[62] N. C. L. C. Minutes, Oct. 25, 1907; "Resolution adopted by the trustees of the National Child Labor Committee, Nov. 26, 1907," Murphy Papers.
[64] N. C. L. C. Minutes, Nov. 26, 1907. A letter of DeForest to Murphy, Jan. 8, 1908, Murphy Papers, indicates that the resolution finally adopted was passed unanimously, and that the first one passed received a two-thirds majority. The minutes of the board only show one resolution passed, the substitute, the wording of which was not given exactly. It was the one submitted in October, on which the final vote was taken in November. A copy of the resolution adopted Nov. 26, 1907, that is, the substitute, is in the Murphy Papers and is referred to here. It passed by a vote of eighteen to ten; Gaston and Neal L. Anderson failed to vote, but it was presumed by the committee that they would have voted in the affirmative. [65] Jan. 8, 1908, Murphy Papers.

of the committee. To the editor of the *Manufacturers' Record* any movement to which the words sociology or social reform were attached deserved condemnation.[66] The *American Cotton Manufacturer* said, "The National Child Labor Committee has never hesitated to misquote, misstate and misinterpret the facts in order to arrive at conclusions which would further its work." As proof of this assertion it pointed to an advertisement in the *Saturday Evening Post* in which the committee quoted the president of the American Cotton Manufacturers' Association as saying that 75 per cent of the spinners in his own state of North Carolina were fourteen years of age or under. This was untrue, in that it had been said by a former president of the association now out of office, and at a time when there was no law against child labor in the state.[67]

A series of articles by Mrs. John Van Vorst, for which the Child Labor Committee was not responsible, appeared in the *Saturday Evening Post* in 1906.[68] They were highly colored pictures of mill conditions, however, and were resented in the South as worse than useless in bringing about reform. "The cotton mill conditions in the South are bad enough and we know it," wrote Professor Bruce Craven in North Carolina, "but we also know that the *Saturday Evening Post* will not help matters much." The editor of the *Charlotte Observer* seconded this attitude.[69] An article similar to the Van Vorst stories in subject matter and emotional presentation appeared in the *Cosmopolitan* from the pen of Edwin Markham.[70] His title, "Child at the Loom," portrayed a lack of information of one kind which the manufacturers were not slow to point out as indicative of the writer's general lack of knowledge of the mill industry. The vast majority of children who worked in mills were employed as doffers, sweepers, or spinners, and only a handful ever handled the looms. When Markham made such erroneous statements as that there "must now be fifty thousand children at the southern looms," there is little wonder that the manufacturers for several years thereafter referred to the article as proof that the reformers did not know what conditions existed. If one southern paper praised the article and declared that every person in the state should read it, this was due as much to the political expediency of making capital of something aimed at the manufacturers as it was to a desire for reform.[71] The National Committee was no

---

[66] Jan. 16, Feb. 23, July 20, 1905; June 21, 1906.

[67] *American Cotton Manufacturer*, Nov. 29, 1906.

[68] "The Cry of the Children," March 10, April 14, 28, May 5, 19, 1906.

[69] June 2, 1906.

[70] "Child at the Loom," Sept., 1906, quoted in Julia E. Johnsen, *Selected Articles on Child Labor*, pp. 75-82.

[71] *Montgomery Advertiser*, Aug. 21, 1906.

more responsible for Markham's statements than for the Van Vorst articles, or for John Spargo's book which appeared in 1906.[72]

The committee did have a number of articles published in a special department of the *Woman's Home Companion* in 1906 and 1907, although some articles had appeared in that magazine before the committee made this arrangement.[73] *Charities* carried regular accounts of all activities of the committee, but since it was a journal of social welfare work it was little read in the South and therefore less commented upon than the articles in more popular magazines. The *Outlook* also noted the progress of state reforms.

With these and other articles on child labor continually appearing, many people in the South felt a resentment against their supposed northern instigators. The idea of federal legislation on child labor had not been widely discussed before the advent of the Beveridge bill, but when its proposals became known textile journals were the first to condemn it.[74] Newspapers like the *Advertiser* that were strongly in favor of child labor reform agreed with Beveridge that conditions were bad, but strongly disagreed with the idea of federal legislation as a suitable remedy.[75] To the *Observer* the intent of the bill was obvious; it was leveled against the cotton mills of the South.[76] The *Constitution*, whose editor was a member of the National Committee, charged Beveridge with extravagance in his statements and upheld Senator Bacon in his replies to him, saying that child labor was subject to state regulation only. "The Beveridge bill is an opening wedge to a dangerous system of centralization of power in the national government at the expense of the state."[77] *The State*, berating Senator Tillman for not opposing the bill with enough vigor, exclaimed, "God help South Carolina if we are dependent on such 'friends' as Beveridge to guide our steps."[78] The *Observer* chose to ridicule the measure rather than to fear it. Commenting on the three-day speech, it said, "By rights, sobs should be heard from the Atlantic to the Pacific" because of the emotional appeal of the subject in which Beveridge chose to do his muckraking—a field which had already been worked "for much money and notoriety."[79]

The cotton manufacturers found a few defenders outside the southern newspaper press. Miss Gertrude Beeks, secretary of the welfare department of the National Civic Association, claimed that her

[72] *Op. cit.*

[73] See Sept., 1906, issue for Jack London, "The Apostate," and other articles; Oct., 1906, for Will N. Harbin, "On Young Shoulders"; articles Jan. to April, 1907, relating to need for federal legislation.

[74] *American Cotton Manufacturer*, Jan. 3, 1907; *Manufacturers' Record*, Dec. 13, 1906.   [75] Jan. 4, 1907.

[76] Jan. 13, 1907.   [77] Jan. 30, 1907.

[78] Jan. 31, 1907.   [79] Feb. 1, 1907.

inspection of southern mills revealed that there was no night work—a statement which McKelway flatly contradicted.[80] Julia Magruder, a writer in the *North American Review,* undertook to show that the Van Vorst descriptions of southen conditions were worthless. "If their inspection of the Southern cotton-mills had been made by going over them in a balloon, it would have been quite as accurate, and a great deal less misleading to the public." The writer for the *Review* reverted to the old defense that child labor was necessary because of poverty; that the mills offered a civilizing influence for the poor whites of the South; that the work in the mill was good training for the children, and not difficult.[81] William P. Few, then a professor at Trinity College in Durham, North Carolina, wrote an article for the *South Atlantic Quarterly,* a Trinity publication, in praise of the social service work being done at the Victor Mill in Greer, South Carolina. He cited it as an example of the progressive work done by the more up-to-date manufacturers.[82] McKelway criticized his views on the Greer Mill in particular and the condition of labor in South Carolina in general.[83]

McKelway had a true reformer's zeal, and he never hesitated to enter into a controversy to uphold his cause. As a consequence he was frequently involved in discussions through the press with those who disagreed with him. *The State* in 1902 under the editorship of N. G. Gonzales had been the most zealous advocate of child labor reform in the South. Six years later it was fighting the Tillman and Blease elements and trying to maintain friendly relations with the manufacturers by advocating very conservative educational and child labor reform. In February, 1909, it criticized the statement of conditions in South Carolina depicted by *Charities and the Commons.*[84] McKelway came to the defense of the article criticized, saying that it was the result of work done under his direction in 1908.[85] McKelway characterized the resolutions of the South Carolina Cotton Manufacturers' Association favoring a fourteen-year age limit for compulsory education and child labor as being intended for "public consumption," since there was no chance for a compulsory school law to be passed. He challenged the manufacturers' declarations that they were

[80] "Welfare Work and Child Labor in Southern Cotton Mills," in *Charities and the Commons,* XVII (1906), 271.

[81] "The Child-Labor Problem: Fact versus Sentimentality," CLXXXVI (1907), 245-56.

[82] "The Constructive Philanthropy of a Southern Cotton Mill," VIII (1909), 82-90.

[83] "Where Southern Students Disagree," in *Charities and the Commons,* XXI (1909), 893.

[84] Feb. 8, 1909.   [85] *State,* Feb. 16, 1909.

living up to their agreements,[86] and pointed to the statements in *Charities* that the Commissioner of Labor in North Carolina had no right to enter any mill, and that South Carolina had no commissioner, no statistics, no inspection, and no other official means of determining the real state of affairs.[87]

The aggressiveness with which McKelway pushed his demands for reform and the unfortunate personal hostility felt toward him by one of the editors of the *Charlotte Observer*, together with the bitter opposition to McKelway and the committee on the part of the *American Textile Manufacturer* of Charlotte, combined to produce a large degree of antagonism toward the work of the National Committee in the Carolinas. Early in 1909 the committee decided to locate its southern branch temporarily in Charlotte. Application was made to the Russell Sage Foundation for funds for this undertaking.[88] Five thousand dollars was granted the committee, which decided to use the sum chiefly in carrying on investigations and a campaign for education of the public in the Carolinas on child labor matters.[89] When the board's committee on district work met to outline a plan of procedure, some of the members believed that the work of the National Committee had been too aggressive to secure the co-operation of the people of the Carolinas and that McKelway's administration had created "an opposition which stood as a barrier to further progress." Owen Lovejoy was appointed to make an investigation in North and South Carolina in order to determine what the future policy of the board should be.[90]

Lovejoy visited the principal cities in the cotton manufacturing area and spent a few days in the mountain districts. He interviewed a number of the more important manufacturers of cotton goods in North and South Carolina, some state school officials, physicians, clergymen, editors, lawyers, and men prominent politically. Neal L. Anderson, who was at that time a pastor at Winston-Salem, and who had been active in support of child labor reform in Alabama and one of the first members of the National Committee, believed that McKelway's leadership was an embarrassment to the work of the National Committee because of conflicts in which he had been engaged before he became associated with the committee. "As teacher, clergyman and editor, he had been actively engaged in the temper-

[86] "The Fight for Child Labor Reform in the Carolinas," in *Charities and the Commons*, XXI (1909), 1224-26.

[87] Florence Kelley, "Child Labor in the Carolinas," in *Charities and the Commons*, XXI, 742.

[88] N. C. L. C. Minutes, Jan. 5, March 8, 1909.

[89] N. C. L. C. Minutes, March 4, 1909.

[90] This and the following statements are from N. C. L. C. Minutes, May 12, 1909.

ence reform, in the fight against bucket-shop gambling and in various other moral movements"—matters in which Anderson agreed McKelway was always on the right side, but which had nevertheless aroused keen personal antagonisms. This criticism related only to McKelway's position in North Carolina, for his work would be very valuable where such hostility did not exist. But Anderson believed it inadvisable to have any representative of the National Committee in charge of the reform movement in North Carolina. He criticized the employment of a photographer to secure evidence against the mills, and disapproved McKelway's interview with President-elect Taft because it was interpreted as a move in behalf of the Beveridge bill. Anderson declared that his criticism was given in a spirit of friendliness and serious concern for the welfare of the reform movement.[91] Yet it indicated the feeling among southerners, even those interested in the National Committee, that the initiative in state reform belonged to local leaders.

Manufacturers to whom Lovejoy went displayed the same feeling. J. W. Fries of Winston-Salem opposed any further agitation on the subject of child labor. D. A. Tompkins, who had shown nothing but hostility to the committee and to McKelway personally, claimed that there had been no effort to seek reform through co-operation with the manufacturers.[92] Lovejoy said that Tompkins avoided making any concrete statements, and while he would not charge that the committee was inspired by New England cotton-mill capital he claimed that there was suspicion of it.[93] Lewis Parker also opposed the work of the committee. Aside from these men, no one offered any criticism of McKelway's work that would tend to justify Anderson's fears. T. N. Ivey, the editor of the *Southern Christian Advocate,* thought that if McKelway could secure the support of a few local speakers in places where his enemies took advantage of the situation, he might continue in charge of the work. Other men gave him even stronger approval. A. J. Graham, treasurer of a Greenville, South Carolina, mill, said that he believed McKelway was largely right in his description of conditions. "Of course we manufacturers do not always agree with him. I suppose like any leader very much interested in his work, he goes further than a man less interested thinks he ought to go." Governor Ansel of South Carolina commended McKelway's work and urged his continuance in co-operation with local officials. Walter Clark, chief justice of the supreme court of North Carolina, said to McKelway, "You are mistaken to think you have

[91] *Ibid.,* Appendix II, letter of Anderson to Lovejoy, April 27, 1909, read at Board meeting.   [92] *Ibid.*
[93] "Interview with Manufacturers in North and South Carolina re Local Child Labor Conditions," April 1-15, 1909, MS in N. C. L. C. Library.

many enemies. There are some people who oppose the ideas you stand for, but they do not oppose you personally. I do not know of any man who has stood as strongly as you for various reforms who has as few enemies." E. L. Cansler, a Charlotte lawyer, said McKelway's former conflicts were assets rather than liabilities, since his old enemies frequently became allies. The pastor of a Presbyterian church in Charlotte said McKelway should be proud of the enemies he made, especially the *Observer*, which was the chief cause of opposition to him in Charlotte.[94] From a number of other men of prominence, W. E. Gonzales of *The State*, former Governor Aycock, and Josephus Daniels of the *News and Observer*, and several clergymen, schoolmen, and others, approval of the committee and McKelway was reported, though a number of them urged that the work of the National Committee be made as inconspicuous as possible so as to avoid arousing local opposition.[95]

Lovejoy reported that he received everywhere the frank confession that young children were employed in the mills, the only justification offered by the manufacturers being that there was a tendency toward steady improvement. He found the general public entirely ignorant of conditions existing in cotton mill villages, even in such large centers of industry as Greenville, South Carolina, and Charlotte. As to the lack of co-operation of the National Committee with the manufacturers which Tompkins charged, Lovejoy and his committee came to the conclusion that the manufacturers were satisfied with the existing laws and seriously objected to any further efforts to change them. They maintained that the employment of young children would gradually disappear, and Lovejoy saw no hope of securing co-operation from them as a class, although a few individuals agreed with the National Committee on some points, such as the advisability of prohibiting night work. The committee realized that the attitude of the manufacturers generally was hostile and it had little hope for improvement. "Captain Ellison Smyth, D. A. Tompkins, W. E. Erwin and others made it plain that all they desire is to be left alone to work out the problem without interference from this committee, or from the general public."[96]

The effort which had just failed to secure an amendment to the child labor law in North Carolina was an example of the co-operation which the committee might expect. The secretary of the state committee was as bitter against the millmen as any of them were toward the National Committee, but he did not have the support of his own

[94] N. C. L. C. Minutes, May 12, 1909.
[95] *Ibid.;* also "Interview with Manufacturers in North and South Carolina re Local Child Labor Conditions," April 1-15, 1909, MS in N. C. L. C. Library.
[96] N. C. L. C. Minutes, May 12, 1909.

group. Speaking of the manufacturers, he wrote to Lovejoy, "If these men are Christians, I am proud to be called something else. I have hired many children away from these men (Elders and Deacons) to keep them from ruining the little tots. . . . We should hereafter make a clear-cut fight. We have lost twice now by compromise."[97]

As regards the comparison of the mountain and mill people, the investigating committee concluded that not all the advantages were on the side of the mill villages. No conclusive statement was made, but the much-talked-of superiority of mill conditions over those from which the workers came was not credited.[98]

Lovejoy and his committee recommended that the National Committee continue its work in the Carolinas, but that it be done as quietly as possible out of respect for local prejudices. The opposition to outside influence there was comparable to that found in Pennsylvania, Connecticut, Ohio, Indiana, and Rhode Island, and the only way to meet it was to have the workers of the committee come into the state in response to invitation from some local group. Local leadership which would or could achieve the aims of the National Committee seemed lacking in North Carolina, however. Neither Anderson nor McGeachy, the Charlotte clergyman who had praised McKelway, knew that a reform bill had just been defeated in the legislature. C. L. Coon, the secretary of the state committee, had sufficient enthusiasm but he was not able to carry his committee with him. McKelway asked that another field secretary be placed in North and South Carolina, and the board concurred in his desire. It wished to avoid any possibility of an implied criticism of McKelway, however, whose activities were considered as being completely vindicated by the report. It was decided to divide the southern field, putting the direction of the work in the Carolinas under an agent who should be technically responsible to the central office, but actually under McKelway's supervision.[99]

Instead of establishing an office at Charlotte the National Committee employed Caroline E. Boone, who had formerly worked for the United States Bureau of Labor, to investigate conditions in the Carolinas and co-operate with local committees.[100] In 1910 John Porter Hollis of Rock Hill, South Carolina, was engaged as an agent of the committee in the southern field.[101]

Although McKelway was completely vindicated by Lovejoy's report in May, he was from then on called on to spend much more of his time in Washington working for a bill for a federal children's bureau, a matter to which he had already devoted himself before

[97] *Ibid.*, letter from C. L. Coon to Lovejoy, April 20, 1909.
[98] N. C. L. C. Minutes, May 12, 1909.   [99] *Ibid.*
[100] *Ibid.*, Sept. 30, 1909.   [101] *Ibid.*, April 12, 1910.

the investigation of his work in the South came up. As a result his direct connection with reforms in the South became less important.[102]

In spite of the sensitiveness of some people to the attempted leadership of the National Committee and the indifference of others to the object of the reforms, there was a slowly growing consciousness among a few people of the need for child labor and other welfare changes. This found expression at first in a series of southern conferences, apart from the national conferences of such organizations as the National Child Labor Committee and the National Conference of Charities and Corrections which were held in the South from time to time. The first of these was called to meet in Nashville, Tennessee, in October, 1907, by a resolution of the state legislature. It was intended to include the manufacturing and labor interests of all the southern states, but the manufacturers of the other states refused to attend. L. D. Tyson of Knoxville, the president of a large woolen mill corporation and prominent politically, presided. The only other states officially represented were Virginia, Louisiana, and Missouri. Governor Swanson of Virginia sent a representative and the factory inspectors of the other states were present. This meeting adopted resolutions approving the fourteen-year age limit for factory work, a sixty-hour week for women and children under eighteen, and the prohibition of night work for children under sixteen. It also recommended compulsory school attendance, better vagrancy laws which would compel able-bodied men to support their families, laws to make it possible to prove the age of children, and the appointment of women factory inspectors.[103]

A more successful conference was called in 1909 by Governor Sanders of Louisiana, at the request of Miss Jean M. Gordon, state factory inspector, who had been largely instrumental in bringing about reforms in Louisiana. Sanders asked the other southern governors to attend personally if possible, or to send as delegates men who were interested in the subject to be discussed, such as manufacturers, members of the labor unions, or members of associations pledged to child labor reform. Governor Comer of Alabama and Governor Campbell of Texas were the only state executives who failed to respond. Noel of Mississippi and Hadley of Missouri came in person. The others appointed representatives, not all of whom were present at the conference, however. Georgia alone of the leading industrial states was represented.[104] Only a few cotton manufacturers were among the two hundred delegates. Compulsory school

[102] *Ibid.*, Oct. 27, 1909.

[103] "Nashville Child Labor Conference," in *Charities and the Commons*, XIX (Oct. 26, 1907), 936; "First Fruits of the Nashville Conference," *ibid.* (Mar. 14, 1908), 1723, 1724.

[104] "Southern Child Labor Conference," in *Survey*, XXII (April 17, 1909), 107.

attendance was eliminated from the discussion, and J. W. VanCleave of St. Louis, the president of the National Manufacturers' Association, opposed the discussion of limitation of hours for children as having nothing to do with the subject; but for this he received little support. McKelway was present and played a leading part in the conference.[105] The resolutions adopted favored practically all the standards offered by the National Committee. A permanent organization, with Governor Sanders as president, a vice-president from each state, and an executive committee was formed.[106]

The second meeting of the "Southern Conference on Woman and Child Labor," as the organization came to be called, met in Memphis in 1910, with Governor Malcolm R. Patterson of Tennessee acting as president. Again Georgia was the only large industrial state represented. The Carolinas and Alabama still ignored the meetings. Resolutions similar to those of the former conference were adopted. The chief new interest of the conference was in the recent reports of Dr. C. W. Stiles of the Rockefeller Hookworm Commission.[107] The child labor reformers unexpectedly found an enemy in Dr. Stiles, who had for several years been making a study of hookworm disease and its effect on the people of the sandy soil regions in the South. He found that many of the cotton mill operatives, fresh from the farms, were infected with the disease. One of his suggestions for remedying it was to stop all restrictive legislation on child labor for a period of years, so that there would be nothing to discourage the movement of the poor farmer class to the mill. Once in the mill village it was easier to treat the cases with the co-operation of the mill management than it would be on the farm. McKelway said Stiles took this position merely to win the friendship and co-operation of the manufacturers, since the proposed child labor legislation, even if enacted, would not affect in any considerable degree the movement from the farm to the mill.[108] The Memphis conference adopted resolutions saying that while it accepted Stiles' statement that the disease was a menace to the South, it did not agree with his plan of suppressing it, which involved stopping child labor legislation for ten years. Instead, the conference suggested that the legislatures force the children into schools instead of into mills.[109] The Memphis conference endorsed the movement for a federal children's bureau and for woman suffrage reform.[110]

[105] N. C. L. C. Minutes, May 12, 1909.

[106] "Southern Child Labor Conference," in *Survey*, XXII (April 17, 1909), 108.

[107] "Child Labor Conference Disagrees with Dr. Stiles," in *Survey*, XXIV (April 23, 1910), 131-32.

[108] Felix Adler, *Conservation of the Human Assets of the Nation*, in N. C. L. C. Pamphlet No. 125, reprint from *Annals* Supplement for Mar., 1910.

[109] "Child Labor Conference Disagrees with Dr. Stiles," in *Survey*, XXIV, 132.

[110] *Ibid.*

A third southern conference on woman and child labor was held in Atlanta in 1911. The labor and child labor organizations were well represented, although the manufacturers were not.[111] In 1912 a similar conference met in Chattanooga.[112] While these conferences showed a growing interest in social problems, the interest was least where the need was greatest, that is, in the leading industrial states.

The investigation of conditions of woman and child labor which Congress had authorized the Department of Labor to make in 1907 had been carried out, but its reports appeared only after some delay.[113] Its finding in regard to the employment of children in the cotton manufacturing industry substantiated in most points the claims made by the National Child Labor Committee. It was condemned by the manufacturing interests, which associated it at once with the reports of the child labor reformers.[114] A quarrel also arose between T. R. Dawley, Jr., one of the men who had been employed by the government, and the Department of Labor officials, who were dissatisfied with his work. Dawley left the Bureau of Labor and wrote a book which he called *The Child That Toileth Not: The Story of a Government Investigation Hitherto Suppressed.* Dawley claimed that he was instructed by the bureau to investigate the mountainous regions in the South in order to determine whether the people there were improved by removing them to the mills, but that his report ran counter to the preconceived ideas of his superiors and when he refused to alter it he was dismissed and the report suppressed.[115] Dawley's attack, which *The State* commented upon in a manner favorable to him, was directed as much against the National Committee as the Bureau of Labor, and the committee immediately replied through McKelway. He said that the resolution providing for the investigation had been introduced in the spring of 1906 and passed one house before Beveridge made his famous speech of January, 1907. Dawley's report, like those of all individual investigators, was tabulated and summarized, and appeared in the first volume of the published report of the Bureau of Labor.[116] The reason for the failure of the report to satisfy the bureau was that Dawley failed to report on the thing he was sent to investigate, which was the condition of the mountain people.[117]

[111] *Constitution*, April 25, 26, 1911.

[112] A. F. of L. Weekly News Letter, No. 53, April 6, 1912.

[113] *Woman and Child Wage-Earners.* Findings of the investigation are dealt with in other chapters.

[114] *Southern Textile Bulletin*, March 7, 1912.

[115] *State*, Dec. 5, 1912.   [116] *Ibid.*, Dec. 13, 1912.

[117] W. L. Stoddard, " 'The Child That Toileth Not,' " in *Survey*, XXIX (1913), 705-8.

Dawley probably hoped to sell his book to the manufacturers. It was reported that he visited a number of them and asked for support. One ordered 140 copies to be sent to the state legislature and another ordered 79.[118]

The only form of federal legislation which the National Committee continued to advocate after the unfavorable reception of the Beveridge bill was for a children's bureau. Such an organization had been first proposed in 1905 by Miss Lillian Wald and Samuel Lindsay in an interview with President Theodore Roosevelt. The President gave his approval and a bill for the establishment of a bureau was introduced at every session of Congress from 1905 until 1912.[119] McKelway spent more and more of his time working for it,[120] and after 1909 the immediate supervision of the committee's work in the southern states was put in the hands of other agents so that he might have personal charge of affairs in Washington.[121] In 1912 the Children's Bureau was established under the Department of Labor, largely as a result of the efforts of the National Committee and other social agencies.[122] The passage of the law providing for the bureau caused little comment in the South, and no very marked hostility beyond the general distrust of federal bureaus and investigations.[123] The *Constitution* called it "one of the most sensible recently undertaken by the federal government."[124]

The membership of the South in the National Committee remained small, although there was an increase over the mere handful in the first years. The total contribution from the South probably never was sufficient to defray more than a fraction of the expenditures of the committee in that section. In 1909 a total of $577 was received from the 129 contributing members. The committee had succeeded in making its influence felt in the South and in keeping alive publicity about the child labor problem. Its progress in legislation was only what the manufacturers were driven to grant by increased pressure of public opinion. Every law was a compromise and no gain was complete, for it did not convert the majority of millmen to an acceptance of the theories that child labor was morally wrong or practically avoidable.

[118] Memorandum re T. R. Dawley in N. C. L. C. Library.
[119] Benedict, *op. cit.*
[120] N. C. L. C. Minutes, Sept. 30, 1908.
[121] *Ibid.*, Oct. 27, 1909.
[122] *Ibid.*, Sept. 30, 1912.
[123] *State*, Dec. 5, 1912.
[124] July 7, 1912.

CHAPTER VIII

NORTH CAROLINA AFTER 1903: REFORM LAWS BY THE MANUFACTURERS

THE NEWLY organized National Child Labor Committee turned its attention to North Carolina first of all in the group of southern states. Dr. A. J. McKelway, the southern secretary for the committee, had lived in North Carolina for several years and had interested himself in the child labor problem there before the formation of the committee. A new legislature was about to meet in 1905 just as the committee was ready to begin its work. Furthermore, there had been no other organization of any strength working for child labor reform in the state as there had been in Georgia and Alabama. The committee was free to begin a campaign without being hampered by the action of other groups.

The Child Labor Law of 1903 had only been in effect a year when the National Committee attempted to reopen the drive for legislation. Its effectiveness in that length of time cannot be judged accurately; the report of the Commissioner of Labor for 1904 fails to record the number of children employed in manufacturing.[1] The general consensus of opinion expressed by the manufacturers to the commissioner was that the law should be accepted in good faith, but that it should also be the last one of its kind.[2]

The prospect for the enactment of a new law in 1905 was never favorable, but McKelway entered upon the work with the optimism of a reformer new to his task. He found the Raleigh *News and Observer*, whose editor, Josephus Daniels, had championed other progressive reforms in the state, willing to give him space for his articles. McKelway had a ready pen, and he published an article advocating a higher age limit,[3] which was reprinted in pamphlet form for distribution.[4] With an appeal to the interest of the older southerners, he used the phrase "Do not grind the seed corn," attributed to Jefferson Davis, as a catchword.[5] He also quoted from Ruskin the lines,

---

[1] N. C. Bureau of Labor, *Eighteenth Annual Report*, 1904, p. 83.

[2] *Ibid.*, pp. 104-10.   [3] Jan. 1, 1905.

[4] A. J. McKelway, *Do Not Grind the Seed Corn.*

[5] When it was proposed to lower the age limit for enlistment in the Confederate army it is said that Jefferson Davis refused, saying, "We must not grind our seed corn." McKelway says, "When I told this story once before a committee of the Alabama Legislature, one of the members of the committee confirmed it by saying

"To be a man too soon is to be a small man," and "It is a shame for a nation to make its young girls weary."[6] The latter recurred time and again in the arguments for a higher age limit.

The article in the *News and Observer* was clearly an effort to forestall prejudice against the National Child Labor Committee. The committee was formed, McKelway said, as a result of the movement in the South, and it had led the North "to do some sweeping before its own door." He gave the names of the men on the committee as most of them were nationally prominent and many were leaders in the South. The child labor problem was presented as a national evil, and its solution in the South a part of a national movement. The bad results of the system of child labor in factories in England were a warning to the South. The reforms asked for by the National Committee at this time were a fourteen-year age limit for girls, the certification of age by the child's teacher, and the requirement of ability to read and write for children under fourteen who were given employment.[7]

Governor Charles B. Aycock had supported the child labor measure in 1903; and again in 1905, in his last message to the legislature, he urged the adoption of the literacy requirement for children between twelve and fourteen. He was a strong supporter of the educational movement in North Carolina, and he considered this as a step toward reducing the percentage of illiteracy. "This amendment will operate as a great stimulus to parents who wish their children to work in the factories as early as the law permits to put them in school and teach them to read and write. It would be a mild form of compulsory education around factory towns and could not work injury to anyone."[8]

As soon as the House had elected a speaker, McKelway went to him and asked for a "square deal" on the Committee on Labor, to which the child labor bill would be referred. In the Senate there was no Committee on Labor, and in the past child labor bills had been referred to the Committee on Manufactures, which was composed of men from cotton manufacturing counties and sometimes manufacturers themselves. This was prejudicial to the child labor bills and usually resulted in an unfavorable report.[9]

The bill which was introduced in 1905 was drawn up by McKelway. He followed in general the principles laid down in the model child labor bill recommended by the National Consumers' League.

that he had joined the Confederate Army so young that he had been nick-named 'Seed Corn Davis' himself."—"McKelway's Account," McKelway Papers.
    [6] *News and Observer*, Jan. 1, 1905.
    [7] *Ibid.*   [8] *Ibid.*, Jan. 6, 1905.
    [9] "McKelway's Account," McKelway Papers.

It provided for raising the age limit from twelve to fourteen for girls, and to sixteen for night work for both girls and boys. It would reduce the hours for children under sixteen to sixty a week. It required the school authorities to issue certificates showing the ages of children who applied for employment. The Commissioner of Labor and Printing, or his deputy, should be factory inspector.[10] This bill was introduced by J. J. Cunningham in the House. He was president of the North Carolina Cotton Growers' Association, and McKelway persuaded him to present the child labor bill because he thought his prominence would give the bill prestige. But the very fact that the measure was introduced "by request" was prejudicial to its interests, as McKelway later realized.[11]

McKelway turned to Edgar Gardner Murphy, who had secured his appointment as secretary for the National Committee, for help in this first campaign which the committee was sponsoring. He asked Murphy to come to Raleigh to speak, but Murphy was unable to do so because of his failing health. He did, however, offer advice from his greater experience as to how McKelway should meet the attacks of his opponents. "They will, of course, make all the capital they can out of your connection with the North. It is sufficient answer for you to be able to point out that you have always been in favor of child labor legislation and that therefore your connection with the North had been in no wise the cause of your present interest. It should also be pointed out that a Committee in which Senator Tillman, Clark Howell, Hoke Smith, Judge Feagin, Judge Gaston and other Southern men are represented can hardly be called a Northern committee. Just in this connection lies one of the largest elements in your service to the country. The Southern men who are in your position are educating the public opinion of the South on a question that lies deeper than labor laws or school development. We are slowly securing a lodgement for the contention that a Southern man has a right to make a national alliance and to assimilate himself with great national forces. The road may be hard for a while but it leads toward the freedom of the Southern publicist to be a citizen of the whole country. The people of the West never think of denying to their leaders the right to be citizens of the United States of America. The South before many years will come to the same standpoint.

"If the logic of our opponents were carried out it would mean that North Carolina and South Carolina ought to refuse to send representatives to sit in the Congress at Washington. The Senators are taking pay from the federal treasury, a treasury which happens

[10] *Ibid.; News and Observer,* Jan. 13, 1905.

[11] N. C., *Journal of the House,* 1905, p. 61; *News and Observer,* Jan. 13, 1905; "McKelway's Account," McKelway Papers.

just now to be under the control of the Republican Party. The justification of this procedure is in essence the same justification which lies back of your work and mine. They are occupying their places in a national organization in order that they may serve the South. That is what you are doing and what every man is doing who works on the theory that the South has a right to representation in every national organization and a right to the broadest national influences which her sons can command."

Coming back to the immediate problem in North Carolina and the effort McKelway was making to secure the co-operation of the leading millmen of the state, Murphy wrote, "I hope that all will be well at home and also that there will be some satisfactory outcome to your conference with Tomkins [sic]. It seems to me that Tomkins ought now to see his opportunity to lead in the right direction. If North Carolina takes this step it will be of great credit to her and of great use throughout the South. If any of the mill men show a disposition to co-operate with you, I think it would be well to show hearty appreciation of their attitude and to make as much of it as possible. This will make your labor seem less like class legislation and will have a good effect generally."[12]

The hope which Murphy expressed of co-operation with D. A. Tompkins was over-optimistic. Tompkins was one of the most influential millmen in the South. A South Carolinian by birth, the son of an Edgefield planter, he had, after the war, taken a technical education in the North. He had returned to Charlotte as a young engineer, and rose rapidly to a position of influence as a builder of cotton mills and joint owner of the influential *Charlotte Observer*. He was a practical worker, and did much to bring about the industrial prosperity of the Piedmont section. He believed that the economic salvation of the South lay in building mills, and he regarded the gathering of the rural whites into mill villages as a form of philanthropy. Like the other more powerful millmen, such as Lewis Parker and Ellison Smyth, he built schools and churches for his people and brought them under a paternalistic system. Tompkins maintained that the work for social betterment and the reform of evils in the factory system were in the process of solution at the hands of the leaders of industry. For all professional reformers he had contempt, as being people who came in to get the glory of achieving a reform the real work of which had been done by others.[13] To this class belonged those who were demanding child labor legislation. "The professional reformers comprise many well-meaning, tenderhearted women, most of whom are living on incomes and have little

[12] Murphy to McKelway, Jan. 23, 1905, Murphy Papers.
[13] Winston, *op. cit.*, pp. 262 ff.

knowledge of practical life. Also of men and women who are thirsty for notariety [sic]. These hate a dull time, and wherever they go there is bound to be trouble. Then there is the grafter pure and simple, who can collect a bigger salary in the name of charity, provided his accounts are left unchecked, than he can get for doing anything else where the measure of his work is reckoned and where his accounts are checked."[14]

With such an attitude toward the reformers there was little hope for co-operation between the National Child Labor Committee and the manufacturers. McKelway was at first under the impression that the legislators were favorable to his measure, but a group of millmen, the hard yarn spinners, met in Charlotte behind closed doors the week before the Cunningham bill was presented in the House.[15] Whether or not plans were then made for opposing the measure, the mill operators appeared in Raleigh before the date arrived for the committee hearing to lobby against it. One of the leading manufacturers was reported to have said that three fourths of the spinners of North Carolina were girls fourteen and under, and that if the bill passed it would close every mill in the state. McKelway claimed that on the day before the hearing the speaker of the House added enough names to the Committee on Labor to insure an unfavorable report.[16]

The hearing before the House Committee took place on January 31, 1905. McKelway appeared as the only advocate of the bill and a number of manufacturers spoke against it. McKelway's argument shows Murphy's influence. He tried to make clear his relation to the National Child Labor Committee and to justify it before his hearers. He had been warned by his friends, he said, that to connect himself with a national organization would discredit him in North Carolina, but he nevertheless based his position on that fact. With less tact, perhaps, than Murphy would have used, but with a straightforward frankness, he stated his case. "I went before that Legislative Committee a Southern man standing for the right to belong to a national organization in the South. I told them that forty years was long enough for people to wander in the wilderness, even for their sins; that the time had come when our people should throw themselves into this movement which should voice the spirit of every representative person in North Carolina."[17]

This appeal to a national spirit struck no responsive note in his hearers. Although the charge of New England interference was an old story in 1905, McKelway seemed to have been taken by surprise

[14] Ibid., p. 265. Winston quotes this as an article by Tompkins but does not cite the source.   [15] State, Jan. 6, 1905.
[16] "McKelway's Account," McKelway Papers.
[17] N. C. L. C. Minutes, Feb. 15, 1905.

when one of his opponents made the statement that the New England millowners were backing the National Child Labor Committee as they had supported the labor organizations in previous years, and hinted that the committee was being financed by northern mill corporations. McKelway cited the names of the southern members of the committee, as he had been advised to do, but they had no effect. They were all mistaken, including Hoke Smith and McKelway himself, said the millmen. Furthermore, the manufacturers felt that they had made a compromise in allowing the law of 1903 to pass, and that the legislature was under a sort of moral obligation not to extend legislation along this line any further, but to leave the regulation of labor to the manufacturers. They belonged to the best people of the state—the people who had solved the Negro problem, and who could handle the labor problem as well.[18]

In his rebuttal to these arguments McKelway failed to take up the point about New England mills financing the National Committee, because, he said, "this slander was such a silly one that I did not think it necessary to reply to it." This was a serious mistake, and a strange one for him to make if he was familiar with the arguments that had been directed against the reformers in the four years previous. Lacking denial, the story spread, until, he said, it was "industriously circulated in North Carolina, growing to the statement that I was personally in the' pay of the New England manufacturers."[19]

The legislative committee reported the child labor bill unfavorably and no further action was taken.[20] There were two bills to regulate hours of labor presented at about the same time but neither received favorable consideration.[21]

The contest had been unevenly divided, one man against many. The time and circumstances were unfavorable because the last law was so recent. Perhaps the most influential argument against the measure was that there had been a tacit agreement in 1903 to pass no laws for regulating child labor in 1905.[22] The measure McKelway proposed had almost no support. The Association of City School Superintendents had adopted resolutions endorsing the bill,[23] and there had been some support from the press. But it had come only in January about the time the legislature opened, too late to help build up a strong public opinion.[24] There was no evidence of any

[18] "Hearing before the Committee on Manufacturers of the House of Representatives, in Regard to the Child Labor Bill, in Capitol Building, Raleigh, N. C., Jan. 31, 1905," MS in N. C. L. C. Library.
[19] N. C. L. C. Minutes, May 12, 1909, Appendix I.
[20] News and Observer, Feb. 1, 1905.
[21] N. C., Journal of the House, 1905, pp. 41, 53, 285, 512, 600, 991.
[22] News and Observer, Feb. 1, 1905.   [23] Ibid., Jan. 29, 1905.
[24] "McKelway's Account," McKelway Papers.

backing whatever from either state or national labor organizations. This was perhaps best for the interest of the bill. Shortly after the campaign had failed, President Gompers of the American Federation assured McKelway that he was fully in sympathy with the movement, but that he realized that advocacy of a cause by organized labor in the South was frequently an embarrassment rather than a help, and he agreed to restrain labor support of a child labor bill when the committee advised him that such support would be harmful.[25] This was an acknowledgment of the wisdom of the policy Murphy had urged on Gompers two years before. So complete was the defeat of the bill that Josephus Daniels advised McKelway to give up his efforts for social legislation and go back to his former occupation.[26] Instead, McKelway turned his attention to building up public interest in further reform, which he undertook to do by calling attention to violations of the existing law[27] and by the organization of a state child labor committee.[28]

An undesirable personal element was introduced into the situation a few months after the defeat of the bill when a difficulty arose between McKelway and one of the owners and editors of the *Charlotte Observer*. The trouble resulted in a suit against the editor which was settled to McKelway's satisfaction.[29] Although it had no direct bearing on the child labor question, the incident served to align the *Observer* clearly against the policies of the committee.

While the lawsuit was in progress McKelway was busily engaged in working for legislation in South Carolina and Georgia, and in establishing a southern branch of the National Committee in Atlanta.[30]

The North Carolina manufacturers were not satisfied with labor conditions existing there. Complaints of the scarcity of labor and the need for immigration in part explain the reluctance of the mills to yield to the demands for restrictive legislation.[31] In his annual report the North Carolina commissioner of labor declared that "in the main, the manufacturers have cheerfully co-operated with the state in carrying into effect the provisions of the measure regulating the child labor question," and that "there is as little child labor in North Carolina as in the New England States, and some of those

[25] N. C. L. C. Minutes, Mar. 23, 1905.
[26] "McKelway's Account," McKelway Papers.
[27] N. C. L. C. Minutes, March 23, 1905.   [28] *Ibid.*, Nov. 16, 1905.
[29] Josephus Daniels to McKelway, April 26, 1904; C. B. Aycock to McKelway, June 27, July 1, 1905; J. P. Taylor to McKelway, Jan. 19, 1906.—McKelway Papers.
[30] "A. J. McKelway's report to the Board of Trustees, Oct. 1, 1906," MS in N. C. L. C. Library.
[31] N. C. Bureau of Labor, *Twentieth Annual Report*, 1906, pp. 254-56; A. J. McKelway to C. P. Neill, U. S. Commissioner of Labor, Nov. 8, 1906, McKelway Papers.

west of the Mississippi River." The greater part of the millmen were opposed to the employment of small children in the mills, but "others, although the number is comparatively small, object to the provisions of the present law, or to any further legislation in this regard."[32] According to the statistics gathered by the commissioner from about three hundred textile mills, 84 per cent of the mill officials stated that there were no children under twelve employed; 3 per cent stated that children under twelve were employed; 13 per cent failed to answer the question. Fifty-eight per cent declared themselves in favor of compulsory education, 15 per cent opposed it, and 27 per cent failed to reply.[33] One mill superintendent declared that the twelve-year age limit was not enforced in 5 per cent of the mills; that in some mills the managers did not put the child's name on the books, while in others they simply ignored the law.[34]

Before the meeting of the legislature of 1907 the manufacturers, realizing that some action would probably be taken, began to consider what form of legislation would be least objectionable to them. The solution on which they determined was to propose a bill which would set the age limit for the employment of children at thirteen years "except when employed in apprenticeship capacity." This was the plan advocated by D. A. Tompkins. He worked out a scheme in which he recommended that children should be admitted as apprentices in cotton factories at the age of twelve years. Those twelve to thirteen years of age should work four months a year in a factory after six months in school; children from thirteen to fourteen should work five months and go to school five months; from fourteen to fifteen they should work seven months and go to school three; from fifteen to sixteen they should work ten months and go to school two months. After that they might become full-time workers.[35] Tompkins proposed this plan, he said, because he thought children should be given the discipline of work at an earlier age than the reformers advocated.[36]

The *Charlotte Observer* reflected Tompkins' ideas. In commenting on the message of Governor Glenn to the legislature in 1907 the *Observer* said, "He is sound on the child labor question in saying that 'tender children should be protected' and that none who cannot read and write should be allowed to work in factories until they are fourteen. There may be difference of opinion as to the proper interpretation of the term 'tender children,' and again, hours of work per day and per year could be so modified that what would be a wrong and hardship if a young child were worked the year round

[32] N. C. Bureau of Labor, *Twentieth Annual Report*, p. 2.
[33] *Ibid.*, p. 208.   [34] *Ibid.*, p. 257.
[35] D. A. Tompkins, *Child Labor and Apprenticeship Training*, pamphlet.
[36] *Charlotte Observer*, Jan. 13, 1907.

for eleven or twelve hours per day would be neither if it were worked three or four months in the year for six hours a day."[37]

On February 13, 1907, a new bill to restrict child labor was introduced in the House.[38] This measure was proposed by the manufacturers and embodied a part at least of Tompkins' plan. It forbade the employment in manufacturing establishments of children under twelve, and of children between twelve and thirteen except in apprenticeship capacity and after having attended school four months out of the preceding twelve. No child under sixteen should work more than sixty-six hours a week; no child under fourteen should work between 8:00 P.M. and 5:00 A.M.[39] McKelway said that at first it was planned merely to forbid employment of children under thirteen except in apprenticeship capacity, without mentioning a twelve-year age limit for all employment, which would have in reality opened employment to all children under that age who could qualify as apprentices.[40] McKelway believed at first that the apprenticeship clause would prove to be of little use to the manufacturers, because the North Carolina law required that the master to whom an apprentice was bound should educate, care for, and support him, and this was hardly practical in the case of minor cotton mill operatives. But the interpretation put on the measure was that there was a difference in employing a child "as an apprentice" and "in apprenticeship capacity." The law was generally interpreted as allowing the employment of any child twelve years old if he was learning the business.[41]

The new law passed the House on March 4 and the Senate on March 8.[42] Since it was a manufacturers' bill, there was no difficulty in securing its passage. The National Committee had hoped to gain enough influence in the state to secure a law for a fourteen-year age limit for girls and a literacy test such as had been advocated in 1905; for a sixteen-year age limit for night work; and for factory inspection. McKelway had organized the North Carolina Child Labor Committee in the fall of 1906. Its officers were Bishop Cheshire of the Episcopal Church, chairman; Clarence Poe, editor of the *Progressive Farmer,* vice-chairman; and Professor C. L. Coon, secretary.[43] The committee attempted to secure the co-operation of the manufacturers.

[37] Jan. 11, 1907.

[38] N. C., *Journal of the House,* 1907, p. 341.

[39] N. C., *Acts of the General Assembly,* 1907, pp. 670-71; *American Cotton Manufacturer,* Feb. 14, 1907.

[40] "McKelway's Account," McKelway Papers.

[41] *Ibid.*

[42] N. C., *Journal of the House,* 1907, pp. 792-93; *Journal of the Senate,* 1907, p. 930.

[43] Clarence H. Poe, "Report of the North Carolina Child Labor Committee," in *Child Labor and Social Progress,* p. 139.

Letters were sent to them, as well as to the press and to the members of the legislature. But the committee failed to bring the manufacturers to an agreement. The members of the committee were not entirely united in their ideas as to what legislation should be enacted. Some of them were inclined to follow the lead of the millmen rather than to assume it themselves. J. W. Bailey, editor of the *Biblical Recorder* and president of the state antisaloon league, was also a member of the State Child Labor Committee. But the *American Cotton Manufacturer,* a textile journal published in Charlotte, expressed much satisfaction over his declaration that if the National Child Labor Committee refused to treat with the millmen or antagonized them, the State committee would act independently.[44] Finding their proposals rejected the State committee accepted the plan of the millmen, under the impression that the apprenticeship clause would not be effective in cotton mills.[45] The law was no substantial gain over the previous one. "Aside from the next to nothing in the proposed law, it has the same fatal defect as the old law—no pretense of a system of enforcement."[46]

In the same session the legislature enacted a law which allowed school districts where a majority of the voters so desired to put in force compulsory school attendance for children between eight and fourteen years of age for sixteen weeks a year. Children over twelve who were legally employed were allowed exemption from this law, so that it did not in any way conflict with the child labor law.[47]

The National Child Labor Committee made a series of investigations in the Carolinas in this period, by methods which sometimes aroused the hostility of the millowners to an even greater extent than already existed. Under McKelway's direction a photographer was engaged to take pictures at a number of mills in North and South Carolina.[48] That the investigations were at times unwelcome and even resisted is not surprising. If permission to take a picture was refused or given reluctantly, the investigators felt that the millowners had something to conceal, and were all the more anxious to find out something about the mill. The material collected was given publicity through the publication of pamphlets[49] and in magazine articles. The friends of the manufacturers, even those who were very much interested in social reform, considered these methods as unjust. "Most of our people had little patience with McKelway's methods, even when they were in sympathy with his purpose," wrote one

[44] *American Cotton Manufacturer,* Feb. 21, 1907.
[45] N. C. L. C. Minutes, May 12, 1909, Appendix I.
[46] *News and Observer,* Feb. 19, 1907.
[47] N. C., *Public Laws and Resolutions,* 1907, pp. 284-85.
[48] L. W. Hine, *op. cit.*
[49] A. J. McKelway, *Child Labor in the Carolinas,* N. C. L. C. Pamphlet No. 92.

of these men years later. "In fact he lined up with a crowd that was notably unfair. They would take pictures and publish them as representative, when they were unusual and exceptional."[50] One of the members of the National Committee, looking back from a perspective of nearly twenty-five years, said, "Unfortunately, in the controversies that later arose, the mill men exploited the best mills as typical of conditions while the representatives of the National Committee persisted in exploiting the worst mills as typical of child labor conditions."[51] The two mills where the committee's agent, Lewis Hine, was forbidden to take pictures were High Shoals and Atherton, of both of which Tompkins was president. A statement to this effect was published in a pamphlet under McKelway's name. The editor of the *American Textile Manufacturer* declared that the statement was misleading, because it made it appear that Tompkins had directly forbidden the photographer to enter the mills, whereas he did not know of the incident until the appearance of the pamphlet.[52] Hine claimed that he saw dozens of children between the ages of nine and thirteen going and coming to the High Shoals mills at the noon hour. He published pictures of children said to be working under legal age.[53] McKelway and the agents working under his direction claimed that the law was not observed; the Commissioner of Labor's report for 1908 shows that only 4 per cent of the manufacturers reported any children employed.[54] It was at about this time that the United States Bureau of Labor was conducting an investigation of woman and child labor. Its agents also reported that the law was violated in all the southern states and that in the Carolinas there was frequent evasion by allowing children who were not employed to work as helpers.[55]

In 1909 the North Carolina Committee again agreed on certain improvements in the law for which they would work. The principal changes desired were for factory inspection, to raise the age limit for night work to sixteen, and to reduce the hours to sixty a week. The committee decided to support any member of the legislature who would propose a bill with these provisions. J. W. Hinsdale, Jr., of Raleigh, introduced a measure[56] which went one step further than the State Committee had proposed in raising the age limit for all child workers to fourteen. This bill was characterized as "drastic"

[50] Letter from J. A. Baldwin to the author, June 13, 1930.
[51] Letter from Neal L. Anderson to the author, Feb. 14, 1930.
[52] *American Textile Manufacturer* (successor to *American Cotton Manufacturer*), Feb. 11, 1909.
[53] A. J. McKelway, *Child Labor in the Carolinas.*
[54] N. C. Dept. of Labor, *Twenty-second Annual Report,* 1908, p. 168.
[55] U. S. Bureau of Labor, *Woman and Child Wage-Earners,* I, 187-97.
[56] N. C., *Journal of the House,* 1909, p. 61.

by the *American Textile Manufacturer*.[57] Meanwhile, the North Carolina Manufacturers' Association met in Charlotte and proposed another bill which made no changes in the law, but provided that as a substitute for inspection the superintendent of every manufacturing corporation should take an oath every six months before the Commissioner of Labor that the law had not been violated in his establishment during that period. Since the manufacturers had only to accept the statement of the parent as to the child's age and no documentary proof was required, the Child Labor Committee regarded this provision as nothing more than putting a premium on perjury.[58]

The manufacturers were opposed to the proposed changes. Governor Kitchin, who represented this class, referred to child labor in his inaugural address. Everyone, he said, opposed child labor in factories. Yet everyone knew that under existing circumstances it was a necessary evil for some children to labor until there were enough orphanages and homes for the aged and infirm to care for the people who were now supported by child labor. He saw no solution for the problem. "Neither the counties nor the denominations are ready to shoulder the expense, however good in theory, of maintaining all those whom children now help to support and such children themselves as now work." Factory work was preferred by this class of people to farm work. Yet the health of the millworkers should be taken into consideration because they were the source of the future labor supply for southern industry.[59]

R. M. Miller, president of the North Carolina Manufacturers' Association, was bitter in his denunciation of the bill, which he characterized as a movement sponsored by paid hirelings of New England. McKelway answered him in the press, saying that no amount of money could hire him to advocate the cause for which Miller stood, which was "nothing less than child-murder. . . . There are men who can never imagine that people can be disinterested even where the welfare of children is concerned."[60]

When the Hinsdale bill was considered by the House committee, Hinsdale spoke in its behalf. But J. W. Bailey, who had been put in charge of the interests of the North Carolina Committee, agreed to accept the terms to which the manufacturers were willing to agree, and opposed the Hinsdale bill. This caused difficulty among the reformers, for Hinsdale charged Bailey with having broken his agree-

[57] Feb. 11, 1909.
[58] N. C. L. C. Minutes, May 12, 1909, Appendix I; *Charlotte Observer*, Feb. 4, 1909; *American Textile Manufacturer*, Feb. 11, 1909.
[59] *News and Observer*, Jan. 13, 1909.
[60] *Ibid.*, Feb. 3, 1909.

ment.[61] The committee accepted the manufacturers' proposals and recommended them as a substitute in place of Hinsdale's bill.[62]

Clarence Poe and the other members of the State Committee took issue with Bailey on his interpretation of the instructions given him by the committee, and Poe telegraphed to McKelway, who was in Washington, to come to Raleigh. McKelway was unable to do so, but he wrote to Hinsdale and the committee and influenced them to offer amendments to the manufacturers' bill for a sixty-hour week and factory inspection.[63] The *News and Observer* also urged these changes. The manufacturers had proposed inspection by the sheriffs of the counties when their first suggestion was discountenanced, but the *News and Observer* declared that there could be no satisfactory inspection except under the Commissioner of Labor. It also advocated a sixty-hour week and no night work for women and children.[64] Both the manufacturers and the friends of the Hinsdale bill realized that the Senate was hostile to the House bill, so they agreed to a compromise arranged between the manufacturers and Hinsdale, Poe, and Daniels of the *News and Observer*. Amendments were agreed to in the House, putting the age limit for night work for girls at fifteen, reducing the hours to sixty-three a week and providing for inspection. The bill then passed and was sent to the Senate.[65]

The bill was favorably reported in the Senate on the basis of the agreement the manufacturers had made, although a minority dissented.[66] The *Observer* said that the manufacturers were divided in their views on the bill, and that the reformers could have gained more concessions had they known it.[67] It was attacked by the Association of Hard Yarn Spinners, which met in Charlotte and voted against a change in the law. The friends of the bill regarded this as a breach of faith inasmuch as the members of this group were also members of the Manufacturers' Association, which had assented to the terms of the House bill.[68] This action caused a shift in the support of the measure and it failed to pass by a vote of sixteen to twenty-three.[69]

The situation in North Carolina was such that it was one of the most difficult states in which to secure reform. The unfortunate per-

[61] N. C. L. C. Minutes, May 12, 1909, Appendix I.

[62] N. C., *Journal of the House*, 1909, p. 251.

[63] N. C. L. C. Minutes, May 12, 1909, Appendix I.

[64] Feb. 7, 1909.

[65] N. C., *Journal of the House*, 1909, pp. 290-91, 401, 420; N. C. L. C. Minutes, May 12, 1909, Appendix I; *News and Observer*, Feb. 10, 1909.

[66] N. C. L. C. Minutes, May 12, 1909, Appendix I; *News and Observer*, March 2, 1909.   [67] Feb. 17, 1909.

[68] N. C. L. C. Minutes, May 12, 1909, Appendix I.

[69] N. C., *Journal of the Senate*, 1909, pp. 560-61, 608-9; *News and Observer*, March 7, 1909.

sonal hostility of some of the manufacturers toward McKelway seriously impaired his influence in the state as long as he personally
directed the efforts for reform. The State Child Labor Committee
included men who were seriously concerned over the question of
reform, but their activity was sporadic and rather dependent on the
National Committee for direction. Its secretary, C. L. Coon, who was
one of the severest critics of the manufacturers, complained that the
committee did little, that the law was weak, and that there was no
way to enforce it.[70]

When the legislature met in 1911 the *Charlotte Observer* issued
a warning that it was an inopportune time to undertake further reform, because the market for cotton goods was demoralized and the
prices of raw material and wages were both high, while labor was
scarce. It still maintained its hostility to "the highly emotional reformers" who "make a trade of reforming things that are already in
process of accomplishment." The legislature might, however, enact
a sixty-hour law and a fourteen-year age limit for night work, and
compulsory school attendance for children in mill villages.[71]

The State Committee presented a bill which provided for a
fourteen-year age limit. Coon and Hollis, the National Committee's
agent from South Carolina, advocated it before the committee hearing,[72] and the *News and Observer* gave its editorial support. "The
milling business is not prosperous now, but that is no sufficient argument to let North Carolina be the exception to a humane child-labor
law that would protect the future hope of the State and its larger
and better milling interests."[73] The child labor bill was debated
at great length in the Senate. The speakers went into detail as to
their position on the subject and indulged in a great deal of oratory. E. R. Pace, the only trade unionist in the North Carolina legislature,[74] spoke on the side of reform.[75] He presented figures to
show the number of children employed in the state, claiming that
there were 202 under twelve, 337 twelve years old, and a total of 2,347
between the ages of seven and fifteen.[76] The speech of General Julian
S. Carr of Durham, who claimed that he controlled more labor than
any other employer in the state, is probably representative of the
attitude of many millmen, and is therefore worth noting. In a
flowery address which began with biblical allusions and ended with

[70] "North Carolina Child Labor Committee," in *Annals* Supplement, xxxv
(1910), 181.
[71] *Charlotte Observer*, Jan. 7, 1911.
[72] *News and Observer*, Feb. 5, 9, 1911.
[73] *Ibid.*, Feb. 14, 1911; also Feb. 24, March 2, 1911.
[74] A. F. of L. Weekly News Letter, April 15, 1911.
[75] *News and Observer*, Feb. 25, 1911.
[76] *Ibid.*, March 4, 1911. Pace gave itemized figures of which these are totals.

the "Man with the Hoe," he defined his attitude. His son was the manager of his mills and as such was a member of the North Carolina Manufacturers' Association. When that organization met in Raleigh the son advocated a sixty-hour week and a law prohibiting the employment of any child under thirteen and of any woman or girl or any boy under sixteen at night. His proposal was voted down, so he felt in honor bound to act in accordance with the will of the convention. While the father felt he must agree with the son, and vote accordingly in the legislature, he urged the other members to vote for the reform bill.[77] Although the child labor bill failed, a law limiting the hours of all employees to sixty a week was passed.[78]

The secretary of the North Carolina Committee urged the National Committee to appoint an agent to spend his whole time in North Carolina in an effort to create a demand for reform. McKelway, who was working almost entirely in Washington at this time, also recommended this step.[79] After considering the advisability of reassigning McKelway to work in the state for a limited time, the Board of the National Committee employed Wiley H. Swift for the year 1912.[80] The Russell Sage Foundation granted the committee $2,500 to cover the expense of this work,[81] and Swift took charge of a campaign to arouse popular interest. He sent out letters to individuals all over the state, receiving replies from more than 5,000 endorsing the bill he proposed and promising support in demanding its enactment. He interviewed two thirds of the manufacturers of the state and a large number of the legislators, and made a number of public addresses.[82] Hine, the same agent formerly employed, made an investigation of a number of mills. He reported that there had been little improvement since the last investigation, and that the idea was still prevalent among the workers that twelve years was the age limit. Not very many children were reported as working at night, however.[83]

The investigation and publicity campaign were scheduled to take place in the months just preceding the meeting of the legislature in 1913. Swift appeared before the Manufacturers' Association and urged a compromise agreement, but the manufacturers adopted resolutions declaring that the existing child labor law was just to both owners and operatives, and should not be changed. Instead they recommended a compulsory education law.[84] The *Observer* said that the

[77] *Ibid.*, Feb. 26, 1911.
[78] N. C., *Journal of the Senate*, 1911, p. 697; *Public Laws and Resolutions*, 1911, p. 253.   [79] N. C. L. C. Minutes, Dec. 6, 1911.
[80] *Ibid.*, March 11, 1912.   [81] *Ibid.*, May 1, 1912.
[82] *Ibid.*, "Brief Summary of the Work of the N. C. L. C. since Oct. 1, 1912," MS in N. C. L. C. Library.
[83] L. W. Hine, "Child Labor Conditions in North Carolina," MS in N. C. L. C. Library.   [84] *Charlotte Observer*, Jan. 1, 1913.

millmen were divided into two classes, those who wished to raise the age limit for night work to sixteen and those who opposed it. They were uneasy over the prospect of coming federal child labor legislation, since the children's bureau bill had been passed, and they were reluctant to yield to more state legislation.[85] They were no more inclined to friendliness toward the State Committee than formerly, and the *Observer* declared that the agitators so harassed the millowners in regard to reforms that it became difficult to carry on the welfare work already planned by the manufacturing companies. The mills were reluctant to yield to state inspection which the National Committee continually urged, and justified themselves by pointing to their good works in building churches and schools, with the insinuation that in so doing they had spent their money more wisely than the National Committee.[86]

The manufacturers were not united in their views on the subject of labor legislation. The association met in advance of the legislature and by a vote of sixty-seven mills to nineteen mills adopted resolutions against the passage of any further labor legislation, and demanded that if such laws were passed they should apply to all classes of labor. The editor of the *Southern Textile Bulletin* regretted that whereas in former years the manufacturers had been so strongly united that the state was one of the last to adopt a thirteen-year age limit and the very last to enact a sixty-hour law for textile mills, they were now divided among themselves, some opposing and some favoring legislation. Some wished to raise the age limit for night work to sixteen while others opposed it.[87] Wiley H. Swift, the agent of the National Committee, also found the millowners divided. There were those who recognized that reforms must come and who would enter into agreements about them; those who wanted to be considered as benefactors and were afraid of hostile public opinion; and those who wanted to be left entirely alone and who fought all legal regulation.[88] To the last class belonged John F. Schenck, the author of a pamphlet entitled *"Child Labor" Legislation,* in which he undertook to destroy the arguments of the reformers. Schenck was the head of the legislative committee of the North Carolina Manufacturers' Association, and while his views were not representative of all the members they probably stood for a fairly large proportion of them. He laid particular emphasis on the assertion that the advocates of reform were "professional and salaried agitators," quite frequently from outside the state. His principles were asserted emphatically. "IN EVERY FREE COUNTRY, EVERY PERSON ENGAGED IN A USEFUL AND PRIVATE BUSI-

[85] *Ibid.,* Jan. 2, 1913.   [86] *Ibid.,* Jan. 6, 1913.

[87] *Southern Textile Bulletin,* Jan. 2, 1913.

[88] Swift, "The Campaign in North Carolina. The Mountain Whites—by One of Them," in *Child Labor Bulletin,* II (May, 1913), 97.

NESS SHOULD BE ALLOWED, IN THE CONDUCT OF THAT BUSINESS, THE
BROADEST LIBERTY CONSISTENT WITH THE PUBLIC GOOD." His definition
of useful business was "that kind which is doing more good than
harm." Second, "legislative meddling, applicable to a whole class,
CANNOT BE JUSTIFIED UPON THE STRENGTH OF A FEW ISOLATED CASES
OF WRONG." "Artificial coercion" to prevent parents from hiring
out children was "a cruel indignity" to an "honorable industrial"
class. Finally, "LABOR LEGISLATION IS CLASS LEGISLATION, AND IF PER-
SISTED IN WILL ULTIMATELY RESULT IN HATRED BETWEEN EMPLOYER AND
EMPLOYEE."[89]

Child labor reform attracted considerable attention throughout
the state in 1913. The Asheville *Citizen,* representing a section outside the manufacturing area, and the *News and Observer* were strong
in support of reform.[90]   The Ministers' Union of Winston-Salem
adopted resolutions favoring a minimum six-month school term for
the state; prohibition of night work for children under sixteen, and
for women; a fourteen-year age limit for day work; and adequate
inspection.[91] The State Committee also had the backing of the wom-
en's organizations, the Farmers' Union, the Junior Order of American Mechanics, and the State Conference for Social Service.[92]   The
bill which was introduced on January 22, 1913, by R. R. Williams of
Buncombe County[93] did not aspire to the standard demanded by the
Winston-Salem ministers. Its terms were much more moderate. It
retained the thirteen-year age limit and the apprenticeship provision
for children between twelve and thirteen; it provided that no person
under sixteen and no woman should work in a factory or mill between 7:00 P.M. and 6:00 A.M.; it required the use of a system of employment certificates issued by school authorities, and if possible based
on documentary proof of age; a board of child labor commissioners
should be formed and an inspector with real powers appointed.[94]

The provision for inspection was the one most objected to by the
manufacturers. Some of them, of the group Schenck represented,
resented it as a reflection on the honesty of the manufacturers.[95] Other
manufacturers had attained a broader view. Julian S. Carr, Jr., who
had on an earlier occasion found himself divided between his personal
beliefs and a feeling of loyalty to the Manufacturers' Association,
appeared before the legislative committee in behalf of the proposed
reform. He declared that inspection would be an advantage for both
the women and children and the mill corporations. He disagreed

[89] John F. Schenck, *"Child Labor" Legislation,* 1913, pp. 1-20. Capitals are
Schenck's.   [90] *News and Observer,* Jan. 15, 1913.
[91] *Ibid.,* Jan. 21, 1913. Neal L. Anderson was at that time pastor of a church in
Winston-Salem.   [92] Swift, *op. cit.,* p. 98.
[93] N. C., *Journal of the House,* 1913, p. 60.
[94] *News and Observer,* Jan. 23, 1913.   [95] *Ibid.,* Jan. 26, Feb. 7, 1913.

with the "unfortunate and unwise and intemperate statements" of Schenck's circular, because Schenck had based his arguments on the assumption that the effort to end night work for women and children was the result of outside influences. Carr championed the State Committee, giving the names of its members in proof that the charges of discreditable motives imputed to them were not true.[96]

The editor of the *News and Observer* replied to those who disparaged the reform movement because of its association with the National Committee. The North Carolina Committee, he said, was affiliated with the National Committee, which was not a northern institution. It had seven hundred and seventy-one contributing members in the South, and therefore North Carolina had a right to call on it for aid in a local contest, just as did any other state.[97] Neal L. Anderson, who had continued to associate himself with the National Committee even though he disagreed strongly with its policy in certain matters, came to its defense through the columns of the *News and Observer,* pointing out the southern men whose names were prominent on the National Committee's roll. To charge them with being under northern influence was absurd. "Hon. B. R. Tillman has been accused of many things by his enemies, but the veteran senator from South Carolina has never before been accused of being friendly to the interests of New England."[98]

The House Committee on Manufactures and Labor reported a substitute for the original bill.[99] It was made the subject of a long debate, and passed only after some of the amendments desired by the most reactionary manufacturers were adopted. The provision for a state inspector was eliminated and the duty of enforcing the law placed on the county school superintendents. The hour after which night work was prohibited for women and boys was made nine instead of seven.[100] The manufacturers were disappointed that the provision for prohibiting night work had been allowed to stand. From their viewpoint it was considered that the elimination of women and children from all night employment would mean that the mills running at night would have to cease to do so, since a large proportion of operatives would be forbidden that employment. This would reduce the output of the mills, many of which had not sufficient capital to increase the size of their plant or the amount of machinery. It would

[96] *Ibid.,* Feb. 9, 1913. The men named by Carr as members of the North Carolina Child Labor Committee were Bishop Strain, Bishop Cheshire, Dr. Foust of the State College for Women, W. A. Erwin, Caesar Cone, Frank Borden, D. Y. Cooper, Will Williams, Eugene Holt, Clarence Poe, and W. H. Swift. Some of these were manufacturers.

[97] *Ibid.,* Feb. 11, 1913.   [98] *Ibid.,* Feb. 13, 1913.
[99] N. C., *Journal of the House,* 1913, p. 268.
[100] *Ibid.,* pp. 440-41; *News and Observer,* Feb. 20, 1913.

also mean that the women and children thrown out of employment would have no means of support.[101] For this condition the agitators from outside the state were held responsible. They had conducted a one-sided campaign throughout the preceding year, in which the mill-men had done nothing. The legislators were charged with holding the mill interests in contempt. Unlike David Clark, the editor of the *Southern Textile Bulletin,* who always assumed that the dictates of the mill association would be followed by the state assembly in matters of labor legislation, the *Observer* lamented that the "outspoken oppo-sition equally of managers and employees hardly weighs with them at all."[102] The responsibility for this was on the selfish manufacturers, who did not run their mills at night, and who believed that to shut their competitors out of night work would glut the market with cheap labor and promote their profit.[103]

In spite of the appeals from the *Observer* the Senate passed the House's child labor bill.[104] The law was substantially the same as the amended bill sent up from the lower house. It required certificates only for children under thirteen who worked as apprentices, to prove that they were at least twelve and had attended school four months in the preceding year.[105] A law was passed requiring children between the ages of eight and twelve to attend school four months during each year. This law applied to the whole state, but children were exempt from its provisions if it was necessary for them to work for their own or their parents' support.[106]

In spite of its efforts the National Committee did not accomplish much more in the way of legislation than the majority of manufac-turers were willing to allow—certainly no more than the more pro-gressive ones admitted as desirable. The very nature of the committee and its work, as it appeared to the manufacturers, set up a barrier against the standards it advocated. The commissioner of labor of North Carolina in 1914 summed up the situation when he said, "I am constrained to believe that so long as the lack of confidence between the advocates of restrictive and corrective measures and the manufac-turers continue to exist, there is small hope for either side of the controversy bringing in a satisfactory bill. As it appears to this Department, it is too much a game of hare and hounds, and the time has come for some member of the General Assembly, who is an inde-pendent thinker, and one who has the courage of his convictions, to draft a bill that will take care of the situation."[107]

---

[101] *Charlotte Observer,* Feb. 21, 1913.   [102] Feb. 23, 1913.
[103] *Charlotte Observer,* Feb. 27, 1913.
[104] N. C., *Journal of the Senate,* 1913, pp. 632, 650.
[105] N. C., *Public Laws and Resolutions,* 1913, pp. 110-11.
[106] *Ibid.,* p. 267.
[107] N. C. Dept. of Labor, *Twenty-eighth Annual Report,* p. 4.

Between 1913 and 1915 the National Committee continued to make investigations of the North Carolina mills. It still found the owners antagonistic and its agents believed children were employed in violation of the law. Since the mills were not running full time and school was in session when the visits were made, fewer children were found than would have otherwise been the case, for the workers felt that the law did not apply when school was not in session. The amount of night work had decreased.[108] The figures of the reports of the Department of Labor for 1914 showed that 296 cotton mills in North Carolina reported a total of almost 59,000 operatives, almost 8,000, or 14 per cent, of whom were children.[109] The figures did not indicate what age group was included in this calculation.

Swift again worked to promote popular demand for reform before the new session of the legislature convened. He sent a questionnaire to three hundred and forty-nine physicians of the state, asking their opinion as to the age at which children could be employed with proper regard for their physical well-being. Three hundred and thirty-eight responded, of whom two thirds advocated a fourteen-year age limit, while a still larger number expressed the opinion that children under sixteen should be limited to working eight hours a day.[110] Evidence of a more widespread general interest in the problem of child labor reform by legislation is seen in the statement issued by the University of North Carolina Bureau of Extension, in which the principal arguments in favor of such legislation and the more reasonable ones against it were stated.[111] The feeling against the National Committee had been kept alive and active by David Clark, who made the editorial columns of the *Southern Textile Bulletin* a medium for attack on the committee in general and McKelway in particular. Feeling among the manufacturers was especially keen at the time the 1915 legislature convened, because the National Congress was at the same time engaged in discussion of the proposed federal child labor law. When the National Committee held its annual conference in Washington early in January, 1915, Clark went before the meeting and demanded what he called a "square deal" for the manufacturers. This aroused comment and interest over the whole state.[112]

The governor, Locke Craig, in his message to the legislature, strongly advocated child labor reform for the sake of the physical

[108] L. W. Hine, "Some Visits to North Carolina Mills—Photographic Investigation," Nov., 1914; and "Summary of 2 Visits to North Carolina, November, 1914 and April, 1915."—MSS in N. C. L. C. Library.

[109] N. C. Dept. of Labor, *Twenty-eighth Annual Report*, p. 115. The workers from nine mills were not classified.

[110] *News and Observer*, Jan. 12, 1915.

[111] *Ibid.*, Jan. 16, 1915.

[112] *Southern Textile Bulletin*, Jan. 7, 14, 21, 1914.

well-being of the child, the enforcement of compulsory school attendance, and the prohibiting of women and children from working at night.[113]   A bill was introduced in the Senate at the beginning of the session, coming again from a member from Buncombe County.[114] It was an "answer to the demand for a child labor bill with teeth," said the *News and Observer*. "The teeth, to be specific, are the Commissioner of Labor and Printing and two factory inspectors." It also proposed a fourteen-year age limit and a system of certificates.[115] Although not coming entirely up to their standard, the bill was approved by the National Committee representatives.[116]   The Federation of Women's Clubs, which in 1913 had supported child labor and education reforms, announced that it would not undertake any legislation in 1915.[117]   The North Carolina Conference for Social Service, of which Clarence Poe was president, adopted resolutions endorsing the fourteen-year age limit as well as a number of other social reform measures.[118]   The third annual meeting of this body was held in January while the child labor bill was under consideration by the Senate Committee on Manufactures.[119]

The manufacturers, not to be forced into more concessions than they could avoid, put an exhibit of welfare work in the mills on display at the public library in Raleigh.[120] While the millmen did not make an outward appearance of serious opposition to the Weaver bill, their influence against it was felt.   The *Observer* prophesied that the agitation for reform would fall through in the 1915 legislature, for several reasons.   "One is the accepted fact that the mill men, on account of the situation growing out of war conditions, have had more than their share of troubles to carry and solve and that they are entitled to a rest.   Another is that there is no demand for a change in existing laws from either the people employed in the mills, or from the owners of the mills—that conditions are satisfactory to all interested except the labor agitators."[121]

The *News and Observer* kept up a steady stream of editorials and articles advocating the proposed legislation during all the time the bill was under consideration.[122] The bill had come from Buncombe County and received support from that quarter.   Gallatin Roberts said the Democratic caucus in his district was in favor of the proposed reform, which he also endorsed.   The party could

[113] *Biennial Message*, p. 9.
[114] N. C., *Journal of the Senate*, 1915, p. 50.
[115] Jan. 16, 1915.   [116] *Ibid.*
[117] *News and Observer*, Jan. 17, 1915.
[118] *Ibid.*, Jan. 24, 1915.   [119] *Ibid.*, Jan. 29, 1915.
[120] *Charlotte Observer*, Jan. 11, 1915; *News and Observer*, Jan. 24, 1915.
[121] *Charlotte Observer*, Jan. 30, 1915.
[122] Feb. 4, 5, 7, 11, 13, 15, 16, 20, 27, 1915.

not be injured by the bill and it would probably need the labor vote in the next election.[123]

At the hearing of the bill before the committee, Swift, McKelway, and Dr. W. L. Poteat, president of Wake Forest College, spoke in its behalf.[124] The bill was not given a favorable report, but it was discussed by the Senate, and a substitute was offered. The substitute failed, and the bill was tabled.[125] When it became apparent that the Weaver bill would fail, the Governor tried to save the situation by appealing to the manufacturers to frame an inspection law to which they could agree,[126] but nothing came of the effort. The child labor bill was dead for another session and the *Observer* rejoiced in its defeat. It now stood on the principle that the millmen did not oppose inspection through an unprejudiced system, but they considered the plan offered by the reformers as dangerous because it would attempt to regulate the problem through state organization and supervision. The millmen, said the *Observer,* would probably now propose a system of their own which would prove satisfactory, but they would not do so under compulsion.[127]

The North Carolina legislature in 1915 enacted a sixty-hour-week law for factories, which forbade the employment of women and minors for more than eleven hours a day or sixty a week, and required the payment of overtime to men who worked longer. Persons who hired children to the mills were required to make a written statement of the age and school attendance of the child.[128]

The enactment of the first federal child labor law changed the situation of the states somewhat in regard to legislation. If the state laws were made to conform to the standards of the national law and proper enforcement machinery was provided, then the new national act would call for a minimum of interference in state affairs. The National Committee and the Children's Bureau, realizing that enforcement of the law would be easier if the state requirements for proof of age were uniform, recommended the embodiment of the rules agreed on by the Department of Labor in state legislation.[129] In the report of the Department of Labor of North Carolina for 1916, Commissioner Shipman recommended that the state amend its law to conform to national standards, and thus relieve a situation which was responsible for a great part of the child labor of the state by stopping

[123] *News and Observer,* Feb. 19, 1915.   [124] *Ibid.,* Feb. 4, 1915.
[125] N. C., *Journal of the Senate,* 1915, pp. 169, 495, 496; *News and Observer,* Feb. 28, 1915.
[126] *Charlotte Observer,* Feb. 24, 1915.   [127] March 1, 1915.
[178] *Public Laws and Resolutions of the General Assembly,* 1915, pp. 232-33.
[129] McKelway to Lovejoy, Sept. 1, 1917, McKelway Papers; McKelway to editor of *Survey,* no date, McKelway Papers.

parents "from shopping among mills for jobs which will employ the greatest number of these children."[130]

The feeling of the manufacturers toward the National Committee was in no way improved by the passage of a federal law which the mills opposed. The mills had succeeded in completely defeating the attempts of the committee to secure reform in 1915, and the reports of the committee's agents and of Charles L. Coon of the State Committee declared that the old law was being violated.[131]

The North Carolina manufacturers were not ready to yield to a state inspection law even under the impending federal law which was to go into effect September 1, 1917. Charlotte was the center of opposition to federal legislation and the first child labor act was no sooner passed than some of the millmen determined to carry a test case through the courts.[132] Feeling that there was a fair chance that the law might be declared unconstitutional, the mill operators were unwilling to bind themselves by a state law for inspection which would stand even though the national law were made void. A meeting, the proceedings of which were kept secret, was held by the Cotton Manufacturers' Association on January 18, 1917. It was reported as going on record in favor of a compulsory school attendance law for children under fourteen. Individual members outside the meeting expressed opposition to legislation that would make the state law coincide with the federal law in providing inspection.[133]

There was an increased interest in social problems in the state which led to the creation of a Board of Charities and Public Welfare. This measure had the approval of the official Baptist, Methodist, and Presbyterian church bodies, the State Sunday School Association, and the women's clubs.[134] The bill was delayed somewhat in the Senate but was passed early in February.[135] It went through the House with little difficulty and became a law.[136] The child labor bills were not so fortunate. Knowing that the federal child labor law which had passed in 1916 would go into effect in a few months, M. L. Shipman, commissioner of labor and printing, announced to the General Assembly through the Governor that he had come to an

[130] N. C. Dept. of Labor, *Thirteenth Annual Report*, 1916, p. 3.

[131] L. W. Hine, "North Carolina Report," and Horace Stacy, "Statement and Affidavit that L. W. Hine's Statements Were True About Lumberton, N. C.," relate to an incident reported by Hine which was disputed by the *Southern Textile Bulletin;* also, C. L. Coon, "Do Children Work in Our Factories?"—MSS in N. C. L. C. Library.

[132] *News and Observer,* Jan. 19, 1917.

[133] *Southern Textile Bulletin,* Sept. 21, 1916.

[134] *Charlotte Observer,* Feb. 4, 1917; N. C., *Journal of the Senate,* 1917, p. 183.

[135] N. C., *Journal of the Senate,* 1917, pp. 220, 271, 280.

[136] N. C., *Journal of the House,* 1917, pp. 344, 425, 489; N. C., *Acts of General Assembly,* 1917, pp. 320 ff.

understanding with the federal authorities in charge of the administration of the new law, so that if the state passed an act which would
provide for enforcement of federal standards it would be allowed to
"manage its affairs without Federal interference."   State officials
could enforce the law and their reports would be accepted by the
federal government officials.[137] The legislature did not consider this
proposal, however. A measure to regulate the employment of children
as delivery agents by telegraph and telephone companies was given
an unfavorable report.[138]   A bill to regulate the hours of employment of females and minors in mercantile establishments was
tabled.[139]

In spite of the refusal of the North Carolina legislature to pass
laws corresponding in standards to the federal acts, the feeling of
many people was undergoing a decided change and it was becoming
obvious that the state could not much longer cling to the old standards regarding child labor which its neighbors were discarding for
more progressive forms of regulation.   The State Conference for
Social Service, which had for the few years of its existence been
recommending progressive social legislation, asked the co-operation
of the National Child Labor Committee in making a study of the
industrial, educational, and family conditions in the state which
affected the exploitation of children.   The names of members of the
state commission were such as to command the respect of the state,
for they included President E. K. Graham of the University of North
Carolina, President Julian I. Foust of the North Carolina College
for Women, J. Y. Joyner, state superintendent of public instruction,
and A. W. McAlister, president of the Southern Life and Trust Company.[140]   The study made under Wiley H. Swift's direction was published by the National Committee.[141]

Inspections made by the Department of Labor under the first federal child labor law resulted in the report that North Carolina standards were lower and the opposition to the federal law more general
than in the neighboring states.   No inspections were attempted by
federal officials in the Western District of North Carolina because the
federal judge there had issued an injunction against the enforcement
of the law pending the hearing of the test case before the Supreme
Court.   In the eastern section where over a hundred cotton, hosiery
and knitting mills, and tobacco stemmeries were investigated, it was
found that ninety-five children under fourteen were at work and one
hundred and forty-four children between fourteen and sixteen were
working more than eight hours a day.   Of these only twelve under

[137] Thomas Walter Bickett, *Public Letters and Papers*, pp. 18-19.
[138] N. C., *Journal of the Senate*, 1917, p. 185.
[139] *Ibid.*, pp. 355, 500, 556.
[140] N. C. L. C. Minutes, Sept. 30, 1917.   [141] *Child Welfare in North Carolina.*

fourteen were working in cotton mills, and forty-one under sixteen were working overtime there. The violations were more frequent in hosiery mills.[142]

The manufacturers also revised their opinions on the desirability of state legislation. After having succeeded in nullifying the first federal child labor law, the North Carolina Manufacturers' Association in 1918 adopted resolutions asking the legislature to enact a law forbidding employment under fourteen years of age. The *Southern Textile Bulletin* explained this stand on the grounds that the other states now had the fourteen-year minimum and for North Carolina to fail to conform to it would merely give ammunition to the advocates of federal legislation. It was still considered desirable to allow the employment of boys from twelve to fourteen during vacation.[143]

Having agreed on the advisability of a fourteen-year age limit, the manufacturers were divided as to the proper machinery to adopt for inspection and enforcement. M. L. Shipman, commissioner of labor, advocated the erection of a new commission composed of the state superintendent of education, the secretary of the board of health, and the commissioner of labor and printing, which should serve without pay, and an appropriation of six thousand dollars for inspection under the direction of the commissioner of labor and printing.[144] Shipman was distrusted by the manufacturers, according to the *Textile Bulletin,* which said that they regarded him as an unsuitable person to be put in charge of inspection, and felt that his efforts to secure an inspection law were for personal gain. They did not, however, agree with Edgar Love, the president of the Saxony Spinning Company and representative from Lumberton, who introduced a bill for the abolition of the Department of Labor.[145] Love was said to oppose the fourteen-year age limit and was therefore out of line with the new policy of the Manufacturers' Association.[146] The chief grievance of the mill interests against Shipman was his friendliness toward the National Committee. "It has never been charged directly against Commissioner Shipman, but at the same time it has been the understanding that he has been too much under influences of the National Child Labor Committee for the promotion of community textile welfare, and that his tendencies toward labor agitation continually threaten disruption of the cordial relations which have been maintained between labor and capital in this State, to make himself a desirable administrator of the law."[147]

[142] Children's Bureau, *Bulletin No. 78,* pp. 70-71.
[143] *Southern Textile Bulletin,* July 11, 1918.
[144] *News and Observer,* Jan. 26, 1919.
[145] N. C., *Journal of the House,* 1919, p. 85.
[146] *Southern Textile Bulletin,* Jan. 30, 1919; also *News and Observer,* Feb. 2, 1919.   [147] *Charlotte Observer,* Mar. 9, 1919.

The selection of an authority to enforce the law was the principal point of debate. There were two bills introduced. The Connor bill in the Senate provided for inspection under the direction of the Labor Commissioner.[148] The Neal bill in the House was approved by the manufacturers. It was introduced February 3, 1919, and was referred to the Committee on Manufacturing and Labor. This committee offered a substitute, which was referred to the Committee on Education.[149] The Neal bill differed from the Connor bill in that it proposed a child labor commission composed of the governor, state superintendent of education, secretary of state, and secretary of the board of health, omitting the labor commissioner.[150] The substitute bill, which included compulsory education provisions as well as the regulation of child labor, was passed in the House late in February, and sent to the Senate, only to be recalled and considered again.[151] On its return to the Senate another substitute was offered proposing to put the administration in the hands of the Commissioner of Labor rather than the Commissioner of Public Welfare, but the bill passed as it had come from the House.[152]

The new act was approved by the *Charlotte Observer* chiefly because it would give future legislatures "immunity from the nagging influences of the New England organization."[153] It combined compulsory school attendance with child labor regulation, an arrangement which many manufacturers had claimed to advocate for several years, and which Governor Thomas W. Bickett had recommended in his message to the Assembly.[154] Parents or guardians were required to send children between the ages of eight and fourteen to school for the entire term, except under certain conditions of distance, poverty, and mental or physical deficiency. Child labor restrictions and compulsory school attendance had not been combined in the same act before, but on two previous occasions, in 1907 and 1913, the standards for both had been advanced at the same time. The employment of children under fourteen was forbidden in any mill, factory, cannery, workshop, manufacturing establishment, laundry, bakery, mercantile establishment, office, hotel, restaurant, barber shop, bootblack stand, or messenger or delivery service, public stable, garage, place of amusement, brick yard or lumber yard. Children under sixteen should not be employed between 9:00 P.M. and 6:00 A.M., nor should they work in mines or quarries. The State Child Welfare Commission,

---

[148] N. C., *Journal of the Senate*, 1919, p. 106; *Charlotte Observer*, Feb. 21, 1919.

[149] N. C., *Journal of the House*, 1919, pp. 123, 214, 278.

[150] *Charlotte Observer*, Feb. 7, 1919.

[151] N. C., *Journal of the House*, 1919, pp. 374, 454, 616.

[152] N. C., *Journal of the Senate*, 1919, pp. 536, 539, 540; *Charlotte Observer*, March 8, 9, 1919.

[153] Feb. 7, 1919.   [154] *Op. cit.*, p. 30.

whose duty it was to enforce child labor laws, should be composed of the state superintendent of public instruction, the secretary of state, the secretary of the board of health, and the commissioner of public welfare. The services of the members should be without compensation. The agents appointed by this commission were to inspect places where employment was forbidden to children. A certificate in the hands of the employer showing that the child was of legal age should be prima facie evidence that the employer was acting in good faith regarding the law.[155]

The manufacturers succeeded by this law in eliminating the labor commissioner from any part in the child welfare administration. This was a disappointment to the State Federation of Labor, which favored the Connor bill, and urged in the summer of 1919 that it be passed at the next session of the legislature.[156] In his departmental report for 1920, Shipman also pointed out that the new law fell short of federal standards, and that in consequence the state officials were "playing 'second fiddle'" to the United States inspectors.[157]

The new Child Welfare Commission chose E. F. Carter as its executive secretary in charge of the administration of the law, and the work of the commission was organized at once. There were certain exceptions to the law allowed at the discretion of the commission. It formulated rules allowing boys between twelve and fourteen to be employed in certain occupations when school was not in session and on Saturdays and outside of school hours, if it did not interfere with their school work. The law was interpreted as not affecting agriculture and domestic service, or the employment of children in places owned and operated by their parents, except during the prohibited hours. The commission adopted a system of certification for the ages of all children employed. Documentary proof of age was required, or if it was impossible to obtain, a physician's certificate as to the physical age of the child. The commission had the same task that appeared in other states when a child labor law of higher standards was adopted, that is, of educating public opinion up to the necessity for enforcement. In 1920 the officers made almost 4,000 inspections and found 738 violations of the law in all types of industry, in which the mercantile establishments and messenger and delivery service were the greatest offenders. Almost 300 prosecutions were instituted under the school attendance and six under the child labor laws.[158] The

---

[155] N. C., *Acts of the General Assembly*, 1919, pp. 273-76.

[156] *Proceedings*, Thirteenth Annual Convention, 1919, p. 49.

[157] N. C. Dept. of Labor, *Thirty-second Annual Report*, p. 5.

[158] N. C. State Board of Charities and Public Welfare, *Biennial Report*, 1919-20, pp. 76-77, 80-81, 90-92; E. F. Carter, "Operation of the Child Labor Law," in *Proceedings*, Eighth Annual Convention of Association of Government Labor Officials, 1921, p. 73.

second federal child labor law was in force at this time. The mill-men were committed to the support of the commission and its work. The Law of 1919 had been passed with their approval and they regarded it as peculiarly their own. They had yielded none of their hostility to and distrust of federal legislation and inspection.[159]

Conditions in the state had shown marked improvement in the few years since the first federal law had been passed, although the requirements of the state for night work and hours were still low in comparison with the large majority of other states.[160] The law so far as the millmen were concerned was being well observed. After a visit to over a hundred factories, a majority of which were cotton mills, in 1922, an agent of the National Committee wrote that the factory men were trying to observe the law, for "the Federal law has put 'the fear of God' in the hearts of many of the mill men." One of the large tobacco companies was among the worst offenders.[161] The textile industry still employed more children between fourteen and sixteen than all other occupations except agriculture and domes-tic service, as might be expected because of the importance of the industry, but the violations were few.[162]

While the observance of the child labor law had improved, the standards were yet low, and further changes were urged by the more progressive people. In an article published in 1923 in the *Journal of Social Forces,* which had just begun to appear from the University of North Carolina Press, Wiley H. Swift pointed out the defects of the law. Children should be required to go to school until they were sixteen years of age or until they had completed the seventh grade and were legally employed. They should not be employed after 6:00 P.M. They should be excluded from hazardous occupations. The sale of newspapers and other street trades should be regulated.[163] The general sentiment of the state was strongly against federal child labor legislation and the proposed constitutional amendment, but the same special session of the legislature which overwhelmingly rejected the amendment passed a law removing the exceptions clause which allowed boys under fourteen to work in textile mills, canneries, and workshops during vacation.[164] Provisions to prevent the employment of children under sixteen who were physically unfit, or in occupations dangerous or injurious to health or morals were also adopted.[165]

[159] *Southern Textile Bulletin,* Oct. 6, 1921.

[160] N. C. Dept. of Labor, *Thirty-fourth Annual Report,* 1924, p. 10.

[161] W. W. Armantrout, "Report on Child Labor in North Carolina Factories," Sept., 1922, MS in N. C. L. C. Library.

[162] N. C. Child Welfare Commission, *Biennial Report,* 1924-26, p. 50.

[163] "Child Labor in North Carolina, 1912-1922," I (1923), 254-55.

[164] N. C., *Journal of the House,* Extra Session, 1924, p. 192; *Journal of the Senate,* 1924, p. 53.

[165] N. C., *Public Laws and Resolutions,* Extra Session, 1924, p. 129.

In 1927 another reform was added when the Assembly enacted a law that no child under sixteen should be employed more than eight hours a day or forty-eight hours a week unless he had completed the fourth grade in school.[166] This provision was so weak as to be of practically no value.

In 1931 the duties of the Child Welfare Commission were transferred to the Department of Labor. At the same time the law was revised so as to set a fourteen-year age limit for both boys and girls for factory and mercantile occupations and a sixteen-year limit for girls in street trades. Newspaper delivery and similar occupations for boys were carefully restricted and the hours during which children might work at night were defined. All children under sixteen were restricted to eight hours a day, forty-eight hours a week, and six days a week, except boys over fourteen who were the "sole support" of themselves or of widowed mothers. A well-defined system of certification was also provided.[167]

In 1937 a new law was enacted, embodying still more advanced provisions. It set the general age limit for gainful employment at sixteen. Exceptions were made to permit children of fourteen and over to work outside school hours and during vacations in certain restricted types of employment. Boys of twelve might also engage in selling papers and periodicals, and other street trades. Children under sixteen were limited to a forty-hour week and six-day week, and eight hours a day, and were prohibited from working at night. Minors from sixteen to eighteen should not work more than forty-eight hours a week or nine hours a day, or for more than six days a week, or after midnight. There were certain minor exceptions. No girls under eighteen were permitted to work at night in factories. Careful provision for employment certificates, inspection of all types of industries, and enforcement of the law were made. While the NRA codes were in effect, children under sixteen were not allowed to have full-time employment. This resulted in an increase in the number of boys engaged in selling papers and other street trades. When the NRA restrictions were abolished, the majority of employers maintained the standards of the codes, but others began to employ children of fourteen and fifteen in full-time work. The Law of 1937 has checked such employment, however. Thus at last the textile manufacturers have ceased to be important as employers of child labor in North Carolina.[168]

[166] N. C., *Journal of the Senate*, 1927, pp. 323, 435, 568, 569, 595; *Journal of the House*, 1927, pp. 761, 857; *Public Laws and Resolutions*, 1927, pp. 618-19; *News and Observer*, Mar. 9, 1927.
[167] N. C. Dept. of Labor, *Child Labor Rules and Regulations*, 1936 (pamphlet).
[168] *Ibid.*, *Biennial Report*, 1936, pp. 36, 44.

CHAPTER IX

SOUTH CAROLINA AFTER 1904: EDUCATION
AND CHILD LABOR

SOUTH CAROLINA adopted a child labor law in 1903, but the labor problem of limiting hours and the educational problem of compulsory school attendance which were so closely associated with it had not been acted upon. The ten-hour-day bill again appeared in 1904, introduced by Representative G. L. Toole of Aiken County. The debate in the House reflected the same line of arguments that had been used in former years. To the opposition all labor legislation was bad and hard times made a change impracticable.[1] This bill failed in 1904 only to reappear in 1905.[2] On February 3 Toole presented a petition in favor of the bill signed by over 1,200 "voters and taxpayers" who begged the legislature, "for God's sake think of the thousands of women and little children of South Carolina who come and go from their work in the night time."[3] The opposition met this challenge a few days later by bringing in petitions from the workers in mills in Anderson, Spartanburg, Pelzer, Piedmont, and Greenville, signed by about 3,000 names, declaring, "We are not overworked, and are satisfied, and only ask to be let alone."[4] *The State*, in an editorial which appeared two days later, commented on the petition from Pelzer as being silent testimony in behalf of the need for an education act. Pelzer was considered one of the show mills of the state, yet 154 operatives who signed the petition made their marks —a pitiful record, said *The State*, to hand down to posterity in the same book in which it was recorded that the state was denied the right to require its citizens to become intelligent.[5] The labor bill was defeated again.[6]

[1] S. C., *Journal of the House*, 1904, pp. 211, 323; *State*, Feb. 3, 1904. Toole was a farmer-lawyer who took a keen interest in the cotton mill population of his section. See Snowden, *op. cit.*, v, 190-91.

[2] S. C., *Journal of the House*, 1905, p. 17.

[3] *Ibid.*, pp. 336-43.

[4] *Ibid.*, pp. 407-22. They were presented through Josh Ashley, who had himself presented one of the first bills to reduce hours of labor in 1892. Ashley was a Tillmanite.   [5] Feb. 9, 1905.

[6] S. C., *Journal of the House*, 1905, p. 476; *State*, Feb. 10, 1905.

In 1905 the South Carolina Child Labor Committee was formed[7] and W. H. Mills, a Presbyterian clergyman, was selected as its secretary. He conferred with McKelway and arranged to conduct a campaign during the legislative session of 1906.[8] The demands which the State Committee expected to make were for a factory inspector, shorter hours for children, the elimination of the exception clause for children of widows and indigent fathers, and the raising of the age limit for girls to fourteen years. These plans reflected McKelway's influence and were similar to the demands which had been defeated in North Carolina.[9]

When the legislature met in 1906 the ten-hour bill continued to overshadow in importance other labor reforms. Both friends and opponents of the bill swamped the House with petitions, though the opposition outnumbered the friends of the bill.[10] In the discussion in committee, Smyth of Pelzer opposed the ten-hour bill on the ground that it was labor legislation introduced by men from Aiken, a district that was disaffected because of its nearness to Augusta, Georgia, where labor unions had a stronger hold than in most cotton mill sections of the South. Lewis Parker of Greenville also opposed the labor bill. Mills, the State Child Labor Committee's secretary, and Walker, a labor union man from Graniteville, urged the passage of the bill.[11] Smyth also opposed the compulsory school law for mill children under fourteen and the prohibiting of employment of children more than ten hours a day, also asked for by the Aiken delegation.[12] Millmen objected to the ten-hour provision because it would limit the entire mill to ten hours a day; and to the compulsory school feature because it was class legislation. "Why not be brave enough to give us what we have asked for, and that is a compulsory school law for all children between 8 and 12 years of age in South Carolina."[13] *The State* made a similar criticism of the educational feature of the child labor bill Mills advocated. "The fault we find with his position is that, being absorbed in the question of labor and laboring children, his educational provision would be class legislation, to the extent that his bill considered only the factory children. The State is a hearty advocate of the law excluding children from the factories. We wish to see that law rigidly enforced; we have no doubt there are frequent violations, but we believe a

[7] N. C. L. C. Minutes, March 23, April 27, 1905.

[8] *Ibid.*, Nov. 16, 1905; also Appendix B.

[9] *Ibid.*

[10] S. C., *Journal of the House*, 1906, pp. 103-4, 131, 133-44, 204, 263, 266, 268, 346-47.

[11] *News and Courier*, Jan. 18, 1906; *State*, Jan. 18, 1906.

[12] S. C., *Journal of the House*, 1906, pp. 59, 150.

[13] *State*, Jan. 19, 1906.

compulsory education law will aid materially in making enforceable the child labor law."[14]

McKelway declared that this attitude on the part of the manufacturers was merely a way for opposing child labor legislation. The millmen realized that compulsory education would be slow in coming because of the Negro problem, and by demanding that an education bill be passed first so as to keep the children out of trouble and off the streets, child labor reform could be postponed indefinitely. As proof of this viewpoint he pointed out a few years later that the compulsory school attendance law was defeated except when it was known that Governor Cole L. Blease would veto it.[15] Both Tillman and Blease were known to oppose compulsory school attendance laws because of their unwillingness to force Negro children to attend school.

The ten-hour bill was debated in the House and again defeated on February 8, 1906.[16] *The State,* sympathizing with the manufacturers' demand for a compulsory school law, expressed the hope that they would take concerted action in the next year to bring about the passage of such a law and thus establish an ideal condition. "With compulsory education and the child labor law enforced, the people of the State can well afford to leave, for a term of years at least, the mills and the operatives to manage their own affairs."[17]

The ten-hour bill was again one of the first to appear in the legislature of 1907, originating this time in the Senate.[18] A similar bill was introduced in the House.[19] On the same day a bill to compel children to attend school twelve weeks a year was introduced in the Senate,[20] and in the House on the day following there appeared a bill to regulate the employment of children, and another to prohibit employment of children under fourteen during the school term unless they were able to read and write.[21]

Hearings on the flood of labor bills attracted attention in Columbia, and mill presidents, cotton mill operatives, and university students came to hear the discussion. The position taken by either side had not changed from that of the previous years. Lewis Parker and Ellison Smyth declared themselves for compulsory education while opposing the ten-hour and child labor laws. The Aiken representatives who were always strong in support of labor legislation

[14] Feb. 5, 1906.
[15] "McKelway's Account," McKelway Papers.
[16] S. C., *Journal of the House,* 1906, p. 606; *State,* Feb. 8, 9, 1906.
[17] Feb. 9, 1906.
[18] S. C., *Journal of the Senate,* 1907, p. 37.
[19] S. C., *Journal of the House,* 1907, p. 37.
[20] S. C., *Journal of the Senate,* 1907, p. 37.
[21] S. C., *Journal of the House,* 1907, p. 43.

declared that compulsory education was no substitute for a child labor law.[22] *The State* adhered to the side of the manufacturers, saying that so far as the child labor law was concerned there was no "necessity or good reason for a change," and that it was useless to provide factory inspection when the inspectors could remedy only the most flagrant cases under existing conditions. "And when gentlemen in political life shower bills upon the legislature to keep children out of factories, and stoutly contend against the 'hardship' and 'iniquity' of a law to force children into school, it appears to us that their sympathy, humanity, and statesmanship are grievously lop-sided. They would run with the hare and hold with the hound."[23]

Mills, the secretary of the State Child Labor Committee, was chiefly interested in reducing the hours of labor, and because of the criticism directed against child labor reform he disbanded his committee and undertook to make a compromise with the manufacturers independently to reduce hours gradually to sixty a week.[24]

Action on the several bills was taken soon after the hearings. Instead of immediate reduction to sixty hours a week it was agreed to continue on the existing basis until January 1, 1907; to reduce to sixty-two hours a week after that, and on January 1, 1908, to begin to operate on a sixty-hour-week basis. The ten-hour bill was passed in this form and sent to the House,[25] where it was amended, and after some debate was passed.[26] The House bill to regulate child labor was unfavorably reported and withdrawn.[27] The Brice bill to prohibit the employment of children under fourteen during the school term unless they could read and write was reported unfavorably in the House, but a minority report in favor of the measure led to its consideration and passage.[28] It was given an unfavorable report in the Senate, however, and was not acted upon.[29] The compulsory education bill was killed in the Senate.[30]

The South Carolina manufacturers were consistently supported in their policies by the Charleston *News and Courier*. In 1907 it published a series of articles by August Kohn, one of its reporters who covered the activities of the legislature. The articles presented a picture of the conditions of cotton manufacturing in the state. They were reprinted in book form through the agency of the State De-

[22] *News and Courier*, Jan. 22, 1907.   [23] Jan. 24, 1907.

[24] N. C. L. C. Minutes, May 12, 1909, Appendix I.

[25] S. C., *Journal of the Senate*, 1907, pp. 276, 281-82; *State*, Jan. 30, 31, 1907; *News and Courier*, Feb. 1, 1907.

[26] S. C., *Journal of the House*, 1907, pp. 387, 396, 454, 515-16, 522, 642, 693, 785; S. C., *Acts of the General Assembly*, 1907, pp. 487-88.

[27] S. C., *Journal of the House*, 1907, pp. 212, 483.

[28] *Ibid.*, pp. 233, 404, 477, 487.

[29] S. C., *Journal of the Senate*, 1907, pp. 444, 644.

[30] *Ibid.*, pp. 86, 253; *State*, Jan. 30, 1907.

partment of Agriculture, Commerce, and Immigration,[31] and used by the opponents of child labor legislation to show that it was unnecessary and undesirable. Since the mill companies owned the houses in which the operatives lived, they wanted as many workers as possible in each family; three was the least number desirable.[32] Since labor was considered scarce in some areas, there were experiments with bringing in workers from outside the state and also using colored labor, which did not prove successful.[33] Kohn said that the operatives were more healthy in the mill villages than on the farms, because of the prevalence of hookworm disease in the sandy soil regions from which many of them came.[34] He acknowledged that the child labor law was violated, but held that it was due to misrepresentations by the parents as to the ages of their children, and to the lack of birth certificates, which were not required by law, so that the manufacturers were not responsible.[35] As to the number of children employed, he said that the statements of the child labor organizations were not borne out by the figures of the United States Census. He estimated fifteen hundred as the number of children under twelve years of age employed.[36]

The only labor bills appearing in the legislature of 1908 were those left over from the previous session. In the Senate the bill to prohibit night work for women and children under sixteen was tabled[37] and the Brice bill was also rejected.[38]

There was a tendency to associate the two Carolinas together in any consideration of cotton mill problems. The geographic and economic unity of the region around Charlotte led naturally to this, and the two states ranked as first and second in the number of mills and employees among the southern states. Perhaps for this reason conditions were found by the investigators of the Federal Bureau of Labor of the United States to be worse there than in other states. In the thirty-six mills investigated there were four hundred and five children under twelve years of age illegally employed, besides forty-two legally employed under the exceptions clause.[39] The National Child Labor Committee conducted investigations in the two states at once and published reports covering both of them. Lewis W. Hine visited five mill towns in South Carolina and nine in North Carolina in 1908, and reported that large numbers of young children were at work.[40]

[31] August Kohn, op. cit.   [32] Ibid., p. 23.
[33] Ibid., p. 24.   [34] Ibid., pp. 75-77.
[35] Ibid., pp. 106-7.   [36] Ibid., p. 119.
[37] S. C., Journal of the Senate, 1908, pp. 141, 735.
[38] Ibid., p. 142.
[39] U. S. Bureau of Labor, Woman and Child Wage-Earners, I, 186, 187, 211.
[40] "Report of a Photographic Investigation of Child Labor Conditions in North and South Carolina, 1908," MS in N. C. L. C. Library.

Alfred E. Seddon, who also investigated mills in Georgia and Mississippi, made a tour of South Carolina, and reported conditions of illiteracy and the employment of children to be as bad as in Mississippi
where no child labor law existed.[41] Investigators found it difficult
to secure information about labor conditions in South Carolina.
"From whatever official source we seek illumination we find only
Stygian darkness. There is no state census, no department of labor
statistics, no factory inspector, no truant officer, no joint legislative
commission of investigation."[42] McKelway went to the Carolinas in
the winter just before the meeting of the 1909 legislatures to interview the governors and other prominent men in the hope of being
able to interest them in the legislation the committee planned to
sponsor.[43] For the actual sessions of the legislature McKelway was
unable to be present as he had been delegated by the National Committee to work in Washington for a children's bureau bill, but he
wrote letters and aided in drafting the bill presented, and distributed among the legislators copies of the article "Child Labor in the
Carolinas," which had appeared in *Charities*.[44]

At the beginning of the legislative session a bill was introduced
by K. P. Smith of Anderson County to repeal the act establishing
the Department of Agriculture, Commerce, and Immigration which
had been passed in 1904.[45] An opposing bill was presented the next
day, proposing to retain the department but to change it by eliminating the word "Immigration" from the name, and substituting
for it "Industries."[46] The measures were debated for several days.
Smith declared there was no need for such a department, while Richards, the author of the second bill, defended the work of the commissioner, and said that while the Farmers' Union and the Labor
Union did not approve of the immigration section they endorsed
his bill.[47] The Richards bill passed so that the department became
the Department of Agriculture, Commerce, and Industries.[48] In the
Senate, F. H. Weston of Richland presented a bill to amend the Department of Agriculture and Commerce law so as to permit the employment of two mill inspectors.[49] The measure passed both houses,
thanks largely to the efforts of Representative John Porter Hollis of

[41] N. C. L. C. Minutes, Sept. 30, 1908.
[42] Florence Kelley, "Child Labor in the Carolinas," *Charities and the Commons*,
XXI (1909), 742.
[43] N. C. L. C. Minutes, Dec. 26, 1908, Oct. 1, 1909.
[44] *Ibid.*, March 4, 1909.
[45] S. C., *Journal of the House*, 1909, p. 66.
[46] *Ibid.*, p. 71.
[47] *Ibid.*, pp. 125, 142, 296, 310, 316, 336-37, 373; *State*, Feb. 5, 1909.
[48] S. C., *Acts of the General Assembly*, 1909, p. 14.
[49] S. C., *Journal of the Senate*, 1909, p. 188; *State*, Jan. 20, 1909, Feb. 11, 1909.

York County.[50] Another act which marked a loss of ground to the reformers allowed the sixty-hour week to be divided into five and one-half eleven-hour days, rather than a straight ten-hour day for six days, as had been provided in the original law.[51]

Before the legislature convened a meeting of the cotton manufacturers was held and Lewis Parker, chairman of their legislative committee, persuaded them to advocate a compulsory education bill with a fourteen-year age limit, and if this passed, to approve a child labor bill with the same age limit, but with proper restrictions. McKelway said that Parker admitted this was a safe proposition, since it was not at all probable that the legislature would pass such a compulsory school law. A bill with a twelve-year age limit was introduced but failed to be acted upon.[52] The state superintendent of education, J. E. Swearingen, was a nephew of Senator Tillman, and like him was supposed to oppose a compulsory school law at that time because of the Negro question. The Commissioner of the Department of Agriculture and Commerce, E. J. Watson, on the other hand, favored it.[53]

A bill in the Senate to prohibit night work for children under sixteen and for women was reported favorably but was not acted upon.[54] Another bill in the House to amend the child labor law was reported unfavorably.[55] The night work bill was carried over to 1910 and passed the Senate,[56] but was rejected in the House.[57]

The State Child Labor Committee in South Carolina had failed to function successfully, and in October, 1909, McKelway went to Columbia and addressed the South Carolina Conference of Charities and Corrections in order to interest them in the committee's reorganization.[58] The committee was reorganized and the National Committee's agent,[59] Miss Caroline E. Boone, was made its secretary.[60] The new committee undertook to establish agreement between its aims and those of the manufacturers. It invited representatives of

[50] N. C. L. C. Minutes, March 4, Oct. 1, 1909; S. C., *Journal of the Senate*, 1909, pp. 218, 412, 484; *Journal of the House*, 1909, pp. 514, 747, 777-78; *Acts of the General Assembly*, 1909, pp. 14-18.

[51] S. C., *Acts of the General Assembly*, 1909, p. 188.

[52] N. C. L. C. Minutes, May 12, 1909, Appendix I; *State*, Jan. 20, 1909; S. C., *Journal of the House*, 1909, pp. 75, 324, 716.

[53] "Interview with Manufacturers in North and South Carolina re Local Child Labor Conditions," April 1-15, 1909, MS in N. C. L. C. Library.

[54] S. C., *Journal of the Senate*, 1909, pp. 115, 175.

[55] S. C., *Journal of the House*, 1909, pp. 108, 228, 713.

[56] S. C., *Journal of the Senate*, 1910, pp. 52, 60, 590.

[57] S. C., *Journal of the House*, 1910, pp. 92, 155, 766-67.

[58] N. C. L. C. Minutes, Oct. 20, 1909.

[59] *Ibid.*, Oct. 27, 1909.   [60] *State*, Feb. 4, 1910.

the millmen to confer on a plan of co-operation. Professor William H. Hand of Columbia presided at the meeting and welcomed the guests. John A. Law, speaking for the manufacturers, recalled that the Manufacturers' Association in 1906 had advocated compulsory education and registration of marriages and births so as to make the enforcement of the child labor law possible, and that subsequently it had endorsed a fourteen-year limit for compulsory education and factory work. The manufacturers present declared themselves in accord with the resolution of the committee to present a bill requiring that no child under twelve be employed either regularly or as a helper in any factory, workshop, or mine; that twelve years be the age limit for work and compulsory education in 1911, thirteen years in 1912, and fourteen years in 1913 and thereafter; and that marriages and births be registered.[61]

The only child labor bill to be debated before the House was the Irby bill, held over from 1909. It proposed a change in penalty for violation of the child labor law by providing that a fifty-dollar fine be recovered by action in court through the child. The bill was objected to because it put the responsibility on the mills for avoiding violations and allowed parents more opportunity for evasion of the law with immunity.[62] This measure passed in the House, but the Senate committee gave it an unfavorable report.[63] In the Senate, Weston presented a bill for amending the child labor law of 1903 which probably had the support of the State Child Labor Committee.[64] It was reported favorably a few days later by the Committee on Commerce and Manufactures,[65] but further action was not taken.

The legislature of 1909 had provided for inspection of cotton mills under the supervision of the Commissioner of Agriculture, Commerce, and Industries, and a report made to the National Committee a few months later said that Commissioner Watson had turned fifteen hundred children under twelve years of age out of the mills with the warning that the manufacturers would be prosecuted for a second offense.[66] The first prosecution under the new law was instituted against a parent for making a false affidavit as to the age of his child. He was fined ten dollars, but was not prosecuted for perjury, since it was a first offense.[67] Commissioner Watson was on friendly terms with the manufacturers, and told the National Committee that they gave him splendid co-operation in the enforcement of the child labor

[61] *Ibid.*, Jan. 19, 1910.
[62] S. C., *Journal of the House*, 1910, pp. 254-55, 262; *State*, Feb. 1, 1910.
[63] S. C., *Journal of the Senate*, 1910, pp. 215, 277.
[64] *Ibid.*, p. 251; *State*, Feb. 4, 1910.
[65] S. C., *Journal of the Senate*, 1910, p. 324.
[66] N. C. L. C. Minutes, Oct. 1, 1909.   [67] *State*, Jan. 27, 1910.

law.[68] In the report for the department in 1910 the factory inspectors said that while the majority of mills were very careful in filing the required affidavits for the ages of children, a few were careless, and instead of warning parents against the danger of violating the law they accepted affidavits which they should have known were incorrect. It was the practice of the department to issue certificates of compliance with the law on the assumption that the affidavits were correct. If it found that they were not, prosecution was instituted, but ordinarily it did not go behind the parent's word.[69] The lack of birth certificates made it difficult to prove an affidavit false but some cases had been prosecuted, and in each case conviction secured.[70] The department felt that since there were only 361 children under twelve employed under the general exemption section of the law there was not "any sound reason why the manufacturers, themselves, should not ask for an amendment to the law, absolutely eliminating the employment of any child under 12 years of age for any cause or reason whatsoever."[71] There were 500 children who worked three months in the summer. The commissioner did not believe that the profit from these children was worth the "adverse criticism" that was "hurled against" the state and which made people believe that the bulk of the operatives were young children.[72]

In 1911 Cole L. Blease was inaugurated as governor of South Carolina. He had eighteen years earlier argued in favor of limiting hours in mills, declaring that "if we have to buy capital by murdering women and children, for God's sake let it go, let it go!"[73] But now he was of another opinion regarding labor legislation. "Much has been said about the enactment of laws in regard to the labor in our cotton mills. These people are our people; they are our kindred; they are our friends, and, in my opinion, they should be let alone and allowed to manage their own children and allowed to manage their own affairs."[74]

In November the State Child Labor Committee, which was now under the leadership of John Porter Hollis, decided to ask for the passage of a bill repealing the poverty exemption section of the child labor law and prohibiting night work under sixteen. The committee wished to provide for gradually raising the age limit for day work to fourteen, but met with opposition from some manufacturers. At a meeting in December the manufacturers said they would not oppose the elimination of children under twelve, but would fight any

---

[68] "Enforcement of Child Labor Laws in South Carolina," in *Annals* Supplement, XXXV (1910), 97.

[69] S. C. Dept. of Agriculture, Commerce, and Industries, *Second Annual Report*, 1910, p. 13.   [70] *Ibid.*, pp. 19-21.

[71] *Ibid.*, p. 13.   [72] *Ibid.*, p. 14.

[73] *News and Courier*, Dec. 6, 1892.   [74] *State*, Jan. 18, 1911.

advance beyond that age unless compulsory education was coupled with it. The Child Labor Committee felt it necessary to compromise with them on these points.[75]

Early in the session of 1911 Osborne introduced a child labor bill in the House which was referred to the Committee on Commerce and Manufactures.[76] It received a favorable majority report, though Josh Ashley presented a minority report against it.[77] The debate on the bill took place about two weeks later and continued two days. It was opened with a motion to strike out the enacting words. Osborne defended the bill because it eliminated features of the existing law which made it easy for parents to make false statements of age for their children and raised the age limit for night work to sixteen.[78] The opposition used the old arguments of the necessity of poverty-stricken families for the wages of children, the dangers of idleness, and the evils of class legislation. The representative from Anderson County called it "paternalism run mad." Irby in defending the bill said that the operatives could not petition for its passage without losing their jobs, so they depended on their representatives to speak for them. Ashley attacked John Porter Hollis, the secretary of the South Carolina Child Labor Committee, and agent of the National Committee, as being employed by the New England mills which were "trying to damn the mills of the South." Irby replied that Hollis was southern born and until two years ago had been a member of the Assembly from York County. Osborne's final word was that the bill had the endorsement of the State Federation of Labor, the State Child Labor Committee, the Cotton Manufacturers' Association and the Commissioner of Labor, none of whom had an axe to grind through its passage. The bill passed in the House and was sent to the Senate.[79] In the upper house it was not referred to a committee, but was read on three successive days and passed without debate.[80] Hollis reported to the National Committee that the chief opposition came from owners of mill stocks, politicians from mill counties, legislators who wanted favors from other legislators, and men who sincerely feared that an inflexible law would work a hardship on unfortunate families. The chief difficulty was that the operatives were believed to be unfriendly to the measure.[81]

[75]John Porter Hollis, "Child Labor Legislation in the Carolinas," in *Annals* Supplement, XXXVIII (1911), 114.

[76] S. C., *Journal of the House,* 1911, p. 52.

[77] *Ibid.,* p. 105.

[78] *Ibid.,* pp. 375-78; *State,* Feb. 1, 1911.

[79] S. C., *Journal of the House,* 1911, pp. 389-90; *State,* Feb. 2, 1911.

[80] S. C., *Journal of the Senate,* 1911, pp. 318, 340, 365.

[81] Hollis, *op. cit.,* pp. 114-17.

The new law provided that no child under twelve years of age should be employed in a mill or factory. No child under sixteen should work between 8:00 P.M and 6:00 A.M. except in order to make up lost time, in which case he might work as late as nine at night. The parent or guardian was required to give the employer a sworn statement in duplicate of the age, birthplace, name, and place of residence of any child under fourteen who was employed. The original copy should be produced by the employer on demand for the inspection of the representative of the Department of Agriculture, Commerce, and Industries, and the duplicate sent to the office of the commissioner at Columbia, in exchange for which the commissioner would issue a permit for employment. The act was to take effect January 1, 1912.[82]

A rather difficult situation in South Carolina due to the high degree of antagonism between Governor Blease and his political opponents led to a hindrance being put in the way of the enforcement of the child labor law in 1911. The factory inspection act of 1909 specified the salaries that were to be paid to the two inspectors which the commissioner was allowed to appoint. In 1911 Governor Blease vetoed this item of the appropriations bill for the year, leaving the department without the funds for the salaries of the inspectors which it had employed in the two years previous.[83] The Governor then appointed L. M. Green of Sumter County, a former newspaper correspondent of Columbia, to inspect the factories, paying him $1,000 from the fund appropriated for the Executive Department. Green published a report of his inspection, the figures for which *The State* claimed he had compiled from the annual report of Commissioner Watson and the columns of *The State* itself. Blease justified his action by saying that he had vetoed the appropriation for inspection because he intended to save the state that much by having the work done by county detectives. But when various counties refused to pay the detectives, he appointed Green, paying him $1,000, which was less than the appropriation of $3,400 which the regular inspectors would have cost.[84] In 1912 the legislature made the necessary appropriation again and it was not vetoed.[85]

In 1911 the National Child Labor Committee decided to make restriction of night messenger service one of its chief goals in the state legislature.[86] Accordingly Howard B. Carlisle, of Spartanburg,

[82] S. C., *Acts of the General Assembly*, 1911, pp. 28-31.
[83] S. C., *Journal of the House*, 1911, pp. 940-41.
[84] *State*, Jan. 22, 1912.
[85] S. C. Dept. of Agriculture, Commerce, and Industries, *Fourth Annual Report*, 1912, p. 4.
[86] N. C. L. C. Minutes, Oct. 4, 1911.

with the support of Hollis,[87] introduced in the Senate a bill to restrict the employment of children in such occupations, as well as in theaters and places of amusement. The bill was favorably reported, with amendments suggested. The age limit for night messenger service was reduced from twenty-one to eighteen and work in theaters was eliminated. The Senate passed the measure on February 8, 1912.[88] A similar bill had been favorably considered in the House, and the Carlisle bill passed with little difficulty.[89] The Governor allowed it to become law without his signature. It forbade employing children under fourteen to work for telephone, telegraph, or other messenger companies, or in the distribution or delivery of goods. Persons under eighteen were not to be employed in such occupations between the hours of 10:00 P.M. and 5:00 A.M.[90]

No effort was made in 1912 to raise the age limit for factory work as the State Committee was not willing to undertake sponsoring it.[91] The absence of legal inspection for a year led to carelessness on the part of some of the manufacturers in observing the law, but the commissioner reported for 1912 a decrease of four hundred and sixty-eight in the number of children employed since the Act of 1911 forbidding employment of children under twelve had gone into effect.[92] The National Committee agent also found that conditions had greatly improved in a few years.[93]

The committee found it difficult to make progress in the Carolinas in the face of the opposition of the manufacturers. Wiley H. Swift, who was engaged in 1912 as an agent for the committee in North Carolina, made numbers of speeches in both states before women's organizations, schools, and church audiences.[94] McKelway was in charge of directing the activities in South Carolina,[95] but he received scant encouragement, even from *The State*, which had been the first champion of child labor reform in South Carolina.[96] The state committees in the Carolinas showed little energy, and were not often willing to go as far in their demands as the National Committee urged. Only a few people, like Judge Joseph A. McCullough

---

[87] *Ibid.*, May 1, 1912. Carlisle was an influential member of the Assembly and championed a number of other reforms such as prohibition, abolition of race track gambling, requiring marriage licenses, and compulsory education. See Snowden, *op. cit.*, III, 230.

[88] S. C., *Journal of the Senate*, 1912, pp. 165, 186, 470, 529.

[89] S. C., *Journal of the House*, 1912, pp. 899, 989.

[90] S. C., *Acts of the General Assembly*, 1912, pp. 705-6.

[91] N. C. L. C. Minutes, May 1, 1912.

[92] S. C. Dept. of Agriculture, Commerce, and Industries, *Fourth Annual Report*, 1912, pp. 13, 22.

[93] L. W. Hine, "Child Labor in South Carolina," MS in N. C. L. C. Library.

[94] N. C. L. C. Minutes, Sept. 30, 1912.

[95] *Ibid.*, Oct. 1, 1912.   [96] Dec. 13, 1912.

of Greenville and C. E. Weltner, a clergyman who was interested in welfare work in one of the Columbia mills, frankly declared that they advocated a fourteen-year age limit and other laws necessary for its proper enforcement.[97]

In 1913 there was some discussion of a fourteen-year age limit for factories but petitions against it came in to the legislature from operatives in some of the mill towns,[98] and no action was taken. A bill presented by Josh Ashley to restore the exemption clause for children over ten years of age even received a favorable report from the majority of the Committee on Manufacturing, although it was not acted upon.[99] In 1914 a flood of petitions from operatives in a number of mills protested against changing the age limit.[100] This was just at the time that the Palmer child labor bill was under consideration for the first time in the National Legislature. A bill to raise the age limit to thirteen in 1915 and fourteen in 1916 was introduced in the Senate. The Committee on Commerce and Manufactures was at first favorable, when members of the Child Labor Committee appeared before it,[101] but later reversed its decision.[102] The chief objection was the provision for an eight-hour day for children which the southern manufacturers generally opposed on the ground that it would limit the working time of the mills and would be a hardship on the employees because of reduced wages. Swift, of the National Committee; J. Whitner Reid, of the State Committee; and H. J. Hardy, district organizer of the American Federation of Labor, urged that the bill be passed. Lewis Parker, Ellison Smyth, a Baptist minister from Pelzer, and J. K. Hood, attorney for the Cotton Manufacturers' Association, opposed the measure.[103] It was rejected "because the mill operatives had a mass meeting and denounced this piece of vicious legislation."[104]

McCullough was elected to the legislature in 1915 and presented two bills in the House. The first was for restriction of hours of work in the mills and the second was to amend the child labor law by raising the age limit to fourteen. The Committee on Commerce and Manufactures made a favorable majority report, and a minority opposed the two bills.[105] They were not reached in 1915, however.

[97] C. E. Weltner, "Social Welfare and Child Labor in South Carolina Cotton Mill Communities," in *Child Labor Bulletin*, II (May, 1913), 85-90; J. A. McCullough, "Conditions of Child Employing Industries in the South—South Carolina," *ibid.*, pp. 133-38.   [98] *State*, Jan. 16, 29, 1913.

[99] S. C., *Journal of the House*, 1913, pp. 328, 394, 784.

[100] S. C., *Journal of the Senate*, 1914, pp. 213 ff.

[101] J. A. McCullough, "A Report from South Carolina," in *Child Labor Bulletin*, III (May, 1914), 80.   [102] S. C., *Journal of the Senate*, 1914, p. 231.

[103] *State*, Jan. 22, 1914; N. C. L. C. Minutes, Sept. 30, 1914.

[104] J. A. McCullough, "A Report from South Carolina," in *Child Labor Bulletin*, III (May, 1914), 80.

[105] S. C., *Journal of the House*, 1915, pp. 174, 335, 964.

While action on child labor was delayed, the state made its first step in progress toward compulsory education in 1915. A law was passed allowing districts where the majority of voters desired it to require compulsory school attendance of all children between the ages of eight and fourteen for the entire term. Exceptions were made for those who were physically or mentally defective, or whose poverty made it necessary for them to work. On the whole it was a weak law, but it was the prelude to a better act a few years later.[106]

The election of Richard I. Manning as governor of South Carolina was a triumph over the Blease faction in state politics and marked a change in attitude of the administration toward social legislation. In 1916 the new governor urged in his message to the Assembly that the child labor age limit be raised so as to correspond to the optional compulsory school attendance age of fourteen, for he said that the mill districts would not vote the education law into effect as long as the children could work.[107] The McCullough child labor bill was debated in the House for two days. The Governor sent a special message urging its passage just before it came up for consideration. On the first day the House refused to pass it by a vote of forty-eight to forty-two. The day following McCullough offered a substitute providing for a gradual raising of the age limit to thirteen after July 1, 1916, and fourteen after July 1, 1917. In this form the bill passed and was sent to the Senate.[108] There the Committee on Commerce and Manufactures returned it without recommendation. It monopolized the time of the Senate for two days. An effort to insert an exceptions clause for children of twelve and over who were dependent on their own support failed. A motion to allow children over twelve to work when school was not in session was also rejected. It was also proposed to pay the child of needy parents a sum equal to what he would earn if allowed to work, but the legislators were not ready for this step. The bill was amended, however, in one respect. Instead of a gradual raising of the age limit, no child under fourteen was to be employed after January 1, 1917.[109] The House agreed through a conference committee to accept this amendment,[110] and the act was approved by the Governor on February 29, 1917.[111]

Marjorie A. Potwin, a recent writer on the life of the Carolina mill people, who is sympathetic toward the manufacturers' efforts to promote the welfare of the mill communities, comments on Man-

[106] S. C., Acts of the General Assembly, 1915, pp. 118-23.
[107] S. C., Journal of the Senate, 1916, p. 9.
[108] S. C., Journal of the House, 1916, pp. 543, 573-81, 612; State, Feb. 9, 10, 1916.
[109] S. C., Journal of the Senate, 1916, pp. 522, 526, 695, 787-88; State, Feb. 19, 1916.
[110] S. C., Journal of the House, 1916, pp. 1122, 1127, 1163-64.
[111] S. C., Acts of the General Assembly, 1916, pp. 655-56.

ning's part in the enactment of this law. "This is a detail of significance to those who recall that by social tradition, economic interest
and family proclivities, Ex-Governor Manning is of the same group
as the cotton manufacturers. Through him, as through them, we see
the functioning of the Old South's 'noblesse oblige.' "[112]

The effect of improved state legislation and the first federal child
labor law was to bring about an improvement in child labor conditions. While these laws were pending, the mills tended to eliminate
children who would not be eligible when they went into effect.[113]
Governor Manning estimated that the number of children under
sixteen employed in mills had decreased 26 per cent at the end of
the first six years of factory inspection.[114] In 1910 there was one cotton manufacturing county, Spartanburg, in which over 1,500 children
under sixteen were employed. In Greenville over 1,000 were employed, in Anderson almost 1,000, and in Union over 600. In each
of fifteen other counties between one and 500 children were employed
and in nine counties less than 100 were employed.[115] In 1918 in no
county were more than 1,000 children under sixteen employed.
Spartanburg and Greenville each had a few more than 700 and Anderson a few more than 500. In eleven counties between one and 500
were employed and in fourteen counties less than 100.[116]

Not all the legislators were convinced that a fourteen-year age
limit with no exceptions allowed was advantageous. In 1919 a compulsory school attendance law was passed requiring children between
eight and fourteen to attend school four months a year. It was a
weak law and contained provisions that would allow children of
twelve and over to withdraw from school to work if it was necessary
for them to support a crippled father or a widowed mother. A clause
was added forbidding the employment of any child under fourteen
during the hours school was in session unless the person employing
the child secured a certificate that he had complied with the school
law for the current year.[117] The House in the same session considered a bill to allow children between the ages of twelve and sixteen
to work in cotton mills when school was not in session, provided they
were not employed more than eight hours a day, or forty-eight hours
a week, or at night. In the debate it was argued that it would keep

[112] *Cotton Mill People of the Piedmont*, p. 141.
[113] S. C., Dept. of Agriculture, Commerce, and Industries, *Eighth Annual Report*, 1916, p. 42.
[114] "The Organization of the Public Welfare of a State," in *National Conference of Social Service*, 44th session, 1917, p. 347.
[115] Compiled from S. C. Dept. of Agriculture, Commerce, and Industries, *Second Annual Report*, 1910, Table of Cotton Mill Employees.
[116] *Ibid., Tenth Annual Report*, 1918, Table of Cotton Mill Employees.
[117] S. C., *Acts of the General Assembly*, 1919, pp. 205-8.

the children out of mischief. The bill passed the House[118] and was reported favorably by the Senate Committee,[119] but did not come up for consideration again.

A growing interest in social problems in the state had resulted in 1915 in the creation of a State Board of Charities and Corrections,[120] which later became known as the Department of Public Welfare. In 1919 the legislature provided for a Child Welfare Commission to be appointed by the governor and composed of ten members: one judge of a juvenile court, two members of the legislature, three members of state boards, two representatives of private child-caring agencies, one teacher, and one labor representative. The object of the commission was to make a general survey of conditions in the state, and draw up a children's code in accordance with its findings. The commission failed to make any report, however, and ceased to function after 1921.[121] Plans were made for an investigation of child welfare conditions in Charleston in connection with the National Committee, but they seem never to have materialized.[122]

In 1923 an effort was made to extend the child labor law to include employment in theaters, stores, offices, hotels, laundries, bakeries, canning factories, and tobacco warehouses as well as the places already specified by law. The bill was intended to raise the state law to meet the federal age and hour standard.[123] It was given a divided report by the Judiciary Committee and late in the session was tabled.[124] In 1925 South Carolina rejected the proposed federal amendment, but subsequent efforts to amend the state child labor law failed.[125]

In 1937 the legislature adopted a sixteen-year age limit for workers in factories, mines, and textile establishments. Night work between 8:00 P.M. and 5:00 A.M. was prohibited for persons under sixteen. The enforcement was placed in the hands of the recently created Department of Labor.[126] The same legislature enacted a more rigid school attendance law for children from seven to sixteen, but still retained an exemption for those who must work because of poverty.[127] In 1938 the law was amended to prohibit persons under eighteen working between 10:00 P.M. and 6:00 A.M.[128]

[118] S. C., *Journal of the House*, 1919, pp. 107, 184, 242-43; *State*, Feb. 6, 1919.
[119] S. C., *Journal of the Senate*, 1919, pp. 202, 273, 716.
[120] S. C., *Acts of the General Assembly*, 1915, pp. 132-34.
[121] U. S. Dept. of Labor, Children's Bureau, *Publication No. 131*, p. 74.
[122] N. C. L. C. Minutes, Dec. 15, 1921, Jan. 24, 1922.
[123] S. C., *Journal of the House*, 1923, p. 378; *State*, Feb. 9, 1923.
[124] S. C., *Journal of the House*, 1923, pp. 406, 625, 1351.
[125] *Ibid.*, 1926, pp. 90, 184, 239, 630.
[126] S. C., *Acts of the General Assembly*, 1937, pp. 531-32.
[127] *Ibid.*, pp. 556-61.
[128] S. C. Dept. of Labor, mimeographed copy of act passed by the General Assembly in May, 1938.

CHAPTER X

GEORGIA AFTER 1904: BELATED ACTION

OF ALL THE leading textile states in the South, Georgia alone failed to enact a child labor law in 1903. It was in this state more than any other in the South that organized labor had championed the cause of child labor legislation. Its efforts over a period of eight years having failed, the state labor convention in 1904 decided on a change in method. The State Democratic Convention had ignored the petitions from labor organizations, and their bills had failed in the Assembly. Therefore at the annual convention of the Georgia Federation of Labor a committee was appointed, composed of a member from each central body in the state, which was to attempt to educate public opinion to demand reform.[1]

The non-labor people had not taken as great an interest in reform in Georgia as in Alabama. They seemingly failed to appreciate the intensity of the effort made by the labor unions to secure legislation. Mrs. A. O. Grainger, chairman of the Child Labor Committee of the Georgia Federation of Women's Clubs, told the National Child Labor Committee that there had not been a real contest for legislation. "There was a bill presented before our Legislature which met last summer, with the help of the labor party. . . . I had the pleasure of . . . hearing the address made by one of the leading manufacturers of the State, which address persuaded the Legislature against passing the bill. . . . That man was a Republican, a wealthy man of Georgia, the head of two mills, and the head of a railroad —and he talked to those people, many of whom were ignorant country people, and told them to beware . . . of the people who wanted to have any laws made about the management of mills, because these dreadful labor people and busy-bodied women who never knew anything about child labor or its effects, after having passed this law would next turn their attention to *their* affairs and would insist upon largely increased taxation, in order to provide schools enough for the children of Georgia and all sorts of fancy things."[2]

The National Child Labor Committee included Georgia in its plans for a reform campaign in 1905, and sent A. J. McKelway, who had just failed in an effort to secure a new law in North Carolina,

[1] *Proceedings*, Sixth Annual Convention, pp. 13, 18.
[2] N. C. L. C. Minutes, Feb. 15, 1905. The man referred to was Major J. F. Hanson.

to study the Georgia situation. McKelway spent a large part of his time in Atlanta, where he undertook to interest the Women's Club in the new movement, but he also visited Rome, which was near one of the largest northern-owned mills. He held conferences with the Georgia members of the National Committee and called together the remnants of the old State Committee which had ceased to function. The state group was apparently unable to furnish a leader willing and capable of directing a program for reform. Although McKelway realized, since his experience of a few months previous in North Carolina, that there was a danger from prejudice against outside influence if he openly assumed leadership, he undertook "the work of organizing public sentiment and harmonizing the different agencies in passing a child labor bill."[3]

The State Committee was reorganized and C. B. Wilmer, who was now also a member of the National Committee, became temporary chairman.[4] McKelway took a leading role at once and in a few weeks secured permission from the National Committee to assume the duties of acting secretary for the Georgia Committee.[5] He interviewed Murphy Candler of DeKalb County, who was candidate for the presidency of the state Senate, and Seaborn Wright, a representative who had been an active supporter of the child labor movement in previous years. Madison Bell, the leading labor exponent of reform in the Assembly, also got in touch with McKelway, and plans for the meeting of the legislature which would take place in the summer of 1905 were made.[6]

The manufacturers in 1905 made the old agreement adopted by the Georgia Industrial Association in 1900 the basis for opposition to legislation. This agreement had provided that the labor of children should not exceed sixty-six hours a week, that no child under twelve should work at night, and that no child under twelve should work except to support disabled or dependent parents. The manufacturers contended that this agreement was a greater protection for children than a law would be. McKelway quoted a manufacturer, who was later a president of the Georgia Industrial Association, as saying, "If you pass the law . . . the mill men will immediately say 'I am no longer bound to keep this agreement. . . . I will run the gauntlet of the law, if I get caught I will pay my fine.' "[7]

The manufacturers claimed that the agreement was enforced, while McKelway undertook to prove that it was not. He took pictures of children who worked and secured statements from them and sometimes

[3] *Ibid.*, March 23, 1905.   [4] *Ibid.*
[5] *Ibid.*, April 27, 1905.   [6] *Ibid.*, March 23, 1905.
[7] "Child Labor in Georgia," MS in McKelway Papers. (Not identical with either pamphlet of the same title.)

affidavits from their parents and other people to show that the children were under the prescribed age limit.[8] On the basis of this evidence the Georgia Committee published a statement that the agreement was not observed and was worthless as a means of protecting children. The Manufacturers' Association denied this and appointed a committee of its own to investigate. The Georgia Child Labor Committee then published the information McKelway had gathered, including the photographs and affidavits, in the Atlanta *Constitution* and *Journal,* both of which were friendly to the reform movement. The initials only of the children were given because the committee said that similar publicity in previous years had caused the parents of the children involved to lose their employment. When this publicity attracted considerable attention, McKelway decided to use the press of the state more widely. He sent short articles on child labor as "ammunition for editorials" to all the papers in the state, and most of them gave a favorable response. Many of the women's clubs throughout the state endorsed the reform.[9]

The line-up of interests on the child labor question was practically the same as in 1903 and previous years. Murphy Candler, a cotton manufacturer who advocated child labor legislation, was a candidate for the speakership in the Senate. A meeting held by Jack J. Spalding and the political opponents of Candler on the eve of the convening of the legislature resulted in his defeat and the election of W. S. West, who was in harmony with the cotton mill interests. One result of the election was the appointment of a Senate Committee on Manufactures and Labor which was hostile to child labor legislation.[10]

Madison Bell introduced the child labor bill in the House when it opened in the latter part of June, and it was referred to the Committee on Labor and Labor Statistics.[11] Bell was a very ardent supporter of reform, but McKelway found him, as a labor man, jealous of the efforts of other agencies in endeavoring to put the child labor bill through.[12] The House Committee held a hearing on the measure on July 14, 1905, and Jack Spalding and representatives from among the manufacturers spoke for three hours in opposition. Spalding's argument lasted an hour and a half[13] and dealt chiefly with the benefits of mill life. As Murphy once described a similar argument, he

[8] In 1905 the manufacturers claimed that their agreement was not to employ children under ten. This age was not specified in the original agreement of 1900. See "The Georgia Gentleman's Agreement Regarding Child Labor" in McKelway Papers and compare with chapter on Georgia.

[9] "McKelway's Account," in McKelway Papers.

[10] *Ibid.*

[11] Ga., *Journal of the House,* 1905, p. 79.

[12] "McKelway's Account," in McKelway Papers.

[13] *Constitution,* July 15, 1905.

represented the mill "as an orphan asylum, a children's training school, a play-ground, a hospital, a college and a trip to Europe, all in one."[14] Spalding did not omit reference to the outside influences demanding legislation. The *Annals* of the American Academy of Political and Social Science, published in Philadelphia and edited by a professor of the Pennsylvania state university, published the proceedings of the annual conferences of the National Committee. Spalding argued that since Philadelphia was a textile center there was a conspiracy there to advocate child labor reform and break up the competition from southern factories.[15]

A second hearing at which the friends of the measure held the floor followed in a few days. C. T. Ladson for the State Federation of Labor presented testimony of photographs and names of children under ten years of age who were employed in Atlanta mills. Ladson's speech represented the matter in the same light as in former years, and the National Committee was apparently left out of the arguments of all the speakers. The report of the Committee was favorable.[16]

The bill was delayed for over two weeks, but came up for final consideration in the early part of August. The amount of publicity it attracted drew a large crowd of visitors to the House for the debate. After some preliminary sparring in an effort to sidetrack the bill, it was agreed to allow each side an hour and a half for debate. Bell, who had worked hard to pledge representatives to the support of his measure, made the leading speech in its favor and indulged in flights of oratory. He was rewarded with flowers and so much applause from the gallery that the speaker had to threaten to clear it of visitors. The opposition then took up the case, and the day ended without coming to a vote on the bill.[17] On the day following, the debate was renewed. The gallery was again occupied by a noisy crowd, chiefly women, whom the speaker was unable to restrain to an orderly quiet. The voting lasted two hours, as twenty-five of the members felt it necessary to explain their votes.[18] One of the five-minute speeches was made by the only Negro member of the legislature. McKelway quoted him as saying, "Mr. Speaker, as you know my people are not particularly interested in this bill. Our children are not employed in the cotton factories, and we are trying to send them to school, and are succeeding tollably well. But we have been here for some time legislating for the protection of the birds of the air and the beasts of the field and the fish of the sea, and I for one, am in favor of doing something for the protection of the little white children of Georgia." This bit of colored logic brought a storm of applause

[14] "McKelway's Account," in McKelway Papers.
[15] *Ibid.*   [16] *Constitution*, July 19, 1905.
[17] Ga., *Journal of the House*, 1905, p. 543; *Constitution*, August 3, 1905.
[18] *Constitution*, Aug. 4, 1905.

from the friends of the measure.[19]   When it was announced that the bill passed by a vote of one hundred and three to sixty-two, the applause from the gallery was renewed and two members embraced for joy in the center aisle of the hall.[20]

The text of the bill passed by the House was moderate, but on a level with the measures in force in neighboring states. It provided for a twelve-year age limit with exceptions for children ten or over whose mothers were widows or whose fathers were disabled. It prohibited night work under fourteen, and forbade the employment of children under fourteen after September 1, 1907, who were unable to read and write.[21] The measure was so weak that McKelway was led to express doubt as to the wisdom of enacting a law which left open a "wide and effectual door for its universal violation." But he felt that this was compensated for by the fact that the House had enacted the principle that the state had the right to interfere between the parent and the child when the parent was ignorant of or indifferent to the child's welfare. It was a victory over the laissez faire tendency of Georgia.[22] McKelway overlooked the fact that in previous years one house had passed child labor bills and the other had defeated them, which was to be the case again.

The bill was immediately sent to the Senate. This was hostile territory, since the speaker was known to be opposed to such legislation and the committee which would consider the bill was supposed to be packed against it. But McKelway attributed the failure of the Committee on Immigration and Labor to make an adverse report to the growing political uneasiness caused by the approaching gubernatorial campaign.[23]   It merely asked that the measure be acted upon at once.[24] The debate and final vote on the measure took place on August 15, 1905. The arguments lasted for several hours and developed into warm debate. Murphy Candler, the defeated candidate for the speakership, made one of the strong arguments in favor of the measure, and the speaker, W. S. West, left the chair to oppose it. Candler was asked if his mill was party to the mill agreement for the regulation of child labor. He replied that it was not as it was not a member of the Industrial Association because he did not wish to pay money to employ attorneys "to fight good legislation."[25] The bill was lost by a vote of seventeen to twenty-three.[26]

The defeat of the child labor bill was not popular. McKelway

[19] "McKelway's Account," in McKelway Papers.
[20] Ga., *Journal of the House*, 1905, pp. 546-48; *Constitution*, Aug. 4, 1905.
[21] *Constitution*, Aug. 4, 1905.
[22] "McKelway's Account," in McKelway Papers.
[23] *Ibid.* ·   [24] *Constitution*, Aug. 14, 1905.
[25] *Ibid.*, Aug. 15, 1905; *Atlanta Journal*, Aug. 15, 1905.
[26] Ga., *Journal of the Senate*, 1905, p. 476.

says that there was an outburst of reproachful comment from the press of the state.[27] The *Atlanta Journal,* which belonged to Hoke Smith, published a cartoon which was a scathing comment on the refusal of the Senate to pass the bill.[28] "Senator Bunn, who had led the fight against the bill in the Senate, afterwards remarked that he believed every man, woman and child in Georgia had cut out that cartoon and mailed it to him."[29]

The question of child labor legislation was a factor of political importance in Georgia in 1905. McKelway declared that if Clark Howell, editor of the Atlanta *Constitution* and member of the National Committee, who also aspired to the governorship, had accepted the invitation extended to him to attend a luncheon meeting of the reorganized Georgia Child Labor Committee, he would have been elected governor. Although this is too sweeping a statement to be accepted literally, McKelway's story is interesting. When he took over the reorganization of the State Committee he invited Howell to attend. Howell replied that he had allowed the National Committee to use his name, but that he had no time for attending meetings or making speeches. McKelway then invited Hoke Smith and he accepted. "After threshing out the question of the child labor bill and its chances under the political conditions that prevailed, the talk inevitably turned toward the necessity of a political revolution in Georgia, before anything could be accomplished, as the cotton mills, the railroads and the liquor interests had hitherto proved an immovable combination where any legislation affecting adversely their interests were [sic] concerned. The talk at the luncheon table grew more personal, without any names being mentioned, looking to the bringing out of a strong candidate to stand for the welfare of the people against this combination. When the meeting adjourned, Hooper Alexander, a member of the [National] Committee, remained talking for an hour or more with Hoke Smith, urging his duty to become a candidate. . . . A few days afterwards, the Atlanta Journal, with James R. Gray, owner and editor, published an editorial describing the kind of man the next Governor of Georgia ought to be. Mr. Gray did not have Hoke Smith in mind, as it was thought that he was out of politics for good."

McKelway did not seem to realize that the *Atlanta Journal* belonged to Smith. "But the description happened to fit Hoke Smith like the paper on the wall, and telegrams and letters and petitions began to pour into his office, asking him to make the race. Then Clark Howell challenged him to run, and Hoke Smith accepted the

[27] "McKelway's Account," in McKelway Papers.
[28] Aug. 18, 1905.
[29] "McKelway's Account," in McKelway Papers.

challenge, made a campaign which carried him face to face with the people in nearly every county in Georgia and was triumphantly nominated in the 'white primary,' which was equivalent to election at the polls, that being merely a ratification of the decision of the primary."[30]

Smith and Howell were not only rival editors; there was political hostility of long standing between them. In 1892 Howell had been bitterly opposed to the nomination of Cleveland for the presidency of the United States and he was later a pronounced bimetallist, while Smith was pro-Cleveland, favored the gold standard, and entered Cleveland's cabinet as Secretary of the Interior. Smith also advocated an educational qualification for voting which would disfranchise the illiterate Negro vote. Howell opposed this qualification because of the possibility that it would disqualify a number of whites. Although Smith and Howell were both Democrats, Smith was helped into office by the Populist following which Thomas E. Watson brought to him.[31] Going back to McKelway's account of the situation: "A year before this historic meeting of the Georgia Child Labor Committee, Hoke Smith had made an address on child labor reform at the State Capitol, and he made this one of the issues of the campaign. The main issue however was the securing, through a new railroad commission, with ample powers, a square deal from the railroads in the matter of freight and passenger rates, and on this issue the cotton mill men divided enough to break the combination, while the Legislature that was elected with Hoke Smith put the saloons out of business by passing a state prohibition law which he signed as Governor, as well as the Railroad Commission bill. The combination was broken into little bits."[32]

The attack made on the railroad interests by Smith as governor was directed against the Central of Georgia and the Southern Railway. Major J. F. Hanson, who had in 1903 made himself prominent as an opponent of the child labor bill, was president of the Central of Georgia. He was also connected with other railroads and steamship companies for which Smith demanded regulation.[33] This is an illustration of the alignment of cotton mill and railroad interests on which McKelway laid the blame for defeat of child labor legislation in the past.

McKelway described Georgia as a state in which "somebody is running for office, either election or re-election, all the time." State officials held office for only two years, and were nominated by primaries which were held a year before the term of office expired. The

[30] *Ibid.*
[31] L. L. Knight, *A Standard History of Georgia and Georgians,* II, 1062.
[32] "McKelway's Account," in McKelway Papers.
[33] Knight, *op. cit.,* II, 1066; VI, 2948.

campaigns for nomination began a year before that. The lower house of the Assembly was composed of from one to three members from each of the hundred and forty odd counties of the state, and was usually responsive to public demands. The Senate, however, was composed of only forty-five members, chosen from senatorial districts of from three to six counties. It was traditional for the counties in each district to rotate in providing the senatorial candidate, so that it was "impossible to reward a faithful servant of the people with re-election or to punish one for bad votes by keeping him at home." The "interests" of the state could control the Senate by controlling the nominations in twenty-three or more counties. The Senate was, therefore, "the graveyard of good legislation."[34]

In the months which intervened between the legislative session of 1905 and 1906 the situation regarding child labor underwent a change. In view of the strength of the demand for reform the Industrial Association agreed at its annual meeting to offer no opposition to the passage of the Bell bill as it stood in 1905.[35] When the legislature convened, the Smith-Howell gubernatorial campaign was being waged. On June 29, 1906, Madison Bell again introduced a bill in the House.[36] About a week later a similar bill was presented in the Senate by Candler, signed by twenty-three senators, including some of those who had actively opposed the bill in 1905. Its chief improvements over the old bill were that it provided for twelve weeks' compulsory school attendance for children under fourteen, and more carefully defined the nature of the dependency of a parent who might be supported by a child between ten and twelve years of age.[37] The House bill passed with only two dissenting votes.[38] Some of the millmen were dissatisfied with the changes which were made in the bill since the preceding year. The president of the Industrial Association, Jeff Davis of Toccoa, said that the senators who signed the bill had been led into a trap, and urged them to strike out the clause relating to compulsory education if they could not go back entirely to the old bill.[39]

When the measure was considered by the Senate Committee on Immigration and Labor, the manufacturers had hopes of defeating it, and several of them appeared to protest against the educational section of the bill. This section required not only that children

[34] "McKelway's Account," in McKelway Papers. The child labor bill of 1905 had been lost in the Senate by a vote of exactly twenty-three against it.—Ga., *Journal of the Senate*, 1905, p. 476.   [35] *Constitution*, July 22, 1906.

[36] Ga., *Journal of the House*, 1906, p. 91.

[37] Ga., *Journal of the Senate*, 1906, p. 100; *Constitution*, July 7, 1906; *Atlanta Journal*, July 9, 1906.

[38] Ga., *Journal of the House*, 1906, p. 317.

[39] *Constitution*, July 22, 1906.

should be able to read and write, but that they should attend school twelve weeks a year until their eighteenth year if they entered employment before their fourteenth year. The vote of the committee was a tie, and was broken by the presiding officer, who favored the bill.[40]

In spite of the narrow margin by which the bill was recommended, there was no opposition in the Senate. It passed on July 30, 1906, with no dissenting voices, but with only twenty-seven votes cast.[41] Besides the educational qualification, the law provided that no child under twelve should be employed unless it were an orphan with no means of support, or unless a widowed mother or aged or disabled father were dependent on its labor. A certificate was required for such children. No child under fourteen should work between 7:00 P.M. and 6:00 A.M.[42]

The enactment of the new law was regarded by the *Constitution* as a particular triumph for Madison Bell. He had been elected to the House from Atlanta two years before and had made child labor legislation his special theme both in his campaign and in the legislature. He was a labor representative, and the labor unions had supported his measure, so they also felt that their efforts for the past ten years were rewarded. Organized labor had learned from experience that too open advocacy of labor legislation by the Federation made the bills unpopular; but the credit for beginning the movement and bearing the burden of it in the hardest years was theirs.[43] The National Child Labor Committee, which had established a southern office in Atlanta and put McKelway in charge for the purpose of supporting reform legislation, also came in for its share of the credit.[44] McKelway had worked for greater publicity for the reform and his efforts were very well rewarded. The Georgia law was regarded by the National Committee as its first success in the South.[45]

The Georgia law was given national prominence almost as soon as it went into effect because of the part it played in the debate in Congress on the Beveridge child labor bill. The manufacturers had recognized that it would, if observed, eliminate a large number of children from the mills. The *American Cotton Manufacturer* estimated the number at a thousand.[46] But in his speech on the proposed federal child labor law, which he made in January, 1907, Bev-

[40] *Ibid.*, July 27, 1906.

[41] Ga., *Journal of the Senate*, 1906, p. 330; *Constitution*, July 30, 1906.

[42] Ga., *Acts and Resolutions of the General Assembly*, 1906, pp. 98-99.

[43] *Constitution*, Aug. 2, 1905; *American Federationist*, XIII (1906), 703.

[44] S. M. Lindsay, "The New Child Labor Law in Georgia," in *Charities*, XVI (1906), 337-38.

[45] N. C. L. C. Minutes, Aug. 3, 1907.   [46] Jan. 10, 1907.

eridge asserted that the Georgia law was a dead letter without a system of inspection or a means of enforcement, and that three thousand applications for permits to work had been filed in Fulton County alone since the law went into effect on January first.[47] There is little doubt that the latter part of this statement was rash and unwarranted by the facts. When Senator Bacon of Georgia telegraphed to Atlanta for an investigation he was informed that the county ordinary, whose duty it was to issue permits, had stated that probably between two and three thousand applications would be made throughout the year, but that only ten had been received during the first weeks of January.[48] This did not indicate, however, that children were not continuing to work in violation of the law. If the ordinary expected even two thousand children to apply for exemption, there must have been a large number to come under the provisions of the law.

The mill officials had been particularly annoyed by the educational requirements of the law, and in June, 1907, President Jeff Davis of the Industrial Association applied to Attorney-General John C. Hart for an interpretation of this section, asking whether attendance at night school would be accepted as a fulfillment of the requirement. Hart informed his questioner that he had no power to give an official interpretation of any law. His personal opinion was that the clause relating to the school requirement for children who entered employment before the age of fourteen was obscure and should be cleared up by a better wording. But in regard to night school he said, "I am not advised of any provision in the law for operating public schools at night. . . . It does not occur to me that a child who works in the mill from 6 a.m. to 6 p.m. could accomplish much by attending school at night. Even children who must work require some sleep, much more than children who do not work. They cannot work both night and day. The legislature, of course, knew that. The act has not for its purpose the requirement that children should do the unreasonable, if not the impossible."[49]

The National Committee decided to continue the branch office which it had opened in Atlanta prior to the campaign of 1906.[50] McKelway urged this action for a number of reasons. A southern office served to identify the South with the child labor cause, and was in line with the policy of appointing southern men to do the committee's work in the South. The argument of northern interference, however unreasonable it might seem to outsiders, was a force

[47] *Congressional Record*, XLI, 1797-98; *Constitution*, Jan. 27, 1907.
[48] *Constitution*, Jan. 30, 1907.   [49] *Ibid.*, June 28, 1907.
[50] N. C. L. C. Minutes, Aug. 3, 1907; A. J. McKelway, "Report to Board of Trustees," Oct. 1, 1909, MS in N. C. L. C. Library.

to be reckoned with in the South, and everything possible had to be done to weaken the prejudice against the national organization. From another viewpoint, it was more practical to distribute literature and gain interest from a southern office than from New York. The work of correspondence for the southern branch had grown to such an extent that it necessitated a permanent office and a stenographer to keep it in order. So far as the location of this office was concerned, McKelway recommended Atlanta rather than Charlotte or any other manufacturing center. Aside from being the largest city in the manufacturing section of the South, it had three daily papers, the *Journal,* the *Constitution,* and the *News,* with a large circulation, that supported child labor legislation. "Georgia, rightly or wrongly, is regarded rather as the leader in social progress by the other Southern States. . . . On account of the long, though unsuccessful, fight for a child labor law in Georgia, there is a large number of people in Atlanta and throughout the State, vitally interested in our cause, and they are men and women of such intellectual caliber that their influence will be felt throughout the South."[51]

The National Committee did not undertake to improve the situation in Georgia by asking for any amendments to the law in 1907. It was considered wiser to wait at least until the 1908 session. Bills to regulate the employment of children were introduced in both the House and Senate in 1907 but were not acted upon.[52] The National Committee employed the Reverend Alfred E. Seddon as an agent to investigate cotton mills and he began his work in the fall of 1907.[53] He did not find himself a welcome visitor in many of the mills. In one small town he was refused a room in the only hotel by the order of the mill manager. Neither was he admitted to the mill, and he was kept practically under guard until he could be put on a train and sent away. Conditions as he reported them were not good. In one town where there were five mills he found two hundred and fourteen children allowed to work under affidavits that they were supporting widowed mothers or disabled fathers. In another town there was no record kept of children employed in such cases.[54]

The National Committee arranged to hold its fourth annual conference in Atlanta in April, 1908, and asked Lewis W. Parker of South Carolina, as a representative of the manufacturing interests, to appear on the program. The committee's welcome from the city officials was somewhat doubtful. The president of the Chamber of

---

[51] A. J. McKelway, "Reasons for Establishing a Southern Office," MS in N. C. L. C. Library.

[52] Ga., *Journal of the House,* 1907, p. 121; *Journal of the Senate,* 1907, p. 95.

[53] N. C. L. C. Minutes, Nov. 26, 1907.

[54] "Investigation of Conditions of Child Labor in Georgia Cotton Mills," 1908, MS in N. C. L. C. Library.

Commerce, Asa G. Candler, said that child labor, "properly conducted, properly surrounded, properly conditioned, is calculated to
bring the highest measure of success to any country on the face of
the earth. The most beautiful sight we see is the child at labor; as
early as he may get at labor the more beautiful, the more useful
does his life get to be." This speech was open to more than one interpretation. The committee chose to consider it as "subtle humor."[55]
Hooper Alexander, while expressing approval of the National Committee with which he was in accord, warned it that the thing which
had retarded progress most was the "limited amount of impotent
scolding from New England" which aroused the popular feeling on
which the "vested interests have shrewdly played for their own purpose."[56] Lewis Parker championed compulsory education as a substitute for child labor legislation. He gave the usual description of
the benefits which the mills provided for their employees and of their
efforts to make them like other citizens. He attacked McKelway's
assertions as to the number of children engaged in manufacturing
in the South.[57] McKelway was presiding at the meeting at which
Parker spoke, and he took occasion to reply to Parker's statements.[58]
Seddon, who came to the meeting fresh from his experiences as an
investigator, told his audience that while the welfare work praised
by Parker greatly improved the conditions in the mills, such work
was the exception rather than the rule, and even where it existed
it could not take the place of a compulsory education law or excuse the presence of children in the mills.[59]

While this meeting served to advertise the child labor reform it
did not create enough new interest to secure additional improvements in the law. The bill which had been introduced in the House
by Wright of Floyd County in 1907 had not been taken up again
in that year. But in 1908 the General Judiciary Committee took it
under consideration. Its chief difference from the Law of 1906 was
the elimination of the exceptions clause which allowed children under twelve to work, and the provision for a ten-hour day for workers
under sixteen years of age.[60] The State Child Labor Committee endorsed the bill and McKelway spoke before the Judiciary Committee
in its behalf. An effort was made in the committee to reduce the

[55] "Proceedings of the Fourth Annual Meeting of the National Child Labor
Committee," in *Child Labor and Social Progress*, 1908, p. 159.
[56] *Ibid.*, p. 160.
[57] Lewis W. Parker, "Compulsory Education, The Solution of Child Labor
Problem," in *Child Labor and Social Progress*, pp. 40-56.
[58] "Proceedings," in *Child Labor and Social Progress*, pp. 167-70.
[59] A. E. Seddon, "The Education of Mill Children in the South," in *Child
Labor and Social Progress*, pp. 70-72.
[60] Ga., General Assembly, House Bills, 1907-1908-1909, Bill No. 115.

hours still further, but it was rejected. Although the committee gave a favorable report, the bill was crowded out by more pressing matters at the end of the session.[61]

The National Committee continued to make investigations through Lewis Hine, the photographer who had done similar work in North Carolina. He found that he was unwelcome in some places, and was "convinced that in every one of these mills there were gross violations of the existing child labor law."[62] In the months that followed, McKelway devoted most of his time to the work of the National Committee in Washington, so that the state philanthropists were left largely to their own devices. The southern office in Atlanta was given up and the center of interest for the time being shifted to the Carolinas.[63]

In 1909 bills were presented to provide for factory inspection and to amend the child labor act.[64] They were killed by the opposition from Jack Spalding who was now president of the Georgia Industrial Association.[65]

In 1910 a new phase of child labor was attacked with the introduction of bills to regulate the employment of minors in messenger service.[66] They met with protests from the attorney for the Western Union and Postal Telegraph companies, and from officers of each corporation, who succeeded in having the age limit cut down from twenty-one to sixteen and in changing the hour after which children might not be employed from 8:00 to 9:00 P.M.[67] The House passed the bill after considerable opposition.[68] The Senate gave it a bare constitutional majority, with seventeen members not voting, just before it adjourned sine die.[69] The act prohibited the employment of minors under sixteen in the delivery of messages for any person or company engaged in the messenger business after 9:00 P.M. or before 6:00 A.M.[70]

Although no amendments to the child labor law were adopted in 1911, other laws having a direct bearing on the child labor situation were passed. One provided for the sixty-hour week in cotton and woolen mills.[71] The other created a Department of Commerce and

[61] N. C. L. C. Minutes, Sept. 30, 1908; Constitution, Aug. 4, 1908; Ga., Journal of the House, 1908, p. 724.
[62] "A Photographic Investigation of Child Labor Conditions in the Cotton Mills of Georgia," 1908, MS in N. C. L. C. Library.
[63] N. C. L. C. Minutes, Jan. 5, 1909.
[64] Ga., Journal of the House, 1909, p. 236.   [65] Constitution, July 20, 1909.
[66] Ga., Journal of the Senate, 1910, pp. 514, 753.
[67] Constitution, July 28, 1910.
[68] Ibid., Aug. 4, 1910.   [69] Ibid., Aug. 11, 1910.
[70] Ga., Acts of the General Assembly, 1910, pp. 117-18.
[71] Ga., Journal of the House, 1911, pp. 169, 646, 707; Acts of the General Assembly, 1911, pp. 65-66.

Labor with a commissioner whose duty it should be to collect information as to the condition of laboring people in the state.[72] These bills had been steadily demanded by the labor organizations ever since the late 1890's and their passage was a distinct triumph for them. The subject of child labor legislation was not pressed very strongly by the State Federation for several years after the enactment of the law of 1906. The few bills that had come before the legislature for limiting hours for minors were possibly endorsed by the labor unions[73] but there was no great effort to push them through. Even when the American Federation of Labor held its annual convention in Atlanta in November, 1911, there was no public discussion of the problem, for the attention of the convention was turned upon its internal problems.[74]

In the summer of 1912 McKelway returned to Georgia to work for the bill which Hooper Alexander had introduced in the House in 1911.[75] Alexander was a member of the State Child Labor Committee and prominent in state politics. He was a member of the House from DeKalb County. During July, 1912, a substitute for the bill was taken up in the House as a compromise between the manufacturers and the reformers. It eliminated the provisions in the original bill relating to certificates and schooling which had been objected to by the millowners. The manufacturers endorsed the substitute in a letter which Alexander read in the House when he made his speech on the bill. It provided a twelve-year age limit for 1913, thirteen years after 1913, and fourteen years after 1915. As this was a compromise measure, opposition was not expected, and it passed the House by a vote of one hundred and eleven to ten.[76] The results in the Senate were not so fortunate. The bill was considered there and defeated. McKelway said that the defeat was due to the influence of individual cotton manufacturers who did not consider themselves bound by the agreement of the group that had arranged the compromise with Alexander, because the House had amended the measure by excepting mercantile establishments from its provisions.[77]

The National Committee again undertook investigations and

[72] Ga., *Journal of the House*, 1911, pp. 174, 514, 630, 1272; *Journal of the Senate*, 1911, pp. 299, 528, 669, 897-903; *Acts of the General Assembly*, 1911, pp. 133-34.

[73] Ga. Federation of Labor, *Proceedings* of the Fourteenth Annual Convention, 1912, p. 42.

[74] Newspaper accounts in *Constitution* throughout November, 1911.

[75] Ga., *Journal of the House*, 1911, pp. 177, 646; N. C. L. C. Minutes, Sept. 30, 1912.

[76] Ga., *Journal of the House*, 1912, pp. 164, 408; *Constitution*, July 17, 1912; N. C. L. C. Minutes, Sept. 30, 1912.

[77] Ga., *Journal of the Senate*, 1912, pp. 310, 410; N. C. L. C. Minutes, Sept. 30, 1912; "McKelway's Account," in McKelway Papers.

publicity in Georgia in 1913. In the spring two investigators made reports on conditions in the state. Lewis Hine covered twenty-five mills and found one hundred and fifty children working who were apparently under twelve, fifty of whom were proved to be so by means of school records, insurance papers, family Bibles, or parents' statements.[78] The reports of the Georgia Commissioner of Labor, which were compiled from information contributed by the manufacturers, did not indicate such a large number of children employed. It listed a total of thirty-five children between ten and twelve, and eleven hundred and twenty-eight between twelve and fourteen.[79] Harvey P. Vaughn, a Presbyterian clergyman from Tennessee, after his visits to a number of mills, reported that he found the hours long and the people apathetic. He did not consider the child labor conditions very unfavorable, however.[80]

The National Committee maintained that the certificates issued by ordinaries in Georgia were unsatisfactory because of carelessness or the wilful violation of the law.[81] A large part of the information gathered by McKelway and his assistants was published in pamphlet form for publicity.[82]

Practically the same action occurred in 1913 in regard to legislation as had taken place in 1912. It was announced by Alexander that the manufacturers had agreed to "an uncomplicated law" to put an end to the labor of young children.[83] When the legislature opened, bills were introduced in both houses on June 27, 1913.[84] The Senate again rejected the measure because it had been amended in the House.[85]

The National Committee was concentrating much of its attention on Georgia at this time. Its recommendation for legislation there was that the age limit be raised to fourteen, that street trades be forbidden to boys under fourteen and girls under eighteen, that the age limit for messenger service be raised to twenty-one, and that an eight-hour day for children be adopted. Compulsory school atten-

[78] "Child Labor in Georgia—Investigation," April, 1913, MS in N.C.L.C. Library.
[79] Ga. Dept. of Commerce and Labor, *Third Annual Report of the Commissioner*, 1914, p. 112.
[80] "Child Labor in Georgia," April, 1913, MS in N.C.L.C. Library.
[81] A. J. McKelway, "Child Labor in Georgia," in *Child Labor Bulletin*, II (Aug., 1913), 53-79; Mary H. Newell, "Proceedings of the Ninth Annual Conference of the National Child Labor Committee," in *Child Labor Bulletin*, II (May, 1913), 157.
[82] A. J. McKelway, *Child Labor in Georgia*, 1913, N.C.L.C. Pamphlet No. 194.
[83] *Southern Textile Bulletin*, May 22, 1913.
[84] Ga., *Journal of the House*, 1913, pp. 131, 418; *Journal of the Senate*, 1913, pp. 101, 396.
[85] *Constitution*, Aug. 6, 1913; Ga., *Journal of the Senate*, 1913, pp. 564, 565.

dance, an efficient system of working permits, and medical inspection for working children were advised.[86]

An enthusiastic ally for the National Committee and the labor unions was found in 1914 in the Hearst paper, the *Atlanta Georgian and News*. The labor organizations in Georgia seemed to take a new impetus in 1914 and the American Federation placed several representatives there to try to organize working women.[87] In June a strike occurred in Atlanta at the Fulton Bag and Cotton Mills, and the strikers declared themselves in favor of increased wages, shorter hours for women and minors, reinstatement of those who had been discharged for joining a union, and prohibition of child labor under fourteen years of age.[88] Beginning with this incident and an editorial reprinted from the Hearst *Sunday American*,[89] the *Georgian* conducted a campaign of sensationalism throughout July and part of August, with daily articles, editorials, and cartoons demanding child labor legislation, which it was supporting in co-operation with the National Child Labor Committee. The Sheppard bill, which had been introduced in 1913, was still on the House calendar,[90] and on July 1, 1914, the *Georgian* featured the bill, in comparison with the old law, on the front page, and gave an account of the activities of the manufacturers who were seeking a compromise. The material for the articles was apparently drawn to a large extent from the agents of the National Committee.

The Sheppard bill was debated in the House on July 23 and 24 and a substitute was adopted in its place. An amendment was added exempting mercantile establishments, hotels, restaurants, bootblacks, and the messenger service from the operation of the law, leaving only mills, factories, manufacturing establishments, and laundries. The age limit was fourteen; certificates of age and school attendance were required for those under sixteen, for which the Commissioner of Labor was to provide blank forms. He was given power to revoke any certificate improperly issued. The bill passed by a vote of ninety-nine to forty-four.[91] In the hearing before the Senate Committee on Labor the vote was a tie, broken by the chairman, who favored the measure.[92] The Senate adopted a twelve-year exemption clause for children of widowed mothers and reduced the age below

[86] "An address to the Citizens of Twelve States on the Child Labor Laws You Should Enact in 1914," in *Child Labor Bulletin*, II (Nov. 1913), 33-43.

[87] S. Gompers, "Georgia's New Child Labor Law," in *American Federationist*, XXI (1914), 869-70.

[88] *Atlanta Georgian and News*, June 17, 1914.

[89] *Ibid.*, June 22, 1914.

[90] Ga., General Assembly, House Bills, 1913-1914, Bill No. 39.

[91] Ga., *Journal of the House*, 1914, pp. 649, 675-80; *Constitution*, July 25, 1914.

[92] *Constitution*, Aug. 4, 1914.

which certificates were required from sixteen to fourteen years and
six months. The educational requirement of ability to read and
write was struck out. In this weakened form the bill passed.[93] The
House very reluctantly accepted the Senate amendments.[94] Besides
the terms already mentioned, the new law forbade night work by
children under fourteen years and six months. It provided that the
county school superintendent and the county ordinary should investigate cases where widows asked for certificates for children to
work in order to determine whether there was actual dependency on
the child.[95]

The duty of issuing employment certificates was placed on the
Commissioner of Commerce and Labor, in co-operation with the
city and county school officials and the ordinaries. This greatly increased the duties of the commissioner, and he at once began to
urge that more assistants be added to his department.[96] He told an
agent of the National Committee that there were few violations of
the law in the South Georgia cotton mills, but that he found forty
children working in Columbus whom he believed to be under the
legal age. He found the school officials indifferent and the certificates issued to children often incorrect, giving an age and a date
of birth that did not correspond.[97]

Two bills for factory inspection were introduced in 1915, providing for two factory inspectors to be appointed by the Commissioner of Labor.[98] The Senate Committee on Commerce and Labor
reduced the number to one,[99] and the measure was left pending before the legislature until 1916. The Governor recommended its passage,[100] and it passed in the House with a large majority of votes.[101]
The inspector was to be appointed by the Commissioner of Labor
and to make reports to him. His salary was twelve hundred dollars
a year and traveling expenses.[102] The enactment of this law was
in all probability hastened because of the movement for federal regulation of child labor.

[93] Ga., *Journal of the Senate*, 1914, pp. 419, 575, 732-38; *Constitution*, Aug. 12,
1914.

[94] Ga., *Journal of the House*, 1914, pp. 1132-44; *Constitution*, Aug. 12, 13, 1914.

[95] Ga., *Acts of the General Assembly*, 1914, pp. 88-92.

[96] Ga. Dept. of Commerce and Labor, *Third Annual Report of the Commissioner*, 1914, p. 4.

[97] "A report of a visit to H. M. Stanley by Lewis Hine, March 10, 1915," MS
in N. C. L. C. Library.

[98] Ga., *Journal of the House*, 1915, p. 599; *Journal of the Senate*, 1915, pp.
294, 435.

[99] Ga. Dept. of Commerce and Labor, *Fourth Annual Report of the Commissioner*, 1915, p. 4.

[100] Ga., *Journal of the House*, 1916, p. 93.

[101] *Ibid.*, pp. 284, 662, 815.

[102] Ga., *Acts of the General Assembly*, 1916, p. 113.

Another measure of importance was the compulsory education law passed in 1916. It required the attendance at school of all children between the ages of eight and fourteen for four months a year. Children who had to work for their own support or that of their parents were exempt from this law.[103] This educational provision supplemented the child labor law of two years previous, although it left loopholes enough for evasions. It was strengthened in 1919 by extending the time required to six months a year, and providing for exemption for children to work only in the case of agricultural labor, for which a temporary excuse might be granted by the local school board.[104]

No further action was taken by the state of Georgia until 1921, when, as in several other states, plans were made for the creation of a children's code commission. A bill to establish such a commission was introduced and passed by the House of Representatives with very little opposition.[105] It was sent to the Senate but was not acted on in 1921.[106] In 1922 it was again taken up and passed in the Senate. The provisions were that the commission should be composed of ten members appointed by the governor. One should be a superior court judge, one a member of the House and one of the Senate, and one member each from the Federation of Women's Clubs, the Council of Social Agencies, the Board of Health, the Board of Public Welfare, the State Federation of Labor, the Department of Education, and the Georgia League of Women Voters. The duties of the commission were to study the laws affecting child life, the conditions of child welfare in the state, and the laws of other states; then to draft bills for presentation to the succeeding legislatures. The members were to serve without salary or remuneration, and no appropriation was made for conducting the investigation.[107]

The commission was organized in 1923. The Council of Social Agencies granted the services of its executive secretary and organized an advisory committee on children's laws. Hearings were held at the capitol and groups interested in special legislation presented their ideas. No recommendations as to legislation were offered in 1923, though a report of the commission's studies was made.[108]

The commission co-operated with the Federal Children's Bureau, calling upon it to make a survey of school children employed outside of school hours in Atlanta. The Federal Bureau in November and December of 1922 also made inspections of certain Georgia textile mills in order to determine whether the removal of the restrictions

[103] *Ibid.*, pp. 101-2.   [104] *Ibid.*, p. 358.
[105] Ga., *Journal of the House*, 1921, pp. 486, 583, 1030-31.
[106] Ga., *Journal of the Senate*, 1921, p. 770.
[107] Ga., *Acts of the General Assembly*, 1922, pp. 71-72.
[108] U. S. Dept. of Labor, Children's Bureau, *Publication No. 131*, p. 37.

of the second federal child labor law had lowered the standards for the employment of children. The report on thirty-nine mills in seventeen localities was that federal standards were violated in all but three and state standards were violated in all but seven. In these mills the state law was violated in 149 cases, 65 of which were in regard to age, 81 in regard to employment without certificate, 3 in . regard to night work. The majority of children under sixteen worked more than ten hours a day.   There were found 57 children under fourteen employed, presumably under the exception clause of the law.[109]   This report indicates that the child labor problem had not yet been solved in Georgia, but another report from the same source showed a decrease of 50 per cent, or from approximately 8,800 children between ten and sixteen in 1910 to about 4,400 in 1920, employed in mills in Georgia.[110]

The Manufacturers' Association, at about the same time that the Children's Bureau investigations were being made, passed resolutions asking the state legislature to raise the age limit for employment to fourteen for day work and sixteen for night work. They did not include reduction of hours in their petition. The *Southern Textile Bulletin* declared that there were only eight children under fourteen years of age employed in Georgia mills, but that these eight gave an excuse for agitation so the manufacturers wished a change in the law.[111]

Bills proposing to amend the child labor law were introduced in 1923[112] and 1924,[113] but they were not supported by the Children's Code Commission or any other organized group and failed to receive much consideration.

By 1925 the Children's Code Commission was ready to make its report and recommendations. It offered eight bills relating to protection of children and based on the principle of a juvenile court in every county.[114] The bills relating to child labor were introduced in the House at the very beginning of the session, with Mrs. Viola Ross Napier of Bibb County taking the lead in advocating them. The child labor bill was drafted by the Commissioner of Labor, H. M. Stanley, and was influenced in part by the Alabama law of 1919. A separate bill provided for two factory inspectors instead of

[109] *Ibid., Eleventh Annual Report,* 1923, pp. 17-19.
[110] *Ibid., Publication No. 93,* Table between pp. 16-17.
[111] Aug. 16, 1923.
[112] Ga., *Journal of the House,* 1923, pp. 490, 585; *Journal of the Senate,* 1923, p. 331.
[113] Ga., *Journal of the House,* 1924, pp. 264, 438, 556.
[114] *Constitution,* June 24, 1925.

one.[115] These measures were supported by a number of prominent men, including several of the superior court judges, whose endorsements were published in the *Constitution*.[116] The bills were debated before the House Committee on Labor on July 14, 1925. The secretary of the Manufacturers' Association expressed the sympathy of his organization with the work of the commission and its desire to see the laws passed. The chief demand for amendment came from William S. Tyson of McIntosh County, where canning of sea food was a leading industry. He demanded exemption for this industry from the provisions of the child labor and inspection bills, arguing, as had the cotton mill men twenty years earlier, that it would ruin this industry in the state to pass such laws. Mrs. R. K. Rambo of the Atlanta Women's Clubs argued with him that exemption for one industry would give the others cause for complaint, but the desired amendment was granted. It was also agreed not to forbid children under fourteen to act on the stage.[117] The House accepted the amendment to the child labor bill and it was passed by one hundred and four to seventy-nine votes.[118] In the last few minutes before the vote was taken, friends of the bill realized that there were not enough present who favored it to give it a constitutional majority. One of the members held off the voting for a while by making various inquiries and motions while Mrs. Napier went through the corridors looking for members who would vote aye. When the vote was finally taken it was necessary for the speaker to vote in order to give the required majority.[119] The bill for two inspectors was reported favorably, but was lost in the House.[120]

In the Senate the child labor bill was delayed for about two weeks, and was then tabled. A few days later it was taken up and after slight amendment was passed by twenty-six votes to fourteen, which was a rather narrow constitutional majority.[121]

The terms of the new law were a marked advance over the former laws. Besides establishing a fourteen-year age limit for day work and a sixteen-year limit for night work in manufacturing establishments, mills, workshops, and laundries, it required that children under sixteen should be excluded from certain specified dangerous employments. A better system of certificates was provided with safeguards to prevent as far as possible fraudulent statements of age. Adminis-

[115] Ga., *Journal of the House*, 1925, pp. 32, 33; *Constitution*, June 27, July 21, 1925.

[116] July 19, 20, 1925.   [117] *Constitution*, July 15, 1915.

[118] Ga., *Journal of the House*, 1925, pp. 473, 475.

[119] *Constitution*, July 22, 1925.

[120] Ga., *Journal of the House*, 1925, p. 425.

[121] Ga., *Journal of the Senate*, 1925, pp. 320, 513, 737, 813, 839-40; *Constitution*, Aug. 12, 1925.

tration continued in the hands of the Commissioner of Labor, who had authority to revoke improperly issued certificates and to enforce the other terms of the act.[122]   The chief weakness left in the law was inadequate provision for inspection. Efforts were made to pass bills providing for the inspectors[123] and to improve the system of certificates[124] in 1927.   Both passed the Senate but were not successful in the House.[125]

The reforms made in Georgia child labor legislation in 1925 were due in large part to the interest of women in social legislation.   The Children's Code Commission was composed of representatives of organizations some of which were composed wholly or in part of women, and the measures in the House in 1925 were championed by a woman representative.[126]   Another factor that led to the passage of better laws was the change in attitude of the manufacturers.   The fear of the proposed federal amendment and the feeling that it was necessary to justify Georgia's opposition to it by showing that the state had the proper attitude toward protection to its children was an influence favorable to legislation. Georgia shared with the other states that awakening of social conscience which was leading not only to negative child labor laws but to constructive legislation for state guardianship and protection of all children.   There have been no changes in the Georgia child labor law since the Act of 1925, but, according to the chief inspector of the Department of Labor, there were no children under sixteen working in the textile mills in 1938.[127]

[122] Ga., *Acts of the General Assembly*, 1925, pp. 292-97.

[123] Ga., *Journal of the Senate*, 1927, pp. 225, 574, 743.

[124] *Ibid.*, pp. 673, 766, 1420.

[125] Ga., *Journal of the House*, 1927, pp. 682, 776, 1329.

[126] *Constitution*, Aug. 9, 1925; Ga. Federation of Women's Clubs, *Year Book*, 1924-25, pp. 166-67, 188.

[127] Letter of W. E. Christie to the author, May 24, 1938.

CHAPTER XI

ALABAMA AFTER 1904; SUCCESSFUL LEGISLATION

THE MOST spectacular child labor campaign of 1903 had taken place in Alabama. After its completion the contest was not allowed to drop. It spread to form the basis of the national movement which after 1904 undertook to set the standard for child labor legislation in all the states. But the law which Alabama had adopted was a compromise. It set no higher standard than was found in the Carolinas. The problem of inspection and enforcement had not been solved and the age limit was seriously weakened by an exemption clause. There would be no further session of the legislature for four years. The leaders of local reform either turned their attention to the problem of organizing the National Child Labor Committee or else let the subject drop for the time being. Murphy's work for the Southern Education Board had taken him away from Alabama, although he kept in close touch with the affairs of the state through correspondence and through visits to Montgomery. He continued to write and speak in the interest of child labor legislation and of better education laws.[1] Other members of the Alabama Committee remained much concerned with conditions in the state. Some of them felt that the increased interest in Negro education in the South was giving colored children an advantage which white children in the mill communities were being denied.[2]

There was no effort to arouse popular interest in the child labor situation in Alabama in 1904 and 1905. The Alabama Federation of Labor at its annual session in 1905 did not take any action or express any views on child labor.[3] The existing child labor law was violated and it is improbable that the offenders were prosecuted in many cases.[4] In 1906, with the approach of elections, public attention was once more drawn to child labor. The State Federation of Labor in that year urged its members to question candidates for office as to their views on this and other labor legislation.[5] A degree of political interest centered around child labor in this campaign because of the

---

[1] Statement of Mrs. E. G. Murphy.   [2] N. C. L. C. Minutes, Feb. 15, 1905.
[3] Ala. State Federation of Labor, *Constitution and Proceedings*, Fourth Annual Convention.
[4] N. C. L. C. Minutes, Nov. 16, 1905; *American Federationist*, XI (1904), 142-43.
[5] Ala. State Federation of Labor, *Constitution and Proceedings*, Sixth Annual Convention, p. 20.

candidacy of B. B. Comer for governor. Comer was the head of one of the largest mill corporations in the state, and was a planter as well. His political ideas were advanced and his enemies called him radical. In 1903 he entered politics as a candidate for the presidency of the railroad commission. His object was to secure a downward revision of railroad rates and to put an end to discrimination against short hauls. In 1906 he became a candidate for governor against R. M. Cunningham.[6]

The *Montgomery Advertiser,* which opposed Comer politically, took advantage of his position as a millman to lead an attack on him on the subject of child labor legislation. A newspaper controversy began in June as to whether Comer had actually opposed child labor legislation in previous years. He was accused of having contributed money to a fund used in opposing the child labor bill of 1900. Comer vigorously denied this, but the *Advertiser* published a letter from E. G. Murphy, in which Murphy said that in the conference between the committee and the manufacturers in 1903 Comer had earnestly opposed legislation in any form and such concessions as he agreed to were made with great reluctance. He had opposed requiring children under fourteen to attend school twelve weeks a year, and while he declared that he did not employ children at night he refused to agree to a sixteen-year limit for night work and had it reduced to thirteen. Murphy said, "Mr. Comer has seemed to me the most bitter opponent of child labor legislation I have ever known."[7]

A. J. McKelway, the southern secretary for the National Child Labor Committee, had been in Alabama early in 1906 for the purpose of reorganizing the Alabama Child Labor Committee, and conferring with Murphy. He took advantage of the opportunity to make an investigation of the Avondale Mills at Birmingham, of which Comer was president.[8] The *Advertiser* got possession of a letter written by McKelway describing the Avondale Mills in which he said that small children were employed there. He gave the names of several children whom he said were ten years of age and working in this mill, and described it as next to the worst one he had ever investigated. During the political campaign the *Advertiser* published this letter, giving it front-page prominence, and added an editorial, "Mr. Comer's Preaching and His Practice."[9]

Comer denied the truth of McKelway's statements through a series of published affidavits. A Methodist minister and a physician of the mill village testified that sanitary conditions there were good, a free school was maintained nine months a year, and children under the

[6] A. B. Moore, *History of Alabama and Her People,* I, 915-20.
[7] *Montgomery Advertiser,* June 29, 1906.
[8] "Report to Board of Trustees," Oct. 1, 1906, MS in N. C. L. C. Library.
[9] Aug. 3, 1906.

legal age were not at work. Several employees said that "no children are employed in said mill under legal age and have not been since the Child Labor Law was passed by the last Legislature." The book-keeper of the mill testified that three of the children whose names were given by McKelway as being only ten years of age had never been on the payroll. The parents of all of them swore that they were of legal age before being employed, or that they were never employed illegally.[10]

The *Advertiser* had supported child labor reform in 1903, but its zeal was increased in large measure because of its political opposition to Comer. Forgetting any dislike it may have had for northern criticism, it quoted an article by Edwin Markham just published in the *Cosmopolitan*. Markham drew chiefly on the stories of Mrs. Van Vorst, Mrs. Macfadyen, and Elbert Hubbard.[11] The *Advertiser* played up the declarations of Cunningham in favor of reform legislation and ridiculed Comer's position.[12]

Comer, whose principal platform was reformation of the railroad laws, was the successful candidate. The railroad problem took precedence over all others in the new session of the legislature. In accordance with the principles of the Democratic platform, which declared that children "of tender years" should be prohibited from employment and that those who were allowed to work should be required to attend school for a certain length of time each year,[13] Comer had to take a stand in favor of moderate child labor legislation. His position on the subject was not unlike that of D. A. Tompkins and other progressive manufacturers of the South. In his message to the legislature he suggested that a gradual limitation of age and some method of compulsory education be adopted. But he continued: "At the same time, I will caution you that a great many people have gone to the mills to work because they have found by experience that they can earn more money and do better than they can elsewhere, and in large families they can better take care of themselves with their earning capacity there than elsewhere, and it is a very serious matter for the State to assume the guardianship as to how and when these people shall work and direct and dictate to them by methods of law as to whether they shall or shall not work where they think to their best interest.

"In the rural districts and in towns and cities there are many poor families, many poor families with children, and any one familiar with the conditions of such things would know that many of them could do better in the mill than elsewhere."[14]

[10] *Advertiser*, Aug. 11, 1906.   [11] *Ibid.*, Aug. 21, 1906.
[12] Aug. 25, 27, 1906.   [13] *Advertiser*, Sept. 11, 1906.
[14] Ala., *Journal of the House*, 1907, p. 145.

The message of the retiring governor when the Assembly convened characterized the existing child labor law as "not sufficiently reformatory," and not very effective, and expressed the hope that an improvement would be made.[15]

The Assembly had a full program when it met after a four-year period of no legislation. There were a number of bills for labor legislation proposed in the first few days. On January 10, 1907, A. D. Kirby of Madison County introduced a child labor bill and Benjamin H. Smith of Franklin County a ten-hour bill in the House of Representatives.[16] Within a few days a compulsory education bill was introduced,[17] and another bill by Kirby requiring all factories to provide school buildings for minor employees.[18]

The Alabama Child Labor Committee, which had reorganized for the new crisis, agreed on a bill at a meeting held about the middle of January. The terms as reported in the *Advertiser* provided for the supervision of the mills by an inspector who should visit each mill twice a year. No boys under fourteen or girls under sixteen should be employed except in order to support a widowed mother, in which case the limit should be twelve years. The president of the Manufacturers' Association was also reported to have a bill ready to present, of which Governor Comer was supposed to approve. It would put the age limit at fourteen with the twelve-year exception for children of indigent parents, and require twelve weeks of schooling a year in order to secure employment.[19] The latter bill did not provide for enforcement, which was the chief point on which the reformers wanted legislation.[20]

The Child Labor Committee bill as it was introduced in the House by Alexander D. Pitts, of Dallas County, provided for a fourteen-year limit for both boys and girls, instead of the sixteen-year limit for girls at first suggested. The exemption clause for children twelve and over who were the support of widowed mothers or totally disabled fathers was retained. No child between twelve and sixteen should be employed unless he attended school twelve weeks a year; no child under twelve should be employed under any circumstances; no child under sixteen should work more than ten hours a day or fifty-six hours a week, or between the hours of 7:00 P.M. and 6:00 A.M.; no child between sixteen and eighteen should work more than eight hours at night. Affidavits of the age of children

[15] *Advertiser*, Jan. 10, 1907.
[16] Ala., *Journal of the House*, 1907, pp. 57, 62.
[17] *Ibid.*, p. 142.   [18] *Ibid.*, p. 224.
[19] *Advertiser*, Jan. 18, 1907. The editor, Frank P. Glass, was a member of the Alabama Child Labor Committee.
[20] *Ibid.*, Jan. 20, 1907, quoting Birmingham *Age Herald*, Prattville *Progress*, Birmingham *Ledger*.

should be made by parents or guardians for all who were employed under eighteen years of age, and affidavits of school attendance should be made by the county superintendent. There were penalties for violation. The governor should appoint a child labor inspector at a salary of $1,800 a year plus traveling expenses up to the sum of $500. Inspections should be made at least four times a year and reports of violations made to the county solicitor. Annual reports of inspection should be printed. Judges of probate, circuit and other courts, and the county superintendent of education should also have authority to inspect.[21]

The joint Senate and House committees on Mining and Manufacturing held a meeting to consider the child labor bills. The chief difference between the Kirby, or manufacturers', bill and the Pitts bill was in the matter of inspection, although the age limits were in some respects different. The lobby for the Kirby bill was made up of mill officials and for the Pitts bill of representatives of the Alabama Federation of Women's Clubs and the State Child Labor Committee. McKelway, the representative of the National Committee, spoke for the Alabama Committee, as did Neal L. Anderson and B. J. Baldwin. Mrs. Erwin Craighead spoke for the women's clubs. G. W. Pratt, the president of the Manufacturers' Association, and other mill officials, represented their interests.[22] After the hearing the bills were not acted on during the winter session of the legislature.

During the first weeks of the session a bill for the inspection of jails and almshouses was passed by the House.[23] In the Senate it was amended so as to include the inspection of cotton mills.[24] The child labor reformers in the House refused to agree to this amendment, because they felt that it would result in the defeat of the child labor bill, which not only provided for inspection but raised the age limit as well.[25] But when the bill went to the Governor, he proposed the same amendment that the Senate had recommended. The House then changed its position and accepted the amendment. This was a defeat in the eyes of the child labor reformers, since the passage of this bill would stand in the way of the improvement of the child labor law without resulting in what they considered as satisfactory provision for enforcement.[26]

In the interval between the winter and summer terms of the legislature of 1907 the people interested in legislation continued to debate the matter. The State Federation of Labor at its annual convention

[21] Ala., House Bills, Legislative Dept., 1907, State Dept. of Archives and History.   [22] Advertiser, Feb. 8, 1907.
[23] Ala., Journal of the House, 1907, p. 1242.
[24] Ala., Journal of the Senate, 1907, p. 1178.
[25] Advertiser, Feb. 27, 1907; Ala., Journal of the House, 1907, p. 1953.
[26] Advertiser, Mar. 3, 1907.

in April declared its interest in the Pitts bill and appreciation of the co-operation of the other interests with labor in endeavoring to secure legislation.[27]   The labor unions were not very active in working for legislation, however.   Despite their protests that they alone had demanded it for years, their interest was more passive now.   They did not receive the stimulation from the American Federation of Labor that had urged them to action a few years earlier.   This was probably best for the child labor reform and it is possible that the president of the American Federation still considered it wise to abide by the policy Murphy had urged upon him.   Also the fact that the attempts to organize southern workers about 1900 had not been very successful had led to a decline in active interest on the part of the national organization in the South.

Edgar Gardner Murphy, in spite of the serious condition of his health, was still vitally interested in the Alabama reform.   He wrote an open letter addressed to the members of the state legislature, dated July 8, 1907.   It was inconsistent, he said, to appoint a state game inspector at a salary of twenty-five hundred dollars and to refuse to provide a child labor inspector.   The existing law was inadequate and the result of compromise.   The demands for reform were not made because of any personal animosity.   "I would deal with institutions and conditions rather than with individuals.   Many of the mill men of my State are men of high character and unquestionable honour.   But there has never been an industrial or social evil, from the beginnings of History, which has not found 'good men,' men who have been really good, to excuse it and to defend it.   Such facts may puzzle us, but they should not mislead us.   They should make us charitable to individuals, but they should make us all the more alert against mental confusion and moral apathy, should rouse us to the closer scrutiny of public conditions and a more careful and consistent enactment of public measures—if the broader welfare of all the people is to be conserved."[28]

Copies of this pamphlet were sent to every legislator in the state, but because of the hostility which the friends of Comer felt against Murphy the Alabama Committee advised Murphy against publishing it in the *Advertiser,* so it did not appear there.[29]

When the bill for inspection was passed in the winter, the Governor immediately appointed Dr. Shirley Bragg as inspector of jails, almshouses, and cotton mills.   Bragg made a report to the Governor

---

[27] Ala. State Federation of Labor, *Constitution and Proceedings,* Seventh Annual Convention, Montgomery, 1907, pp. 24, 44-47.

[28] *The Child Labor Question in Alabama,* July 8, 1907.   This pamphlet was republished by the N. C. L. C. as Pamphlet No. 59.

[29] McKelway to Murphy, Jan. 17, 1911, in Murphy Letters, endorsement in Murphy's hand giving this explanation.

in July before the legislature reconvened, but the Governor did not submit it to the Assembly until the Senate requested it in the latter part of July when the child labor bills were again brought up.[30] It was not a complete or well-organized report, but it was sufficient to show that there was extensive violation of the existing child labor law.[31] Governor Comer recommended that a method of enforcing the child labor law be adopted. This, he said, could be easiest done by empowering the inspector to discharge any girl or boy who in his judgment was under the legal age or not fit to work, and providing a penalty for re-employing such a child without the inspector's permission. The Governor was unwilling to agree to the more advanced legislation advocated by the Alabama Committee. "Will caution you that by an extreme provision of the law you can easily hurt the parties that we are trying to help. We have the poor with us always, and it is as much incumbent upon the business of the State to provide methods of work, and perhaps would be more beneficial to this class of our fellow citizens, than to provide ways how they should work; and we should be exceedingly careful along this line."[32]

When the Assembly reopened, the Pitts bill was on the House calendar, but it continued to be delayed. The *Advertiser* renewed its attack on the administration for blocking legislation. A clever cartoon represented the child labor measure as buried under a mass of legislation for the relief of individuals.[33] The remaining days of the session were growing short and friends of the bill felt that it was being unduly delayed. The *Advertiser* asserted that for forty-two of the fifty legislative days the question of child labor had received no attention. The responsibility was placed on the Governor because the administration opposed the age limit proposed in the bill. It was hinted that the Governor had warned the speaker of the House that unless certain features were changed the bill could not become law.[34]

On July 16, 1907, the House bill had been recommitted to the Committee on Mining and Manufacturing without losing its place on the calendar.[35] On July twenty-third the subject was taken up again in the House, but instead of the original Pitts bill a substitute was put in its place. Representative S. W. John of Jefferson County, a friend of the Comer administration, asked that all amendments to the original bill be withdrawn and his substitute adopted. The substitute went back to the twelve-year age limit without exceptions, instead of the fourteen-year limit with an exceptions pro-

[30] *Advertiser*, July 24, 1907; *Age Herald*, July 24, 1907.
[31] Ala., *Copies of Reports of Dr. Bragg, Inspector of Jails, Cotton Mills and Almshouses.*
[32] Ala., *Journal of the Senate*, 1907, p. 1571.
[33] July 13, 1907.   [34] July 23, 1907.
[35] Ala., *Journal of the House*, 1907, p. 2853.

viso. It required children between twelve and sixteen to attend school eight weeks a year, instead of the twelve weeks called for in the original. It advanced the number of hours of work a week for minors from fifty-six to sixty, and reduced the age limit for this provision from sixteen to fourteen. It retained the provision that no child under sixteen should work between 7:00 P.M. and 6:00 A.M. and no child under eighteen more than eight hours at night. Affidavits of age were required for all under eighteen, to be filed with the employer, and to be open to inspection by the grand jury of the county or the inspector of jails, almshouses, and factories. The inspector was empowered to inspect all mills and to prosecute the management for violation of the child labor laws. He was allowed one assistant. The bill provided penalties for those who "knowingly" violated the law, which the reformers considered a loophole for the manufacturers to escape prosecution.[36]

The committee that reported this substitute was accused of yielding to the lobby against the bill. One of the members defended its action, saying that it "had been insulted, threatened and bullied in a way that he never saw a committee treated before." The substitute was frankly a compromise, he said, as the committee had tried to suit everyone. The new measure had been submitted to the Governor and he had approved it. This was one point which caused dissatisfaction to the opponents of the administration, as they considered the substitute as dictated by the Governor. But every effort to amend the bill was promptly defeated, including the proposal to establish the fourteen-year limit for girls. The objection was that the new inspector, Dr. Bragg, stated that work in the factory was no more dangerous for girls than work in the schoolroom. The substitute bill passed the House with a vote of seventy-three to three. The reformers yielded to the compromise since they could hope to do no better.[37]

In the Senate two child labor bills had been introduced in the middle of July. One of them received no consideration.[38] The other was in most respects like the House substitute advocated by the administration and had the endorsement of the new prison and factory inspector. It was considered by the committee, and accepted at about the time the House bill was received.[39] All efforts to raise the standards set in these bills failed in the Senate, and there was only one

[36] Ala., House Bills, Legislative Dept., 1907, State Dept. of Archives and History, H. 558; Ala., *Journal of the House,* 1907, pp. 3426-30; *Advertiser,* July 24, 1907.

[37] Ala., *Journal of the House,* 1907, pp. 3430-34; *Advertiser,* July 24, 1907.

[38] Ala., *Journal of the Senate,* 1907, p. 1928.

[39] Ala., Senate Bills, Legislative Dept., 1907, State Dept. of History, S. 612.

opposing vote.[40] The manager of the bill opposed all amendments because the measure was a compromise and its terms once agreed on should remain as they were.[41] An amendment suggested by the Governor that the new law should go into effect January 1, 1908, was concurred in by both houses.[42] The act was ratified August 9, 1907.[43]

The new law was below the standard which had been set by the State and National committees. Like practically all the child labor laws passed in this period, it represented a compromise. Two years later the representative of the National Child Labor Committee stated that it was only through the influence of Neal L. Anderson and B. J. Baldwin of the State Committee that Comer had been persuaded to compromise,[44] but Comer had always represented himself as being in favor of "moderate" action. Although the law fell short of McKelway's expectations, he made the most of it, considering any gain as worth the effort, and reported to the National Committee that the result was satisfactory.[45] The state labor organization was not so well pleased, for its president termed the law so altered as to be unrecognizable as the original endorsed by the union.[46] The Labor Federation was not represented at the legislature when the contest took place because the executive committee felt that the Assembly was too much interested in the liquor question to have time for labor problems.[47] In reality the whole question of child labor legislation in 1907 hinged more on politics than on the activities of the reformers. It had played a part in the preceding elections and the enactment of a law depended on the consent of the dominant political faction. The National and State Child Labor committees were both interested, but the relations between them may have been a bit strained because Murphy and Anderson strongly disapproved of the action of the National Committee in regard to the Beveridge bill in Congress.

The long and full session of the legislature in 1907 did not complete the work that the new administration intended for it. Governor Comer called for a special session in 1909. Its principal object was to consider railroad legislation, but in his proclamation convening the Assembly the Governor named the "re-enactment" of the child

[40] Ala., *Journal of the House*, 1907, pp. 2351, 2464, 2777-82.

[41] *Advertiser*, Aug. 2, 1907.

[42] Ala., *Journal of the House*, 1907, p. 3026.

[43] Ala., *Acts of the General Assembly*, 1907, pp. 757-62.

[44] McKelway, Memorandum as to the co-operation of the manufacturers in the South, N. C. L. C. Minutes, May 12, 1909, Appendix I.

[45] Report of McKelway to Lovejoy, Aug. 3, 1907, N. C. L. C.

[46] Ala. State Federation of Labor, *Constitution and Proceedings*, Eighth Annual Convention, p. 24.　　　　　[47] *Ibid.*, p. 39.

labor law as a matter to be dealt with.[48] On the first day of the session a bill was introduced in the House by S. W. John which embodied the terms of the law of 1907.[49] The club women had been expected to make some demands for improvement, but they took no active part in demanding changes.[50] The bill went through the House with little comment or opposition, although some efforts to raise its standards by amendment failed. It passed with only three opposing votes.[51] In the Senate there was no opposition[52] and the act was approved on August 26, 1909.[53]

The first inspector of jails, almshouses, and factories appointed by Governor Comer under the new law was Dr. C. F. Bush. His first report was published in December, 1909. He estimated that there were 14,606 employees working in the 63 cotton mills, 1 woolen mill and 7 knitting mills of the state. Of this number 4,525, or 31 per cent, were between the ages of twelve and eighteen; 2,535, or 17 per cent, were between twelve and sixteen. He reported that the sanitary conditions in the mill were good, but that the sixty-hour week in most cases was interpreted to mean any number of hours a day and a half day on Saturday. He believed that parents were guilty of fraud in making affidavits of age for their children, and he had removed a number of children from employment, but since he had no proof of their ages he was unable to prosecute. In making his investigation he found that 115 of the children of school age had not fulfilled the educational requirement before going to work. Night school was not regarded as fulfilling the law. His chief complaints were not that the law was poor or incapable of enforcement, but that the people who had urged reform legislation failed to give him co-operation and encouragement in carrying it out. There was only one inspector and one clerk for the sixty-nine jails, seventy-one factories, and fifty-five almshouses, or a total of 195 institutions which must be inspected.[54]

The agent of the National Child Labor Committee who made investigations of some of the mills of Alabama in 1910 also reported that the age limit was evaded, although he failed to get the open admissions that were made in the Carolinas. In the mills around Huntsville and Anniston he found a number of such cases, and the

[48] Ala., *Journal of the House*, Extra Session, 1909, p. 7.
[49] Ala., House Bill No. 49, Legislative Dept., 1909, State Dept. of Archives and History.   [50] *Advertiser*, July 28, 1909.
[51] Ala., *Journal of the House*, Extra Session, 1909, pp. 46, 120, 505, 507.
[52] Ala., *Journal of the Senate*, Extra Session, 1909, pp. 319, 387, 580-81.
[53] Ala., *Acts of the General Assembly*, 1909, pp. 158-162.
[54] C. F. Bush, *First Annual Report of the Department for the Inspection of Jails and Almshouses and Cotton Mills, Factories, etc.*, for 1909 (Montgomery, 1910), pp. 5-13.

attitude of the mill managers was not friendly toward his activities. He criticised Governor Comer's Birmingham mill, where he was naturally not very welcome, and where he took photographs before securing permission from the manager.[55]

Popular interest in child labor reform reached a low ebb after the passage of the laws in the Comer administration. The State Committee was again inactive. The labor organizations showed no interest. The women's clubs agreed "that Alabama, so far as its women could do it, was to have a rest from further reform bills, until the present dose had taken effect."[56] Having secured a law, it was easy to let the whole subject slip into the background and to leave enforcement and improvement to take care of themselves. The state inspector complained that he received no moral support from the erstwhile reformers and his complaint was probably well founded. The legislature met in regular session in February, 1911, and although a child labor measure was presented it attracted little attention and no support. The whole public interest was centered on the struggle over prohibition and local option. The *Advertiser* did not mention child labor in its editorial columns. The Stollenwerck bill provided for the amendment of the child labor law so that no child under fourteen years of age should be employed in manufacturing. It had no support and was unfavorably reported by the Judiciary Committee.[57] A Senate bill to amend the enforcement provisions of the existing law met with no opposition and passed both houses, although it was delayed somewhat.[58] The new provision declared it a misdemeanor knowingly to employ children in violation of the law or to refuse to give information to the inspector. The prison inspector or his chief clerk was required to inspect every mill and factory in the state four times a year, if practicable without previous notice.[59] At the same time a law was passed requiring county school boards to maintain a school in every mill community where fifty or more children were employed, and requiring these schools to be in session wherever possible as long a term as the other schools in the districts. The purpose of this act was to enable children to comply with the compulsory attendance provision of the child labor law.[60]

[55] Lewis W. Hine, "Report of Photographic Investigation into Child Labor Conditions in Tennessee and Alabama," and "Alabama Investigation," MSS in N. C. L. C. Library.

[56] Ala. Federation of Women's Clubs, *Year Book*, 1910-11, p. 27.

[57] Ala., House Bill 526, Legislative Dept., 1911, State Dept. of Archives and History; *Journal of the House*, 1911, pp. 970, 1877.

[58] Ala., *Journal of the House*, 1911, pp. 1733, 2544; *Journal of the Senate*, 1911, pp. 551, 780, 1290.

[59] Ala., *Acts of the General Assembly*, 1911, p. 546.

[60] *Ibid.*, pp. 247-48.

Before these bills had gone through the legislature, the National Child Labor Committee met in Birmingham during the second week in March for its seventh annual convention. The State Child Labor Committee, which had been quiescent for a while, was reorganized[61] and appeared as host to the convention.[62] The general subject for the meeting was uniform child labor laws.[63] The chief attraction offered was former President Roosevelt, who was then on a speaking tour through the South.[64] The committee felt greatly encouraged by the reception it received in Birmingham. The executive secretary wrote, "Two years ago the fifth conference met in Atlanta. The South had not been sufficiently aroused and informed. It resented the implications of many of the reports on southern conditions, especially in the cotton mills. A polite, but rather cold, hearing was given and the attendance of southern people of influence was meager and unsatisfactory. Official reports and the persistent and better organized efforts of the National Committee in the interval have made an impression."[65] In Birmingham there was a satisfactory attendance at the meetings. Three hundred business men came to a luncheon to discuss child labor and at each of the two mass meetings at least fifteen hundred people were reported to be present.[66]

McKelway went down to Montgomery from Birmingham with an exhibit on child labor. It was displayed in the hope of influencing the legislators. It presented the child labor problem as national rather than sectional, and illustrated the evils found in the cotton mill and canning industries with photographs. Again the Avondale Mill of which Comer was president was represented in a bad light.[67] The *Advertiser,* whose interest in child labor had lagged somewhat published some of the photographs and comments from the exhibit.[68] But in spite of the apparent interest Birmingham showed in the national convention, the legislature failed to take any action on the bill to raise the age limit and to remove the clause in the law which used the word "knowingly" in connection with violation of the age limit.

However poor the Alabama law may have been, its provisions for factory inspection did something toward promoting the regulation of conditions, and if nothing else, presented annual evidence that children were still employed in the mills in considerable numbers. The report of 1912 showed that the inspector, Dr. W. H. Oates, had visited 54 mills. In them he found over 1,900 children employed

[61] Conference of Charities and Corrections, *Proceedings,* Thirtieth Convention, p. 445.
[62] *Advertiser,* March 5, 1911.
[63] *Ibid.*
[64] *Ibid.,* March 10, 1911.
[65] S. M. Lindsay, "Seventh Annual Child Labor Conference," in *Survey,* xxvi (1911), 124.
[66] *Ibid.*
[67] *Advertiser,* March 15, 1911.
[68] March 16, 1911.

legally.[69] The greatest numbers were found in a few counties: in Chambers, where Lanett was located on the Chattahoochie River just opposite the great West Point, Georgia, mills; in Etowah, where the Dwight Manufacturing Company of Alabama City employed 218 children legally; in Madison where a number of mills centered around Huntsville. Other localities where large numbers of children were employed were Florence in Lauderdale County on the Tennessee River, Anniston in Calhoun County, and Pell City in St. Clair, and in Walker and Elmore counties. There were a few scattered mills elsewhere, but these represented the areas that were most seriously concerned with cotton mill child labor, and that had opposed the passage of restrictive legislation.

Oates was fully aware of the difficulties of his office. He characterized the child labor laws as "conspicuous by their ambiguity, inefficiency, inexplicitness and inadequacy."[70] In his experience he found the parents indifferent to education and anxious to put their children to work. The affidavits they made concerning the ages of children were worthless and yet in the absence of vital statistics it was almost impossible to bring together the evidence necessary to prosecute offenders. The inspector removed forty-two children whom he believed to be under twelve years of age from working in factories. For this condition he held the parents more responsible than the mill managers. Yet the latter allowed children to do piecework with their parents and did not put their names on the pay roll. Contrary to the report of the first inspector, he found the provisions for sanitation and fire protection inadequate.[71] The inspector endeavored to enforce the educational provision, and posted in the mill lists of children who were eligible for employment and those who were not, according to this clause of the law.[72]

The four-year period between meetings of the legislature in Alabama gave the reformers an opportunity to build up new demands for improvement and to arouse the social conscience of the state more fully. The child labor law was an imperfect instrument, but its enactment had been a considerable achievement in the face of the opposition which it received. The early reforms had been directed against child labor in the one great offending industry, and the vigorous defense made by the cotton mills had centered public

[69] Ala., Factory Inspector, *Children Eligible for Employment . . . in 1912.* The copy in the possession of the Alabama Child Welfare Department has certain additions written in by hand as the investigations were carried further after the report was printed.

[70] Ala., Factory Inspector, *Annual Report* (Montgomery, 1913), p. 5.

[71] *Ibid.*, pp. 8-9, 11, 16-22.

[72] Ala., Factory Inspector, *Children Eligible for Employment in . . . 1913;* and *Children Ineligible for Employment in . . . 1913.*

interest there. But with its expanding program and gradual change of standards the National Child Labor Committee began to agitate for reforms in other occupations employing minors. In the Gulf States along the coast, oyster and shrimp canning were profitable industries in which children could be exploited. The investigations made by the National Committee turned some public attention on conditions along the coast which had hitherto been ignored.[73] The committee was also giving attention to the employment of boys in the night messenger service, which was regarded not only as injurious from the standpoint of night work, but as being a serious threat against the moral welfare of the boys employed.[74] The cotton mills were beginning to receive divided attention, but they were not neglected. The committee's agent continued to visit mills and his reports bore out the statements of the factory inspector that the law was insufficient. In some mills it was evident that the owners used various schemes to circumvent the educational requirements of the child labor law, and the committee's agents in confidential reports charged them with actual dishonesty.[75]

By 1914 some of the local reformers began to arouse themselves from the apathy that had settled down after the meeting of the legislature in 1911. Some of them, particularly a few members of the women's organizations, co-operated with the National Committee in planning and carrying out an extensive investigation of child labor conditions throughout the state.[76] One of the most prominent women working in this connection was Mrs. W. L. Murdoch. She was the most active member of the Alabama Child Labor Committee as it then stood, although it was not at that time functioning to any great extent. She tried to keep alive the interest of the Women's Federation, and this body gave the investigation theoretical support, though for a time its actual activity was very limited. There was in fact some friction between the Federation of Women's Clubs and the child labor reformers.[77] It may well have been that some of the prominent club leaders who were connected with prominent manufacturers resented the constant criticisms of the cotton industry. This

[73] E. F. Brown and L. W. Hine, "The Child's Burden in Oyster and Shrimp Canneries," MS in N. C. L. C. Library; Edward F. Brown, "The Neglected Human Resources of the Gulf Coast States," in *Child Labor Bulletin*, II (1913), 112-16.

[74] Edward F. Brown, "The Demoralizing Environment of Night Messengers in Southern Cities," in *Child Labor Bulletin*, II (1913), 138-41.

[75] L. W. Hine, "General Statement—Investigation of Merrimack Mfg. Co., Huntsville, Ala.," and "Special Investigation of Child Labor Conditions in Alabama," MSS in N. C. L. C. Library.

[76] N. C. L. C. Minutes, Nov. 23, 1914.

[77] L. W. Hine, "Special Investigation of Child Labor Conditions in Alabama," MS in N. C. L. C. Library; Ala. Federation of Women's Clubs, *Nineteenth Annual Convention*, Nov., 1913, p. 8, and *Twentieth Annual Convention*, Nov., 1914, p. 10.

was the opinion of Mrs. Murdoch, who was herself able to see and sympathize with this view.[78]

Mrs. Emmons Blaine was interested in the proposed investigations and secured a gift of a thousand dollars from her sister, Miss Mary V. McCormick, of the wealthy Huntsville McCormick family.[79] In the fall of 1914 Lewis W. Hine of the National Committee and eleven other investigators, ten women and one man, undertook a state-wide study of the child labor problem, not only in cotton mills but in other industries as well. An effort was made to establish harmonious relations and a spirit of co-operation between the committee and the women's clubs. Interviews with officials of the clubs as well as superintendents of schools, factory inspectors, and business men helped to bring about desired results. Mrs. Murdoch concluded from her part in the investigation that the number of children under fourteen years of age who were employed was relatively small, and that economic necessity was not the force driving children to work. The newspaper carriers and the other street trades had not yet been reached by any law. Neither had child workers in department stores or in messenger service been protected. Lewis Hine made special inquiries into the messenger service and his report on existing conditions made reform there appear as a necessity.[80]

The investigations were completed just in time for the material to be used in agitating for a new law in 1915. The National Committee sent Herschel H. Jones to Alabama to take charge of organizing the campaign and to work with the other interested groups. He was elected secretary of the Alabama Committee and organized the legislative program of the reformers.[81] The results of the investigation were given publicity through the press. The evil conditions under which messengers worked at night were especially emphasized. Cotton mills, which had for fifteen years borne the brunt of the attack, were relieved somewhat, though certainly not exonerated, by the emphasis placed on other evils. An effort was made to present the National Child Labor Committee in a favorable light. It was represented as "a kind of clearing house, which supplies expert and absolutely correct information upon all subjects pertaining to the subject of child labor, from the necessity of such laws to the enforcement of them." The standard law for which the committee was

[78] Letter from Mrs. W. L. Murdoch to the author, July 14, 1931.

[79] N. C. L. C. Minutes, Nov. 23, 1914.

[80] L. W. Hine, "Special Investigation of Child Labor Conditions in Alabama, MS in N. C. L. C. Library, which includes Mrs. Murdoch's report; also, Hine "Notes on the Messenger Service of Birmingham," MS in N. C. L. C. Library, and Mrs. W. L. Murdoch, "Conditions of Child Employing Industries in the South,' in Child Labor Bulletin, II (1913), 124-28; and "Child Labor Reform in Alabama," ibid., Vol. III (1914), No. 1, pp. 82-84.

[81] N. C. L. C. Minutes, Nov. 23, 1914; Jan. 26, 1915

asking enactment in Alabama was the one approved by the American Bar Association, which called for a fourteen-year age limit and an eight-hour day for all children under sixteen. The committee also proposed that the superintendent of schools be made the main factor in enforcing the law; this would necessitate no new department for enforcement, but it was recommended that three inspectors instead of one be provided. It also proposed that the school attendance requirement be increased. An effort was made to meet and defeat the old arguments that work of children was a necessity for the support of widowed mothers. Less than a third of the families in the Birmingham district whose children worked were found to be really dependent on them for necessities. "If there are twenty women in the state who would actually starve to death, if this law were passed, let them go on and starve rather than jeopardize the welfare of thousands of children in the state who are now working when they should be going to school." The state could care for such cases as these and free two thousand children from the mills.[82]

Besides publicity through the newspapers, Jones wrote a pamphlet which was published under the name of the Alabama Child Labor Committee and which also appeared as a pamphlet of the National Committee.[83]

In his report to the National Committee, Jones said that other occupations than cotton manufacturing would receive the greater emphasis in the movement for a new law. He expected opposition chiefly from the representatives from the rural districts, who, he said, saw the problem only in local terms. The Negro child also complicated the matter of legislation. Jones realized that the demands the committee was making were higher than there was probability of getting, but they might make for a more favorable compromise. He felt that he had the support of Mrs. Murdoch and the Alabama Committee, the Federation of Women's Clubs and the State Federation of Labor, and two of the leading papers, the *Advertiser* and the *Birmingham News*. Another problem causing difficulty was the threat of certain elements to bring about the abolition of the office of state prison inspector on whose direction the enforcement of the child labor law was dependent. The reformers were asking for two additional inspectors, and were prepared, in case the office of prison and factory inspector were abolished, to introduce a special bill for inspection.[84]

The Alabama legislature opened the second week in January.

[82] *Advertiser*, Jan. 11, 1915; also Jan. 5, 1915.
[83] H. H. Jones, *Child Labor in Alabama*.
[84] H. H. Jones, "Plans for the Campaign for a New Law in Alabama," MS in N. C. L. C. Library. See *Advertiser*, Jan. 12, 1915, for support Women's Federation was giving the movement.

Governor Emmet O'Neal in his message recommended the enactment of a law, specifying the terms in accordance with the reform
program.[85] A few days later the committee's bill was introduced into
the House by Representative John B. Weakley of Jefferson County
and in the Senate by H. T. Hartwell of Mobile. It was based on the
uniform child labor law endorsed by the National Child Labor Committee and the American Bar Association. A bill was also introduced
by Representative S. W. John, who had supported the Comer measures in former years, but it differed in most essentials from the
"women's" bill.[86]

Before any action was taken on the bills the new governor, Henderson, was inaugurated, and endorsed the reform program.[87] Every
effort was being made to give the subject publicity. The *Advertiser*
published accounts of the lobbying activities of the women who were
busy interviewing legislators, distributing campaign propaganda, and
studying the terms of the bill and the arguments to be used in its
favor. The committee and the Federation of Women's Clubs put a
child labor exhibit in the rotunda of the capitol. It consisted of
pictures illustrating the various employments of children, the ignorance of families allowing children to work, and the poor schools
provided for the education of the children. It also offered answers
to the questions of what to do with families dependent on children
for support; whether child labor did not furnish good training; and
whether it did not keep children out of mischief.[88] Some of the clergy
took the matter up and sermons were preached on child labor in
the pulpits of both Montgomery and Birmingham.[89] The demand
for legislative reform had become widespread, and the *Advertiser*
anticipated that the legislature would respond by enacting a new
law.[90]

Although the reform measure contained provisions which would
restrict the employment of children in practically all occupations in
the state except agriculture and domestic service, it would also
place more stringent limitations on the cotton mills, and the manufacturers, as on all such previous occasions, sought to defend themselves. They claimed that the Hartwell-Weakley bill was too drastic,
since to limit the hours for children to forty-eight a week would mean
that the whole mill would have to run on that schedule; that it
would drive their operatives out of the state; that the workers did
not want such a law; and that in the depressed state of business then
existing the mills would be crippled by it. There was nothing new
in these arguments, but a group of mill operators came to Mont-

[85] Ala., *Journal of the House*, 1915, pp. 132-35.
[86] *Advertiser*, Jan. 16, 1915.
[87] *Ibid.*, Jan. 20, 1915.   [88] *Ibid.*, Jan. 17, 18, 21, 1915.
[89] *Ibid.*, Jan. 25, 1915.   [90] Jan. 24, 1915.

gomery to appear before the legislative committee. Prominent among the speakers for reform were the women, including Mrs. Murdoch and Mrs. Erwin Craighead. R. E. Gann represented the Alabama Federation of Labor. The most notable fact about the hearings was that opposition to reform on the grounds that it was labor legislation or northern interference did not appear at all. It was also significant that the only industry represented in opposition was textile manufacturing. There was apparently no strong objection from the canning or messenger companies or from the department stores and newspapers.[91]

The legislative committee was favorable in its attitude, but the manufacturers, as on all previous occasions of this kind, had the strength to force the reformers to compromise. They absolutely refused to agree to a forty-eight or even a fifty-five hour week for minors, and the committee and Women's Federation had to yield or lose their whole reform.[92] They also agreed to lower the night messenger service to eighteen years as a concession to the telegraph companies who then withdrew their opposition. This industry had not presented any strong demands before the committee as had the cotton mills. Such concessions were no more than the reformers expected.

The bill was reported favorably by substitute.[93] The principal opponent was Representative John. After a heated debate the measure passed by a vote of eighty-two to ten.[94] In the Senate the vote was thirty to five.[95]

The new law was more comprehensive and detailed than any heretofore proposed, and in spite of the House amendments it raised the standards of regulation. It had certain weaknesses, however. For the year from September, 1915, to September, 1916, the age limit was placed at thirteen, and thereafter at fourteen for all gainful occupations except agriculture and domestic service. The clause was worded so as to exclude the possibility of evasion by allowing children whose names were not on the pay roll to work. The only exception to the age limit was that boys of twelve and over might work in business offices or mercantile establishments in towns under twenty-five thousand during vacation. No child under sixteen could be employed more than six days a week, or more than sixty hours a week, or eleven hours a day, or between 6:00 P.M. and 6:00 A.M. The hour

[91] *Advertiser*, Jan. 28, 29, 1915.
[92] Ala. Federation of Women's Clubs, *Year Book*, 1916, pp. 50-51. The N. C. L. C. placed responsibility for this opposition on former Governor Comer. See N. C. L. C. Minutes, March 15, 1915.
[93] Ala., *Journal of the House*, 1915, p. 956; *Advertiser*, Jan. 31, Feb. 2, 1915.
[94] Ala., *Journal of the House*, 1915, pp. 1210-30; *Advertiser*, Feb. 12, 1915.
[95] Ala., *Journal of the Senate*, 1915, pp. 1015, 1196.

limit asked for had been forty-eight. The presence of a child under sixteen in any mill or factory was to be regarded as prima facie evidence of his employment there. The mills were required to keep copies of the law posted in prominent places where children worked. No person under eighteen years of age was allowed to work as a messenger for any telegraph, telephone, or messenger company between the hours of 9:00 P.M. and 5:00 A.M. in cities of twenty-five thousand or more, or after 10:00 P.M. in cities of smaller size. No person under twenty-one was allowed to work in any establishment where intoxicating liquors were made or sold. A number of occupations involving danger from the use of machinery or other causes, and employment in theaters and concert halls were closed to children under sixteen. Boys under twelve years of age and girls under sixteen were excluded from selling papers or employment in other street trades. No boys under sixteen should be so engaged between 8:00 P.M. and 5:00 A.M. Children employed legally in such occupations were required to wear a badge. Boys ten and over were allowed to deliver newspapers in residence sections.

The system of employment certification adopted provided that the employer should keep on file certificates for the children he employed for the inspection of the state officials. If the inspector found a child employed without a certificate he should require the employer to present proof of the child's age in ten days. If this were not done the child was dismissed, and any continuation of employment was illegal. Children under sixteen were required to attend school eight weeks a year, six of which should be consecutive, in order to be eligible for employment. The person in charge of issuing certificates was the superintendent or principal of the school in the city or district where the child lived, or lacking such an official, the county superintendent. These officers could delegate their duties to some other person. In order to secure a certificate the child, accompanied by his parent or guardian, should appear before the issuing officer and present a school record signed by the teacher or principal of his school, stating that he had attended school at least sixty days in the preceding year. The acceptable evidence of age for a certificate was a birth certificate, passport, or baptismal certificate. But because of the general lack of laws requiring registration of births throughout the South, it was necessary as a last resort to accept the affidavit of the parent. When the employment of the child terminated, the certificate should be returned to the child if he asked for it, or to the officer who issued it.

The enforcement of this law was continued in the hands of the state prison inspector who was also known as the factory inspector, and of his deputies. It was his duty to institute prosecution against violators and to require that prescribed sanitary regulations be complied with. The inspector was given free access to any place where children were employed at any time, and penalties were provided against giving false statements or refusing admission to establishments, as well as for other violations.[96]

The most serious defect of this law was in the low school attendance requirement. A compulsory school law was passed by the same legislature requiring children between the ages of eight and fifteen inclusive to attend school eighty days a year, unless the county or city board reduced the time to sixty days. Children who had to work because of extreme poverty were exempt from school attendance.[97] The child labor law required only forty days' attendance at school. The continuation of inspection in the hands of the prison inspector was also a cause of weakness. It placed a burden on a department that had other heavy duties and an insufficient force, and whose primary purpose was not the regulation of the employment of children. The new law did not pass without criticism of its provisions from the *Advertiser,* which charged the legislature with being unduly prejudiced in favor of its manufacturing friends.[98]

The interest of Alabama people in child labor and the problems of regulating it was now thoroughly aroused. The weakness of the Law of 1915 had still to be removed and the work of bringing about a change in the next legislative session four years later was taken up by the women's clubs and the National Committee. The co-operation of these two agencies had produced the Law of 1915, and it was through them that further reforms were to be made. The State Federation of Women's Clubs in the next year renewed its demands for shorter working hours for children and a sufficient number of inspectors to enforce the law.[99] Mrs. Murdoch, who had been the most active Alabamian in securing legislation in 1915, now began to agitate for a bill to require physical examinations for children. As chairman of the Alabama Committee, Mrs. Murdoch worked largely at her own expense. The National Committee was now called on to help, in this respect.[100] Another source of help was again found in Mrs. Emmons Blaine, who, as trustee of the Virginia McCormick fund, agreed to finance an investigation of child welfare in Alabama to the amount of $6,325.[101] The McCormicks lived in Huntsville and had taken an interest in social work among the mill people there, establishing Y. W. C. A.'s that were in reality settlement houses.[102]

[96] Ala., *Acts of the General Assembly,* 1915, pp. 193-200.
[97] *Ibid.,* pp. 534-35.   [98] Feb. 12, 17, 1915.
[99] Ala. Federation of Women's Clubs, *Year Book,* 1916, p. 35.
[100] N. C. L. C. Minutes, Feb. 13, 1918.   [101] *Ibid.,* Mar. 20, 1918.
[102] Statement of Mrs. Lorraine B. Bush, who became Mrs. A. M. Tunstall, head of the Child Welfare Department of Alabama.

The investigation which was carried out with the aid of the McCormick fund took the form of a survey of conditions in the state. The survey indicated the progress made in thought on social problems in Alabama. It dealt not only with child labor but with the larger problems of care and education for dependent, delinquent, and defective children. Similar evidence appeared in the study of penal and taxing systems of the state, which was conducted by the Russell Sage Foundation at the invitation of the newly elected governor. The Child Welfare investigation was a thorough piece of work, conducted under the direction of the National Committee's agent, Edward N. Clopper, with the aid of the state university and of Mrs. Lorraine B. Bush.[103] Mrs. Bush, who was the widow of a former factory inspector, appointed during the Comer administration, and who was familiar with the child welfare problems of Alabama, was made a representative of the National Child Labor Committee, and a deputy factory inspector as well. She and Wiley H. Swift, the committee's agent for the southern states, planned a legislative campaign for 1919.[104]

Governor Kilby had outlined legislation for a board of control, along the lines suggested by the recent investigations. He had not, however, included a children's bureau in the plan, and when it was first suggested to him by Mrs. Bush he objected to a change in the program he had announced. When Mrs. Bush and Thomas M. Owen, head of the Department of Archives and History of Alabama, drew up such a bill and presented it to him they secured his approval. The club women of the state again gave their support to reform.[105]

The prospect of another reform bill was no more pleasing to the cotton manufacturers than before. They had hoped the Law of 1915 would be final, and had been given to understand by Mrs. Murdoch that no new demands would be made in 1919. The National Committee had given no such assurance, and its representatives went ahead with the preparation of a bill. Donald Comer, son of the former governor and now head of his father's mills, was much disturbed, and he asked Mrs. Bush to come to Birmingham and discuss the matter with the millmen there. At this conference Mrs. Bush presented each of the men with a copy of the bill, which had not as yet been made public. It was then that the argument that northern interests were interfering in the affairs of the state was made for probably the last time in connection with the enactment of a state child labor law in Alabama. A certain manufacturer lost his temper somewhat and declared that he was tired of having a northern or-

[103] Edward N. Clopper, *Child Welfare in Alabama*, N. C. L. C. Publication; also N. C. L. C. Minutes, Sept. 30, 1919.

[104] N. C. L. C. Minutes, Sept. 30, 1919.

[105] Mrs. Tunstall's (Mrs. Bush) statement to the author.

ganization with its headquarters in New York coming into Alabama every time the legislature met and telling the state what to do. Alabama was capable of handling her own problems. This was the cause of some laughter at the expense of the man who made the remark, for Mrs. Bush, who was very well known to the men present, was a native of Clarke County, Alabama, while the man who made the assertions about northern interference was forced to admit that he was born in Massachusetts.[106]

Opposition to child labor reform and child welfare work had weakened to a remarkable degree in the four years since 1915. The two measures introduced into the Assembly encountered very little opposition. The first was to regulate child labor so as to remedy some of the defects of the old law, and the second was to create a child welfare department and put the enforcement of child labor laws under its direction. The measures passed without a dissenting vote in the House and only slight opposition in the Senate.[107] One reason for the new attitude toward child labor legislation may have been the desire to meet the federal standard.[108] But there was also a general feeling of the need of such laws for the good of the state. Alabama had become conscious of her responsibilities toward the children of the State. The war may have had a part in bringing this about as it seemed to arouse people to an effort to remedy social ills,[109] but it was no less true that the laws were the result of years of effort on the part of a few people.

The law relating to the employment of children kept the same age limit for work. It cut down on the hours to meet the forty-eight hour week provided for in the federal statutes. Careful regulation of work certificates was provided for and the additional requirement for a health certificate made. Practically the same restrictions were made on hours during which children might be employed as in the former law.[110] The regulation of school attendance for working children only was no longer necessary since a compulsory school attendance law had been enacted which required children between eight and sixteen to attend the entire term, though those over fourteen were excused if they were legally employed or had completed grammar school.[111] Most important of all, the enforcement of the child labor law was transferred from the hands of the prison inspector to the newly created Child Welfare Department. This department was under the control of a board consisting of the governor of the

[106] Statement of Mrs. Tunstall to the author.
[107] Ala., *Journal of the House,* 1919, pp. 1164, 1298, 1651, 2117, 2524-25; *Journal of the Senate,* 1919, pp. 751, 911, 1006-7, 1151, 1429, 1430, 1435.
[108] *Advertiser,* Aug. 1, 12, 1919.   [109] *Ibid.,* July 11, 1919.
[110] Ala., *Acts of the General Assembly,* 1919, pp. 867-76.
[111] *Ibid.,* p. 619.

state, the state superintendent of education, the state health officer, and six other persons appointed by the Governor. This new body not only controlled the administration of child labor laws but had supervision of all the laws relating to the welfare of children.[112]

The Alabama Child Welfare Department proved an efficient agency in enforcing the child labor laws. All difficulties were not immediately solved by the passage of a good law. While its enactment was popular, its enforcement frequently met with indifference. Local officials were often unwilling to prosecute the violators. The department began a policy of building up public sentiment in favor of enforcement. They worked to interest the employers in co-operating with the department in the enforcement of the law rather than undertaking to force compliance by police methods. The problem of the mill child was no longer the most difficult one. The manufacturers had learned through previous laws to abide by regulations. It was the miscellaneous establishments, the stores and shops, that employed only one or two children, that proved most difficult.[113] The work of the department was made immeasurably easier by the changed attitude of the manufacturers. Men who had once opposed legislation and either evaded laws or offered passive resistance now joined in co-operation with the department in enforcing the provisions of the law. The Cotton Manufacturers' Association, the heads of the chain stores, and the Western Union officials were named along with the State Federation of Labor by the chief child labor inspector as agencies that gave their co-operation in enforcing the child labor law.[114] Mrs. Bush, who had been largely responsible for securing the laws of 1919, became the first head of the Child Welfare Department.

In 1935 a reorganization of state departments took place in which the Child Labor Division of the old Child Welfare Department was transferred to the new Department of Labor. Unfortunately, under the new arrangement there was provision for only one inspector for the state instead of the two previously employed, but there has been every effort made to uphold the high standard of enforcement set by the original Child Welfare Department.[115] The inspector finds that since the NRA regulations were in force for a time the manufacturers have employed fewer children under sixteen than previously.[116]

[112] *Ibid.*, p. 695.

[113] Esther Lee Rider, "Child Labor and Vocational Education," in *Proceedings, Eighth Annual Convention of Association of Government Labor Officials,* 1921, pp. 22-27.

[114] Statement of Miss Ruth Scandrett, chief child labor inspector of Alabama, to the author [1931].

[115] Ala., Dept. of Labor, *First Annual Report,* 1935-36, pp. 26-30.

[116] Letter of Mrs. Daisy Donovan to the author, May 18, 1938.

CHAPTER XII

CHILD LABOR LEGISLATION IN SOME OTHER SOUTHERN STATES

THE NUMBER of cotton mills outside of the manufacturing area of North and South Carolina, Georgia, and Alabama was small. Virginia, Tennessee, and Mississippi had a few, though cotton manufacturing never reached the importance there that it had in the states that bordered them to the south and east. All the coast states had the problem of child labor in the industry of canning sea foods. Florida, with practically no cotton mills, put up a fight against the child labor reforms because of this industry. Tennessee and Virginia were among the first southern states to achieve child labor reform. Mississippi and Florida were among the later group. In 1900 the rank of the southern states according to the number of cotton mill employees was as follows: North Carolina, South Carolina, Georgia, Alabama, Virginia, Tennessee, and Mississippi. The rank according to the proportion of children employed was North Carolina, Alabama, South Carolina, Georgia, Mississippi, Tennessee, and Virginia.[1]

Mississippi was essentially an agricultural state. There were no cities of any considerable size, and only a few large towns. With one half of its population Negro, its people were engaged principally in raising cotton. According to the Census for 1900 there were about 98,000 children employed in the state, almost 89,000 of whom were in agriculture, 7,000 in domestic service and 1,163 in manufacturing and mechanical employment. Although the legislature was about to meet in 1906 when McKelway made a report to the National Committee on conditions in the state, he advised that "effort here would be wasted, considering pressing conditions elsewhere."[2]

In spite of this report the National Committee undertook an investigation of the Mississippi cotton mills in 1908, and organized a state committee there. Conditions found in the mills were on a par with those in South Carolina. Young children were employed, parents were indifferent, and illiteracy was common.[3] In the same year the state legislature had enacted a law prohibiting the employment

[1] U. S. Dept. of Labor, *Census Bulletin No. 69*, p. 43.
[2] N. C. L. C. Minutes, Nov. 16, 1905, Appendix B.
[3] A. E. Seddon, "Investigation of the Conditions of Child Labor in the Cotton Mills of Mississippi," MS in N. C. L. C. Library.

of children under twelve in mills, factories, or manufacturing establishments, and restricting the employment of persons under sixteen to not more than ten hours in one day or fifty-eight hours in one week, and forbidding their employment between 7:00 P.M. and 6:00 A.M. Affidavits of the age of children were required from parents and guardians. The sheriff of each county was required to visit each factory once a month and the county health officer was required to visit each one twice a year, or oftener if requested to do so by the sheriff. The Circuit Court Judge was required to instruct the Grand Jury at each session of the court to investigate violations of the child labor law.[4] With all its weaknesses this law was in advance of the laws of the larger manufacturing states on some points. None other provided for the ten-hour day or fifty-eight-hour week, and the provision for inspection by the local sheriffs and health officers, while not providing much in the way of efficiency, was more than the Carolinas or Georgia could boast of.

The National Committee's agent, after visiting Mississippi in 1911, reported that he found conditions there better than they had been a few years earlier, but the workers were anxious to put their children in the mills. The same stories of poor farmers who had failed at agriculture and who looked to the mills for salvation were told here as elsewhere. They willingly violated the law, declaring their younger children to be twelve years of age, and put them to work.[5] Nor was the attitude of the manufacturers different from their Carolina and Georgia contemporaries. The president of a large mill located at Stonewall, which was operated on a paternalistic system, called McKelway's statements "a pack of lies"[6] and the National Child Labor Committee an agent of the East to undermine southern prosperity. He described the charitable work which he did as justification for conditions in his village, and he refused to allow the committee's agent to go into the mill. The physician of the place supported his claims that the children and other employees were in good health, but the teacher at the school where mill children were supposed to attend declared that many of them were totally illiterate.[7]

In 1912 the committee sent Edward N. Clopper to Mississippi where he spent several weeks in propaganda work for a fourteen-year age limit.[8] The women's organizations such as the United Daugh-

[4] Miss., *Laws of the State*, 1908, pp. 88-89. Hereafter cited as *Laws*.

[5] L. W. Hine, "Child Labor in the Cotton Mills of Mississippi," April-May, 1911, MS in N. C. L. C. Library.

[6] A. J. McKelway, *Child Labor in Mississippi*, N. C. L. C. Pamphlet No. 169.

[7] Alexander Fleisher, Stonewall, Miss., "Report, Jan. 2-4, 1912," MS in N. C. L. C. Library.

[8] N. C. L. C. Minutes, May 1, 1912.

ters of the Confederacy, the W.C.T.U., and the State Federation of Women's Clubs, also worked to arouse publicity.[9] A law was passed raising the age limit to fourteen for girls and leaving it at twelve for boys. An eight-hour day and forty-eight-hour week for boys under sixteen and girls under eighteen was established. Canneries were also included under the law's provisions. In other respects it re-enacted the Law of 1908.[10]

The investigators from the National Committee in the winter of 1913-14 found the child labor law was unenforced. H. H. Jones reported that not a single county sheriff had inspected the factories once a month as the law required, and only two had made any inspections at all. In one town which the sheriff had inspected, Jones reported seventy-four violations in two mills. Only two health officers were found who had ever visited the factories. The age, hour, sanitation, and fire protection laws were all found to be violated.[11] The lack of interest characteristic of the sheriffs and health officers extended to other people who were inclined to accept the manufacturers' view that the operatives were in the mill "because they like it" and that it was a means of working out their salvation with which it was not wise for outsiders to interfere. The millmen were regarded as public benefactors in that they provided an industry which "opens its doors to the helpless and penniless women and children . . . and gives them that useful and profitable employment without which they would suffer want."[12]

The other large industry in which Mississippi was an offender in regard to child labor was in oyster and shrimp canning. At the coast towns of Biloxi, Pass Christian, and Bay St. Louis, conditions similar to those in Alabama and Florida occurred. There was no regard for the legal restriction of hours and no affidavits of the ages of the children at work kept on file. Numbers of children were found to be employed in violation of the law.[13]

H. H. Jones, who made these investigations, was not made welcome by the Mississippi Child Labor Committee, so he left the state.

[9] Mrs. E. L. Bailey, "Conditions of Child Employing Industries in the South," in *Child Labor Bulletin*, II (May, 1913), p. 129.

[10] Miss., *Laws*, 1912, pp. 173-75.

[11] H. H. Jones, "Notes on the Need for Factory Inspection in Mississippi," Dec., 1913-Jan., 1914, MS in N. C. L. C. Library; also, *idem*, "Stonewall Cotton Mills," Jan. 15, 1914, MS in N. C. L. C. Library.

[12] *Statements of Mississippi King's Daughters, Professor O. A. Shaw, President of Winona High School; and Dr. B. F. Ward, as to Conditions of Health and Sanitation at the Winona Cotton Mill*, leaflet, extracts from the *Meridian Dispatch*, Jan. 28, 1914.

[13] H. H. Jones, "Violations of the Child Labor Law in the Oyster and Shrimp Canneries of Biloxi, Pass Christian, and Bay St. Louis, Miss.," Jan. 10, 1914, MS in N. C. L. C. Library; L. W. Hine, "Baltimore to Biloxi and Back," in *Survey*, XXV (May 3, 1913) 167-72.

The State Committee was disapproved of by some other people, however, who urged that it be disbanded and matters of reform left altogether to local initiative.[14] There was, in spite of this, enough feeling favorable to reform to secure the enactment of a law providing for a state factory inspector. The State Board of Health was empowered to appoint an inspector at a salary of fifteen hundred dollars a year plus traveling expenses. His duties were to inspect factories and canneries three times a year, collect evidence of violations of the law, and furnish it to the county or district attorney.[15] The same legislature reduced the age limit below which the eight-hour law applied to fourteen for boys and sixteen for girls.[16]

In spite of the law providing for inspection, conditions in Mississippi factories and canneries were slow to improve. Politics no doubt played a part in this. In January, 1916, the state inspector, David McDowell, told the National Committee's agent, Lewis Hine, that Governor Theodore G. Bilbo had cut off his appropriation for two months. The inspector had been in office two years but had never prosecuted anyone for violation of the child labor law, on the theory that people should be led and not driven. He said that he used "common sense" in enforcing the law in the shrimp canneries since it was not very harmful work. Another man told Hine that McDowell did not enforce the law because he was afraid of political opposition in the Gulf Coast region. The principal of the high school at Jackson said that Bilbo had made an unsuccessful attempt to oust McDowell from office, and that if he could be made to fear that he would lose his position the inspections might be more efficient.[17] Hine believed the conditions in the canneries to be worse in 1916 than they had been five years before. He found one hundred and sixteen violations of the age and hour law, and evidence that others were successfully hidden from inspectors.[18]

There was not such great opposition to national legislation from Mississippi in this period as from the Carolinas and Georgia. The small number of mills meant that the cotton manufacturers were a less powerful class than in the other states, and the canning industries of the South never put up a fight against the federal laws. In the same year that the constitutional amendment was proposed, Mississippi raised the age limit for work in mills, factories, workshops, canneries, and manufacturing establishments to fourteen for boys as well as girls and provided an eight-hour day and forty-four-hour

[14] N. C. L. C. Minutes, April 20, 1914.
[15] Miss., *Laws*, 1914, pp. 209-12.   [16] *Ibid.*, p. 212.
[17] L. W. Hine, "Some Information about the State Factory Inspector of Mississippi," Feb. 29, 1916, MS in N. C. L. C. Library.
[18] "Law Enforcement in Mississippi Canneries," Feb.-Mar., 1916, MS in N. C. L. C. Library.

week for workers under sixteen. Exemption was allowed to the employees of fruit or vegetable canneries, an industry which was just beginning to assume importance in the state.[19] The salary for the inspector had been increased a few years earlier to $2,400 in a general salary revision.[20] The law provided for no regulation of newspaper or street trades; it applied only to a limited number of occupations; it made no provisions against employment of minors in dangerous occupations; its educational requirement under the compulsory attendance law was low; and no proof of age of the child other than the parents' affidavit was required for employment. The state ranked forty-ninth in the percentage of children not employed, but this included the large number of child agricultural workers. The Census of 1920 indicated only 1,570 children in manufacturing and mechanical occupations, or an increase of about 400 over the previous decade.[21]

The era of child labor legislation in Tennessee began ten years earlier than in the Carolinas and Alabama. The situation in this state was different from that in the more southern states. There were a few cotton mills, chiefly in the eastern part, where mining was also of considerable importance. Labor unions entered the state earlier than they did further south. In 1890 there were a few trade unions in Nashville, and demands began to appear for a child labor law.[22] In 1893 a law was enacted prohibiting the employment of children under twelve years of age in workshops, mills, factories, or mines. The employer was allowed to ask the parent of a child employed for a sworn statement of its age.[23] This law was on a par in its requirements with the laws of 1903 in the Carolinas. Efforts were made by the labor interests in each successive legislative year to enact a law which would set higher standards and provide for enforcement. When the State Federation of Labor was organized it secured from both the Democratic and Republican parties a pledge for child labor reform.[24] The legislature in 1901 passed a law with very little opposition.[25] This law was directly the result of the demands of organized labor,[26] and there was no organized opposition from any industry. It

[19] Miss., *Laws*, 1924, pp. 542-43.   [20] *Ibid.*, 1920, p. 159.

[21] *Child Labor Laws and Child Labor Facts*, N. C. L. C. Publication, 1929. Not paged. States arranged alphabetically.

[22] C. P. Fahey, "No Children in Tennessee Factories," in *American Federationist*, VIII (Oct., 1901), 401.

[23] Tenn., *Acts of the State*, 1893, pp. 315-16. Hereafter referred to as *Acts*.

[24] C. P. Fahey, "No Children in Tennessee Factories," in *American Federationist*, VIII (1901), 401.

[25] Tenn., *Journal of the House*, 1901, p. 346; *Journal of the Senate*, 1901, p. 515.

[26] Gompers to C. P. Fahey, April 5, 1905, Telegram, Letter Book of Gompers, Vol. XLI; Gompers to Fahey, July 22, 1901, Letter Book, Vol. XXV.

raised the age limit to fourteen, declared false swearing as to age on the part of the parents to be punishable as perjury, and empowered the grand juries to investigate violations of the act.[27] In 1908 provision was made for the gradual reduction of hours for women and children under sixteen so that by 1910 sixty hours would constitute a week's work.[28] In 1909 police power with full authority to enforce all labor laws relating to factories was conferred on the factory inspector.[29] These changes gave Tennessee a higher standard of legislation than any of the other southern states had at that time. It was also here that the movement for conferences on the child labor problem began. For this reason the National Committee paid little attention to the state for several years.

In 1911 events occurred which drew attention to Tennessee. The case of a child who received an injury in a cotton mill was carried to the State Supreme Court. The judge declared the law unconstitutional because of technical defects. This necessitated the re-enactment of the state law.[30] A few months later a child worker in a Knoxville mill attempted suicide. It was asserted that she revealed a suicide pact which a number of children had made because of the long hours of work required of them. The story was soon widespread.[31] The National Child Labor Committee earlier in the year issued a pamphlet relative to conditions in mills, mines, and the messenger service.[32]

As a result of the Supreme Court decision, the legislature re-enacted its child labor law in June, 1911, expanding its provisions so as to include within the fourteen-year age limit laundries, telephone and telegraph office work, and messenger and delivery service, as well as factories. Dangerous occupations and night messenger service were forbidden to children under sixteen.[33] In 1913 a gradual reduction of hours to fifty-seven a week was provided for children under sixteen and women, but a ten-and-a-half-hour day was allowed instead of ten hours.[34] In 1917 when the first federal child labor law was about to go into effect the Tennessee law was amended in several respects to meet its requirements. The canneries were added to the list of establishments forbidden to offer work to children; an eight-hour day and six-day week and prohibitions of night work were provided for children under sixteen; and documentary evidence of age was required

[27] Tenn., *Acts*, 1901, p. 49.

[28] *Ibid.*, 1907, pp. 1060-61.   [29] *Ibid.*, 1909, p. 406.

[30] "Mary Alma Jackson versus Welsh Manufacturing Company," Certified Transcript from Court Record, MS in N. C. L. C. Library; A. F. of L. Weekly News Letter, May 27, 1911.   [31] Atlanta *Constitution*, July 14, 1911.

[32] A. J. McKelway, *Child Labor in Tennessee*, N. C. L. C. Pamphlet No. 150.

[33] Tenn., *Acts*, 1911, pp. 108-10.

[34] *Ibid.*, 1913, pp. 407-8; 1915, p. 403. A technical error called for the second act.

for the issuing of an employment certificate.[35] This law made no provision for street trades, but in so far as manufacturing employment was concerned it put Tennessee in the rank of states with laws acceptable according to federal standards.

While Alabama was the first state to pass a law regulating the hours of labor for women and children, Virginia followed with a similar act a few years later. In 1890 it was declared that no female and no child under fourteen should work in a factory or manufacturing establishment for more than ten hours a day.[36] This was probably in response to the same wave of demand for labor legislation that was in evidence all over the South at that time, but unlike the Alabama law it was allowed to remain on the statute books of the state.

In 1903, just as the first child labor laws were appearing in the Carolinas and Alabama, Virginia passed a law forbidding the employment of children under twelve years of age in manufacturing, mechanical or mining operations, and of children under fourteen at night.[37]

When the National Committee first turned its attention to Virginia in 1905 it found that the chief industries employing children were cigar making, woolen mills, and cotton mills. As in all southern states, by far the largest number of children were employed in agricultural and domestic service, occupations which were not touched by legislation anywhere at that time. The National Committee urged the improvement of the state's law at the meeting of the 1906 legislature.[38] The labor unions also continued to stand back of the child labor movement. The State Federation had been formed in 1896 at about the time Georgia union workers took the same step. It supported the bills which came up from time to time, and tried to influence the members of the state legislature in behalf of reform.[39]

A report to the National Committee in 1908 indicated that the child labor laws of Virginia were being disregarded.[40] A law was passed the same year to raise the age limit. Children under fourteen were forbidden employment except in the case of those between twelve and fourteen who were orphans or dependent on themselves for support, or whose parents were invalids and solely dependent on them. In such a case the county court, mayor, or justice of the peace

[35] *Ibid.*, 1917, pp. 233-35.

[36] Va., *Acts and Joint Resolutions Passed by the General Assembly*, 1889-90, p. 150. Hereafter cited as *Acts*.

[37] *Acts*, Extra Session, 1902-3-4, p. 233.

[38] N. C. L. C. Minutes, Nov. 16, 1905, Appendix B.

[39] Va. State Federation of Labor, *Eighth Annual Session* (1903), p. 15; *Tenth Annual Session* (1905), pp. 13-14, 36-37.

[40] Marie Hunter, "Investigation of Virginia Cotton Mills," MS in N. C. L. C. Library.

could give the permit for the employment of the child. Fruit and vegetable canneries and country stores were also excepted from the provisions of the law.[41] Three years later the National Committee found children employed in the cotton and knitting mills, glass factories, and cigar and cigarette factories, although the Department of Labor was making every effort to enforce the law and had prosecuted violations all over the state. Even when manufacturers tried to observe the law, the parents claimed the right for their children to work under the exemption clause when there was no real need for them to do so.[42] The labor unions, which had always stood strongly back of child labor legislation in Virginia, were advised by the American Federation officials that an attempt to secure the passage of a drastic child labor law would meet with a lobby from the manufacturing interests.[43] The State Federation was urged by its secretary, however, to undertake to get the age limit raised.[44]

In 1910 the manufacturers had undertaken without success to have repealed the old ten-hour-day law for women and children which was passed in 1890.[45] In 1912 the law was re-enacted so as to include workshops and mercantile establishments as well as factories and mills.[46] The manufacturers succeeded in their effort to defeat a more strict method of issuing permits to working children.[47]

The attitude of a large part of the business and professional men, the clergy, school superintendents, social workers, and newspaper press was favorable to the enactment of an improved child labor law. The greatest difficulty apparently lay in the state Senate, for a number of people told the agent of the National Committee that many of the state senators were members of the political machine or opposed to the state prohibition act, and would probably oppose child labor reform.[48] The reform act was passed, however, removing the exceptions clause for children between twelve and fourteen, and forbidding the employment of children in any way during school hours or at night. The ten-hour day was extended to all under sixteen. The fourteen-year age limit for messenger service and eighteen-year limit for night messengers was established. Fruit and vegetable canneries

[41] Va., *Acts,* 1908, p. 542.

[42] L. W. Hine, "Photographic Investigation of Child Labor in Virginia," May-June, 1911, MS in N. C. L. C. Library; A. J. McKelway, *Child Labor in Virginia,* N. C. L. C. Pamphlet No. 171.

[43] A. F. of L. Weekly News Letter, June 3, 1911.

[44] Va. State Federation of Labor, *Sixteenth Annual Session,* 1911, p. 26.

[45] Mrs. John H. Lewis, "Report on Work at Richmond," 1910, MS in N. C. L. C. Library.   [46] Va., *Acts,* 1912, p. 558.

[47] A. J. McKelway, "Fighting Child Labor in Three States," in *Survey,* XXVIII (April 20, 1912), 122.

[48] H. M. Bremer, "Report on Trip to Virginia in the Interest of Better Child Labor Law for the State," Nov.-Dec., 1913, MS in N. C. L. C. Library.

were exempt from the operation of the law between the first of July and the first of November. Employment certificates were to be issued by a notary public, and required documentary proof of age.[49]   The last provision was found violated a few months later in Suffolk when the labor inspector found over two hundred Negro children apparently under twelve working for a peanut company on permits which had been sold them by the local magistrate at fifty cents apiece.[50]

The movement for federal legislation found the Virginia representatives in Congress favorable to it, and while the state was not ready to do so all at once, it gradually raised its standards to meet the federal regulations.   In 1918 the fourteen-year age limit was extended to a wider variety of occupations.[51]   In 1920 the eight-hour day for children under sixteen was adopted, although vegetable and fruit packing or canning places were permitted to allow children over twelve to work eight hours a day when school was not in session, and twelve-year-old children could be employed to run errands or deliver parcels during the day under the same conditions.[52]   In 1922 the fourteen-year age limit was extended to include all gainful occupations except those on farms, in orchards and in gardens, and for fruit and vegetable canneries as under the former law. A forty-four-hour week for children under sixteen was provided, physical examination required for certificate, and certain dangerous occupations prohibited to children under sixteen.   The administration of all the law was in the hands of the Commissioner of Labor.[53]

Florida was the only state in the South without a cotton manufacturing industry which made a strong protest against child labor legislation for industry.   The canning of sea foods and manufacture of cigars were the two industries in which a great many children were employed.   There were no restrictions on such employment when the National Child Labor Committee first interested itself in the state. McKelway went to Florida in 1905 and undertook to secure the enactment of a child labor law.   He considered such action a preventive rather than a remedial measure, as there were no cotton mills and the extent of child employment in other fields was not yet realized.[54] The proposal for a law had the support of the State Federation of Labor, and that body believed it had the promise of a favorable vote from the legislative committee that was considering the bill.   Its defeat was credited by the labor men to the railroad interests.[55]

McKelway did not blame the railroad interests, which he believed

[49] Va., *Acts*, 1914, pp. 671-73.

[50] A. J. McKelway, "Protecting Negro Child Laborers in Virginia," in *Survey*, XXXII (August 15, 1914), 496.   [51] Va., *Acts*, 1918, pp. 347-48.

[52] *Ibid.*, 1920, p. 840.   [53] *Ibid.*, 1922, pp. 855-60.

[54] "McKelway's Account," McKelway Papers.

[55] Fla. State Federation of Labor, *Sixth Annual Convention*, 1906, p. 45.

were out of power at that time. He attributed the defeat, probably correctly, to the activity of John G. Ruge, of Apalachicola, the owner of the largest oyster packing company in the state.[56] Ruge's industry would have been directly affected by any restriction of child labor, and he systematically undertook at each legislature to prevent the passage of such a bill. In 1907 he appeared before the legislative committee on organized labor to oppose restrictions.[57] The legislature enacted a law which established the twelve-year age limit for children in any factory or workshop, bowling alley, barroom, beer garden, place of amusement where intoxicating liquor was sold, or mine or quarry. Employment in canneries was not referred to, but children under twelve were forbidden to work for wages at any occupation at any time when public school was in session in the city or school district in which they lived. The duty of enforcing the provisions of the act devolved upon the local sheriff or police officers.[58]

Bills to raise the age limit to fourteen were proposed in 1909 and 1911. In each case the opposition came chiefly from Ruge and was strong enough to defeat the measures.[59] In 1911 Ruge went to New York and expressed his resentment toward McKelway in a personal interview with the officers of the National Committee. He claimed among other things that the canneries had not employed children under fourteen for a number of years; that they had not been running for three years because of organized labor interference; that shrimp was not poisonous and did not injure the workers as had been claimed; that he opposed the child labor bill because it was proposed by organized labor in an effort to secure factory inspection.[60] He made a definite proposition to Lovejoy to withdraw his opposition to the fourteen-year age limit if the committee would agree to an exemption clause for children working with perishable articles and employed with one or more parents, and would make the compulsory school session come in summer and not in the oyster season.[61] This position was inconsistent with his assertions that he employed no children under fourteen. The National Committee then secured a number of affidavits from people in Apalachicola which seemed to discredit Ruge.[62]

[56] "McKelway's Account," McKelway Papers.

[57] "Child Labor Legislation: Speech Before Committee on Organized Labor at Tallahassee," April 27, 1907, MS in N. C. L. C. Library.

[58] Fla., *Acts and Resolutions Adopted by the Legislature*, 1907, pp. 194-96. Hereafter cited as *Acts*.

[59] A. J. McKelway, "Notes on Child Labor Laws in Florida," July 19, 1911, MS in N. C. L. C. Library.   [60] *Ibid.*, July 17, 1911.

[61] O. R. Lovejoy, "Notes on Child Labor Laws in Florida," Sept. 11, 1911, MS in N. C. L. C. Library.

[62] Affidavits of C. H. Lind, Sept. 12, 1911; Jno. W. Bishop, W. B. Rogers, G. D. Folks, Sept. 19, 1911; E. G. Newmann, S. Jenkins, Sept. 22, 1911; J. W. Bishop, Nov. 3, 1911, in N. C. L. C. Library.

Two years later the question of legislation again came up and Ruge insisted that the secretary of the National Committee had agreed to support a bill that would exempt the oyster canning industry from the fourteen-year age limit. Lovejoy denied entering into any such agreement, saying the committee would work for the best law it could get.[63]   The only open opposition encountered in 1913 came from the Western Union and Postal Telegraph companies.[64]   The law passed in 1914 included a fourteen-year age limit for factory work, twelve for stores, offices and messengers in cities, eighteen for night messengers, and required employment certificates for persons under sixteen.   The law established a fifty-four-hour week or nine-hour day and prohibited night work between 8:00 P.M. and 5:00 A.M. for children under sixteen.   The office of State Labor Inspector was created at a salary of twelve hundred dollars and traveling expenses.[65] This law was more strict than any in the neighboring states, at that time.   Canning was again not specifically mentioned.   The labor inspector in his first annual report made no reference to this industry. He reported that the employers in other businesses had co-operated with him in enforcement of the law, although the parents were indifferent.[66]   From that time the problem of child labor in industry drew little attention in Florida.

The reforms in the less important manufacturing states followed in general the same lines as in the more important ones.   There was in each of them except Mississippi a labor movement back of the child labor reform.   In each except Florida the principal opposition came from the textile industry, although the others joined in and their opposition was probably more noticeable than it would have been if the cotton interests had been stronger.   In all, the peak of reform was reached by the time the federal amendment was defeated, if not sooner.

[63] J. G. Ruge to Lovejoy, Jan. 18, 1913; Lovejoy to Ruge, Jan. 27, 1913; Ruge to Lovejoy, Feb. 11, 1913, MSS in N. C. L. C. Library.
[64] A. J. McKelway, "The Florida Child Labor Campaign," in *Survey*, xxx (July 12, 1913), 497-98.   [65] Fla., *Acts*, 1913, I, 301-10.
[66] Fla. State Factory Inspector, *First Annual Report*, pp. 7-11.

CHAPTER XIII

THE SOUTH AND FEDERAL CHILD LABOR LEGISLATION

IN THE early years of the National Child Labor Committee its efforts in the South had been directed wholly to the investigation of the employment of children in textile mills and the securing of legislation to prevent it. The committee had certain standards for legislation from the outset, but they continued to grow from year to year. In the first few years the ideal bill which was offered to the local interests as a model sought to prevent the employment of children under fourteen; to limit hours for children between fourteen and sixteen to eight a day, and to forbid certain dangerous or harmful employments to them; and to require evidence of good health and of elementary education.[1] Obviously the bills championed by the committee in the South seldom came up to this standard, for the terms proposed in state legislatures had to be governed by expediency.[2] By 1911 the committee broadened the scope of its work to include child labor in other fields. While not lessening its persistent demands for cotton mill reforms, it also turned attention to the restriction of night messenger service and street trades.[3] By 1913 the committee was conducting investigations of the oyster and shrimp canneries on the Gulf Coast. Every year several thousand immigrant workers were taken from Baltimore to the southern coast cities to work during the canning season. The committee found children from four and five years to fourteen employed in such places under very undesirable conditions.[4] This was the first time an extensive examination of conditions in this industry had been carried out.[5] The canning industry did not come under the provisions of the child labor laws which usually specified mining and manufacturing as the industries within their scope. The

---

[1] O. R. Lovejoy, "A Six Years' Battle for the Working Child," in *Review of Reviews*, XLII (1910), 593-96.

[2] "McKelway's Account," McKelway Papers.

[3] N. C. L. C. Minutes, Oct. 26, 1911; E. F. Brown, "The Demoralizing Environment of Night Messengers in Southern Cities," in *Child Labor Bulletin*, II (May, 1913), 138-41.

[4] E. F. Brown and L. W. Hine, "The Child's Burden in Oyster and Shrimp Canneries"; E. F. Brown, "Child Labor in the Gulf Coast Canneries"; L. W. Hine, "Report on Child Labor in the Canneries of the Atlantic Coast," Jan.-Mar., 1913. —MSS in N. C. L. C. Library.

[5] McKelway had visited the canneries at Pass Christian, Miss., in 1909.—N. C. L. C. Minutes, May 8, 1909.

explanations offered by the employers for the presence of child workers were much the same as those given in other industries. It was said that the parents required the children to work and would not come to the canneries without them. The children were merely helping the family and were not on the pay roll. One superintendent said that he objected to parents bringing their children because the Child Labor Committee "would be lying about us as they do up in New York. We don't want them to know about this because they would not understand that it is better for these low people to be at work. They don't want school. The children who grow up and can't read and write are always better off than those who can because as soon as they get a smattering of education they want to strike for higher wages."[6] The canning interests did not put up a strong fight in the state legislatures, however. There were only a few protests, the most notable of which was in Florida where one firm maintained a lobby for some time at the state capitol.[7]

The leaders of the National Child Labor Committee recognized the fact that a gradual change in the aims of the committee was taking place. Lovejoy outlined the stages through which they passed as being first for legislation; second, for honest enforcement; third, for efficient administration; and fourth, for the correlation of protection from premature employment with practical educational opportunities.[8] The aims of the committee were changing in another way as well. When it was organized Murphy was its leading spirit, and his influence, coupled with the desire to hold the interest and approval of its southern members, had led the entire group to agree to the exclusion of national legislation from its program. The first break from this policy, as has been seen, came in 1907 when the committee undertook to support the Beveridge bill and Murphy felt compelled to resign in order to remain consistent with his principles. When this measure was admittedly a failure, the committee had resolved not to support any federal legislation other than bills for a children's bureau and a District of Columbia child labor law until the results of the investigation which the Bureau of Labor was authorized to make were known. The nineteen-volume report of this investigation appeared between 1910 and 1913, and it revealed conditions which undoubtedly called for remedial measures. The investigations by the agents of the committee also continued to show that large numbers of children were employed in industry.

The National Committee was ten years old in 1914. The decade covered by its activities had seen improvements in child labor condi-

⁶ E. F. Brown, "Child Labor in the Gulf Coast Canneries," MS in N. C. L. C. Library.   ⁷ Ibid.
⁸ O. R. Lovejoy to Robert W. DeForest, Nov. 27, 1912, N. C. L. C. Minutes.

tions to which it had contributed in large measure through its propaganda to arouse popular interest. In 1904 there had been thirteen states with a fourteen-year age limit law for factory work, one with an eight-hour day for workers under sixteen, five that prohibited night work by persons under sixteen, and thirteen that provided for factory inspection. In 1914 thirty-five states had fourteen-year age limits, eighteen had an eight-hour day for workers under sixteen, thirty-four prohibited night work under sixteen, and thirty-six provided for factory inspection.[9] But it is noticeable that a relatively small proportion of this progress had been made in the South and almost none of it in the more important manufacturing states. Year after year the secretary of the committee reported failures or weak compromises in these states. The state committees which the National Committee sponsored had not generally proved successful in either North or South, and even when well organized, as in the Carolinas, their policies sometimes ran counter to those of the National Committee.[10] In 1913, after success seemed assured in Georgia, the bill for a fourteen-year age limit failed. In South Carolina, where the manufacturers had promised to promote a child labor law if compulsory education were adopted, the school act was vetoed by the governor, and the child labor law remained unamended. In North Carolina, where the age limit was practically twelve because of the law which allowed children from twelve to thirteen to be employed in apprenticeship capacity, every effort to secure some form of inspection was repulsed.[11]

The repeated failures brought the National Committee back to its position in favor of federal regulation of child labor which it had repudiated after the Beveridge bill affair in 1907. There was not in 1914 the opposition within the committee to this move that had been evidenced seven years earlier. The opposition then came from southern members or those who had sympathy for the southern view of federal legislation. But with the withdrawal of Murphy from the committee, whatever influence such ideas may have had gradually disappeared. The manufacturers were not altogether unjustified in calling the committee a northern organization. While the membership of the committee included a few southerners, the predominant influence was northern. In 1910 there were only two southern members on the board, Chancellor Kirkland of Vanderbilt and Francis

[9] N. C. L. C. Minutes, Sept. 30, 1914. This does not include states with exemption provisions which served to nullify the benefits of the law.

[10] N. C. L. C. Minutes, April 20, 1914.

[11] *Ibid.*, Sept. 30, 1913. McKelway said at the Southern Sociological Congress in 1913 that the four cotton manufacturing states were practically where they had been ten years earlier so far as child labor reform was concerned.—"The Extent of Child Labor in the South and Needed Legislation," in *The South Mobilizing for Social Service*, p. 240.

Caffey, who was no longer living in the South, and after a few years there was none except Caffey, for Kirkland dropped out in the early part of 1913. The large majority of members were New York men.[12] It was because of this situation that the committee could draw up a federal child labor bill which it presented to Congress through Representative A. Mitchell Palmer of Pennsylvania and Senator Robert L. Owen of Oklahoma.

The Palmer-Owen bill was not the first one of its kind to appear in Congress since the Beveridge bill. There had been some such measure before the national legislature almost constantly since 1907. The Kenyon-Taylor bill was possibly one of the best known of these and the Cullop bill was another. Only a few months earlier, Representative Ira C. Copley of Illinois had proposed a measure for denying to interstate commerce the right to carry the products of child labor.[13] The National Committee did not choose to support any of the earlier bills because they fell short of the minimum standards the committee set, or, as in the case of the Copley bill, were weak in enforcement provisions.[14]

The National Child Labor Committee was prepared to give the Palmer-Owen bill all the support and publicity it thought necessary to secure its passage. The bill was taken under consideration by the House Committee on Labor, and at the first hearings Owen R. Lovejoy, Mrs. Florence Kelley, Wiley H. Swift, and Alexander J. McKelway testified to the need for federal legislation to remedy the conditions existing in the child employing industries. They were supported by Miss Julia Lathrop of the Federal Children's Bureau and Arthur E. Holder, representing the legislative committee of the American Federation of Labor.[15] The Committee on Labor then offered to hear the opponents of the measure, and three prominent South Carolina manufacturers, Lewis W. Parker and W. E. Beattie of Greenville, and Alexander Long of Rock Hill, came to present their reasons for opposing federal legislation.

The discussion of federal child labor legislation caused both its friends and its opponents, the manufacturers, to restate their views on child labor. The old arguments that had been used since the child labor controversy began did not disappear, but there was a change in emphasis. The question as to whether child labor was a result of

[12] Names of members of the board appear on almost all publications of the committee.

[13] N. C. L. C. Minutes, Sept. 30, 1914.

[14] "Federal Control of 'Anti-Social' Labor," in Survey, xxx (Aug. 16, 1913), 615-16; "To Prohibit Interstate Trade in Child Labor," in Survey, xxxi (Feb. 7, 1914), 539.

[15] U. S. Congress, House Committee on Labor, Child Labor Bill, Hearing on H. R. 12292, Feb. 27, Mar. 9, 1914, pp. 11-83.

poverty or a cause of it was one which drew attention. For years the manufacturers had pointed out the poverty of the families which came to their mills to work as a justification for giving employment to the children. A writer in the *Outlook* declared that it was the poor father of a family who was unable to make a living wage under the existing economic system, and who perforce hired out his child, that was deserving of sympathy.[16] McKelway replied to this with the theory which he repeatedly stated. Child labor was a cause of poverty in that it depressed the wage scale so the adults were unable to make a living wage. Abolish child labor and wages would rise.[17] The manufacturer as well as the trade unionist knew this to be true and therefore opposed child labor legislation which would result in higher adult wages. A doffer boy of twelve in South Carolina received $3.54 a week, and one of fifteen received $4.75. But one who was twenty received only $2.52.[18] This view was also supported by Jerome Jones, the editor of one of the South's few labor publications, the Atlanta *Journal of Labor*.[19] Wiley H. Swift said that the millmen no longer claimed that the mills needed children, or that to remove them would cripple industry; they no longer talked about educating the poor mountaineers; or contended that the question should be left to the parents. They now based their opposition on the ground that the workers were so poor that they could not possibly live without the wages earned by children. It was this argument that had recently defeated a law in South Carolina. But if the mills could not pay a living wage, Swift said, what became of the manufacturers' theory that the mill life was far superior to that from which the workers came.[20]

But Swift saw that the sole reason for the persistence of child labor in the South did not lie in the greed of the manufacturers for cheap labor. It was a part of the social heritage of the South, a tradition which died hard. Slavery, he said, had created a large class of poor whites and produced the feeling that the advantages enjoyed by the rich were not properly intended for the poor. "The old civilization was shattered, but the thoughts and feelings of that time remain. We have fallen heir to these. Some of the old families survive. Many

[16] George Frederic Stratton, "The Man Behind the Child," in *Outlook*, cv (Sept. 20, 1913), 137-40.

[17] A. J. McKelway, "The Child Against the Man," in *Child Labor Bulletin*, II (Nov., 1913), 52-59.

[18] A. J. McKelway, "Child Wages in the Cotton Mills: Our Modern Feudalism," in *Child Labor Bulletin*, II (May, 1913), 7-16; also see A. J. McKelway, "The Modern Feudalism," in *Boston Common*, III (Mar. 22, 1913), 17.

[19] "Child Labor and Low Wages," in *Child Labor Bulletin*, II (May, 1913), 52-55.

[20] W. H. Swift, "The Last Stand of the One Business Which Opposes Child Labor Legislation in the South," *Child Labor Bulletin*, III (May, 1914), 85-89.

men from the poorer white class have pushed themselves up through the shattered shell of the old civilization. They have been successful. They have made money. They began to establish business. Mills were built and the doors were thrown open for help. It was only the poor class who came to work in these mills. They brought their children with them. The manufacturers said: 'They are children of poor ignorant people. They can never amount to much at best. It will be a piece of good luck for them to find an opportunity for their children to earn money.' So the working of young children became a custom.

". . . It has seemed right and no crime to place children at an early age in our mills. They were the ignorant children of ignorant parents and would, in the opinion of many, never amount to much. The child that was employed in the mill belonged to a type that frequently depend upon charity. Thinking perhaps, that we were doing good we suffered the child of the poor to be hired. Money was made from this labor through long hours, and that money was used to dress and educate the other man's child. The best explanation that we can give of this attitude is that it is the fruit of thought developed in our earlier civilization, for this code of morals could hardly be built up now. Without being conscious of it we have lived not only in neglect but in the exploitation of our children."[21]

There were other features of the southern attitude toward social problems which made reform difficult. The South was averse, said Swift, to making inquiries into the life of the state or community. "Mr. Walter Page's speech on the Forgotten Man was bold. When Dr. Stiles said we had hookworm the lie was all but passed." The parents of children who worked made no protest against the system. They were not organized and they lacked "the ability to buck-up." They even sought the mills so as to have an opportunity to put their children to work. Again, the South regarded its manufacturers as leaders whose views were worthy of respect. When child labor was called to the attention of people they saw it, "but the manufacturer said it was all right, and the manufacturer was one of the leading men of the state and of the community; he was a man of wealth. . . . We preferred to accept the statement . . . that the cotton mill was a sort of orphanage as well as a business institution." However much the manufacturers might deny that they wanted to employ children, they continued to do so. Swift said, "I am thoroughly convinced that the child is there because the owner of the mill wants him there. They do not want negroes, and we do not find

---

[21] "Why It Is Hard to Get Good Child Labor Laws in the South," in *Child Labor Bulletin*, III (May, 1914), 73-74.

negroes. Wanting this child, the cotton manufacturer has been able to keep him."[22]

Finally there was the political power of the mill-owning class to be taken into consideration. "A man who runs a cotton mill has direct control over a large number of votes. Under ordinary circumstances he can turn a great many of these votes just as he will. Recognizing this fact public officials and political parties make terms with him and, as perhaps he later contends, place themselves under obligations to these cotton manufacturers."[23]

This statement of a southern representative of the National Committee constituted the committee's indictment against the South for responsibility for child labor. It was against these conditions that the committee had struggled rather unsuccessfully in its effort to secure legislation.

In justification of its effort to secure national legislation the committee had to defend its bill from the standpoint of need or desirability and of constitutionality. To prove its first point the conditions in the various states were pointed out. Forty states, containing a very large majority of the people of the whole country, had adopted the fourteen-year age limit for child labor in industry. Those that failed to conform to this standard were chiefly the southern manufacturing states. Uniformity of legislation was desirable because child-made goods from one state were sold in other states. They were thus forced upon consumers who were unwilling to use goods made under such circumstances. The only remedy lay in federal legislation. But this brought up the problem of what form of legislation to adopt. It was contended that Congress could regulate child labor through three channels: interstate commerce, taxation, and the use of the mails. The last two were regarded as less practical than the first. Therefore the first was chosen as the basis for the Palmer-Owen bill. The question of constitutionality depended on the interpretation of the interstate commerce clause of the federal constitution and touched the long-debated problem of state rights.[24]

Although the South Carolina manufacturers were the first to appear in opposition to the Palmer bill, the most vigorous attacks against federal legislation came from David Clark, the editor of the *Southern Textile Bulletin*. When the movement for federal legislation began to be pushed by the National Committee, Clark took steps

[22] *Ibid.*, pp. 75-77.   [23] *Ibid.*, p. 77.
[24] O. R. Lovejoy, *The Federal Government and Child Labor*, N. C. L. C. Pamphlet No. 216, pp. 1-23, *passim;* see also Felix Adler, "The Child Labor Movement: A Movement in the Interests of Civilization," in *Child Labor Bulletin*, III (Mar., 1914), 8-10; A. J. McKelway, "Law without Enforcement," *ibid.* (May, 1914), 34-41; Anna Rochester, "The Consumer and the Federal Child Labor Law," in *Survey*, XXXII (July 18, 1914), 412-13.

to organize the southern manufacturers in opposition. A conference was held in Greenville, South Carolina, and an organization formed which called itself the Executive Committee of Southern Cotton Manufacturers. Clark was elected its secretary and treasurer and former Governor W. W. Kitchin was employed to look after the interests of the manufacturers in Washington.[25] When the National Committee held its annual conference in Washington in January, 1915, only a few weeks before the child labor bill was to come up for consideration, Clark decided it was time for the southern manufacturers to come to their own defense against the "misrepresentations and false statements" of the committee.[26] He wrote to the secretary of the committee asking for a place on the program and a hearing was arranged for him.[27] His speech constituted the double indictment against the committee which he had made before through his paper, namely, that the committee misrepresented conditions in the mills deliberately and maliciously, and that it had no right to interfere in the internal affairs of the southern states, especially since conditions worse than any found in the South were prevalent in New York, within a stone's throw of the offices of the National Committee.[28]

The reply to this speech on the floor of the convention in the discussion led by McKelway answered Clark's charges in detail. The committee's agents were careful to verify the truth of statements they made, for they knew that misstatement would lead to dismissal. The committee could not justly be held responsible for statements of irresponsible people which were sometimes blamed on it. It admitted that it laid special emphasis on the cases of young children found employed, but held that this was permissible so long as any such children were found, even though it obscured the fact that a majority of the child workers were over twelve. So far as the evils of New York tenement work were concerned, it was pointed out that some of the strongest statements against them had been made by the National Committee. The manufacturers insisted on national protection for their industry through tariff laws, but objected to national protection for child workers as being an infringement on state affairs.[29]

The House Committee on Labor returned the Palmer bill with a favorable report on February 13, 1915, appending a large part of the testimony of its supporters.[30] The debate on the bill and its passage occurred two days later. The principal speeches against it came from

[25] *Southern Textile Bulletin,* June 6, 1918.
[26] *Ibid.,* Jan. 7, 1915.   [27] *Ibid.,* Feb. 4, 1915.
[28] "A Demand for a Square Deal," in *Child Labor Bulletin,* IV (May, 1915), 37-44.
[29] "Statement by National Child Labor Committee," in *Child Labor Bulletin,* IV (1915), 44-54; *Survey,* XXXIII (Jan. 16, 1915), 413-15.
[30] *Child Labor Bill,* Report No. 1400 to Accompany H. R. 12292.

Representatives Byrnes and Ragsdale of South Carolina. Together with Tribble of Georgia they tried to filibuster, since it was known that a caucus of the Democratic members had been called to meet in the House at eight o'clock in the evening. The friends of the bill prevented adjournment until a vote had been taken. It stood at two hundred and thirty-seven for the bill and forty-five against. Although the measure had been introduced by the Democrats, the Republican minority stood strongly back of it, and the vote was on sectional rather than party lines. Only one Republican, Parker of New Jersey, voted against the bill, while the other votes came chiefly from southern Democrats.[31] The vote was sectional, however, not in the sense of the whole South against the whole North, but rather of the manufacturing South against the rest of the country. Only from the Carolinas, Mississippi, and Georgia were a majority of votes cast against the measure. Alabama was divided, though a majority voted for the bill, and in the delegations from Kentucky, Tennessee, and Virginia the vote was as strong for the bill as any of the other delegations were against it.

The child labor bill did not get through the crowded Senate calendar in 1915, because Senator Lee Overman of North Carolina refused his consent when a unanimous vote was necessary to put the bill forward to an earlier date.[32] It was reintroduced in the House in 1916 by Edward Keating of Colorado. The opposition came again from Carolina manufacturers and the representatives from manufacturing districts. The vote by which the measure was passed shows a definite alignment of the southern manufacturing areas against it as in the year before. The ten representatives from North Carolina and seven from South Carolina voted against the bill. Nine of the eleven Georgia members opposed, one failed to vote, and one voted in the affirmative. Four of the representatives from Alabama favored the bill, two opposed and three did not vote. From the other southern states where manufacturing was not so firmly entrenched but where the state rights appeal was presumably strong, there was no such united opposition. Louisiana cast seven votes for the measure. The eighth representative was absent but was paired in favor of it. Mississippi cast two votes for and four against, with Representative Harrison failing to vote. Tennessee gave eight votes for, one against, and two not voting. Florida was equally divided, one for, one against, two not voting.[33]

The Senate Committee immediately took up consideration of the child labor bill, and held hearings for the friends and opponents to

[31] *Congressional Record*, Vol. LII, Pt. 4, pp. 3827-36; "Federal Child Labor Bill Passes the House," in *Survey*, XXXII (Feb. 27, 1915), 569.

[32] N. C. L. C. Minutes, Mar. 15, 1915.

[33] *Congressional Record*, Vol. LIII, Pt. 2, pp. 2007-35.

give their views.[34]   The bill was reported favorably on April 19, 1916.[35]   The passage depended on whether or not it was given a favorable place on the Senate program, and it appeared that the opposition Democrats would be able to prevent its coming up for action.   After the Republicans had announced their willingness to co-operate with the Democratic Steering Committee in its passage, the Democratic Caucus, under the influence of Smith of South Carolina, Hardwick, Overman, Vardaman, Bryan, and Shields, left the bill off the program.   McKelway wrote to President Wilson setting forth these facts and urged him for the sake of the progressive record of the party to use his influence to bring the bill up for consideration.[36] Wilson responded to this appeal and the measure was acted upon in spite of the southern Senators.   The extensive debate showed that it had no chance of being defeated, and the vote was fifty-two in favor to twelve against.   The opposition votes included both senators from North Carolina, Overman and Simmons; from Georgia, Hardwick and Hoke Smith; from Florida, Bryan and Fletcher; and from South Carolina, Ellison D. Smyth and Tillman.   The vote from Alabama was divided, Underwood favoring and Bankhead opposing the meas-ure.   The only votes against it from outside the South came from the two Republican senators from the manufacturing state of Pennsyl-vania.   Two southern states, Kentucky and Virginia, gave their votes for the bill.[37]

In the hearings and debates on the child labor bill the strongest argument which its opponents had to put forward was that it was unconstitutional. The fact that the bill was based on the interstate commerce clause of the Constitution, under which the pure food and drug acts and other such measures had been passed and sus-tained, made the constitutionality of the bill seem plausible to its friends. The other acts had been passed to prevent the transporta-tion of goods that were injurious or immoral in themselves, while the manufacturers contended that this rule could not be applied to child-made goods which were in themselves harmless. W. W. Kitchin, former governor of North Carolina, presented this argument be-fore the House Committee on Labor,[38] and it was reiterated in the debate in the House by representatives from North and South Caro-lina. The regulation of labor, they said, was a state problem, rather than a national one, and for Congress to attempt to legislate on the subject was an infringement of state rights.[39] The friends of

[34] U. S. Congress, Senate Committee on Interstate Commerce, Hearings on H. R. 8234, Feb. 15-17, 1916.   [35] *Ibid.*, Report on H. R. 8234.
[36] McKelway to President Wilson, July 17, 1916, McKelway Papers.
[37] *Congressional Record*, Vol. LIII, Pt. 12, p. 12313.
[38] *Statement before the Committee on Labor*, on H. R. 8234, pp. 3-17.
[39] *Congressional Record*, Vol. LIII, Pt. 2, pp. 1569-70, 1576, 1578, 1579, 2012, 2034.

federal legislation replied that the manufacturers and other opponents of the bill were merely taking refuge in the state rights defense as a means of hiding their true motives for opposition. The mill interests were forced to admit that in the Carolinas children twelve years of age were allowed to work eleven hours a day.[40]

The Carolina senators took the same position in regard to constitutionality as did the representatives from those states. Tillman of South Carolina declared himself heartily in favor of the standards which the child labor bill proposed if they were enacted by state legislation, but opposed federal regulation of labor as a usurpation of state rights and a dangerous tendency toward centralization which would result in the destruction of the old system of government and the substitution for it of bureaucratic control.[41] While the argument for state rights coincided with the desires of the manufacturing group, it was, none the less, one which ordinarily carried weight in southern politics, and it is hard to doubt the sincerity of a part of the men, at least, who used it in this case. Tillman had been a member of the National Child Labor Committee, though his supposed championship of this reform was somewhat marred by his hostility to compulsory education. But Senator Hoke Smith of Georgia, who had seriously concerned himself ten years earlier with the enactment of a state child labor law, voted against the federal bill.[42]

While the manufacturers regarded federal child labor legislation as unconstitutional, a few Carolinians declared that since the states had failed in their duty the national government was entitled to act. Such opinions came from Judge Joseph McCullough of Greenville, South Carolina, a lawyer and a member of the National Committee;[43] from Josephus Daniels, editor of the *News and Observer* of Raleigh, and Secretary of the Navy in Wilson's cabinet, who had seen all his efforts in behalf of state legislation go down before the opposition of the manufacturers;[44] from Clarence Poe of Raleigh, editor of the *Progressive Farmer* and an active member of the North Carolina Child Labor Committee which had failed to secure legislation;[45] and from Dr. George T. Winston, former president of the University of North Carolina, who said, "As a citizen of North Carolina by birth, by education, and by residence, as a Southern man, as a Democrat, as a states' rights man, I say, if the fathers and mothers of little chil-

[40] U. S. Congress, House Committee on Labor, Report on H. R. 8234, p. 7; *Congressional Record*, Vol. LIII, Pt. 14, p. 206.

[41] *Congressional Record*, Vol. LIII, Pt. 12, pp. 12194-200, 12294-95.

[42] *Ibid.*, p. 12313; "The Democrats' Child Labor Law," in *Literary Digest*, LIII (Sept. 2, 1916), 547-48.

[43] *Supporters of the Keating-Owen Bill*, N. C. L. C. Pamphlet No. 256, p. 1.

[44] *Congressional Record*, Vol. LII, Pt. 5, p. 5338.

[45] *Ibid.*, Vol. LIII, Pt. 14, p. 242.

dren will not take care of them, if the communities where they live will not take care of them, if their states will not take care of them, then, in God's name, let them have the protection and the care of the great United States!"[46]

Julian S. Carr, Jr., of Durham, North Carolina, one of the more progressive manufacturers who had been an advocate of child labor legislation in the state, disagreed with the other millmen, for he approved the first federal law, and declared that the plea of states rights was a cloak behind which to hide delay or non-action.[47]

Senator Keating introduced into the *Congressional Record* a long list of extracts from editorials in southern newspapers to show that the southern press was friendly to the federal child labor bill. But he was able to include in his list few of the leading papers from the cotton manufacturing sections. The Asheville *Citizen*, edited by James H. Caine, and the *News and Observer* in North Carolina are two of the most outstanding for the section. But the large number of smaller papers which were listed from the Carolinas and Georgia as well as from states that did not present such decided opposition to the proposed bill indicate that there was a fairly widespread sympathy with the idea of federal regulation of child labor.[48]

Another form of defense offered by the opponents of federal legislation was to say that such laws were unnecessary. Much was said in praise of the good work done by the millowners for their employees in the way of welfare work and education, and testimony was introduced to show that the workers were satisfied and did not want federal child labor legislation. David Clark and Ellison Smyth were the chief witnesses to this.[49] This was essentially the same kind of argument offered before the state legislatures, especially in South Carolina. In reply to the statements regarding the attitude of the mill operatives, the report of the House Committee on Labor said that Clark's own testimony indicated that the workers signed petitions against the federal bill under a misapprehension, believing that it established a sixteen-year age limit, and that the petitions were prepared by the millowners and in many cases signed in the presence of the pay-roll man.[50]

[46] *Child Labor in North Carolina*, N. C. L. C. Pamphlet No. 262, p. 4.

[47] "Mills Will Obey Federal Law," in *Child Labor Bulletin*, v (Nov., 1916), 136-37.

[48] *Congressional Record*, Vol. LIII, Pt. 15, pp. 1806-11. Keating referred to the "Raleigh (N. C.) Observer," but quite obviously this was a mistake and the *News and Observer* is the paper intended.

[49] U. S. Congress, House Committee on Labor, Hearing on H. R. 12292, May 14, 1914, pp. 85-124; and on H. R. 8234, Jan. 10-12, 1916, pp. 3-12, 16-31; Senate Committee on Interstate Commerce, Hearing on H. R. 8234, Feb. 15-17, 1916; *Congressional Record*, Vol. LIII, Pt. 2, pp. 1570, 1578, 1581-82, 2021-22.

[50] U. S. Congress, House Committee on Labor, Report on H. R. 8234, pp. 7-8.

Another line of defense less frequently used was the old argument that the work done by children in mills was not really harmful. The *Southern Textile Bulletin* contended that it could not be shown that cotton mill work caused tuberculosis or in other ways injured the health.[51] Ellison Smyth asserted repeatedly that the work was not unhealthy.[52] Webb of North Carolina said that the light work in the mills was better for children than loafing on the street,[53] and Doughton of the same state declared that the millmen were the best people of the community, they were not coining money out of the labor of children, and they took every interest in their welfare.[54] Former Governor Kitchin of North Carolina took the same position he had supported while in the state's chief executive office. Poverty made it necessary for the children of poor families in the South to work, and it was better for them to work in the cotton mills than elsewhere.[55]

The greatest objection of the manufacturers to the terms of the bill was that it provided an eight-hour day for children under sixteen. The limitation of hours for certain age groups had always proved one of the most difficult points in state legislation because the mills claimed that a short workday for a part of the working force would of necessity cut down the day for the whole plant. They claimed that since the mills were unable to operate on an eight-hour basis entirely such a clause in effect would raise the age limit for children to sixteen instead of fourteen.[56] This was an injustice not only to the mills but to the children since the compulsory education laws did not extend to sixteen and the child would therefore be left in idleness.[57]

Clark and the *Charlotte Observer* took the attitude that the southern factories were the victims of persecution by the National Child Labor Committee, which, through misrepresentations and half-truths had played upon the feelings of the people and so led to a widespread support for the Keating bill. Clark testified before the Senate Committee on Industrial Relations that McKelway's statements before the committee were largely false and that the manufacturers regarded the members of the National Child Labor Committee as parasites and grafters who took advantage of courtesy shown them

[51] Mar. 2, 1916.

[52] U. S. Congress, Senate Committee on Interstate Commerce, Hearing on H. R. 8234, pp. 7-28.

[53] *Congressional Record*, Vol. LIII, Pt. 2, p. 1571.

[54] *Ibid.*, pp. 2021-22.

[55] U. S. Congress, House Committee on Labor, Hearing on H. R. 8234, pp. 12-13.

[56] *Ibid.*, pp. 3-12; Senate Committee on Interstate Commerce, Report on H. R. 8234, pp. 7-8; Hearing on H. R. 8234, p. 10.

[57] *Southern Textile Bulletin*, Nov. 11, 1915.

to misrepresent and falsify conditions.[58] In his *Textile Bulletin* he said, "We can never be made to believe that Dr. McKelway has any real interest in the welfare of the children and we honestly believe that his motive aside from the financial benefits to himself have been to seek revenge upon the cotton manufacturers through whose influence he was driven from North Carolina."[59] The *Charlotte Observer* declared that nothing good could be expected for the South from the agencies which backed the federal bill.[60] Congressman Webb practically repeated Clark's charges against the Child Labor Committee on the floor of the House. The whole purpose of the child labor movement as these men represented it was to destroy the effectiveness of the southern competition with northern mills.[61]

There is nothing in the history of the National Child Labor Committee to indicate that it was ever actuated by any motives other than those of the humanitarian reformer. This does not mean, however, that there was not more self-interest on the part of some who supported its legislative measures. Southern manufacturers had for sixteen years been accusing New England manufacturers of trying to destroy the mill interests of the South by promoting labor legislation. Whether or not the New Englanders ever took any active steps in that direction they certainly looked with interest on the struggle in the South. From the viewpoint of the Massachusetts mill-owner who complied with a fourteen-year age limit and other child labor restrictions, the absence of such restrictions in the South which would seem to permit a lower wage scale and cheaper production was an unfair advantage for that section, and it came to be regarded as one which nothing except federal regulation could remove. This attitude found expression in Congress in the debates on the child labor bills, not only from representatives from Massachusetts but from some of the other industrial states. Husting of Wisconsin represented this view in the Senate,[62] Gallivan[63] and Carter[64] spoke for Massachusetts on the subject in the House, and Ricketts[65] and Cooper[66] for Ohio.

The question as to the constitutionality of the Keating bill had occupied more time and space than any other phase of the problem in the discussions before the passage of the law. The National Committee and the members of Congress in charge of the bill strongly

---

[58] "Testimony before the U. S. Committee on Industrial Relations," May 26, 1915, MS in N. C. L. C. Library.

[59] Aug. 17, 1916.   [60] Feb. 18, 1915.

[61] *Congressional Record*, Vol. LIII, Pt. 2, pp. 1570-71; U. S. Congress, House Committee on Labor, Hearing on H. R. 8234, pp. 30-31.

[62] *Congressional Record*, Vol. LIII, Pt. 12, p. 12208.

[63] *Ibid.*, Pt. 14, pp. 220-21.   [64] *Ibid.*, pp. 183-84.

[65] *Ibid.*, pp. 184-85.   [66] *Ibid.*, p. 204.

maintained its constitutionality; some other people who were equally concerned with securing reform admitted that the constitutionality of the measure was questionable, but they were willing to give the reform the benefit of the doubt. There was a tendency for some, with the disregard for constitutional limitations of government which has often characterized reform, to assume that the supposed great need for the legislation placed it above constitutional limitation. Such was the attitude of Samuel Gompers, the president of the American Federation of Labor, which had stood as strongly back of the National Committee as any other organization. "Whether the child labor law may be held legally constitutional is not the potential consideration. Child labor is morally wrong, economically improvident and nationally unwise. And a law enacted by the United States Congress and signed by the President solemnly so declaring cannot be disregarded."[67]

This was far from being the spirit of the Carolina manufacturers whom Clark had organized to oppose the Keating bill. A few weeks after it became law, the manufacturers announced that they would test its constitutionality in the courts.[68] This was the natural consequence of the long debate as to the right of Congress to pass such a law. The federal law was to go into effect on September 1, 1917, and some of the mills began rearranging their plans of operation so as to conform to it,[69] while the factory inspectors in Georgia and South Carolina took steps to impress on the mill managers in their district the necessity of complying with the federal regulations.[70] There was also a movement during the months the Keating bill was under consideration and after it had passed to raise the standards of state legislation.[71] The News and Observer urged this action on North Carolina,[72] but the manufacturers were unwilling to make such an admission that the federal law was right or that it would stand the test of the courts.[73]

A month before the law was to become effective the Fidelity Man-

[67] "Lift the Burdens from Child Life," in American Federationist, XXIII (Sept., 1916), 844.

[68] Southern Textile Bulletin, Sept. 21, 1916.

[69] E. J. Watson, "Administration of Child Labor Law," in Textile World Journal, LII (June 16, 1917), 3301-2; Grace Abbott, "How to Meet Child Labor Law," ibid., p. 3304; "Hearing on Child Labor Law," ibid., LIII (July 28, 1917), 321; Eugene Szepesi, "Preparing for the Keating Child Labor Law," ibid., LII (June 16, 1917), 3295.

[70] Ga. Dept. of Labor, Federal Child Labor Laws and Supplement to Labor Laws of the State of Georgia and Laws Affecting Children, 1916; S. C. Dept. of Agriculture, Commerce, and Industries, Eighth Annual Report, 1916, p. 42.

[71] See chapters on these states; also McKelway to Miss Julia Lathrop, June 22, 1917, McKelway Papers.

[72] Feb. 25, 1917.   [73] News and Observer, Jan. 19, 1917.

ufacturing Company of Charlotte posted the Keating child labor law in its mill, and notified its operatives that after September first no person under fourteen would be employed and no person under sixteen would be employed more than eight hours a day. On August 9, Roland H. Dagenhart filed a bill of complaint in the United States District Court for the Western District of North Carolina on behalf of his two sons, Reuben and John, against the Fidelity Manufacturing Company and William C. Hammer, the district attorney. The charge made was that Reuben, who was fifteen years old and worked sixty hours a week, was to have his hours reduced, while John, who was under fourteen but old enough to work under the North Carolina law since his family needed the income, would lose his job. The father claimed that this was depriving him of his rights, which entitled him to the earnings of his children until they were twenty-one years of age.[74] The Dagenharts were merely figureheads, chosen because the case presented all the points of the law which it was desired to test. Clark said he had some difficulty in persuading Dagenhart to allow his name to be used, and that he was not even employed by the Fidelity Company when the case came before the Supreme Court.[75]

The case was heard before Judge James E. Boyd of the Western North Carolina District Court. The Dagenharts, or the manufacturers, were represented by the law firms of O'Brien, Broadman, Harper, and Fox of New York; Manley, Hendren and Womble of Winston-Salem; and W. P. Bynum of Greensboro.[76] The United States Department of Justice was represented by Thomas I. Parkinson, a member of the Legislative Drafting Bureau of Columbia University who had outlined the constitutional defense of the law for the National Child Labor Committee when it was under consideration in Congress; Roscoe Pound, dean of the Harvard Law School; and the United States district attorney, William C. Hammer. The services of Parkinson and Pound were secured through the National Committee.[77]

The complainants sought a permanent injunction against the Fidelity Manufacturing Company to prevent the discharge of the two Dagenhart boys and against Hammer to prevent the enforcement of the federal child labor law in the Western North Carolina District. They argued that the federal law was unconstitutional, for the following reasons: it was not a regulation of commerce such as Congress is empowered to make under the Constitution; it attempted to regulate the conditions of manufacturing, and not commerce; it

[74] N. C. L. C. Minutes, Sept. 30, 1917. The report of the secretary reviews the case.—Southern Textile Bulletin, Aug. 16, 1917.

[75] Southern Textile Bulletin, June 6, 1918.

[76] Ibid., Aug. 16, 1917.   [77] N. C. L. C. Minutes, Oct. 3, 1917.

was not included among the delegated powers of Congress; it was an attempted usurpation of power; its enforcement would deprive the plaintiff of property without due process of law. Judge Boyd entered a decree making permanent the injunction against the mill from discharging the children and the district attorney from enforcing the law in Western North Carolina on the day before the act was to go into effect.[78]

Clark was gratified by this decision, for he took to himself the credit for preparing the case, employing the lawyers, and raising the necessary funds. He indignantly denied that the large tobacco companies had contributed in any way to the success of the first round in the contest. He called a conference of the Western North Carolina mills and succeeded in getting them to pass resolutions that they would continue to operate under the North Carolina law, but not under the federal law, and that they would not take advantage of their competitors by soliciting operatives from outside the Western District so long as the injunction was in force.[79]

In the months which elapsed between Judge Boyd's injunction and the decision of the Supreme Court on the child labor law, Clark busily worked to keep the matter before the Carolina manufacturers. Meanwhile McKelway, who had devoted fourteen years to work for child labor legislation, and who had done more than any other person to help promote federal legislation, died suddenly in April, 1918.[80]

The Supreme Court on June 3, 1918, handed down a decision supporting Judge Boyd's position and declaring the law unconstitutional on the grounds that it was not a regulation of interstate or foreign commerce and that it conflicted with the fifth and tenth amendments. The vote of the court was five to four, with Justices Holmes, McKenna, Brandeis, and Clarke dissenting.[81]

The overthrow of the federal child labor law led immediately to steps on the part of the National Committee to re-enact the principle of federal legislation in another form. The history of the passage of the second child labor law was in many respects a repetition of the first. The committee had chosen to base the first law on the right of Congress to regulate interstate commerce, rather than on its right to tax. It now fell back on the taxing power as an expedient for regulation of child labor. Four days after the decision of the Supreme Court on the Keating law became known, the National Committee held an impromptu meeting to decide on the proper steps to take,

[78] N. C. L. C. Minutes, Sept. 30, 1917; *Southern Textile Bulletin*, Sept. 6, 1917.

[79] *Southern Textile Bulletin*, Sept. 6, 1917.

[80] Owen R. Lovejoy, "Dr. Alexander Jeffrey McKelway," in *Child Labor Bulletin*, VII (May, 1918), 21-27.

[81] N. C. L. C. Minutes, Sept. 30, 1918; 247 U. S. 251.

and appointed a committee to consider further legislation.[82] The committee, in collaboration with the Consumers' League and the American Federation of Labor, drew up a bill based on the war power, proposing to restore the conditions of the Keating Act as a temporary measure.[83] This proposal did not prove expedient, however.

The second federal child labor law was not introduced in the Senate as a separate bill, but as an amendment added to a revenue bill of 1918. The debate centered entirely on the question of constitutionality, for the measure proposed to levy a 10 per cent tax on all child-made goods, defining the requirements in the same terms as were used in the Keating Law. Senators Hardwick of Georgia, Smith of South Carolina, and Overman of North Carolina debated the amendment with Senators Kenyon, Lenroot, Lodge, Pomerene, Kellog, and France. The vote taken with thirty-four members not voting was fifty to twelve in favor of the tax. The opposition votes came from all the senators of Alabama, Georgia, South Carolina, North Carolina, and Kentucky, and one each from Colorado and Mississippi.[84]

In the House the Mississippi representatives, Venable and Humphreys, debated the provision with Gard of Ohio and Rainey of Illinois. The vote on February 8, 1919, was overwhelmingly in favor of the amendment, as there were only eleven against it. Four of these were from Mississippi and only one from Alabama. The majority of the delegations from Georgia, Alabama, and the Carolinas voted for the measure, and it is evident that its opponents preferred to leave the matter up to another court decision since opposition in the face of such a large majority would have been useless.[85]

Before the second federal child labor law had come up for consideration in the House of Representatives, David Clark announced that he would undertake to raise funds to fight it in the courts,[86] and soon after its passage steps were taken to secure attorneys and decide on the best method of testing the act.[87] The same lawyers were engaged by the mill association as had served in the Dagenhart case.[88] Meanwhile, North Carolina was in the process of enacting a law which fulfilled a part of the federal standards, although not providing for an eight-hour day for all workers under sixteen.[89]

[82] N. C. L. C. Minutes, June 7, 1918; "Planning a New Child Labor Law," *Survey*, XL (June 15, 1918), 323-24.
[83] N. C. L. C. Minutes, Sept. 30, 1918.
[84] *Congressional Record*, Vol. LVII, Pt. 1, pp. 609-21.
[85] *Ibid.*, Pt. 3, pp. 3029-35.
[86] *Southern Textile Bulletin*, Dec. 26, 1918.
[87] *Ibid.*, Feb. 20, 1919.
[88] *Southern Textile Bulletin*, April 10, 1919.
[89] See chapter on North Carolina.

The case proposed by the manufacturers to test the child labor law was the one of Eugene T. Johnston *vs.* the Atherton Mills, for refusing employment to his son, John W. Johnston, who was fifteen and a half years old, for more than eight hours a day.[90] As in the case of the first law, the hearing was held before Judge Boyd, who granted an injunction restraining the district attorney from enforcing the law in Western North Carolina. The decision by Judge Boyd was made on May 2, 1919, seven days after the law went into effect.[91]

The decision on the second federal law was delayed from month to month by the Supreme Court. The hearing on the Johnston case was consolidated with the Drexel Furniture Company *vs.* J. W. Bailey, which had also been brought up to test the law.[92] Finally the case of Vivian Mills *vs.* J. W. Bailey was added, and the hearing, after more than two years' delay, took place in March, 1922.[93] In May the court gave an adverse decision against the child labor law.[94] David Clark again congratulated himself on his success in behalf of the manufacturers.[95]

The child labor law was in force from May, 1919, to May, 1922, everywhere except in the Western District of North Carolina. The group that was seeking to defeat it had difficulty in keeping up the interest of all the manufacturers through this long delay.[96] But the attitude toward the problem of child labor was undergoing a change in the nation at large. Raymond G. Fuller, in writing of this change, which had begun before the war, but which had been greatly accelerated by it, said, "The present emphasis is placed not only on the nationally *harmful* effects of child labor, but on the nationally *beneficial* effects of such public action—including the abolition of child labor—as will 'develop all the children of the nation to be healthy, intelligent, moral and efficient citizens.' "[97]

This difference of feeling was as perceptible in the South as in any other part of the nation. Beside the awakening social conscience in the South, there were economic reasons for the changing attitude which Broadus Mitchell in 1919 prophesied would succeed in remedying the child labor evil where social propaganda had been only partially effective.[98] The growing industrialism of the South was bring-

---

[90] *Southern Textile Bulletin*, April 17, 1919.
[91] *Ibid.*, April 24, 1919; *American Child*, I (1919), 176.
[92] *Southern Textile Bulletin*, Dec. 23, 1921.
[93] *Ibid.*, Mar. 9, 16, 1922. [94] 259 U. S. 20.
[95] *Southern Textile Bulletin*, May 18, 1922.
[96] *Ibid.*, Dec. 4, 1919.
[97] "Child Labor—Now," in *Review of Reviews*, LIX (June, 1919), 630-32.
[98] "The End of Child Labor; How Labor is Finishing What Social Work Began," in *Survey*, XLII (Aug. 23, 1919), 750.

ing the problems of labor more acutely to the attention of the manufacturers, while experience under the federal law was proving that successful operation without child labor was possible.

The Supreme Court action of May, 1922, undid the labor of several years of the National Child Labor Committee. The leaders of this organization did not admit that the problem of federal regulation was settled. Some of the reformers claimed that the period during which the federal laws were enforced showed the advantages of such legislation, while the return of children to work in some states after the restrictions were removed emphasized the need of uniformity.[99] Seven months before the decision of the Supreme Court was made, the secretary of the National Committee proposed that in case its opinion was adverse the committee should be ready to resume its campaign, and advised that a special committee be appointed to consider whether further restrictive legislation or a constitutional amendment should be sought.[100] The committee to whose consideration this was finally given was composed of William Draper Lewis, Samuel M. Lindsay, and Francis Caffey. The first two favored working for an amendment, while Caffey opposed it.[101] The secretary sent an inquiry to the members of the Board of Trustees and the Advisory Committee, asking for an expression of their attitude on the question of an amendment. Twelve members of the board favored and four opposed working for the amendment, while seven did not vote. Eighteen of the Advisory Committee favored, eight opposed, and thirteen did not vote. A variety of opinions were expressed. Dr. C. P. Neill said that state legislation had been successful, while national legislation to be consistent should include women as well as children in its provisions. D. F. Houston thought national legislation turned attention away from state legislation which was more effective. Dr. Charles W. Eliot said that the public should be allowed to get used to the woman suffrage and prohibition amendments before another was tried, especially as there was no emergency demanding the child labor amendment. Julia G. Lathrop, former chief of the Children's Bureau, thought the time was unfavorable for another constitutional amendment. A few were willing to accept an amendment only as a last resort. The majority, however, favored the movement.[102] On June 19, 1922, the Board of Trustees formally went on record in favor of an amendment by a vote of fourteen to five.[103]

[99] Raymond G. Fuller, "Child Labor and Federal Legislation," in *Review of Reviews*, LXVI (July, 1922), 67-69; Florence Kelley, "Industrial Conditions as a Community Problem with Particular Reference to Child Labor," in *Annals*, CIII (Sept., 1922), 60-64.

[100] N. C. L. C. Minutes, Oct. 1, 1921.   [101] *Ibid.*, May 29, 1922.

[102] *Ibid.*, May 31, 1922.   [103] *Ibid.*, June 19, 1922.

A number of resolutions for a constitutional amendment were introduced in Congress in the winter of 1922-23. In the Senate the Committee on Judiciary held hearings on them. Many of the same people came to testify who had appeared in behalf of the first federal child labor law. Gompers, Mrs. Kelley, and Owen Lovejoy were among the first. Representatives from a long list of organizations, including the National Catholic Welfare Council, the National League of Women Voters, the National Women's Trade Union League, the Parent-Teachers Congress, the Council of Jewish Women, the Federation of Business and Professional Women, and the Democratic National Committee, testified that the organizations they represented favored the amendment.[104]

The first opponent heard was a representative of the American Constitutional League of New York. The principal opposition was again brought forward by David Clark. He brought to Washington A. H. Gilbert, Jr., the chief factory inspector for South Carolina, Mrs. K. B. Johnson and E. F. Carter of the Welfare Department of North Carolina, and State Senator W. L. Long of North Carolina.[105] The resolution for an amendment was favorably reported in the Senate,[106] but action was not pressed through. New hearings were held before the Senate Judiciary Committee. The chief of the Children's Bureau, Miss Grace Abbott, submitted evidence to show that after the first federal law had been declared unconstitutional many children were allowed by the states to work at ages below the federal standard or for more than eight hours. The chief offenders in regard to age were North Carolina in factories and Maryland in canneries; in regard to the eight-hour day North Carolina, South Carolina, Virginia, and Rhode Island led the others in violations. Georgia and Alabama were not reported as being offenders in either regard.[107]

In the House, Joint Resolution 184 was given a favorable report, although a minority submitted a report declaring the amendment unwise centralization of power under a bureaucratic system.[108] The debate in the House took place on April 25-26, 1924. Almost all the opposition came from southern states, although Connecticut, Massachusetts, and Pennsylvania were represented. The chief objection urged was that such an amendment would be an unwise extension of federal power tending too much toward centralization of government and development of bureaucratic control, and at the

[104] U. S. Congress, Senate Committee on Judiciary, *Hearings before a Sub Committee . . . on Child Labor Amendment to the Constitution*, pp. 21-66.

[105] *Ibid.*, pp. 95-116.

[106] *Ibid.*, Report to Accompany S. J. Res. 1, Child Labor Amendment.

[107] *Ibid.*, p. 37.

[108] *Ibid.*, House Committee on Judiciary, Child Labor Amendment to the Constitution of the United States, Report, H. J. Res. 184, Pt. 2, Mar. 29, 1924.

same time reducing the control of the states over internal affairs. It was also argued that it would interfere with labor in agricultural sections in that it would allow Congress to prohibit the work of children on farms, even those of their own parents. The amendment allowed Congress to prohibit or regulate employment of persons under eighteen, a grant of power which its opponents said would give Congress blanket control over all occupations both domestic, agricultural, and industrial, and which would in effect remove the young person from the authority of both the parent and the commonwealth. Some of the southerners pointed out that this would be particularly unfortunate in the case of Negroes in rural districts.[109] The resolution passed by a vote of two hundred and ninety-seven to sixty-nine. The votes from the southern cotton manufacturing states formed about one third of those cast against it. The opposition was apparently as strong on the state rights and agricultural grounds as from possible interference with manufacturing, for Alabama and Virginia, which had given a majority of their votes in favor of each of the two child labor laws, gave a majority against amendment. North Carolina, the greatest opponent of the first child labor law, gave four votes for the amendment to five against.[110]

The Senate debate followed the same line of arguments that had been presented in the House.[111] The vote was sixty-one for and twenty-three against the amendment, twelve not voting. Of the negative votes twelve came from the Southeastern States: two each from Louisiana, Florida, North Carolina and South Carolina, and one each from Alabama, Georgia, Mississippi, and Virginia. Six of the other negative votes came from the Northeastern Industrial States, four from the West, and one from Missouri. Harrison of Mississippi was the only senator from the lower Southeastern States to vote for the amendment, although both the Texas senators did. The senators from Tennessee and Kentucky gave their votes for the amendment as did Glass of Virginia.[112]

The proposed amendment to the Constitution had few friends in the South Atlantic States. Georgia was the first state to reject it.[113] A month later the North Carolina legislature, which was meeting in extra session to consider other matters, voted it down by overwhelming majorities.[114] It was characterized by one speaker as subversive

[109] *Congressional Record*, Vol. LXV, Pt. 7, pp. 7166-7294.

[110] *Ibid.*, p. 7295.

[111] *Ibid.*, Pt. 10, pp. 9858-64, 10001-10142.

[112] *Ibid.*, p. 10142.

[113] Ga., *Journal of the House*, 1924, pp. 74-76, 102-4, 288; *Journal of the Senate*, 1924, pp. 36-38, 72, 383.

[114] N. C., *Journal of the House*, Extra Session, 1924, pp. 192, 215, 216; *Journal of the Senate*, Extra Session, 1924, pp. 155, 171.

to the principles of the Democratic party, and by another as a move-ment sponsored by "misguided individuals and organizations, whose socialistic, communistic and bolshevistic efforts are influenced by propaganda originating in Moscow." Another thought the other sec-tions of the country wanted to retaliate on the South for "ramming the Volstead Act down their throats."[115] Even the *News and Observer* admitted that the action of the legislature represented the opinion of the majority of North Carolina people.[116] South Carolina, through its legislature, declared that the amendment would practically take the parental control of children under eighteen away; that it would seriously impair the rights of the state and lead to centralization; and that it would destroy personal and family liberty and the prin-ciple of local self-government.[117]

The southern states were not alone in their opposition to the amendment. The *Literary Digest* quoted from about a dozen leading newspapers from cities throughout the North and West that con-demned it, although as many more were in favor of it.[118] The op-position of the manufacturing interests was of course taken for granted. The *Southern Textile Bulletin* condemned it in almost every issue in 1924, while the *Manufacturers' Record* of Baltimore, an old opponent of labor legislation reform, devoted a whole issue to the subject in January, 1925. Noel Sargent explained why the manufac-turers opposed the amendment in the *American Industries*, published by the National Association of Manufacturers.[119] Senator Duncan U. Fletcher of Florida summed up the opposition which the South had to offer in an article in the *North American Review* which was coupled with one on the other side by Miss Grace Abbott of the Children's Bureau.[120] By the end of 1925 the amendment had come before the legislatures of forty-three states. Three had ratified and twenty-one rejected it, thus making it impossible for it to become a part of the Federal Constitution.[121]

With the establishment of NRA codes in 1933, most of the em-ployment of children under sixteen in industries was stopped. After the codes were invalidated, some manufacturers re-employed workers under sixteen, but the indications seem to be that many of them retained the code age standards even when state laws did not require it. There was also a brief revival of interest in the proposed child labor amendment, but there are still twenty states which have not ratified it.

[115] *News and Observer*, Aug. 22, 1924.   [116] Aug. 23, 1924.
[117] S. C., *Journal of the Senate*, 1925, pp. 24-25, 26.
[118] Nov. 29, 1924, pp. 31-32; Dec. 6, 1924, pp. 12-14.
[119] *Why Employers Are Opposed to the Twentieth Amendment*, a reprint from the *American Industries* for Feb.,·1925, in pamphlet form.
[120] "The Child Labor Amendment, II," ccxx (Dec., 1924), 238-44.
[121] *American Year Book*, 1925, p. 678.

CHAPTER XIV

CONCLUSION: THE OUTCOME OF REFORM

THE DEVELOPMENT of child labor laws in the South from the weak beginnings in 1903 followed similar lines in the several industrial states. Reference to Table XII[1] shows that the early laws set low standards with no provisions for inspection or enforcement of the laws. As the age limits were gradually raised and the hours shortened, inspection and a system for issuing employment certificates were developed in each state. New machinery was not at first set up for this purpose. In Alabama it was made a function of the inspector of jails, and in South Carolina it became a part of the duties of the Department of Agriculture, Commerce, and Industries. In Georgia and North Carolina enforcement devolved on local school agencies.

The improvement of child labor legislation by the states went on throughout all the period of experimentation with federal legislation. Spurred by a desire to improve the social welfare of the state, the fear that the administration of federal laws would bring undesired inspections and centralized control, and the feeling that it was necessary to justify their actions in rejecting the national laws, the manufacturing states one by one during the decade between 1915 and 1925 adopted laws with fairly acceptable standards. North and South Carolina in recent years made marked improvements. There were still deficiencies in inspection in some states, but the advances made were real and effective, including not only higher age limits but the creation of special agencies for the administration of child labor laws. The restrictions which were applied to cotton mills were more strict than those for occupations which had not figured so large in the reform movement.

The period of greatest gain in legislation coincided with the period of most marked prosperity in cotton manufacturing. The decade which included the wartime industrial expansion saw a marked development in the southern cotton mills. The increase in the number of mills and the size of the factory population which had been going on steadily since the last quarter of the nineteenth century was accompanied by a slowly growing consciousness of the social problem they presented. Coincident with this there developed a realization of the dangers of widespread illiteracy and efforts were

[1] See p. 275.

made to provide for the education of the masses of people. It was no mere accident that the compulsory education laws were enacted almost simultaneously with the improved child labor laws. They were the product of the same spirit of reform and their success in many communities was interdependent.

The Census of Manufactures taken in 1919 shows statistically a remarkable decrease in the employment of children in the preceding decade. An examination of Table XI shows that the reductions in the per cent of children under sixteen employed in the four leading southern manufacturing states were so great as to put them almost on

TABLE XI[2]

AVERAGE NUMBER OF WAGE EARNERS, WITH PER CENT UNDER 16 YEARS

State	Census Year	Average Number Wage Earners	Per Cent under 16
Alabama	1919	18,102	1.8
	1914	13,697	16.7
	1909	12,731	18.7
Georgia	1919	38,283	3.4
	1914	30,719	18.7
	1909	27,803	15.0
South Carolina	1919	48,079	6.3
	1914	46,448	15.3
	1909	45,454	18.7
North Carolina	1919	67,297	6.0
	1914	53,703	13.3
	1909	47,231	18.9
Massachusetts	1919	124,150	5.8
	1914	113,559	3.9
	1909	108,914	5.7
Rhode Island	1919	36,336	6.0
	1914	29,483	5.6
	1909	28,786	6.0
Connecticut	1919	16,483	4.8
	1914	15,466	4.3
	1909	14,360	4.8

a par with the New England manufacturing states. South Carolina and North Carolina were respectively .2 per cent and .5 per cent higher in the number of this class of laborers than Massachusetts, where 5.8 per cent of the cotton mill workers were under sixteen. Georgia, which had approximately the same number of textile workers as Rhode Island, had 2.6 per cent less than that state. Ala-

[2] U. S. Bureau of the Census, *Manufacturers, Fourteenth Census*, x, 161.

bama had an advantage of 3 per cent less workers under sixteen than Connecticut, the state nearest her size in the cotton industry. There was also in each of these New England states a slight increase from 1914 to 1919 in the per cent of children employed, which was not true in the case of the southern states, as their period of greatest reduction came in these years.

The long period of agitation against child labor seemed to end with the failure of the federal amendment. This was a natural result of the defeat. The state reformers felt that the new state laws constituted a real achievement and were content to let the matter rest. It is not probable that the majority of them in the South desired federal action. The manufacturers on the other hand had consented to reforms gradually and more or less grudgingly. At no time were they willing to go the whole way and make the sweeping changes asked of the legislatures by the National Committee. The federal laws had brought the states to an acceptance of changes, but the Supreme Court decisions and the defeat of the amendment effectually removed such incentives to action and the manufacturers were free to return to their former attitude of opposition to social legislation. This was especially true in the Carolinas, where the mill interests were predominant, though it was scarcely noticeable in Alabama, where there were fewer mills but where progressive changes in the laws continued to be made. This reaction set in at a time when the cotton manufacturing industry was beginning to suffer a decline from the prosperity of the previous decade.

When the Institute for Research in Social Science of the University of North Carolina in December, 1925, asked the permission of the North Carolina Board of Manufacturers to make a study of the textile industry, it was refused, and the *Southern Textile Bulletin* advised the University not to engage in "breeding radicals and reformers."[3] The editor of the *American Child,* official organ of the National Child Labor Committtee, in 1929 expressed the view that it was still impossible to get "cool consideration" for child labor laws in the legislatures of either of the Carolinas.[4]

The mill operatives were little concerned over child labor legislation. The reforms that were accomplished came about through the efforts of disinterested men and women, organized state and national child labor committees, and women's clubs, and through the consent and co-operation of the manufacturers, however ungraciously and reluctantly for the most part it may have been given. But the mill laborers themselves seldom gave voice to their opinions after the first laws were passed.

[3] "Keep to Your Knitting," in *American Child,* VIII (Feb., 1926), 6.
[4] "The Carolina Textile Strike," XI (May, 1929), 2.

While occasional articles depicting the evils of child labor have appeared since 1925 and some special studies have been made, the demands for reform have turned more and more to the remedying of abuses in agriculture and in other occupations than cotton manufacturing. The movement now includes much more than the simple prohibition of children from working prematurely or for long hours. It extends to the positive phases of child welfare in promoting health, education, and recreational activities and the proper care for children of dependent classes.

TABLE XII*

FACTORY CHILD LABOR AND COMPULSORY EDUCATION LAWS: 1903-1938

Year	Alabama	Georgia	South Carolina	North Carolina
1903	Age limit: 12 yrs. Exceptions: 10 yrs. Age limit: 7 p.m.-6 a.m. 13 yrs. Hour limit: 66 a wk. for children under 12 yrs. Proof of age: Parent's statement.		Age limit: 10 yrs. in 1903; 12 in 1905. Exceptions: no age limit. Age limit 8 p.m.-6 a.m. 12 yrs. Proof of age: Parent's affidavit.	Age limit: 12 yrs. Hour limit: 66 a wk. under 18 yrs.
1906		Age limit: 12 yrs. Exceptions: 10 yrs. Age limit 7 p.m.-6 a.m. 14 yrs. Proof of age: Parent's affidavit. Requirements: 12 wks. school a yr. for employed children under 14 yrs. of age. Inspection by Grand Juries allowed.		
1907	Age limit: 12 yrs. no exceptions. Age limit 7 p.m.-6 a.m. 16 yrs. Hour limit: 60 a wk. under 14 yrs. Requirements: 8 wks. school a yr. for employed children between 12-16 yrs. Inspection by jail inspector.		Hour limit: 10 a day for all mill workers.	Age limit: 13 yrs. Exceptions: 12 yrs. (for apprentices). Age limit 8 p.m.-5 a.m. 14 yrs. Hour limit: 66 a wk. under 16. Requirements: 4 mo. school a yr. for employed children 12-13 yrs. Compulsory school attendance: Local option for children 8-14 yrs. for 16 wks. a yr.
1909			Two inspectors allowed.	

* Compiled from the preceding chapters.

TABLE XII (Continued)

Year	Alabama	Georgia	South Carolina	North Carolina
1911		Hour limit: 60 a wk. for all mill workers.	Age limit: 12 yrs. no exceptions. Age limit 8 p.m.-6 a.m. 16 yrs. Certificates from Dept. Ag. Commerce, Indus.	Hour limit: 60 a wk. for all mill workers.
1913				Age limit 9 p.m.-6 a.m. 16 yrs. Requirements: Ch. 12-13 submit certificates of compliance with compulsory ed. law. Enforcements: County school superintendent. - - - - - - - - - - Compulsory school attendance: Children 8-12 yrs. 4 mos. a yr. Exceptions: mental and physical deficiency, poverty, distance.
1914		Age limit: 14 yrs. Exceptions: 12 yrs. Age limit 7 p.m.-6 a.m. 14½ yrs. Requirements: Certificate under 14½ yrs. from Department of Commerce and Labor. Inspection of special cases by county ordinary, and school supt.		
1915	Age limit: 14, no exceptions. Age limit 6 p.m.-6 a.m. 16 yrs. Hour limit: 11 a day; 60 a wk. under 16 yrs. Requirements: 8 wks. school a yr. for employed children under 16. Certificates from school supt. or documentary proof of age.		Compulsory school attendance: Local option for children 8-14 yrs. for entire school term.	Hour limit: 11 hr. day; 60 hr. wk. for women and minors. Proof of age: Parent's statement.
1916		Inspection: One inspector under Dept. of Commerce and Labor. - - - - - - - - - - Compulsory school attendance for children 8-14, 4 mos. a yr. Exceptions for mental	Age limit: 14 yrs.	

TABLE XII (Continued)

Year	Alabama	Georgia	South Carolina	North Carolina
1916		and physical deficiency, poverty, distance.		
1917	Compulsory school attendance: children 8-15 yrs. for 80 days. Exceptions for mental and physical deficiency; poverty; distance. (Law passed 1915, effective 1917.)			Compulsory school attendance: children 8-14 yrs. 4 mos. a yr.
1919	Hour limit: 48 hr. wk. under 16. Inspection and enforcement by Child Welfare Dept. Certificates of health and age. - - - - - - - - - - Compulsory school attendance: children 8-16 for entire term. Exceptions for children 14 who complete 7 grades or are employed.		Compulsory school attendance: children 8-14, 4 mos. a yr. Exceptions for physical and mental deficiency; distance; poverty for children over 12 at work.	Compulsory school attendance: children 8-14 for whole term. Age limit: 14 yrs. Exceptions: 12, for vacation, etc. Age limit 9 p.m.-6 a.m. 16 yrs. Inspection and enforcement by Child Welfare Commission.
1924				Age limit: 14 yrs. No exceptions.
1925		Age limit: 14 yrs. Age limit 7 p.m.-6 a.m. 16 yrs. Certificates based on documentary proof.		
1927				Hour limit: 48 hr. wk. under 16. Exceptions: Children who complete 4th grade.
1931				Age limit: 16 yrs. for girls in street trades. Hour limit: 8 hrs. a day, 48 a wk., 6 days a wk. for all under 16, except: boys 14 supporting self or mothers.
1937			Age limit: 16 in factory, mine, textile est. Night work prohibited 8 p.m.-5 a.m.	Age limit: 16, except for restricted employments outside school hrs. 18 for girls at

TABLE XII (Continued)

Year	Alabama	Georgia	South Carolina	North Carolina
			Inspection by Dept. of Labor. - - - - - - - - - - Compulsory education 7-16, except in extreme poverty.	night. Hour limit: Under 16, 8 hrs. a day, 40 a wk., 6 days a wk. Under 18, 48 hrs. a wk., 9 hrs. a day, 6 day wk. Complete certification and enforcement provisions.
1938			Age limit: 18 for nt. wk. 10 p.m.-6 a.m.	

BIBLIOGRAPHY

BIBLIOGRAPHICAL LISTS

Griffin, Appleton Prentiss Clark. List of Books Relating to Child Labor. Washington: Government Printing Office, 1906.

Loughram, Miriam E. The Historical Development of Child Labor Legislation in the United States. Washington, 1921.

Meyer, H. H. B. and Thompson, Laura A. List of References on Child Labor. Washington: Government Printing Office, 1916.

Thompson, Laura A. References on Child Labor and Minors in Industry, 1916-1924. Washington: Government Printing Office, 1925.

UNPUBLISHED SOURCES

Alabama. Legislative Papers, House and Senate Bills, in State Department of Archives and History.

American Federation of Labor. Copies of the letters of Samuel Gompers. In A. F. of L. Building, Washington, D. C.

———— Letter Files. In A. F. of L. Building, Washington, D. C.

Craighead, Lura H. Data Concerning the Alabama Federation of Women's Clubs. In Alabama State Department of Archives and History.

Georgia. General Assembly, House Bills, Senate Bills, Calendar of Original Bills. In Georgia State Department of History.

McKelway, A. J. Collection of Papers and Letters. In possession of Mrs. A. J. McKelway, Washington, D. C.

Morgan-Malloy Mill, Laurel Hill, N. C. Correspondence. In Duke University Library.

———— Time Book. In Duke University Library.

Murphy, Edgar Gardner. Correspondence. In possession of Mrs. Edgar Gardner Murphy, New York, N. Y.

National Child Labor Committee. Manuscripts in N. C. L. C. Library, including reports of agents, letters, etc. In Committee's Office, New York City.

———— Minute Books, 1904-1930. In Committee's Office, New York City.

North Carolina. Legislative Papers. In State Historical Commission Office, Raleigh, N. C.

Turnersburg Mill, Turnersburg, N. C. Time Books. In Duke University Library.

STATE PUBLICATIONS

Alabama. Acts of the General Assembly.
——— Annual Report of the Factory Inspector of the State, Montgomery, 1913.
——— Copies of Reports of Dr. Bragg, Inspector of Jails, Cotton Mills, and Almshouses. Montgomery, 1907.
——— Department for Inspection of Jails and Alms Houses and Cotton Mills, Factories, etc. First Annual Report. Montgomery, 1910.
——— Department of Labor. Annual Reports.
——— Factory Inspector. Children Eligible for Employment . . . in 1912. Montgomery.
——— Children Eligible for Employment in . . . 1913. Montgomery.
——— Journal of the House of Representatives of the State.
——— Journal of the Senate of the State.
Bickett, Thomas Walter. Public Letters and Papers, 1917-1921. Raleigh, 1923.
Craig, Locke. Biennial Message. Raleigh, 1915.
Florida. Acts and Resolutions Adopted by the Legislature.
——— State Factory Inspector. First Annual Report. 1914.
Georgia. Acts and Resolutions of the General Assembly.
——— Annual Reports of the Commissioner of Commerce and Labor, 1912-1930.
——— Department of Labor, Federal Child Labor Laws and Supplement to Labor Laws of the State of Georgia and Laws Affecting Children, 1916. 10 pp.
——— Journal of the House of Representatives of the State.
——— Journal of the Senate of the State.
Mississippi. Laws of the State.
North Carolina. Bureau of Labor and Printing (Bureau of Labor Statistics, or Department of Labor). Annual Reports.
——— Child Welfare Commission. Biennial Reports.
——— Journal of the House of Representatives of the General Assembly of the State.
——— Public Laws and Resolutions.
South Carolina. Acts and Joint Resolutions of the General Assembly.
——— Department of Agriculture, Commerce, and Industries. Annual Reports.
——— Journal of the House of Representatives of the General Assembly of the State.
——— Journal of the Senate of the General Assembly of the State.
Tennessee. Acts of the State.
——— Journal of the House, 1901.

———— Journal of the Senate, 1901.

Virginia. Acts and Joint Resolutions Passed by the General Assembly.

UNITED STATES GOVERNMENT PUBLICATIONS

Bureau of the Census. Reports.

Bureau of Labor. Report on Conditions of Woman and Child Wage-Earners in the United States. 19 vols. Vol. I, Cotton Textile Industry, Washington, 1910; Vol. VI, The Beginnings of Child Labor Legislation in Certain States; a Comparative Study. Washington, 1910-13.

Congressional Record.

House Committee on Labor. Child Labor Bill, Hearing on H. R. 12292, Feb. 27, March 9, May 14, 1914.

———— Child Labor Bill, Report No. 1400 to Accompany H. R. 12292, Feb. 13, 1915.

———— Hearing on H. R. 8234, Jan. 10-12, 1916.

———— Report on H. R. 8234.

———— Statement of W. W. Kitchin on H. R. 8234.

House Committee on Judiciary. Child Labor Amendment, Report on H. J. Res. 184, Pt. 2, March 29, 1924.

Senate Committee on Interstate Commerce. Hearings on H. R. 8234, Feb. 15-17, 1916.

———— Report on H. R. 8234, April 19, 1916.

Senate Committee on Judiciary. Hearings before Sub Committee . . . on Child Labor Amendment to the Constitution.

———— Report to Accompany S. J. Res. 1, Child Labor Amendment.

Department of Commerce and Labor, Bureau of the Census Bulletin No. 69, Child Labor in the United States. Washington, 1907.

Department of Labor. Children's Bureau Publications.

Industrial Commission. Report of the Industrial Commission on the Relations and Conditions of Capital and Labor. Vol. VII. Washington, 1901.

NEWSPAPERS AND PERIODICALS

Age Herald. Birmingham, Ala.

American Child. N. C. L. C., New York City.

American Cotton Manufacturer (changed to the American Textile Manufacturer). Charlotte, N. C.

American Federationist. Washington, D. C.

Atlanta Georgian and News. Atlanta, Ga.

Atlanta Journal. Atlanta, Ga.

Biblical Recorder. Raleigh, N. C.

Boston Evening Transcript. Boston, Mass.

Central Presbyterian. Richmond, Va.

Charities (changed to Charities and the Commons, and to Survey).
New York City.
Charlotte Daily Observer. Charlotte, N. C.
Christian Advocate. Raleigh, N. C.
Constitution. Atlanta, Ga.
Industrial Journal. Charlotte, N. C.
Manufacturers' Record. Baltimore, Md.
Mobile Daily Register. Mobile, Ala.
Montgomery Advertiser. Montgomery, Ala.
News and Courier. Charleston, S. C.
News and Observer. Raleigh, N. C.
Outlook. New York City.
Presbyterian Standard. Charlotte, N. C.
Southern Textile Bulletin. Charlotte, N. C.
State. Columbia, S. C.

PAMPHLETS, MAGAZINE ARTICLES, AND NATIONAL CHILD LABOR
COMMITTEE PUBLICATIONS

Abbott, Grace. How to Meet Child Labor Law. Textile World Journal,
LII (June 16, 1917), 3304.
Address to the Citizens of Twelve States on the Child Labor Laws
You Should Enact in 1914. Child Labor Bulletin, II (Nov., 1913),
33-43.
Adler, Felix. The Child Labor Movement: A Movement in the In-
terests of Civilization. Child Labor Bulletin, III (March, 1914),
8-10.
———— Conservation of the Human Assets of the Nation. N. C. L. C.
Pamphlet No. 125.
———— The Evil of Child Labor—A Crime Against Humanity: an
Address. Social Service, VI (Dec., 1902), 107-15.
Alabama's Appeal to New England. Outlook, LXIX (Nov. 2, 1901),
524.
Ashby-Macfadyen, Irene M. Abolish Child Labor. American Federa-
tionist, IX (1902), 19-20.
———— Child Labor in Alabama, Report to the Executive Com-
mittee of the State on the History of Child Labor Legislation in
Alabama. Alabama Child Labor Committee Pamphlet. 1901.
———— Child-Labor in Southern Cotton Mills. World's Work, II
(1901), 1290-95.
———— Child Life vs. Dividends. American Federationist, IX (1902),
215-23.
———— The Fight Against Child Labor in Alabama. American Federationist, VIII (1901), 150-57.

———— The Last Stronghold of Infant Mill Slavery. Social Service, IV (1901), 202-5.

Bailey, Mrs. E. L. Conditions of Child Employing Industries in the South. Child Labor Bulletin, II (May, 1913), 128-33.

Baldwin, J. A. Evils of Southern Factory Life. Gunton's Magazine, XXII (1902), 326-37.

Battles over the Child Labor Amendment. Literary Digest, Dec. 6, 1924, pp. 12-14.

Brown, E. F. Demoralizing Environment of Night Messengers in Southern Cities. Child Labor Bulletin, II (May, 1913), 138-41.

———— Neglected Human Resources of the Gulf Coast States. Child Labor Bulletin, II (May, 1913), 112-16.

Carter, E. F. Operation of the Child Labor Law. Proceedings of Eighth Annual Convention of Association of Government Labor Officials, 1921.

Child Labor. Independent, LIV (Aug. 21, 1902), 2032-33.

Child Labor Again. Independent, LIV (Sept. 11, 1902), 2205.

Child Labor and "Politics." Reprint from Montgomery Advertiser, Oct. 29, 1902.

Child Labor—A Symposium. American Federationist, X (1903), 339-60.

Child Labor Conference Disagrees with Dr. Stiles. Survey, XXIV (April 23, 1910), 131-32.

Child Labor in Alabama. Annals of the American Academy of Political and Social Science, XXI (1903), 179-80.

Child Labor in Alabama. Outlook, LXIX (Dec. 14, 1901), 957-58.

Child Labor in Factories. Harper's Weekly, XLVI (Sept. 13, 1902), 1280.

Child Labor Reform by "Voluntary Agreement." Outlook, LXXII (Sept. 20, 1902), 144-45.

Clark, David. A Demand for a Square Deal. Child Labor Bulletin, IV (May, 1915), 37-44.

Clopper, Edward N. Child Welfare in Alabama. N. C. L. C. Publication. N. Y., 1918.

Coon, C. L. North Carolina Child Labor Committee. Annals of the American Academy, XXXV, Supplement (1910), 181.

Crowell, John F. The Employment of Children. Andover Review, IV (1885), 42-55.

Democrats' Child Labor Law. Literary Digest, LIII (Sept. 2, 1916), 547-48.

Dodging the Child Labor Issue. Gunton's Magazine, XXII (1902), 246-52.

Dowd, Jerome. Cheap Labor in the South. Gunton's Magazine, XVIII (1900), 112-21.

———— Textile War Between the North and the South. Forum, xxv (1898), 438-44.

Ellis, Leonora Beck. Child Labor Legislation in the South. Gunton's Magazine, xxi (1901), 45-53.

———— Child Operatives in Southern Mills. Independent, liii (Nov. 7, 1901), 2637-47.

———— Model Factory Town, Forum, xxxii (1901), 60-65.

———— Movement to Restrict Child Labor, Arena, xxviii (1902), 370-78.

———— Study of Southern Cotton-Mill Communities. American Journal of Sociology, viii (1903), 623-30.

Ely, Richard T. An American Industrial Experiment. Harper's Monthly Magazine, cv (1902), 39-45.

Factory Labor in the South. Gunton's Magazine, xiv (1898), 217-28. The author's name is not given.

Fahey, C. P. No Children in Tennessee Factories. American Federationist, viii (1901), 401.

Federal Child Labor Bill Passes the House. Survey, xxxiii (Feb. 27, 1915), 569.

Federal Control of "Anti-Social" Labor. Survey, xxx (Aug. 16, 1913), 615-16.

Few, William P. The Constructive Philanthropy of a Southern Cotton Mill. South Atlantic Quarterly, viii (1909), 82-90.

First Fruits of the Nashville Conference. Charities and the Commons, xix (March 14, 1908), 1723-24.

Fletcher, D. U. The Child Labor Amendment. North American Review, ccxx (1924), 238-44.

Flower, B. O. Topics of the Times. Arena, xxviii (1902), 305-17.

Fuller, Raymond G. Child Labor and Federal Legislation. Review of Reviews, lxvi (1922), 67-69.

———— Child Labor—Now. Review of Reviews, lix (1919), 630-32.

Gompers, Samuel. Child Labor in the South. American Federationist, viii (1901), 262-63.

———— Child Labor Verified by Disaster. American Federationist, x (1903), 576-77.

———— Children of All Ages Employed. American Federationist, viii (1901), 277.

———— Crime of '94-5. American Federationist, iv (1898), 278.

———— Georgia's New Child Labor Law. American Federationist, xxi (1914), 869-70.

———— Lift the Burdens from Child Life. American Federationist, xxiii (1916), 843-44.

———— Subterfuge and Greed in North Carolina. American Federationist, viii (1901), 163-64.

———— To Abolish Child Labor. American Federationist, x (1903), 835.

[Gordon, F. B.] F. B. Gordon, President Mill, Columbus, Ga., Answers "the Last Stronghold of Infant Mill Slavery." Social Service, v (1902), 148-49.

Graffenried, Clare de. Child Labor. Publications of the American Economic Association, v (1890), 193-271.

———— The Georgia Cracker in the Cotton Mill. Century Magazine, XLI (1891), 483-98.

Greene, Prince W. Southern Textile Workers. American Federationist, VI (1899), 126.

Guild, Curtis. Address before the Child Labor Committee. Leaflet. Boston, 1910.

Gunton, George. [Child Labor in the South.] Gunton's Magazine, xx (1901), 253-54.

———— The South's "Labor System." Gunton's Magazine, XVIII (1900), 234-39.

———— What Can Be Done About It? Gunton's Magazine, XVIII (1900), 112-30.

Harben, Will N. On Young Shoulders. Woman's Home Companion, XXXIII (Oct., 1906), 9-10, 60.

Hearing on Child Labor Law. Textile World Journal, LIII (July 28, 1917), 321.

Herring, Harriet L. Cycles of Cotton Mill Criticism. South Atlantic Quarterly, XXVIII (1929), 113-25.

Hine, L. W. Baltimore to Biloxi and Back. Survey, xxx (May 3, 1913), 167-72.

Hollis, John Porter. Child Labor Legislation in the Carolinas. Annals of the American Academy, XXXVIII, Supplement (1911), 114-17.

Hubbard, Elbert. White Slavery in the South. Philistine, XIV (1902), 161-78, reprinted as Slaughter of the Innocents. American Federationist, XII (1905), 205-9.

Hunter, Robert. Child Labor: A Social Waste. Independent, LV (Feb. 12, 1903), 375-79.

Johnsen, Julia E. Selected Articles on Child Labor. N. Y., 1925.

Jones, H. H. Child Labor in Alabama. N. C. L. C. Pamphlet No. 242.

Jones, Jerome. Child Labor and Low Wages. Child Labor Bulletin, II (May, 1913), 52-55.

Kelley, Florence. Child Labor in the Carolinas. Charities and the Commons, XXI (Jan. 30, 1909), 742.

———— Industrial Conditions as a Community Problem with Particular Reference to Child Labor. Annals of the American Academy, CIII (1922), 60-64.

Lindsay, Samuel McCune. New Child Labor Law in Georgia. Chari-
ties, XVI (Sept. 1, 1906), 537-38.
———— Seventh Annual Child Labor Conference. Survey, XXVI
(April 22, 1911), 124-26.
London, Jack. The Apostate. Woman's Home Companion, Sept., 1906.
Lovejoy, Owen R. Dr. Alexander Jeffrey McKelway. Child Labor
Bulletin, VII (May, 1918), 21-27.
———— Federal Government and Child Labor. A Brief for the
Palmer-Owen Child Labor Bill. N. C. L. C. Pamphlet No. 216.
N. Y., 1914.
———— Schoolhouse or Breaker. Outlook, LXXX (Aug. 26, 1905),
1011-19.
———— Six Years' Battle for the Working Child. Review of Reviews,
XLII (1910), 593-96.
McCullough, J. A. Conditions of Child Employing Industries in the
South. Child Labor Bulletin, II (May, 1913), 133-38.
———— Report from South Carolina. Child Labor Bulletin, III (May,
1914), 78-84.
McKelway, Alexander Jeffrey. The Child Against the Man. Child
Labor Bulletin, II (Nov., 1913), 52-59.
———— Child Labor in Georgia. Child Labor Bulletin II (Aug.,
1913), 53-79.
———— Child Labor in Georgia, N. C. L. C. Pamphlet No. 194.
———— Child Labor in Mississippi. N. C. L. C. Pamphlet No. 169.
———— Child Labor in Tennessee. N. C. L. C. Pamphlet No. 150.
———— Child Labor in the Carolinas. N. C. L. C. Pamphlet No. 92.
———— Child Labor in Virginia. N. C. L. C. Pamphlet No. 171.
———— Child Wages in the Cotton Mills: Our Modern Feudalism.
Child Labor Bulletin, II (May, 1913), 7-16.
———— Do Not Grind the Seed Corn. Pamphlet, 1905.
———— Evil of Child Labor. Why the South Should Favor a Na-
tional Law. Outlook, LXXXV (Feb. 16, 1907), 360-64.
———— Extent of Child Labor in the South and Needed Legislation.
The South Mobilizing for Social Service, Nashville (1913).
———— Fight for Child Labor Reform in the Carolinas. Charities
and the Commons, XXI (Mar. 20, 1909), 1224-26.
———— Fighting Child Labor in Three States. Survey, XXVIII (Apr.
20, 1912), 121-22.
———— Florida Child Labor Campaign. Survey, XXX (July 12, 1913),
497-98.
———— Law Without Enforcement. Child Labor Bulletin, III (May,
1914), 34-41.
———— Modern Feudalism. Boston Common, III (Mar. 22, 1913), 17.
———— Protecting Negro Child Laborers in Virginia. Survey, XXXII
(Aug. 15, 1914), 496.

——— Welfare Work and Child Labor in Southern Cotton Mills. Charities and the Commons, XVII (1906), 271-73.

Magruder, Julia. The Child Labor Problem: Fact Versus Sentimentality. North American Review, V (1907), 186, 245-50.

Manning, Richard I. The Organization of the Public Welfare of a State. National Conference of Social Work. Forty-fourth Session.

Mills Will Obey Federal Law. Child Labor Bulletin, V (Nov., 1916), 136-37.

Mitchell, Broadus. The End of Child Labor; How Labor is Finishing What Social Work Began. Survey, XLII (Aug. 23, 1919), 747-50.

——— Why Cheap Labor Down South. Virginia Quarterly Review, V (1929), 482-91.

Murdoch, Mrs. W. L. Child Labor Reform in Alabama. Child Labor Bulletin, III (May, 1914), 82-84.

——— Conditions of Child Employing Industries in the South—Alabama. Child Labor Bulletin, II (May, 1913), 124-28.

Murphy, Edgar Gardner. Appeal to the People and Press of New England. Pamphlet, 1901.

——— Case Against Child Labor—An Argument. Pamphlet, 1902.

——— Child Labor and Business. Pamphlet, 1902.

——— Child Labor and the Public. Pamphlet, 1902.

——— Child Labor as a National Problem; with Especial Reference to the Southern States. Thirteenth National Conference of Charities and Corrections. Proceedings, 1903, pp. 121-34.

——— Child Labor in the Southern Press. Pamphlet, 1902.

——— Child-Labor Law, A. Pamphlet, Aug. 17, 1902.

——— Child Labor Legislation. Review of Laws in United States. Pamphlet, 1902.

——— Child Labor Question in Alabama. Pamphlet, July 8, 1907.

——— Editorial about Child Labor. Pamphlet, 1902.

——— Federal Regulation of Child Labor. Alabama Child Labor Committee. Pamphlet, 1907.

——— Open Letter on Suffrage Restriction, and Against Certain Proposals of the Platform of the State Convention (1900). Alabama State Department of Archives and History.

——— Pictures from Life, Mill Children in Alabama. Pamphlet, 1902.

——— South and Her Children, The. Pamphlet, 1902.

——— Southern Conference for the Discussion of Race Problems. Alabama State Department of Archives and History. Pamphlet, 1900.

——— The White Man and the Negro at the South. Alabama State Department of Archives and History, 1900.

Murphy, E. G. and others. The National Child Labor Committee (A Suggested Organization). Leaflet, 1903 (?).

Nashville Child Labor Conference. Charities and the Commons, XIX (Oct. 26, 1907), 936-37.

National Child Labor Committee. Child Labor Laws and Child Labor Facts; An Analysis by States, 1929.

——— Child Welfare in North Carolina. N. Y. *ca.* 1918.

——— Constitution. Pamphlet No. 148 (1907).

——— Leaflet 1.

——— Objects of the Committee, 1904.

——— Supporters of the Keating-Owen Bill. Pamphlet No. 256, 1916.

Newell, Mary H. Proceedings of Ninth Annual Conference of the National Child Labor Committee. Child Labor Bulletin, II (May, 1913), 157.

Parker, Lewis W. Compulsory Education, The Solution of Child Labor Problem. Child Labor and Social Progress, pp. 40-56. N. C. L. C. Publication. N. Y., 1908.

Planning a New Child Labor Law. Survey, XL (June 15, 1918), 323-24.

Poe, Clarence H. Report of the North Carolina Child Labor Committee. Child Labor and Social Progress, pp. 139-48.

Proceedings of the Fourth Annual Meeting of the National Child Labor Committee. Child Labor and Social Progress, pp. 155-75. N. C. L. C. Publication. N. Y., 1908.

Progress in Child Labor Legislation. World's Work, V (1903), 3264.

Raphael, M. Child Labor. American Federationist, III (1896), 157-59.

Regulating Child Labor. Charities, VII (Sept., 1901), 225.

Reports from State and Local Child Labor Committees and Consumers' Leagues. Annals of the American Academy, XXIX (1907), 142-83.

Rider, Esther Lee. Child Labor and Vocational Education. Proceedings of the Eighth Annual Convention of Association of Government Labor Officials. 1921.

Rochester, Anna. The Consumer and the Federal Child Labor Law. Survey, XXXII (July 18, 1914), 412-13.

Sargent, Noel. Why Employers are Opposed to the Twentieth Amendment. Pamphlet, reprint from American Industries, Feb., 1925.

Seddon, Alfred E. The Education of Mill Children in the South. Child Labor and Social Progress, pp. 72-79.

Schenck, John F. "Child Labor" Legislation. Pamphlet, 1913.

Southern Child Labor Conference. Survey, XXII (Apr. 17, 1909), 107-9.

Southern Protest Against Child Labor. Outlook, LXXI (Aug. 9, 1902), 906-8.

Spahr, Charles B. Child Labor in England and the United States. Chautauquan, xxx (1899), 41-43.

Statement by National Child Labor Committee. Child Labor Bulletin, IV (Jan., 1915), 44-54.

Statements of Mississippi King's Daughters, Professor O. A. Shaw, President Winona High School; and Dr. B. F. Ward, as to Conditions of Health and Sanitation at the Winona Cotton Mill. Pamphlet, 1914.

Stoddard, W. L. "The Child that Toileth Not." Survey, xxix (Feb. 15, 1913), 705-8.

Stratton, George Frederic. The Man Behind the Child. Outlook, cv (Sept. 20, 1913), 137-40.

Swift, Wiley H. Campaign in North Carolina—The Mountain Whites —By One of Them. Child Labor Bulletin, II (May, 1913), 96-104.

———— Child Labor in North Carolina, 1912-1922. Journal of Social Forces, I (1923), 254-55.

———— Child Welfare in North Carolina. N. C. L. C. Publication. N. Y., 1918.

———— The Last Stand of the One Business which Opposes Child Labor Legislation in the South. Child Labor Bulletin, III (May, 1914), 85-89.

———— Why It is Hard to Get Good Child Labor Laws in the South. Child Labor Bulletin, III (May, 1914), 72-78.

Szepesi, Eugene. Preparing for the Keating Child Labor Law. Textile World Journal, LII (June 16, 1917), 3295.

Tompkins, D. A. Child Labor and Apprenticeship Training. Pamphlet, 1906.

———— The Sociological Work of the Cotton Mill Owners. Thirtieth National Conference of Charities and Corrections (1903), pp. 157-66.

To Prohibit Interstate Trade in Child Labor. Survey, xxxi (Feb. 7, 1914), 539.

Tutwiler, Julia S. Reports of State Corresponding Secretaries—Alabama. Proceedings of the National Conference of Charities and Corrections, Twenty-eighth Session (1901), 37-39.

Valesh, Eva McDonald. Three Notable Lines of Child Labor Work. American Federationist, VIII (1901), 457-62.

Van Vorst, Mrs. John. The Cry of the Children. The Saturday Evening Post, CLXXVIII (Mar. 10, 1906), 1-3, 28-29; (Apr. 14, 1906), 3-5; (Apr. 28, 1906), 10-11; (May 5, 1906), 11-13; (May 19, 1906), 12-13, 26-27.

Watson, E. J. Administration of Child Labor Law. Textile World Journal, LII (June 16, 1917), 3301-2.

———— Enforcement of Child Labor Laws in South Carolina. Annals of the American Academy, xxxv, Supplement (1910), 96-102.

Weltner, C. E. Social Welfare and Child Labor in South Carolina Cotton Mill Communities. Child Labor Bulletin, II (May, 1913), 85-90.

Where Southern Students Disagree. Charities and the Commons, XXI (Feb. 20, 1909), 893.

Winston, George T. Child Labor in North Carolina. N. C. L. C. Pamphlet No. 262, 1916.

Worst Crime of Civilization. World's Work, IV (1902), 2475-76.

Would Congress Spoil Our Children? Literary Digest (Nov. 29, 1924), pp. 31-32.

Wright, Carroll D. An Historical Sketch of the Knights of Labor. Quarterly Journal of Economics, Vol. I (1887).

OTHER PUBLISHED MATERIALS

Alabama Federation of Women's Clubs. Annual Conventions.
———— Year Books.

Alabama State Federation of Labor. Constitution and Proceedings of the Annual Conventions.

Alden, Edwin, Co. Central South Advertising Mediums. Cincinnati, 1887.

American Federation of Labor. Proceedings.
———— Weekly News Letter, 1911-12. (Bound mimeographed sheets.) 2 vols.

American Year Book.

Arnett, Alex Mathews. The Populist Movement in Georgia. N. Y., 1922.

Bader, Louis. World Developments in the Cotton Industry. N. Y., 1925.

Conference of Charities and Corrections. Proceedings.

Dawley, Thomas R., Jr. The Child That Toileth Not. N. Y., 1912.

Dunn, Robert W. and Hardy, Jack. Labor and Textiles. N. Y., 1931.

Faulkner, H. U. The Quest for Social Justice, in A History of American Life, Vol. XI. N. Y., 1931.

Florida State Federation of Labor. Proceedings of the Annual Conventions.

Georgia Federation of Labor. Proceedings of the Annual Conventions.

Knight, L. L. A Standard History of Georgia and Georgians. Chicago, 1917.

Kohn, August. The Cotton Mills of South Carolina. Columbia, 1907.

Mitchell, Broadus. The Rise of Cotton Mills in the South. Baltimore, 1921.
———— William Gregg: Factory Master of the Old South. Chapel Hill, N. C., 1928.

Moore, A. B. History of Alabama and Her People. Vol. i. American Historical Society, Inc., 1927.

Murphy, Edgar Gardner. Problems of the Present South. N. Y., 1904.

North Carolina State Federation of Labor. Proceedings of the Annual Conventions.

Owen, T. M. History of Alabama and Dictionary of Alabama Biography. 4 vols. Chicago, 1921.

Potwin, Marjorie A. Cotton Mill People of the Piedmont. N. Y., 1927.

Rhyne, J. J. Some Southern Cotton Mill Workers and Their Villages. Chapel Hill, N. C., 1930.

Scherer, J. A. B. Cotton as a World Power. N. Y., 1916.

Simkins, Francis Butler. The Tillman Movement in South Carolina. Durham, N. C., 1926.

Snowden, Yates (ed.). History of South Carolina. 5 vols. Chicago, 1920.

South in the Building of the Nation, The. 12 vols. Richmond, Va., 1909.

Spargo, John. The Bitter Cry of the Children. N. Y., 1906.

Thompson, Holland. From the Cotton Field to the Cotton Mill. N. Y., 1906.

Vandiver, Louise Ayer. Traditions and History of Anderson County. Atlanta, 1928.

Van Vorst, Mrs. John and Van Vorst, Marie. The Woman Who Toils. N. Y., 1903.

Virginia Federation of Labor. Proceedings of the Annual Conventions.

White, George. Statistics of the State of Georgia. Savannah, 1849.

Winston, George T. A Builder of the New South. N. Y., 1920.

INDEX

ABBOTT, Grace, 269, 271
Addams, Jane, 123
Adler, Dr. Felix, 123, 130, 137
Aiken County, South Carolina, 178, 179, 180-81
Alabama
    child labor laws, 18-21, 50-51, 122, 215, 223, 224-25, 232-34, 236
    child labor legislation, proposed, 22-23, 30-32, 218-19, 221-25, 230-32, 236; relation to politics, 215-16, 223; loss of interest in, 225; new attitudes toward, 236
    children employed in, 27-28, 216-17, 221, 224-25, 227
    Child Welfare Department, 235-37
    compulsory school attendance, 234
    Department of Labor, 237
    opposed Beveridge bill, 136
Alabama Child Labor Committee, origin, 32-34; early work of, 40, 41-42, 46, 49-50, 68, 79; later work of, 122, 129, 215-30, *passim*
Alabama Cotton Manufacturers' Association, 218, 219, 231-32, 237
Alabama factory inspection, 225-26, 233-34, 237
Alabama Federation of Labor, 30, 47, 215, 219-20, 223, 225, 230, 232, 237
Alabama Federation of Women's Clubs, 31, 43, 50, 219, 225, 228-29, 231-35
Alamance County, North Carolina, 103, 112
Alexander, Hooper, 80, 199, 205, 207, 208
American Bar Association, 230, 231
American Child, The, 127, 274
American Constitutional League, 269
American Cotton Manufacturer, 138, 158, 202
American Cotton Manufacturers' Association, 138
American Federationist, The, 21, 28, 37, 65, 116

American Federation of Labor, in Alabama, 15, 45-46, 79, 220; and child labor reform, 21, 23-24, 96, 116, 122, 190, 209, 245-52, 266; organization in South, 21-22, 23, 58-59, 71, 95, 113, 207; Dr. Murphy on, 34
American Industries, 271
American Textile Manufacturer, 141, 159, 160
Anderson, Neal, in Alabama, 27, 32-33, 219, 223; on National Child Labor Committee, 124, 166; on Dr. McKelway, 141-42, 144; on Beveridge bill, 223
Anderson County, South Carolina, 183, 187, 192
Annals of the American Academy of Political and Social Science, 127, 197
Ansel, Governor Martin F., 142
Appeal to the People and Press of New England, 57, 65, 81
Ashby, Irene M. *See* Macfadyen, Mrs. Irene M. Ashby
Asheville Citizen, 165, 260
Asheville New Era, 112
Ashley, Joshua W., "Citizen Josh," 90, 99, 101, 187, 190
Association of City School Superintendents, 154
Association of Hard Yarn Spinners. *See* North Carolina Association of Hard Yarn Spinners
Atherton Mill, 159
Atlanta Constitution, 56, 72-73, 77, 78, 79, 80, 139, 148, 196, 199, 202, 204, 213
Atlanta Federation of Trades, 71, 81
Atlanta Georgian and News, 209
Atlanta Journal, 57, 196, 199, 204
Atlanta Women's Clubs, 213
Avondale Mill, 216, 226
Aycock, Governor Charles B., 100, 114, 119, 128, 143, 150

Federal Regulation of Child Labor, The, 133-34
Few, William P., 140
Fidelity Manufacturing Company, 263-65
Fletcher, Senator D. U., 258, 271
Florida, child labor legislation, 247-48
Florida Federation of Labor, 246
Folks, Homer, 125
Foust, Dr. Julian I., 172
Fowler, G. B., 89
France, Senator J. I., 266
Fries, J. W., 114, 142
Fuller, F. L., 107-8
Fuller, Raymond G., 267
Fulton Bag and Cotton Mills, 209
Fulton County, Georgia, 203

GALLIVAN, J. A., 262
Gann, R. E., 232
Gard, Warren, 266
Garrett, Mr., president of Georgia Federation of Labor, 74
Gaston, Judge J. B., 33, 50, 124, 133, 151
Gaston County, North Carolina, 104, 113
Georgia
  Board of Health, 211
  Board of Public Welfare, 211
  child labor laws, 129, 201-2, 206, 209-10, 213-14
  child labor legislation, proposed, 70-74, 76-78, 80, 83-84, 87-88, 196-98, 201-2, 204, 208
  Children's Code Commission, 211-12, 214
  compulsory education, 211
  Council of Social Agencies, 211
  Department of Commerce and Labor, 206-7
  Department of Education, 211
  labor legislation, 69-70, 73, 84, 206
  politics of, 200-1
Georgia Central Committee, 80, 81, 82, 84, 129
Georgia Child Labor Committee, 195-96, 205, 207; McKelway on leadership of, 204
Georgia Commissioner of Labor, 208, 210, 212, 214
Georgia Factory Inspector, 210

Georgia Federation of Labor, 71, 86, 209, 211; support of legislation by, 74-76, 194, 197, 202, 207; effect of support, 84-85
Georgia Federation of Women's Clubs, 73, 85, 194, 211
Georgia Industrial Association, 198; opposes legislation, 87, 195-96, 201
Georgia League of Women Voters, 211
Georgia Manufacturers' Association, 212, 214
Gilbert, A. H., Jr., 269
Gilliam, Donald, 120, 121
Glass, Senator Carter, 270
Glenn, Governor R. B., 156
Gompers, Samuel, 21, 23, 45, 63; Mrs Macfadyen agent of, 24-25, 28-29, 30, 41, 82; relations with Dr. Murphy, 47-48; other agents of, 113, 116, 120; relations with Dr. McKelway, 128; on federal legislation, 263, 269
Gonzales, N. G., 99, 100-1, 140, 143
Goodwin, D. T., 50
Gordon, F. B., 66
Gordon, Jean M., 145
Gordon, General John B., 80
Graham, A. J., 142
Graham, Dr. E. K., 172
Grainger, Mrs. A. O., 194
Gray, James R., 199
Graydon, Ellis G., 98
Green, L. M., 188
Greenville County, South Carolina, 192
Greer (S. C.), 92
Gregory, S. S., 93
Guild, Curtis, Jr., 129
Gunton's Magazine, 37, 56, 64, 65, 117

HADLEY, Governor H. S., 145
Hall, T. J., 48-49
Halsted, J. W., 102
Hammer, William C., 264
Hand, William H., 185
Hanson, Major J. F., 55, 85, 86-87, 200
Hardwick, Senator T. W., 258, 266
Hardy, H. J., 190
Harris, Hugh W., 107-8
Harrison, Senator B. P., 270
Hart, Attorney General John C., 203
Hartwell, H. T., 231
Henderson, Governor, 231
Herring, Harriet L., 3

www.ingramcontent.com/pod-product-compliance
Lightning Source LLC
Chambersburg PA
CBHW021809270326
41932CB00007B/119